THROUGH THEIR EYES

447 Broadway, 2nd Floor
New York, NY 10013
www.throughtheireyesbooks.com

Publisher's Note: Some names and identifying details have been changed to protect the privacy of individuals.

Our books may be purchased in bulk for promotional, educational, or business use. For information, please email us at info@throughtheireyesbooks.com.

Edited by Laura Dragonette
Book Layout © 2018 BookDesignTemplates.com

The Eternal Outsider 10 Years Black In Japan/ Trevor David Houchen.
FIRST EDITION

Library of Congress Control Number: 2018949874

ISBN 978-0-9997754-1-7

THE ETERNAL OUTSIDER

10 YEARS BLACK IN JAPAN

A JADED MEMOIR

Trevor David Houchen

THROUGH THEIR EYES
BOOKS

NEW YORK

Dedicated to my 3 beautiful and amazing children, Naya Amari'el, Taiyo and Asia.

"Take Every Chance You Get In Life, Because Some things Only Happen Once"

- KAREN GIBBS

Table of Contents

INTRODUCTION

My Japan wasn't all cherry blossoms, green tea, *hanami* and sushi. Mine was more edgy, psychedelic, seedy, *dangerous*.

My Japan was nightclubs, street fights, copious sex, drugs, marriage, children, divorce, humiliation, exhilaration, rage, depression, friendship, renewal, jealousy, betrayal, music, fame, art, notoriety, extreme loneliness, unbound creativity, and ultimately a search for self in a land where the self is denied in favor of the group.

It was also thousands of young Japanese faces, chalkboards, colors, letters, numbers, shapes, children's songs, animal noises, textbooks, lunchrooms, lesson plans, and a never-ending array of *jikou shokai-* self-introductions. Oh, and there was this one time a Japanese girl named Mika grinded herself to an orgasm on my ankle while I was watching music videos on her computer. Then there was the time a 9.0 earthquake (the second largest recorded in history) swept across the coastline of Japan, resulting in a massive Tsunami that claimed the lives of thousands.

My Japan was decadent, sensual, and indulgent, while at the same time humbling, emptying, and spiritually revealing. It was the time of my life, a lifetime of experiences crammed into just about ten years, and I am a wiser, better human being as a result.

Even though during the vast majority of my time in Japan I was deemed "sensei" by my English students, it was I who was the student, and Japan itself was the true sensei in every definition of the word. I went to Japan to teach, but instead, I was taught. Vices and fetishes I never knew I had came to the fore. Addictions and sordid passions took me over and ruinous behavior resulted. But *oh how good it all was*, and *I wish I were doing it now*...maybe.

It was all impossibly romantic and visceral. But it was real.

Japan, *arigatou gozaimasu*, for your beauty, harmony, silence, safety, selflessness, kindness without bound, and your hypnotic uniqueness.

I am forever in your debt.
This is my story.

PROLOGUE

I didn't hold out any special hope for Japan or the Japanese to come rescue me from my little acting hellhole of a life in LA. But they did. Ten years' worth, baby.

Flashback:

Japanese PTSD syndrome.

The effect of which is at any random time your mind transports you back to that island archipelago. The people you met and knew, the places you were, and the things you were doing. You wonder: Was any of it real? The kind and generous, nobly humble people. The misty mountaintops in the countryside, the pristine and cold flowing rivers. The energetic, colorful, sometimes indulgently perverted thrill of living in Japan is intoxicating for many "Western" men, and it's also addictive.

The peace and simultaneous electricity of life there. The harmonious assortment of people, places, and things.

Do I really have two children there? Two little half-Japanese, half-Jamaican American kids running around in Japan? Where are they now? What are they doing? Do they miss their daddy? Does my Japanese ex-wife ever think of me? Would she know me if she bumped into me on the street?

Do I still exist in her heart?

Did I really teach my own language to literally thousands of Japanese, young, old, and in between? Did anyone learn anything?

Did I?

Did I almost drown in a white-water rafting fiasco that left a three-inch scar on my shin? Was that me frying my brain smoking "spice" on the set of my early-morning music video shoot with the Japanese Suicide Girl? Did I just see a twenty-foot-tall poster of myself at the airport and in the subways of my Japanese home city Nagoya? Was my bed on fire and did she just squirt on my carpet? Was that another earthquake?

The images take over my mind like some cheap cinematic special effect, where polaroids come flipping onto the screen of my brain and come to life in heavy and sometimes haunting psycho cuts. These edits momentarily splatter a different reality in front of my mind's eye for a few seconds, or minutes, or hours, and suddenly I'm Back In Japan, riding my bike through tiny backstreets looking for . . . who knows what.

Japan flashbacks, I call them.

You ever been to Mars?

Part 1

WELCOME TO MARS

Chapter 1

AN ALARMING SITUATION

"Should I turn myself in to a cop shop or what, mate?!"

I t's 6:30 A.M. on a cold November morning in Nagoya, Japan. Nagoya was recently voted the "*Most boring city in Japan*" by none other than the *Japan Times*. I had recently written an article for the *Japan Times* on a Brazilian hip-hop band called MDG, which is short for Mundrungos, which means 'street kid' in Portuguese. MDG represents for the "052," which is Nagoya's area code, and they are one of the *coldest* Brazilian crews to ever bless the mic. Shout-out to Khalil and crew.

Back in Nagoya, boring is a state of mind. You bring your perspectives and experiences with you wherever you go. Nagoya might not be the first city that comes to mind when considering outwardly and obviously "fun and exciting" locales in Japan, but again, that depends on perspective. Lurking underneath the staid, small-town outer appearance of Nagoya, beats the heart of a vibrant, economically powerful and artistic city searching for its own identity. Just like any major metropolitan area in the world, Nagoya is imaginative with people trying to make a name for themselves and working hard at it. I salute the city of Nagoya and the people who live and/or lived there. Nagoya, baby.

There's always action just around the corner. You just have to know where to look for it. I always knew exactly where to go.

My Phone Was Ringing

My main chick, H34, was sound asleep next to me under about four blankets on our futon. We were both naked. Japan is cold as an ice pick during winter, and November brings it too. Her alarm was about to go off, which meant we were about to have our usual morning sex session, except my phone was ringing. *Who the hell calls at 6:30 A.M.?* Had to be bad news, fucking *trouble*. Someone must have died. I didn't want to answer the phone, but I had to. *Fuck.*

I looked at the screen on my phone, it was B, my wing nut Australian friend. B was one of the first friends I made when I got to Nagoya almost ten years ago. We met on the twelfth floor of Freebell, "*Gaijin* Ghetto," a huge old apartment building that at the time, and maybe still, was home to a large percentage of foreigners who had come to Nagoya. Freebell is famous and infamous. If you're a foreigner in Nagoya chances are either you've lived at Freebell, or you know someone who has.

When I first met B, he had a frenetic happy-go-lucky attitude, and I guess I did too. He told me about his past as a horse trainer in the Australian outback, and had lots of wild stories about exotic animals, drinking, and his eight brothers who used to kick his ass constantly. I told him about smoking blunts in Brooklyn and about my sporadic appearances on television. B said he was the runt of his family—that's how he referred to himself. His stories always ended with him trying to get a "root," which means orgasm in Australian. Short, wiry, loud, and more than a little nuts, B looked kind of like that Aussie actor Guy Pearce, the skinny dude from that flick *Memento,* but more ragged. Or rugged. Whatever. B was a decent friend, but he'd been kind of missing in action for a few months. No one had seen or heard from him for a while, but today, his name was showing up on my cell phone at 6:30 A.M., just as I was about to give it to my girlfriend on this cold November morning in Japan. Fuck. *What does he want?*

I picked up the phone: 'B, what the fuck do you want, man? It's six thirty! Where the hell have you been, man?" B screams into the phone, "I gotta see you, mate, *loik roight naow!*" He sounded frantic, more frantic than usual, plus there was that Crocodile Dundee accent. One of my other Aussie friends Larry called it "one of the top five sexiest accents in the world." GTFOH.

A Bit About Larry

Larry fancied himself an "erotic photographer," but hadn't taken any erotic photos in years. He spent his time holed up in his semi-subterranean windowless apartment on the backstreets of Kakuozan, chain-smoking Marlboro Reds and watching British sitcoms. Larry claimed to be a professional cyclist, but he was carrying about a hundred pounds more than any pro cyclist I'd ever seen.

Larry and I both had no direction, but at least I was getting pussy. Sometimes I felt sorry for Larry because he got *no* pussy but he didn't seem to really want any pussy, and he didn't seem bothered by this in the least, a trait I admired in him. Besides that, Larry was a great cook, appreciated great food and he wasn't an asshole, which a great many foreigners in Japan were, myself included. It was cool to chill with Lar all the time.

However, there was this one young, really foxy Japanese girl Larry did hook up with for a few months. My dude Jason and I were Larry's best, maybe only friends at the time. Jason was a brother from St. Louis who I had met on the street in Sakai. We were both stunned at how hot this girl was that Larry had managed to rope in. She was in her early 20's, maybe even in her late teens, wore only designer clothing and had a nice rack and a tight ass. *Foine,* actually. Larry rearranged his apartment for her and squired her around town in his drop-top black Benz for a few months, and then, poof, just like that the girl disappeared, leaving Larry shell-shocked. Japanese broads, man, *fucking* vanishing acts.

Japanese girls are famous for that. You'll be deep in their guts one day and suddenly they'll vanish off the face. Larry was gutted about it for a couple weeks, maybe a month. He kinda walked around looking stupefied and shell-shocked for a while and sometimes wouldn't answer you when you spoke to him. Japanese girls will do that to you. Real easy. They can be absolutely gorgeous, angelic creatures one minute, and totally soulless, indifferent machines named *Yoshimi* the next. Robotrons. "Evil-natured robots/programmed to destroy us"—this is exactly what they can become. Check out the Flaming Lips' track "Yoshimi Battles the Pink Robots"—pretty dead-on.

Last I heard, Larry had bounced Japan and wound up in Colombia hanging out on the beach and taking naked pictures of Colombian hookers. Nice come up. Score Larry.

This one time, me, Jason, Larry, and a couple of cute Japanese girls Larry had managed to rustle up, were trying to get into "ID Bar," the biggest nightclub in Sumiyoshi, Sakae's club district. Getting the girls past security was going to be an issue, even though they were 19 and 20, the girls looked like they might have been 17. Problem was, the girls were underage so they couldn't get in anywhere.

Larry and I are outside pleading with Big T, a former male stripper who actually looked like Drago from Rocky V. Big T moved to Japan from California and quickly transformed himself into a professional kickboxer and unofficial enforcer of the entire nightclub district in Sakae. Big T was also the head of security at ID—and who was also my dude. Big T became Nagoya's 'Golden Boy', partly because he ran shit on the street, *and* was connected to African thugs, the Brazilian mafia and Japan's own mafia, Yakuza. Whomever was considered bad or dangerous, Big T was connected to them. Most of the time he showed madd love to me and whomever I rocked with, but...

Problem. Big T is known to fly off the handle at any given moment and start kicking, punching, choking, and thrashing anyone within arm's reach, and on that particular night, Larry, unfortunately, was within arm's reach.

So what happened? T gets sick of Larry asking if the girls can get in the club and suddenly throws Larry to the ground. With fire in his eyes, Big T towers over him yelling, "I TOLD YOU NO ALREADY WHAT THE FUCK DO YOU WANT FROM ME?? GET THE FUCK OUTTA HERE BEFORE I REALLY GET PISSED AND DO SOMETHING I DON'T WANT TO DO!" Larry is looking up at him from the ground, terrified, shaking, confused and embarrassed. All this in front of the two cute Japanese girls Larry is escorting around Sakae. Shame. Big T was my dude at the time, but I wasn't about to try to reason with the dude in this moment—his nose was flaring and I could have been caught in the crossfire.

The girls we were with disappear down the block while Larry, Jason, and I head to a local convenience store. Larry copped some Chu-Hi and Reds, I copped some hot tea, and we forwarded home and watched some British sitcoms, smoked some Marlboro Reds, looked at his erotic picture books and bullshitted the night off.

Either way, it happened that Larry was my best friend in Japan for my last few years there. It also happened that Larry erroneously thought that his totally *wack* Australian accent was cool, which it was most definitely not. That was my point. Anyway, that is another story for another time.

Back to B and the Mysterious Phone Call

Right now B is on my phone breathing heavy and sounding like someone's been chasing him or like he'd been chasing someone. However, unbeknownst to him he's interrupting my early morning fuck.

Every morning my girl H wakes up half an hour earlier than she has to so we can get it on before she goes to work. I love these morning sex sessions because after H gets her nutt off, she goes off to work and I either go back to sleep or I call over *another* honey. However, today, neither one of these scenarios is going to happen. B is on the phone breathing like a friggin' racehorse and my girl H is rustling in the bed next to me wondering why my phone is ringing so damn early. I softly place my hand on her smooth posterior to let her know not to get up *just yet,* there's still a chance I can give her what she needs before she gets up for work, but B has other plans.

"*Mate, you don't understand me, man, I need to see you roit naow, I'm roit outside your doh-ah, please Tre-vah, please, please op'n the doh-ah, mate. Please...*" Nutty Aussie accent. "*Please Tre-vah, please mate...*"

Come on B, it's six thirty- can't you call me later? My girl's here, man. I'm pleading with B on the phone, but B's not trying to hear it.

B. Dude is either the coolest, most alpha male you ever met, or, a complete and total meathead. Over the top *Crocodile Dundee* motherfucker if there ever was one. Australian dudes come off like they just walked in from the bush, cocky and sure. B's like that, but today, dude is whimpering on my phone and *not letting me bone.*

*All right, man-*I tell him *-wait a minute, let me wake H up and after she goes to work you can come up. After you see her leave just come knock on the door and I'll let you in, but B, this better be important, man.*

I tell my girl that B is on the phone and something is really wrong. I ask her if she could please get ready for work and I'll text her later about whatever is happening. She sits up and wipes her eyes softly. Her perky cinnamon nipples stare at me, and I can almost smell her- and it all makes me more pissed at B...and then the phone rings *again.*

"Did she leave yet, mate?"

NO DUDE...SHE HASN'T LEFT...DID YOU SEE HER LEAVE MAN? I TOLD YOU I'D CALL YOU WHEN SHE LEAVES SO WAIT A COUPLE MINUTES, OKAY? I end the call. *Jesus Christ.* I'm heated.

My girl takes a quick shower, puts on her clothes and leaves for work. What a fucking waste. I throw on my thermals. A cold November morning in Japan, like I said.

The minute she leaves, B is knocking on my *doh-ah.* I open the door in my thermals to see B standing there looking like he just had a fight with an alley cat. *Look what the cat dragged in* for real. His eyes are bulging, chest is heaving, hair is scraggly and he's wearing a yellow raincoat.

His face has scratches and looks red and irritated. He looks like he'd been awake for days trying to pull his own skin off. He's scratching his head and bouncing from foot to foot like he needs to piss. He's jittery and frazzled. His hair is fucked, more fucked than usual, and he's sporting a beard, which I'd never seen on him before. His hands are dirty with tiny blood stains. He's wearing a big yellow fisherman rain-coat and it's wet—and it isn't raining—and shorts, and a pair of those goofy-ass shoes that look like big Martian alligator feet with the toes and webs. He's holding a laptop.

He comes inside and starts walking towards my kitchen without taking off his shoes, which is an absolute *do-not-do* in Japan, which begs me to question *has this fucker totally lost his mind?*

What the fuck are you doing man-I say, looking down at his Martian, alligator feet shoes.

"Sorry, mate, I'm all out of sorts . . ." he says, and slips off his shoes. His real feet looked exactly like the dirty ass feet shoes. *May as well have kept them on, fucker,* I think to myself.

B walks over to my tiny kitchen table with his dirty bare feet and big, mysteriously wet, yellow raincoat. He quickly plugs in his laptop, and starts frantically pounding on his keypad. He's banging away at his laptop, while I'm leaning against the doorframe leading into my kitchen, wondering *what in the hell is going on.* I fold up my futon and linens, *–Shit, it all smells like my girl.* I get momentarily pissed again.

H has been staying the night with me pretty regularly. She's pretty much my live-in girlfriend, even though she goes back to her parent's place out in Gifu sometimes. Whenever she takes that trip, I usually have another girl over. However, lately it's been pretty much H and I keeping it tight. *Pretty much.*

What are you looking for? I ask B. No answer.

He's hunched over the laptop with his eyes bulging at the screen, punching madly at the keypad, standing up, strutting around, sitting down while scratching at his beard and pulling at his hair like a madman. He looks like a psychopathic Australian Sherlock Holmes gone mad. *Want some tea?* I ask him. No answer.

He's concentrating. Maniacally. He's glaring bug-eyed at the laptop, punching the keys like a maniac, scratching his head and wiping his face, which I notice is sweating like he might have run all the way to my house. He looks like he's boiling up. *No tea then?* No answer. I set out to fix myself a cup.

He's punching the keypad but whatever he's looking for isn't coming up and suddenly it's all too much and he drops to his knees with his face in his hands and starts full-on crying. Sobbing. Bawling like a baby. Tears are exploding out of his eye-sockets. It's shocking and very weird to see a grown man cry so boldly.

My kettle is whistling and I'm thinking *What the fuck.* It's 8am, the kettle is screaming and B is bawling in my kitchen in his wet raincoat, and my girl was just here and...*huh?*

His face is buried in his arm, sprawled across his laptop, sobbing. I ask him if he's okay.

"*It was just the-ah!*" he says in his Aussie accent, gesturing to the computer through tears, "*Just a few minutes agaow! I swe-ah it was the-ah but naow I cah'nt foind it! Dee-ah Gaad please woi ahh you doin' this to me naow? Woi woi?*" He's full on sobbing into his hands.

What the fuck is God doing to you? I'm thinking. He's down on his knees in my kitchen, looking up at the ceiling, tears streaming down his face, frothing at the mouth.

I don't know what to do. I pour myself a cup of green tea and take a look at his laptop, which has a bunch of unintelligible (to me) numbers, symbols, and codes displayed on the screen. I look back over at him and he's down on his knees with his face still in his hands, and I'm wondering what I should do. What I *wanted* to be doing was banging my girl, but I wasn't doing that because B was on my kitchen floor crying in his raincoat and there was a laptop on my kitchen table with something on it, or not, that he was trying to find, which he could not.

Woi me. Come on, B, you gotta tell me what is going on, man, I say to him. He looks up at me, eyes huge, swollen and red, wipes his face, gets up slowly, and says:

"Tre-vah, oi don't want you to hate me, mate, but oi don't know what else to do. Oim losing mah moind, mate, I'm really losing it and I want to maik sure I'm not goin' crazy, but I think I've lost it, mate . . ."

And then he starts sobbing again. But he's not only crying, he's also pleading, and it's a drawling, hyper, super-terrified, paranoid and panicked plea with me, God and whomever else-to please help him find whatever he's looking for. Eventually, I'm able to calm him down long enough for him to start talking.

He tells me, *"Tre-vah, oi think oi've be-cahm what they coll a pedophoile. You know what that is?"* I'm shocked, taken aback. *Of course I know what a pedophile is man, but why do you think you've become one? Are you having sex with kids, B?"*

"Naow, I'm not," he says. *Whew.* So, well, man if you're not having sex with kids, then you're not a pedophile-okay, B? So what's the deal, man? *"Well, you know oi've been sma-okin' spoice roight?"* He's wiping his eyes, composing himself.

Spice

Synthetic marijuana. Sold all over the place in bright, shiny, colorful little packets in various shops in Nagoya and elsewhere in Japan. Not quite legal, but not quite illegal either. Spice falls through some drug/paraphernalia loophole in Japanese law. It's supposed to be used as incense, but many people, like B, use it to get high. There are spice bars aplenty in Japan, semi-legal crack houses, where people go to buy and smoke spice together. I went to this one place in Sakae that was on the third floor of this building that also had sex shops and "health clubs." Health clubs are legal blowjob places.

Yes, I did it. I eagerly, and quite often, patronized the "health" shops and Spice Shops of Nagoya. Yes, it was great, sometimes.

Back To B

B is in my kitchen, down on his knees while pounding the keys of his computer through teary eyes. B's telling me he's been holed up in his house smoking spice "oll dai and noight fo the lahst few weeks" watching child porn, which, he said anyone could get, at any local video store, which I knew was true. You walk into the porn section of any video store in Japan and there on the shelves are dozens of smiling young Japanese girls. These girls look as young as eight or nine years old, wearing bathing suits or the typical Japanese schoolgirl outfit.

There's a famous Japanese, teenage girl group named AKB48, whose fan base is overwhelmingly grown-ass Japanese men. At their regularly sold-out shows in Japan, the audience is almost exclusively these grown Japanese men singing, dancing, and literally crying to show their adoration for these young girls. Let me state here for the record that the indiscretions that dudes are allowed to get away with in Japan—like being fucking *herbivores*—is astounding.

These herbivore freaks are a new breed of young Japanese men who don't want anything to do with women, sexually or otherwise. They don't want the "hassle and expense" of girlfriends, they don't want and aren't even remotely considering marriage or children. They are allowed and encouraged to be fey, hermaphroditic, eyeliner-wearing weirdos. Then you have the guys who are at AKB48 concerts crying their eyes out, waiting in line for hours to get autographs from some skinny Japanese girl who is probably in junior high school. Then you have the dudes who are squeezing girls' asses on the trains, known as "*chikan*," then you have the others who are taking videos of women as they go up the stairs or the escalators. There are probably millions of

Japanese men who have fetishized the young Japanese schoolgirl's uniform of black penny loafers, short black pleated skirt, white shirt, socks/stockings, and tie, and B is in my kitchen telling me he had become one of them. Except for one big difference. Where Japanese men fantasize about mostly teenage girls, and it is implicitly accepted, B says he's been fantasizing about even *younger* girls-elementary school girls—and this is taboo, even in Japan. And pretty fucked up.

This whole scenario presented a major dilemma. Hear me out. One reason B didn't want to make me mad was that he knew that I had two small children of my own in Japan at the time. I have a six-year-old son and a four-year-old daughter, my babies, products of my failed three-year marriage and subsequent hairy, heinous, harrowing, and humiliating divorce. He'd even met them, held them, played with them, and he was at my wedding. He knew coming to me admitting to being a pedophile, or a pedophile in the making, might have caught him a beat down, or maybe me running to the cops. He also knew I'd find it most disgusting that he wanted to fuck kids *just because it is*. He was taking a chance coming to me with it, not sure if I'd throw him out, throw him down, curse him out, call the cops, or what, but there he was at 6:30 fucking A.M. asking for my help, crying in my kitchen, begging for salvation, or something. This is how fucked up and desperate he was. He was on his last straw. I could see it in his eyes and his behavior. I'd felt like that before myself, like I'd fucked up so bad that maybe this was the last day of my fucking life. I felt like that after my divorce, like "maybe this is really it, maybe after today, there'll be no more 'me' . . ." That's how B looked and was acting, but he was my friend. I couldn't stand there and pass judgement at this needy moment in his life. I had to just put my judgement aside for a moment, and just act like a friend. So I did. But it was hard.

I ask him exactly how young the girls he's been fantasizing about were. "Eight, nine, ten years old, mate," he says matter-of-fact. I ask him if he's ever actually done anything with a girl that young, not really wanting to hear his answer. "No, never, oi just watch the videos, but that's what oi want to show you on me laptop," he said, returning his attention to his computer on my table, "but it won't facking work, will it?" He's staring at the computer screen, more tears explode, banging on his keypad.

Frantic now, he gets up and starts flailing at the keys again. Apparently, it still isn't working. He starts pulling out his hair, stands up and starts literally screaming. It's not even 9 am yet. Suddenly, B charges into my living room area, which is littered with all kinds of shit, because I had decided to move out of Japan and back to Los Angeles. B falls to his knees on top of all my shit, slams his face onto my *tatami* mat, balling like a kid who's been caught stealing. I'm sitting at my tiny kitchen 'table', sipping my green tea in my long johns wondering what the *fuck is going on.* It's cold, it's early, and I'm confused.

Eventually, B calms down long enough to tell me that, somewhere in between watching kiddie porn, a woman online asked him to tutor her children. Turned out the woman is the landlord of the old Japanese house B has been living in—and smoking spice in, and watching child porn in—and he tells me that he's actually been teaching the woman's children at her/his house for a few months already. B tells me that he had grown "fond" of the woman's young daughter, who wasn't even in her teens yet. B says he told the woman he wanted her children to "come over and play" at his house without her, but his "play" meant the dirty pedophile type of play. Now, in B's spice-induced paranoia, he had gotten the idea that this woman was spying on him, watching him prey on her children, and that she had subsequently alerted the authorities who were no doubt on their way to get him *right now.*

How is she spying on you, B?-I bemusedly ask him. "W-well..," he says stutteringly, "...she's the landlord, so, she could have installed cameras in the house to watch me." *Why would she do that B?* I ask. He's flustered. "Because, fack, mate, because I'm a *goi-jin*! You know how these Japanese ahh . . ." he says, pissed that I seemingly didn't already know that.

Gaijin

"Goijin" is the Australian approximation of "*gaijin*," which is a shortening of the word "*gaikokujin*," which means "foreigner" in Japanese. Many non-Japanese in Japan are offended by this term. Most Japanese do not fully understand why the term *gaijin* might be offensive to a foreigner, since by definition, it simply means "foreigner." It becomes offensive when Japanese use the term to humiliate foreigners. Gaijin is a weighted word.

B Is Losing It

I ask him, *so B, you think the lady, who is your landlord, whose kids you have been teaching, and whose kids you want to 'play' with, has installed some spying device in your house, and you think she's been watching you while you're watching the kiddie porn, and you think she knows that you want to . . . do whatever you want to do with her young daughter. Right? And you want to show me exactly what on the computer, B?*

He softly looks over at me, stands to his feet, wipes his eyes, and slowly walks over to his computer sitting silently, defiantly, on the table. "WOI ME, GOD, WOI? Should I just turn moiself in to a cop shop or what, mate? I'm done foh-ah! Done, oim tellin' ya! Done it to mi self naow 'aven't oi!!"

I'm sipping my tea. My long johns are itchy. *I hope H washes these today*, I think to myself.

I ask him how it had come to him wanting to have sex with little girls. He launches into a long monologue, almost like he's explaining something I should already understand.

"...It's nature, mate..." he says, "...it just got youngah and youngah and now, *oim facked*..." He says this like he's describing a flat tire that pissed him off. I ask him again if he's actually ever done it, had sex with a minor; he says no, but admits that the only way he can "properly get off" now is by watching the kiddie porn flicks, even if he's with a "real woman,". I ask him if "real women" are cool with his fetish, to which he responds almost gleefully, "Oh, mate, you wouldn't believe 'ow many women there ahh aowt theh who ahh okay with it. That's another thing oi wanted to sha-ow ya on the compu-tah, I wanted you to see oll the women *on-loin* oi've been chattin' with who don't 'av any problem with it . . ." Oh, okay.

He continues-"The compu-tah has the email exchange oi've 'ad with the land-lohd and I want you to see it to make sho-ah oim no' goin' croizy thinkin' she's been watching me, BUT NAOW OI CAHN'T FIND THE FACKING EMAILS AND OI DON'T KNOW WHAT OI SHOULD DO, MATE! IS IT WRONG, MATE? IS IT? SHOULD I JUST TU'N MOI-SELF IN TO A COP SHOP OR WHAT, MATE?! TELL ME WHAT OI SHOULD DO TRE-VAH!!" And then, knees, tears, hair, et cetera.

So I stand up, approach him with my tea cup in my hand and my itchy long johns drooping off my waist and I say, "Listen, B. Calm down. If she's been watching you, she wouldn't let you take care of her kids, man. She'd probably have called the police the first time she saw you doing it. She's not 'watching you,' bro—for what? Or at the least, she'd have told you to move out of her house if she didn't like something you are or aren't doing. No woman is going to allow some dude she thinks is a degenerate watch her kids. You think she's getting off watching you watch kiddie porn dude? And she's still sending you her kids? *Come on, man.* The spice has you fucked. I don't think she knows you're watching kiddie porn. So calm down." He does. A little.

On a roll now, I keep talking. "..And if all you said in the emails is that you wanna play with her kids, and you've never touched them before, then she has no reason to think you want . . . whatever it is you want from her kids, and her kids have never said anything to her about something weird you did, then you're all good, okay? So just calm down." And he does, a little more. And I hear myself say this and I'm thinking, *Trevor, are you fucking serious, man? Is this what it's come to, dude? You're standing here in your long johns at eight o'clock in the morning trying to convince both yourself and this fried Australian cat that it may somehow be okay that he wants to fuck eight-year-olds? W. T. F. Man?*

I look around at my boxes and clothes in piles all over the floor. I look at my children's' desks up against the wall, and their pictures and toys and books and drawings and crayons on the desks, and I'm sipping green tea. B is in my kitchen down on his knees at my tiny, little wooden kitchen table, whimpering because he's a spice addict, junkie pedophile in the making. A super creep who wants to fuck his landlord's 8 year old daughter, and is afraid his landlord *knows* his intentions. In that moment, I *knew* beyond a shadow of a doubt that I had to get the hell out of Japan as soon as possible. Once you compromise your morals, morality becomes a slippery slope. It's said that you are the friends you keep, therefore, I knew I *had to take a flight out* because I did not want to become like B. Ever.

Suddenly, B says in a fit of inspiration, "Oi've gotta sell m'cah, d'ya know anyone who moight wanna boi moi cah?" *Last I heard your car doesn't run, B, still the same?*

"Yeh, but moibee oi c'n git a few thousand yen for it, boi a plane ticket, and get outta this country . . ." He's ruminating.

Nah, man, I don't know anyone who wants to buy a car that doesn't work.

"Hm. Roight, roight . . ." He's thinking hard now, like he's making a plan. I'm thinking too. *What should I do? Should I call the cops? But he hasn't technically done anything wrong, right? At least that's what he says. Fuck, what if I heard someone had touched my son or my daughter? I'd want to kill the fucker. Right? Shouldn't I call the cops to stop him from doing it, even if he hasn't already?*

But he's my friend, right? Am I as fucked up as he is? I am, aren't I? I'm at least an accomplice to his uncommitted crime(s) right? What if he does some wild shit and someone finds out that I knew he was planning to do some wild shit? What then? I'm partially responsible aren't

I? Fuck. But I can't snitch on him either—and for what exactly? Watching child porn? He got it at the fucking video store on the corner! Hm.

Should I just tell him to go home? Tell him not to tell me anymore? What kind of friend is that? Fuck. Dilemma.

Meanwhile, he's pounding on the computer keys again. It's approaching 9am now, this has been going on for over an hour. I tell him, *dude, look, you can chill at my house for a few hours, try to find whatever it is you're looking for. I'm going to the gym. I'll be back in a little while, and we can try to figure out what to do when I get back.* His eyes bulge and his body stiffens, he looks both terrified and completely resolved. He stops banging his keypad, stands up, approach me, looks me in my eyes and says matter-of factly: "No way, mate! No way yo-ah leaving me alone to-dae, mate. Anywhere you go oi'm going with ya. That's it, Tre-vah. Decision made! Oi won't take no for an an-sah. I cahn't be alone today, mate, oi just cahn't . . .", and he falls into my chest and starts sobbing all over again. *Fuck.* I don't want to babysit dude all day, but I also can't just leave him in this condition. I figure going to the gym might take his mind off the situation, if there even was a situation.

He says he'll walk with me but we'll wait outside while I do my thing. I say okay, hop in the shower, change into some sweats, B scoops up his laptop and we head out towards the gym. It's cold.

B is soaking wet from crying. There's steam coming off his forehead. He's wearing shorts, an oversized yellow raincoat and those stupid alligator-feet shoes. He looks exactly like what he has become, a tweaked-out, potential sex predator, junkie foreigner, and I'm walking down the street with him at 9 o'clock in the morning. In Japan. *This is my life?*

On the way, perplexed and still not understanding, I ask *B, man, I mean, little baby girls, man? What the fuck, man? Why? I mean, I just don't get it.* He tells me again that in Japan it's more "acceptable" for a grown man to have sexual feelings for young girls than it is in Western countries. He says he feels like it has just become the "natural course of events as a man," to want a girl at that young age. He's not apologizing for how he's feeling, he's convinced himself that *he's* normal and that the rest of us are fucked up. I wonder momentarily if he's right, shake it off, and we continue walking.

He tells me he has a shitload of child porn at his house, and he doesn't know how to get rid of it. He says he's sure the authorities are on their way to his place "*roight naow*", and that he has to leave the country in the next few days somehow. As we're walking, I notice that he's walking way too close to me, as if we're attached at the shoulder. With every other step, B is turning around looking behind us to see something or someone that doesn't exist. He thinks we're being followed. He's paranoid looking back at nothing. I'm now becoming paranoid, looking behind us at absolutely nothing. As a result, I pick up the pace and lo and behold, so does he.

B is cradling his old-ass laptop in both arms, so close to him it looks like he's either carrying a baby, or like he's holding a dozen loose eggs in his arms. As we get closer to the gym, he's looking around furtively, jumpy and irrational, nervous and spastic, thinking he's doing his best to *not* get noticed, while in fact he looks exactly like what any normal Japanese person might consider to be a paranoid drug infested, pedophile, foreign sex predator. And then there's me, the tall, skinny black guy with dreadlocks and sunglasses, wearing black long johns and grey sweats, walking down a suburban Japanese street towards the gym, alongside the junkie Australian sex predator pedophile.

How has it come to this? I think to myself. *Just a short while ago, B was happily telling me stories about riding horses and catching roots in the Australian outback with his brothers. Why does he want to fuck 8 year old Japanese girls now? And why is he wearing that raincoat?*

I work out for about forty minutes, during which time B calls me repeatedly on my cell phone. There are 8 text messages and 10 missed calls from him. I listen to the first message, it's him saying "You almost done, mate? Oim still he-ah, aowtside waitin' foh ya . . ." in a hoarse whisper. His voice sounds like a car creeping up a stone covered driveway. With an Australian accent.

I finish, head outside, and there he is standing exactly where I'd left him, like he hadn't moved an inch. He was too paranoid to move from that spot. We start walking back towards my house, B is silent, head low, brow furrowed as if he's in deep thought. I'm wondering what's going to happen next, are we going to go upstairs and...what? Is he going to keep trying to find whatever on his laptop? Should I call the cops? Should I be angry at him? Should I try to talk him out of his...fetish? Should I, suddenly, just as we round the corner to my apartment, B stops in his tracks, looks at me maniacally and says in a flash, "Mate, oi think oi've got an oi-dea, oi'll be roight back . . .", and he takes off running in the opposite direction, holding his laptop, yellow raincoat blowing in the wind.

I watch him get smaller and smaller thinking, *man, I hope you work it out*, and feeling relieved that the issue was going away, for the moment at least. That image of B running down the block in his frog feet, alligator shoes, shorts, and wet yellow raincoat, clutching his laptop was the last I ever saw of my Aussie friend B, who was becoming a pedophile after living in Japan for just about the same amount of time I had been living there. He vanished.

I went inside and sat at my son's desk and looked at pictures of him and his sister for about an hour, staring at their soft half black, half Japanese faces wondering if it was a good idea for me to leave Japan after having been there for a decade, knowing there were weirdo freaks like B running around. I'd been wondering if it was time for me to bounce Japan for the last few years, and had decided it was time to go. It was crazy for me to imagine leaving my two babies in Japan, not just because there were weirdos out there, but also, how *could* I leave them? *They need me*, or at least, *I needed them*. Fuck. *Should I stay or should I go?* I'd been having this conversation with myself the last six years. But now that I'd set the wheels in motion already, there was no turning back. Or was there?

I told myself I could still stay. I didn't have to leave just yet, it hadn't been exactly ten years. What's so bad anyway? *I've got it going on here in Japan.* I can drag this out and no one can ever say I didn't live it plush. Or, at least I could stay until my birthday and then leave-that'd be exactly 10 years. Another six months, right? Leave in the fall, when I arrived, yeah, that sounds like the move.

Confusion is a bitch and decisions are hard, even if they're easy sometimes. One thing I knew was, I didn't want to fuck little girls. I was grateful. Grateful that I hadn't morphed into a raving lunatic, spice-smoking, raincoat-wearing, junkie pedophile. I made myself more tea and silently wished the best for B. Soon, my thoughts returned to my girl H, I hoped she wasn't spooked by the whole situation.

Chapter 2

THE CASE TO LEAVE AMERICA

"Been though the desert on a horse with no name..."

Things are really getting real here in these dis-United States.

You get caught up in the noise of America. White noise, black noise, red noise, yellow noise, brown noise. Relaxation and peace are anathema. It's a cutthroat, dog-eat-dog death race competition. *Game Of Thrones, Hunger Games, Total Recall,* dystopian *Mad Max* nihilistic battle for life every day, everywhere. Everyone screaming at the top of their lungs all the time whether it's necessary or not. Outrage and vitriol. Taxes rise, prices rise, tensions rise, blood pressures rise, and we consume it all ravenously every night in our living rooms, bedrooms, kitchen counter laptops and our 50 inch flatscreens siphon off our energy—and then we wash it all down with a Coke and a smile. *Free refills everywhere?*

"America" is a myth. It's an idea much more than it is a country. It's a place that exists in history books, movies, wishes, hopes, and dreams. Vast swaths of The Real America are a jangly juxtaposition of racist, paranoid, jingoistic, bureaucratic, dangerous, gun totin', high maintenance, aggressive, divided, obnoxious, loud, lazy, ignorant, deluded, violent, racist goofballs, except when and where it isn't, which isn't often. I'm a "proud" American.

We are living in the time of "alternative facts," lies by any other name.

The air is poisoned and whereas it used to be a caveat that we never talk about politics, right now, the only thing anyone is talking about is politics.

I was bought and sold into the American Dream, a dream that may never really have existed, or if it did, it was a short-lived dream, and it doesn't seem to exist today. There's no middle class, barely a shot at it. Our political parties spar with one another and rather than actually try to get something done, they'd rather block the other party from getting anything done.

Whatever. It's all fucked up and you know it and we all know it, but if you're black, it's extra fucked up. There's an extra-thick coating of darkness, danger, and degradation black people in America live their entire lives with.

You could say it's our "skin." Funny, huh? Not really, not fucking really.

If you're American, especially a Black American, it feels like there's always something out to get you. The system, the police, your own brothers living up the block from you, the food, the IRS, your landlord, Armageddon, the second coming of Christ. Doomsday politics is an American thing, every few months there's a new prediction that the world is about to end, in America the end is always near. But if you're a Black American male, it seems even nearer.

I'm not just saying Black America is more dangerous than it is for White America, I'm saying it's *way* more dangerous. If you could slip on the "one ring to bring them all and in the darkness bind them" like Frodo did in The Lord of The Rings, you'd see the swirling miasma of hostility blacks in America face on a daily basis. Life in America for black people is one big shadowy realm.

When I came back from Japan I had hoped all this overt, violent, stupid, self-destructive but more so black-destructive, dumbass American racism between black people and white people would have disappeared. Fuck was I thinking? The block is hotter than ever right now.

Black Americans live with a kind of fear of the cops you see in movies about apartheid South Africa. Abject paranoia, yo. From the moment we're born.

Without fear, or even with much less of it, your mind literally changes. Your options grow, choices you make become unlimited, and you transcend your program. You are able to access more subtle realms of yourself. You can succeed. But you must overcome, or be allowed to live in a society where you are not afraid. In Japan, for the most part of my time there, I wasn't afraid of the cops coming after me. Instead of being afraid, I was creating.

Them Japanese cops weren't out to get me. They weren't profiling me, weren't looking at me sideways, weren't giving me dirty looks, they looked at me for sure, I could never escape being gaijin, but, they weren't about to shoot me either.

My mind and posture both straightened up. I wasn't checking behind my back every few steps to see if the cops were following me, or radioing something into headquarters. The one run-in I had with cops was my own fault. Overwhelmingly though, the cops in Japan had absolutely no effect on my life there, and the lack of my having to think about them freed me up, body, mind, soul, and spirit.

I had more space in my brain psychology to work with. I was doing all kinds of wildly creative things I had only dreamt about doing when I was in America. I was making more money too. Those yen were flowing. I was making 4 to 5 hundred thousand yen in one month—the equivalent in dollars is 4 or 5 thousand bucks monthly. This is no king's ransom by any means, but in Japan, it was coming in steadily, every month. I had this dough in my pocket, shooting through the city like a rocket, and the cops weren't fucking with me at all. Sure, they noticed me, but they aren't packing heat, *first of all*, and second, they don't look menacing, they look benign, and they weren't fucking with me.

"Fear not, for when you fear you die a thousand small deaths, but real death comes but once." Fear is a killer.

New Work Ethic

In America, I had a weak work ethic—if it even existed—and a disdain for authority that exacerbated the already "us vs. them" mentality that exists as part of the fabric of life in the US amongst the two 'dominant' races.

What I mean is that after a while in Japan, strangely, I started to loosen up, relax, let go of certain invisible results of living in America—the fear of cops was one of the first "American" things to go. Weird to be scared of something your whole life then, suddenly, notice that fear goes away, or more precisely, the thing which you feared no longer exists.

I had decided to work hard. I looked around in Japan and it seemed like everyone was working—day after day, month after month, year after year, long hours with very little leisure time, at least as far as we Americans see it.

I saw very few slackers; what I did see were Japanese folks waking up early, working long hours, and doing it steadily with very little complaint and a great deal of pride in their jobs.

Chin up. Shoulders back. Long strides. Deep breaths.

This is how I felt a few years in. Walking tall, feeling proud, working hard, and succeeding as someone useful *in another country.* When I noticed I wasn't afraid of the cops, because they didn't seem afraid of me, I noticed at the same time that I wasn't feeling bitter either. I didn't feel like I had to *take* in order to receive. I felt like no one owed me anything, because I didn't feel like society at large was mistreating me based solely on my skin color. I was getting opportunities based on being unique, and I guessed, therefore, useful. I wasn't being marginalized because I wasn't of the dominant race; I was being put to work, tested on my own laurels and challenged for my valor.

Something For Nothing

Another prevailing attitude in the US, that I hadn't noticed until it was absent, is the attitude that somehow we deserve something for doing nothing. Again, I hate to indict my own race, but I guess the history of Black Americans having been slaves, having been dirt poor, having been legally and illegally discriminated against, having had to deal with second- and third-class citizenship and dirty water fountains and backs of buses, has left this stain in our brains that has us always expecting something—in many cases, for having done nothing. Black Americans sometimes expect "special treatment" just for being black. *We deserve it* is at the back of the brain of Black America, *as long as it's free.*

I think this particular trait goes beyond color though. I think Americans in general just expect lots of free shit, and if shit ain't free, Americans are more than willing to take what isn't theirs and make it theirs.

In Japan, you don't get shit free, and no one is expecting to get shit free. Everyone is working, or almost everyone—Japan's unemployment rate hovers just over three percent, and "welfare," in the way Americans know it, doesn't exist there. There are no Japanese mothers pumping out babies in order to collect that government check monthly. Well, there are, but it isn't a cottage industry like it is in America.

Homelessness exists in Japan, but nowhere near the degree to which you see it in major American cities. Japanese teenagers are not wandering around with nothing to do after school, being nuisances or petty thieves. Twentysomething Japanese are not, for the most part, getting high/drunk/stoned, with nothing to do, all the while expecting something from someone for having done nothing. Some are, but most aren't. It isn't part of the culture like it is in America.

I'm not saying *all* American young people—or minorities, or which-ever marginalized demographic you'd like to slip in here—are doing all of these things, but it sure seems like a lot of them are.

'Private' Property?

The notion of private property in America is odd. Americans steal shit like it's going out of style. Leave your bag/purse/wallet somewhere for five minutes in almost any major American city, chances are that piece of property is not going to be there when you return for it. Fuck five minutes, five *seconds* is more like it in some places.

Japan, totally different story. *Opposite* story. I left my phone on the train several times, only to have the train company locate me and mail my phone to my house. In Japan, I left my bag sitting in parks over-night, only to return the next day to find it exactly where I'd left it. I have to admit having had my bicycle stolen, but I chalk this up to my own overly trusting attitude towards Japanese, as a result of seeing firsthand how they respect other people's property. I learned, however, it ain't smart to keep an expensive bicycle, or inexpensive for that mat-ter, unlocked at the train station for four or five days in a row—even in Japan. Bicycles are hot commodities in urban Japan. I tried to play "no one is going to take my shit, even if I leave it there for a week" one too many times, and my shit got *took*.

By and large, there's no comparison when it comes to respect for private property between Japanese and Americans. They do, we don't, simple. Again, the feeling of knowing your stuff is essentially safe, that no one is eyeing you and what you have, that you don't have to watch over your belongings like a friggin' miser 24/7, is freeing to the mind and spirit. Again, it's liberating. It unlocks previously knotted emo-tions and diffuses paranoia and fear and all the attendant negative tendrils associated with those emotions. This release was mentally, emotionally, and spiritually orgasmic. I give thanks and praise in abundance to the Japanese for showing me what life without these fears is like, and for giving me safety for a while.

Black Americans Don't Travel. Much.

Black Americans don't travel. They might go to the Caribbean, might go on a cruise or might hit up Brazil looking to hook up with Brazilian women, but for the most part, Black Americans stay put, right in America, thinking America is some kind of Promised Land. Why? They're afraid. They know it ain't great in America, but at least they know how it is. There's nothing more terrifying than the fear of the unknown, and what's beyond the borders of America is absolutely unknown to most Black Americans—hell, most Americans, black or white.

Props go out to the brothers overseas who have made the next level jump, to actually leave their own country to go live in a different country than their own. It's a mind expanding leap into the unknown.

Beyond all the reasons not to leave America, or anywhere, there are positive reasons for leaving as well. There's expansion, learning, growth, *enlightenment*.

Jimi Hendrix, Jonathan Livingston Seagull, Plato & Outkast Or *Escape, Disappear, Be Gone, Bounce.*

Jimi Hendrix was a virtuoso guitar player that "got no love" here in the US—that is, until he left his home country and traveled to England, where his guitar playing was recognized and honored. After being discovered by Chas Chandler, Jimi returned home a superstar hero, and has since become a legend.

Chapter 3

TRUE HOLLYWOOD STORIES

A small shitty neighborhood, where dreams go to die

I'd been living in Los Angeles for about three and a half years, pursuing a mildly successful acting career. I was in the movie, *Vanilla Sky* and worked right next to Tom Cruise. I also appeared in the "Survivor" video for Destiny's Child back when Destiny's Child was still a thing. However, notwithstanding these sporadic windows of opportunity, my career as an actor was bitter sweet. Mostly bitter.

The Nutty Actor Who Pissed Away a Great Opportunity

One of my first acting gigs was for the film, 'The Nutty Professor II' starring Eddie Murphey and Janet Jackson. We were shooting an outdoor scene in downtown LA at night. At the time, LA's downtown was a cesspool of drug addicts, crazies, and the largest homeless population you've ever seen. People openly shooting up dope, fighting, pissing, shitting, and fucking right there on the sidewalk. All this is happening while we're shooting a big Hollywood movie. Cool.

In the film, I was cast as a photographer in the pivotal scene where Eddie unveils his latest scientific formula to the press. In the scene, the formula gets into the wrong hands and chaos ensues during the press conference. Everyone, myself included, was supposed to run out into the street when Eddie's plan goes haywire. So we did that.

After about 40 takes though, I had to piss. So I did. I walked around the corner to where the homeless folks were, whipped out my shit and let it fly. I then promptly returned to production and waited along with everyone else to be called back to set. As soon as we were called, I felt a tap on my shoulder. Some dude with a walkie-talkie strapped to his ear ask me to follow him to the production office, which was really a mobile home trailer. I'm thinking, *maybe someone spotted me and I got upgraded, maybe I'll get a line or two with Eddie or Janet. Maybe I'll get my own trailer.* Nope. Once inside the production office/mobile home trailer, walkie-talkie dude sits down behind a desk, eyes me scornfully, and finally says to me,

"Mr. David, someone spotted you...uh...relieving yourself on the street. Is that true?"

I'm thinking, *someone spotted me? Like who? Some homeless dude snitched on me? Complained that I pissed on his street? You have got to be joking.* But he wasn't. I'm standing there shell-shocked that someone is asking me if I took a leak on the street. Hell, in NYC, we take a leak wherever the hell we want.

Walkie-talkie man is staring through me, so eventually I had to come clean,

"Yeah man, I had to go, the port-a-potties were too far away from set, so I...I just...I...peed."

As soon as I admitted the deed, dude immediately pulled out the sign in sheet, scratched my name off it and tore up my voucher in front of my face, like he was angry at me. He then instructed me to wait there in the office/trailer. He gets on his walkie and exits the trailer. Moments later, he returns and tells me that security would be there momentarily to escort me off set. *Escort me off set?*

He exits again and I'm left standing in the trailer thinking, *hold up Trev, you pissed on a street where pissing in the street is what folks do, and now, you're not going to get your shot with Janet? Word?!*

Well, at least I got escorted. *Nutty Professor II* sucked anyway. Janet was really pretty though.

Vanilla Sky - How I Met Tom Cruise

Somehow, I scored a gig as a 'featured extra' on the set of Tom Cruise's '*Vanilla Sky*' film. Featured extras, are extras whose faces you can actually see for more than a few seconds on screen. They're customers standing in line next to the main actor at Starbucks, or a doctor dealing with a patient as the main actor runs into the hospital after getting shot. Or a bar patron who's standing directly next to the main actor pretending to be overly amused by fake conversation. This was me. But it wasn't supposed to go down how it did.

I got booked to do one day's work on 'Vanilla Sky'. A day's work on a SAG feature film in LA paid a little over a hundred bucks at the time. If you were lucky, you'd get some overtime, which was about an extra fifty bucks. For 12 hours of work, a hundred fifty bucks is just over 12 bucks an hour, *before taxes*. Extra work pays shitty money, unless you book lots of commercials, which pays better than movies and television shows. Much better.

So, we're shooting at Paramount Studios on the set of Vanilla Sky. The scene is set in a bar. Cruise and his co-star is having a sort of face off. In character, Cruise tells everyone to 'shut up', to prove to his nemesis that he is not actually living in the real world, but rather a world of his making. Somehow, the first AD (Assistant Director) placed me directly behind Tom. I'm clearly on camera; denim shirt, flowing locks, while having a fake conversation and pretending to consume alcohol.

We did take after take of the scene. Apparently, there were some nuances that the director, Cameron Crowe wanted to get out of Cruise's character. Time and again, "action!", "cut!", "back to one!", "ready-sound, rolling, camera rolling, speed, Vanilla Sky, bar scene, take 47, 48, 49..."---

Everyone was exhausted, including Tom Cruise. In between every take, he'd slip on a pair of headphones and get lost listening to music on his CD Walkman. He'd stand on his mark listening intently to the music until someone tapped him on his shoulder to let him know we were ready to shoot. Tom would then hand over his headphones and Walkman to a production crew member and we'd shoot the scene again. And again. And again.

By the end of the day, Cameron Crowe still hadn't gotten quite what he wanted from Mr. Cruise. As we're signing out for the day, the AD expressed to me that I would need to return tomorrow because I was featured in the scene and they'd need me in order to maintain continuity. But I had other plans the next day.

I was booked for a commercial, and it was a Saturday, which guaranteed me a payday of at least 400 dollars. As I said, commercial extra work pays more than film extra work, and even though I was 'featured' in the footage we'd shot with Tom, there was no telling whether or not I'd actually end up in the film.

So for me, it was a no brainer. I couldn't return to Paramount the next day, not only because I had already been booked on a commercial, but also because I would have been taking a financial loss. Again, it was 100 bucks for the Cruise flick verses 400 bucks for the commercial, and since I couldn't afford to be star struck, I went with the commercial.

I let the AD know that I couldn't return the next day and he looks at me disdainfully and says, "Well, we might need you, so just keep it open..."

"Sure" I say. *Fuck that*, I'm thinking. I'm going to my 400 dollar commercial shoot.

Next morning, I wake up at 7 in order to get to my 9 a.m. call time on set of the commercial in Newport Beach. Newport Beach, taking the 405, is about an hour drive from Hollywood.

I'm sitting in the makeup chair on the set of this commercial for some famous brand, chatting languidly with the pretty make up woman patting my face. My phone rings. I answer it, and whose voice is on the other end---? It's Cameron Crowe, director of *Vanilla Sky*.

"Hey Trevor, could you do us a big favor? We really need you on set. If we can't match the scenes from yesterday we've got to trash all the film we shot yesterday. That's gonna throw our budget by tens of thousands of dollars..." Cameron Crowe tells me.

Holy Fucking Shit...Cameron Crowe's on my phone asking me to come to Paramount Studios to do a scene with Tom Cruise.

"Well, Mr. Crowe, I'd love to help you out but I'm already on the set of my commercial, I'm actually about to go in front of the camera..."

"Listen," he says, all serious. "I'll pay you whatever they're paying you, if you'll come to my set. We're all standing here waiting for you Trevor, including Tom..."

I think for a split second.

"Okay. I'll be there. See you in about an hour..." I say before hanging up the phone.

I jump out of the makeup chair and tell the makeup lady that I've got to go. She's temporarily startled but she's not the producer so she doesn't really give a shit. I walk outside the trailer, find the first AD and tell him I've got to go do a gig with Tom Cruise and Cameron Crowe at Paramount Studios.

"Cool dude! Good luck" he says.

An hour later, I pull up to the gate at Paramount, give my name and immediately I'm allowed access. I head towards the soundstage and walk upstairs to the bar set we'd worked on the day before. On set, I find everyone, including Tom Cruise, standing in exactly the same positions they all had been in the day before. Except this time, they were all staring at *me*. I truly felt special. It was surreal.

I walk over to take my place next to Tom. He's wearing his headphones while glaring directly into my eyes. It's that really intense, wide-eyed glare that Tom gives in almost all of his movies. It means he's *really, really* listening, or looking, or looking *through* you. I extend my hand,

"I'm sorry..." I start.

Tom immediately grabs my hand and swipes off his headphones with his other hand like the movie star he was. He then flashes the famous Tom Cruise smile, pulls me in close and says,

"Sorry for what brother?"

At that moment, I imagine Tom and I are best friends. He's happy I'm there, and I am too. I signed my voucher as "featured extra", strolled off the set buzzed about having met Tom Cruise, and having earned 400 bucks to boot. *What commercial?*

Beyoncé Believed in Me

I met Beyoncé when I was an extra on the hip hop remake of the French opera, "Carmen". Beyoncé was playing the lead in the movie, she spotted me in the crowd, and had her assistant invite me into her trailer. I sat a few feet across from her, she introduced herself and I thought, *damn this girl has a deep voice.* She had a big beautiful smile and was friendly and gracious. She told me that Destiny's Child was about to shoot a music video for one of their songs, "Survivor" on Zuma Beach. She asked me if I'd like to take part in the shoot. I told her, of course. We shot the video on the beach one cold November morning. California beaches are always cold. Beyoncé, Kelly, and Michelle went into the cold Pacific Ocean repeatedly while the director repeatedly yelled "action" and "cut!" Lucky for me, my scenes consisted of me standing on a cliff, over-looking the ocean, and then walking and dancing through a fake "jungle", which was really the botanical gardens of Los Angeles. She was gregarious and warm, and Oh yeah, Beyoncé was thick and fine as well.

Almost Famous

I had moved to Los Angeles after my film, *Love Goggles* won the best narrative prize at the first ever Black Hollywood Film Festival. I played the lead character, "Topcat" in the film. The Topcat dude was an asshole club owner with a deep distrust of women. At the time of filming, I was going through some crazy stress in my personal life, living in Brooklyn, trying to make ends meet while shuttling back and forth into Manhattan looking for a break. The Topcat character in the movie mirrored my own life, filled with self-doubt, coupled with delusions of grandeur. When *Love Goggles* won the best film award, I thought my acting career was going to take off in LA. I thought I'd be up on the big screen with Denzel Washington, Morgan Freeman and Samuel Jackson, doing movie star things in Hollywood. I camped out on my friend's couch in Studio City, and went at the acting. I never returned to Brooklyn.

I was in a few commercials and music videos. I'd had a few guest star roles on several television shows, but I was working as an 'extra' more than anything else. The money in being an extra isn't enough to survive in Los Angeles, and the acting bug is a parasite that if you're not careful, can suck your soul out through your back, leaving you hollowed out and bent over. After too many "almost" auditions, I was burnt out and decided I needed something different.

Chapter 4

CHRISTINE

The Vegan Vampire

At the end of my stint in LA, I had a girlfriend, Christine, a bisexual, hyper-feminist, vegan, self-proclaimed vampire that I'd met at a bus stop while riding my bike on Ventura Boulevard. Christine was standing at the bus stop but wasn't waiting for a bus. I didn't know that at the time.

Christine was a young, half black, half white, Stevie Knicks type with brown hair and a pretty face. She was on vacation from New York when we met. As I rode by on my bike, our eyes locked and fate took its course. I circled around and pulled up in front of her.

"Hey", I say.

"Hey", she smiles. I notice she has fangs. Real life Dracula fangs. I wasn't sure if they were natural or not but there they were, gleaming white through her smile, and that was enough.

Ties That Bind

LA had me feeling like a fish out of water. My acting "career" was in a drawer somewhere, and I was living alone in Van Nuys. I was feeling lost and alone in LA, and when I met Christine it seemed like we were both desperate for something. Desperation is the thing that binds people together in Los Angeles. She needed help, I needed help. She told me she was staying in a hotel on Ventura Boulevard for a few days with some "asshole", and asked me right at the bus stop if she could come stay with me. I said yes. She flew back to New York, packed her bags and a few months later, she arrived at LAX.

I picked Christine up at the airport in my white, 1985 Toyota Supra, which I had recently bought for one thousand dollars cash. It was running fine, until the night I picked up Christine at the airport.

As we're on our way back to my studio apartment, cruising down the 405 freeway, I'm thinking, *this could be heaven or this could be hell*.

Christine is happy. I believe I'm happy too. However, the truth was that I couldn't stop looking at her vampire teeth through her hopeful smile. Suddenly, there's a loud CLUNK in the engine. The car sputters and decelerates until I have to pull over. Needless to say, it was supremely embarrassing to be picking up this girl from the airport, who is ostensibly about to become your live-in girlfriend, then to have your car die on the road on the way home. But that is exactly what happened. I had no money at the time, and Christine ended up having to fork out two hundred dollars to have my car towed. She also covered the cost of the taxi to take us to my, our, place.

Christine was direct, she told me immediately that I owed her the two hundred dollars, while I thought, *babe, you're moving into my apartment for free*. Things didn't get off to a great start between us.

A couple weeks later, Christine's truck arrived from New York City. She had it shipped via auto-train. Her truck became our transportation since my stupid Supra was now history. I suddenly was in debt to Christine, and now, I was in the passenger seat of *her* truck everywhere we went.

My Vegan Likes Hamburgers

Christine and I did not get on well. She was a bisexual vegan and had unique philosophies regarding men and women's relationships. She was extremely talkative, and would talk to me incessantly about the "fact" that a woman's menstrual cycle was the true and real 'clock', or calendar by which humanity ought to structure itself. She talked about the cycles of the moons and how it relates to a woman's menstrual cycle and proclaimed herself to be a 'white witch'. She practiced pagan rites and ate parsley sandwiches and expected me to do the same. She was insanely committed to this theme, until, that is, once in a while, when she'd gorge herself on hamburgers, French fries, Coke, and chocolate cake at this deli located down in Santa Monica a couple blocks off the beach. Christine would stuff the cake into her mouth as fast as she could as if someone was watching her. She'd gulp down the Coke and then sit there until she burped. This was startling, this "vegan", pounding cake and hamburgers down her throat but would yell at me whenever I wanted a Snickers bar.

"Trev-uh, what's going to happen to ow-ah kids when you die? You want me to tell them their faw-thuh killed himself eatin' Snickuzz bahz?" she'd say in her thick New York accent.

Kids?! What the fuck are you talking about Christine? I'd think to myself.

I wished she'd have just made me some chicken. Or meatloaf. Or fried eggs. Something. But all she ever 'made' were these fried vegetable patties that tasted like hot dirt.

Her grandmother called the apartment nearly every day. If Christine was out, she'd talk to me on the phone for an hour, telling me how much she loved Christine, how "innocent" Christine was, and how thankful she was that I was "taking care of" her Christine.

"I'll do my best", I'd say, and hang up, hungry.

Have You Ever Had Sex With A Vampire?

When Christine and I made love, she'd insist I pleasure her with my fingers first. For 45 minutes to be exact, give or take.

She'd position herself sitting naked and upright on the edge of the bed. She'd then have me kneel in front of her and put my index and middle finger inside her. I'd work my fingers until she squirted copious amounts of clear milky fluid. Sometimes, Christine flushed out so much liquid that it would form a filmy pool in my palm and cascade down my forearm. There were lots of times I actually gagged. It was a sight to behold.

Immediately following the mandatory trip to Niagara Falls, Christine would hand me a purple dolphin shaped dildo that I had to use on her. She'd lay back on the bed and guide the dolphin inside her. She'd instruct me exactly how fast to go, how hard, how deep, etc. Only after the fingering and purple dolphin dildo was I "allowed" to actually have intercourse with Christine.

She would lie underneath me, look directly into my eyes, *defiantly*, as though we were fighting, not making love. Usually, I'd stroke long enough to force Christine into submission or sensual enough where she'd succumb to the feeling.

She'd release a huge sigh, as though she'd been holding her breath, grab me and yell, "...okay, okay!"

She'd force me on my back, then grind me *way too hard*, while pounding on my chest with her fists. It was as though Christine was angry that what we were doing felt good to her. Or maybe she was angry that she had told me that as a bisexual she "preferred women to men", but there she was, enjoying a man that was inside of her. Either way, her banging on my chest was traumatic and painful for me. I can't allow a women on top of me to this day.

Woman Of Mystery

Christine and I went to skeezy parties up in Franklin Village and hung out at Venice Beach. Sometimes at these parties in Hollywood, Christine would disappear for a while, 30 minutes, an hour, and then magically reappear as if nothing happened. I'd ask her where she was and she'd always say, "...oh, I just met some really cool artists...", and leave it at that. Things happen in dark rooms of Hollywood mansions, and parties all the time. Christine was a mystery to me. Most importantly though, *I was hungry*.

Christine fancied herself an actress and a musician who actually played a killer guitar and had a sick little mixtape of songs she'd written. I had a blue electric Fender Stratocaster guitar at the time, which I had hoped I could just wake up one day and play like Jimi Hendrix on that bitch, but that never happened. The truth is, Christine played my guitar better than I did. We stayed up at night and wrote songs and poems and ate her veggie patties. We had fights too. We went for walks along Sherman Way,

"Tell me you love me" she'd say.

"Chris, I mean, you just got here. I mean, I really like you a lot you know..." I'd attempt to reply.
"TELL ME YOU LOVE ME!" she'd yell.

"...okay man, I love you okay? Jesus..." I'd say.

Christine demanded my affection, beat my chest when we fucked, *had fangs*, and wouldn't make me a freakin' sandwich. Sexually, she was demanding, self-serving, and violent. Ruthless, almost. She seemed indignant about the fact that I was a man and her "I'm a Witch" thing had gotten old quick.

Christine was an ultra-feminist bisexual lesbian-leaning vegan, who loved pleasuring *herself* with a purple dildo and eating gobs of chocolate cake and hamburgers whenever she *wasn't* being a vegan. *Why am I doing this*, I wondered. It was no good.

An Opportunity Awaits

Two months later, we were at each other's throats and I was wishing she'd either get out of my place, or a miracle would come my way. At this point, I was broke, rent was due, and Christine was pissed. So, I decided to give acting another try.

I picked up a paper copy of Backstage and came across an ad that read:

"Do You Want Adventure? Travel? Glamour? How Would You Like To Teach English And Drama In Japan?"

I thought to myself *sure,* that sounds about right actually.

I threw together a package of pictures and a resume, and they asked me to come in for an interview. Christine drove me to Hollywood and parked her truck outside the building on Hollywood Boulevard and told me she'd keep the car running.

Inside this LA office, I was first interviewed by a young Japanese woman in a business suit. She wasn't especially beautiful, but she was excessively polite. She was professional, gracious, extremely attentive, and had a hyper feminine air about her. A stark contrast to Christine, who had a hyper *feminist* air about her.

After our interview, the lady told me she was going to call Mr. Kosugi and that I'd speak to him directly on the phone. Mr. Sho Kosugi, as it turned out, was a well-known movie star in Japan, who, during the 80's, played a ninja assassin in a string of highly successful Japanese martial arts movies. On the heels of his fame, he'd opened up a handful of international martial arts/acting schools, and he was interviewing actors in Los Angeles to come to his school in Nagoya to teach his students acting, English, drama, and whatever else.

Mr. Kosugi was in Tokyo at the time of the interview but minutes later I'm on the phone with him discussing plans for a new life in Japan.

"What do you know about Japan" he asked me.

What I knew at the time was that the Japanese woman who interviewed me was much nicer than Christine had ever been, and that Godzilla did not like Japanese people, and that Japan had bombed Pearl Harbor, and also that Japanese people loved sushi. That's it. However none of those qualify as answers one can give in a job interview.

"Not much", I said,

"But I'm a quick learner and able to adapt to new people, places, and environments, and I'm a great communicator and I've always been interested in Japan and blah blah blah...", and somehow I got the job.

Right there, on the phone, on that late summer afternoon in that building on Hollywood Boulevard, with Christine waiting for me downstairs with her truck running. My destiny was laid out before me by some dude named Sho Kosugi talking to me from Tokyo, Japan.

I was told that I'd have exactly one month to prepare my things and leave my apartment, my friends, my career, and my life in Los Angeles. I was leaving it all behind in order to fly out to Japan to become an English and Drama teacher.

Why me? Japan? Teach English? *For real?* I didn't know how to teach anything. I floated out of the office thinking, *Hey Trev, you're going to Japan dude. Wow.* Japan. I bolted downstairs and couldn't wait to tell Christine. I'm bopping along Hollywood Boulevard with the Walk of Fame underneath my feet.

Christine's truck is parked ahead, a few blocks east of Highland. I reach her truck, it's running, and Christine is sitting in the driver's seat wearing a flannel shirt and jeans. I swing the truck door open and blurt out,

"Hey! I think I just got that job! They asked me to come to Japan in a month!"

"Great! I've never been to Japan! I've always wanted to go, when are we leaving?" Christine says.

Confusion. *What? Who is "we"?* It seemed as though, somehow, Christine thought *we* had gotten a job in Japan, not me. I climbed in, feeling a mixture of elation and surprise about getting the job, and weird paranoia about whatever was going to happen with Christine.

We drove back to my apartment with her demanding over and over again, that I 'let' her come to Japan with me. She said that I ought to bring her with me, as if it was my decision to make.

She told me again and again while we were driving, how selfish I was for not telling them I had a girlfriend and that she'd *have to* come with me.

I kept saying, "Chris, I can't take you, I don't know anything about Japan, or about where I'll be living, what I'll be doing, I can't be responsible for you over there..", but she wasn't having it. She pounded on her dashboard and her eyes bulged and she balled up her fists and told me I was selfish. I didn't care.

When I finally convinced her that I didn't have the option to take her, she demanded that I give her my guitar.

"GIVE ME THAT GUITAR. I WANT THAT GUITAR!" she's screaming at me while we're driving back to my Van Nuys studio apartment that we called 'home' for the last two months.

"I WANT THAT GUITAR BECAUSE I WANT IT AND YOU WON'T TAKE ME TO JAPAN. I DESERVE TO HAVE IT!"

Christine didn't get my guitar. It, along with all the other stuff I couldn't take went packed up to my Uncle Ron's garage in Baldwin Hills. Baldwin Hills is LA's "Black Beverly Hills". My Uncle Ron lived there with my Aunt Carolyn, who once threaten to shoot me because I entered her house at 3 A.M., high, looking for water and toaster pastries. I was supposed to be staying in their backhouse but I was high, and extremely hungry.

After I received the news about the gig in Japan, Christine stayed in my Van Nuys studio for a few more days, then one day she came home and informed me that she was moving into a commune-style house in Franklin Village that she'd found on her own. Over the course of a day or two, Christine packed her stuff and moved out of my place. A few days later, Christine returned and silently handed me a card that said "Heal Yourself," and vanished. And that was it, I never heard from her again. Vegans.

A few weeks after, I was on an airplane bound for Japan.

>Chapter 5

WELCOME TO JAPAN

Sail Away

You never know where you'll end up, how you'll get there, or how long you'll stay. I had no idea what to expect. None whatsoever, other than what I was told, which was that I'd have an apartment, and I had to report for work at 8 A.M. the very next day. I hadn't taught anything ever before in my life, let alone English to Japanese people. I didn't know if I'd be able to do it. I didn't speak a single word of Japanese. No, that's a lie, I had learned how to say *arigatou* and *onaka ga suita,* which means, respectively, "thank you" and "I'm hungry." I figured those were pretty important things to know how to say, so I learned them. But that was it.

It was early October, and I had no idea of what the weather was like in Nagoya, Japan at this time of year. I figured I'd wing it. I'd been winging it my whole life until this point, so why fuck with a good thing? The whole thing was a grand experiment—the resume, the interview, the pictures, everything. I figured why screw with the genius momentum I had going? Learn nothing before you go, and then once there, blow it open. That was my plan. And you know what? I did *just* that.

The Four Seasons

I had imagined Japan was like Thailand, or Hawaii, or someplace like that, tropical and warm, but with technology and fast trains. No one had ever told me Japan actually gets COLD. It does. *Friggin' cold.* Freezing actually. One thing Japanese are proud of (insanely proud, I might add) is their four seasons. Japanese like to brag that their country experiences all four seasons, as though that should be some kind of massive attraction, and as though Japan is the only country in the world that experiences four seasons. GTFOH. I didn't get it really, but they do indeed have four seasons, three and a half of which absolutely suck ass. Winter is cold, grey, windy, wet and brittle. Summer is a sweltering hotbox, brutally hot and humid. It feels like you're being smothered by a hot wet Japanese blanket. Spring always starts with the most ferocious allergy season you can imagine. It's insane. It's allergies times forty. They call it "kafunshou", and it has something to do with some "gift" of cedar trees that the US gave to Japan after World War II, coupled with "yellow sand" that supposedly blows in from China. Japanese don't like to take the blame for anything, even their own allergy season, so China and the US get the blame.

Kafunshou

Kafunshou is the Japanese word for "pollen allergy". If you are unfortunate enough to suffer pollen allergies in Japan, you're doomed. It feels like a thick snake has crawled inside your nasal cavities, blocking all oxygen going into your nose that lasts weeks, sometimes months. I experienced Kafunshou every spring, and it was tortures.

I had allergies so bad that I had laser surgery done on the inside of my nostrils every other year for the last six years I lived there. Imagine this: some weird, old gangly Japanese doctor with bad teeth who smells like *natto* (a slimy traditional Japanese food of sticky, gooey, vile-smelling fermented soy beans, which they ferment with *bacillus sub-tilis,* and yes, it is exactly as disgusting as it sounds, but Japanese, especially the men, swear by this shit), cigarettes, and alcohol. Who is standing about four inches from your face, peering up your nose, holding a long, skinny laser torch, which he uses to burn away layers of your inner nostrils, so that when the allergies hit, your inner nose can't completely swell. Also, as a precursor to the nostril burn, the doctor shoves two-foot-long tissues drenched with anesthetic up your nose and down the back of your throat for half an hour, so you can't feel the burn inside your nose. I did this four times. Willingly. To avoid the head-and-face-exploding trauma that is the Japanese allergy season. Four times.

I know this *kafunshou* bullshit was part and parcel of the demise of my marriage, because each time it hit, I was insane. I could not breathe, which meant I could not sleep, which meant I could not function like anything resembling a normal human being, which most likely I am not to begin with. I'm sure my *kafunshou,* and attending neuroses, made my pretty Japanese ex-wife take sharper notice of what a fucking *lunatic* she had married. I guess. Whatever.

Take your four seasons and shove them, Japan.

I digress.

I hadn't properly packed for autumn in Japan. I definitely wasn't ready for Japanese winter either.

I'm In the Air Tonight

I'm a fan of harsh smash cuts, going directly from one scene to the next. I don't shrink from radical changes of scenery. Here one minute, gone the next, that's how I like it. *Total teleportation.*

On the flight over to Japan, I was just ... tired. I just wanted to sleep and looked forward to sleeping in my own bed, wherever or whatever it may have been. I could barely imagine what my new "apartment" in Japan might look like. But I was too tired to work my brain. The month prior had been a whirlwind. Dealing with and leaving Christine, sorting out my stuff, wondering if what I was doing was right, and wondering just what I was doing altogether. I was nervous, but not scared. More tired than anything. I'd never been on a 9 hour flight.

As we were landing I noticed a young-looking white dude with dark hair. He looked like a poor man's Tom Cruise. I went over to him and we struck up a conversation. He told me when I settled down in Nagoya that I'd need to meet a gentleman named Dash. Dash was a notorious musician, I was told,

"Notorious for what?" I asked.

"Notorious for just being notorious" he said.

I was told that this musician named Dash would be able to get me anything I needed. He said all I had to do was meet Dash and I'd be set in Nagoya. And he warned me.

He told me to be very careful, or the women in Japan would ruin my life. He was more serious about this warning than he was about Dash. He looked me directly in my eyes when he said it, but immediately turned away once he caught himself in thought.

He spilled his guts in the back of that airplane, but I didn't understand any of it. All I knew was that he was hurt.

Don't Let the World Change Your Smile

When I landed at Nagoya Airport, I was greeted by two, cute, smiling young Japanese women. Their faces were filled with warmth, and they were very polite. They greeted me with acceptance, and more importantly they called me "sensei" right off the bat.

In America, I had been accustomed to seeing mostly western style faces; wide noses, thin noses, big eyes and angular features. Aki and Eiko, however had large, round, flat faces, punctuated by tiny eyes and buck teeth. These two women had the absolute, buckest teeth I had ever seen until that point. Nonetheless, buck teeth and flat faces notwithstanding, Aki and Eiko were very beautiful to me. They showed me love from the very beginning, even though they didn't know who I was or where I was from.

It isn't common knowledge that Japanese people, as a whole, have bad teeth. However, in my most humble but accurate opinion, Japanese teeth make British teeth look like a show stopping, Hollywood smile. It could be that their dental aesthetics are just different. *Crooked teeth are in.* Straight white teeth are important in the west but not so much in Asia, particularly Japan. You'll see more Japanese women on the train wearing eye patches, than you'll see wearing braces. Having "big eyes" is a major beauty point in Japan. Eye surgery to widen the eyes is more popular than clean, straight white teeth.

There are countless posters on Japanese trains, in department stores, walls, et cetera, with Japanese celebrities, politicians, and models smiling at you with the most mangled teeth you have ever seen in your life. In fact, many Japanese feel those imperfect teeth are a "best feature", they call it a "charm point". An analogy would be if western women felt proud about having bad skin. Japanese women feel proud if they've got a few perpendicular right-angle teeth.

None of the Japanese that I encountered seemed to care so much that everyone's teeth were so mismanaged. I thought this was pretty cool. Not that I myself have bad teeth, but it made me feel like maybe Japanese are a little less self-conscious about certain aspects of appearances.

Aki and *Eiko*

Their names didn't sound so much like names, as much as they did *sounds. What was I expecting?* I guess I was expecting them, and there they were.

"Hajimemashite!" they bowed to greet me in unison and hurried my one bag into their tiny car.

"Welcome to Japan," they said graciously before climbing into the front seat of their little car. Seconds later, we drove off to my new adventure in Japan.

Me, my eighty bucks, my one bag of T-shirts, socks, underwear, and a couple of my favorite CDs.

I'd made it this far.

I was in a new country.

I was happy to meet Aki and Eiko.

I was even delighted with their imperfect teeth.

And I was spent.

>Chapter 6

HIGASHI-KU

I think I'm turning Japanese, I really think so

S tupid song.

Everyone knows Japan is small. The people are small, their cars are small, the houses are small, food portions are small, small tits, mostly, and yes, Japanese dudes have small dicks. I'm not saying that I have the biggest dick nor am I saying the opposite, what I am saying is that I know because several Japanese women have told me so. I mean, look, as dicks go sizes run the fucking gamut and *who gives a fuck* anyway. However, certain physical attributes belong to certain races, it's simple genetics. Everything is smaller in Japan.

My apartment was no exception. Shit was tiny. Had this small area which I supposed was the bedroom, because there was a dingy futon in that area. There was another small area which I guessed was the living room/dining room, because there was *a kotatsu* in it (a small wooden table with a heat source underneath, which Japanese use to warm themselves during winter; some *kotatsus* work, some don't, mine didn't), and a small 1952 black-and-white TV. There was also a tiny kitchen with a Bunsen burner for a stove and a three-foot-tall fridge—both of which, I later came to find out, are de rigeur for almost all Japanese apartments—and there was a tiny little plastic bathroom, with a plastic tub, a plastic sink, plastic toilet, plastic shower. I could hardly turn around in that bitch, and the tub—wtf—shit looked like a baby's bassinet.

But I'll tell you what, all that smallness, all that plastic shit, that dingy futon, it was like heaven to me. It was where I'd make my next move, where I'd plan my attack on the next phase of my life. It was my secret hideaway from the whole fucking world. It was as if I'd literally landed on another planet, with some kind of mission to remake myself, to learn about the inhabitants, to suss out the scene and find my place in it. It was my bat cave, my own private Idaho, and I was at peace with it all immediately. My tiny dirty futon was my own bed and my small plastic apartment was to me a palatial mansion of privacy and peace. My sanctuary.

That first night, I went out and around, checked out the environment. There was a bakery across the street from my house in one direction, and in another direction, there was a ramen shop. Off down the street, there was a Denny's, a fucking Denny's. I came to find out later, Japan has Denny's all over the place, not the kind of Denny's we're used to in America, but a different kind of Japanese Denny's where you can get miso soup and fish for breakfast. And there was a gas station right down below my place.

I returned to my Japanese plastic Playskool apartment after my little walk and unpacked a bit. Tried to get to sleep, but couldn't because of the excitement of being in my new home, in a new country, and because of the fucking street lights down below my apartment was making noise all night. Street lights and crosswalks all over Japan gives off this annoying "beep beep" sound when pedestrians are allowed to cross. Unlike New York City, almost no one in Japan crosses the street without the light being green ("blue" in Japan, although the shits looked green to me the entire ten years I was there)—Japanese will stand at a red light for however long it takes for the light to change, whether or not there is one speck of traffic anywhere to be seen. This is a perfect example, in tiny form, of the Japanese personality: do not do anything that isn't legal, or socially accepted, ever, for any reason, even if it's something as innocuous as crossing the street without a green, er, blue light.

I didn't know what that "beep beep" was for weeks, maybe months, until one night I was standing underneath one of the signs and noticed it. Everything makes some kind of noise in Japan—the street lights, the parking garages, the subway platforms, the taxis, the rice cookers, the vending machines—*every freakin' thing* talks to you and it makes for a cacophony of small, tinny, robotic Japanese voices coming at you from all angles, everywhere you go, all day long, and it either becomes background noise that you ignore, or it annoys the hell out of you. For me, it was a little of both. Urban Japan is a lot like being caught in a tiny little plastic electronic Japanese Playskool, remember those plastic cityscapes you played with as a kid? Small little people, small round heads, small little cars, plastic and cute. Japan is a lot like that.

All I knew was, that I was happy as hell to be out of Los Angeles and rid of Christine's B.S. And to be honest, I was also happy to put away the dream of becoming a famous actor, and happy to not have to deal with Hollywood anymore, at least for however long the Japan thing was going to last. Mr. Kosugi had told me my contract was for one year, so I figured I'd be in Japan for one year, and that was fine with me.

Heal Yourself

Nobody ever got rich being an English teacher, but I figured it was a better gig than what I was doing at the time, which was basically starving while trying to be some kinda freakin' "actor" in Los Angeles. So I left. I had been wishing silently to be somewhere else, and it happened.

Trippy how the universe answers questions you put out there, whether consciously or not.

Day Two

Wake up. Early. Get dressed. The beeping sound is going off every ten seconds. *What the fuck is that?* Out the door. Elevator. My place is on the seventh floor. Downstairs. Walk down the street, a guitar shop, convenience store, small restaurants and bars. Bakery. Gas stations. Ramen shops. A few clothing shops and lots of Japanese people.

I made it, somehow, to the school, which was located along one of the main streets, parallel to what they called Central Park, which was a tiny four-block-long replica of New York's Central Park.

At my gig, Aki and Eiko are there, and they point me to the classroom where I'll be teaching. I still wasn't sure of what I'd be teaching nor to whom, or how, but they kept referring to me as "sensei" so I guessed what the fuck, I *am* a sensei. This moment was key, because I decided that I was going to be a sensei even if it kill me.

I met Jack that first day. Jack's a Chinese dude, much more raw and outspoken than Japanese. At the time I hadn't yet learned to tell Japanese and Chinese apart physically. Jack immediately took me under his wing and told me Shane was an asshole and that the whole fucking school was dying. Shane Kosugi had been managing the school to death, and Sho Kosugi, his father, the dude who hired me, though famous, hadn't made a movie in years. *The school is dying?* I thought to myself. Hm. Didn't feel great to get this news.

I had gotten here the day before, and this Chinese cat is telling me the *school is about to go under.* When Jack told me the school was going under, it didn't quite register. I kind of thought, *well whatever, I'm here and we'll see how long we can make this whole Japan thing last.*

Jack and I became good friends. We still are.

Japanese hate Chinese and Chinese hate Japanese right back, and Jack never missed a chance to tell me exactly how he felt about Japan, Japanese, Shane, Sho, the whole fucking kit and caboodle. There's a lot of racism in Asia with one group of Asians hating another. Japanese consider themselves the cream of the crop, kind of the "white" Asians of Asia, which isn't so far from the truth actually, considering how the Japanese Imperial Army ran around Asia and pretty much slaughtered, butchered, and ran roughshod over almost every other Asian country. My first day on the job.

Jack tells me that for a long time the school has been losing students, due to bad management by Shane. There were four Sho Kosugi "institutes" in existence at the time, three of them located in Japan. One in LA, one in Tokyo, one in Osaka, and one in Nagoya. The Tokyo and Osaka schools were doing well, the Nagoya school had been faltering, and I'd been brought in to help save it. The LA branch was just an office. I did not know any of this.

Shane had no idea how to deal with the parents of the students going to the school, which was a crucial element for the school's success. His personality was like wet cardboard, useless and irritating. He smiled a lot and flexed his little muscles and not much else. He was immediately an asshole to me and exemplary of the Japanese male personality trait of being overly polite and pretentiously gracious, but essentially irritating, condescending, and pretty much prickish. Shane was the kind of dude who is lucky enough to inherit a successful business from his father and then railroad said business into the ground almost immediately. We didn't get along from the start.

The first day at any job is nerve-racking. There are new people to meet, rules to learn, duties and responsibilities to absorb, protocol to follow. There are people watching you and your every move, making snap judgements. You're silently frantic. Trying to learn all this new stuff, trying to fit in, trying to absorb and make a decent impression without letting on that you're terrified, dumbfounded, and essentially in a state of shock.

Imagine all that in a different country. Multiply whatever your experiences have been at a new job by a hundred, and that's how I felt in Japan.

You've just landed on this different planet *the day before* and on the next day you're expected to produce, that's just how it is.

You're in a daze, you've got that *I-just-got-here-yesterday-I-don't-know-where-to-go-or-what-to-do-and-why-is-everyone-looking-at-me* feeling. Again, imagine that times a hundred. Imagine you're on a mission to Mars or Jupiter, and you've just arrived, and the Martians or Jupiterians step to you and tell you to get to work. *Immediately.* Your job is to teach little Martians and Jupiterians how to speak English, and you can't speak their language one lick.

Why have you done this? What made you think you could leave the safety of your home country to come to this foreign land where you essentially know nothing? The simplest of tasks becomes a gargantuan puzzle to solve. Food, even, becomes a mystery. I had eaten sushi exactly once in my life before going to Japan, at some restaurant in West Hollywood with my dude Brad, and I remember marveling at how nimble Brad was with the chopsticks. *Why didn't they just use forks? Do they have forks?* So much easier to use forks, I thought. You ask yourself over and over *why do they do it that way and not this way?* This is part of culture shock.

What else can I not do here? What else is different? What habits of mine do I have to change? Will they be able to cater to my various vices and addictions?

What about weed? Is it illegal here? Do they know what weed is? Do they have dealers? Weed spots? *How am I going to be able to get high?*

I'm Your Sensei

I had no idea what to teach or how to teach it. I remembered some games (Red Light, Green Light, 1-2-3) and songs ("This Old Man"), phonics (short "e," long "e," and "sometimes y") and basic rules of my own language. I went to a local bookstore and bought a book I found called *Acting and Drama Games For Young Children.* I played a game with the children wherein I'd yell "action!" and the kids would have a minute or so to run around and pretend to be anything they wanted to be. I had kids pretending to be animals, astronauts, cops, divers, baseball players, sumo wrestlers, princesses—all kinds of stuff.

Genius, I thought. Then I'd yell "STOP," and they'd have to stop in whatever pose they were in in the moment. Then I'd yell "action!" again, and they'd start over. They loved it. I came to love it, and it was cool. Kids love to run around and act wild, and that's just exactly what I encouraged. It passed the time anyway.

My students were all children, some as young as three years old. Most three-year-old Japanese children look like tiny living human porcelain dolls. There can be nothing cuter. That porcelain doll is trying to speak English and is repeating everything you say almost perfectly with your inflection and everything, the kids had much better accents than the adults I'd later teach, because their ears were unprejudiced. They copied me exactly and often had perfect pronunciation It was adorable to see them looking up at me with their huge Japanese porcelain doll eyes. I loved every one of my students and they had absolutely no fear of me. They came close to me and sat on my lap and asked me questions and were terribly cute and played with my hair and smiled at me. They had no fear of me.

Fitting In

Japanese expect proficiency. They expect you to be good at whatever they've hired you to do immediately. They expect results fast. They'll give you leeway with formalities and customs for a minute, but not so much with your job. You have to know what you're doing. Thing is, it's not so difficult to fake knowing what you're doing with Japanese, because they think you're a weirdo and you are a weirdo and so a weirdo's behavior is unpredictable. I'm basically saying that, a weirdo can get away with stuff. Sometimes. This is pretty much the Japanese take on foreigners. They think anyone who isn't Japanese isn't really quite human. I know this sounds weird, but it's absolutely one hundred percent true. This is the Japanese form of racism I experienced. At first the release from skin color based discrimination is liberating but after a few years of being made aware how not Japanese you are, it begins to grate on your nerves. It was life changing not to have to worry about being black, but insert the word foreigner instead of black and it's still discrimination. If you stay in Japan long enough, it becomes vexing and intolerable. You find yourself allied with folks from different countries who might have discriminated against you if they met you in their home country.

Cultures vary worldwide and they are all very different. In a foreign country *you* are the one that is different because you are in their country. Though their customs and culture may seem strange to you, you are in the minority so it's actually your culture that is strange to them. Among first world nations, Japan has one upped the modern world on having "different" or "strange" culture and customs. The interesting thing is that Japanese *know* they are different and *enjoy* being as different from the rest of the modern western world as they can. But still, when you're there, you're different and they are all the same.

And they're watching you. Everyone is making note of everything you do. *All Eyez On You.* Japanese have perfected the art of looking without being noticed. They see what you're doing and in Japan, if you're not Japanese, mostly what you're doing isn't right because you're not doing it the Japanese way, and the Japanese way is sometimes stupid, sometimes weird, sometimes hard, sometimes unnecessary. This all creates anxiety. At first, being watched is kind of a thrill, but also kind of strange. It's like you're performing life karaoke with everyone watching you. Then it becomes disconcerting and weird, at some point you want to put the microphone down and step off the stage and return to your seat unnoticed, but you can't. It's like everyone is silently screaming at you "hey, sing another one!!", when you don't want to sing anymore. Then it becomes irritating, *hey, can a brother just live?* Then it becomes annoying and gratuitous, instead of noticing it less, you notice it more, and *they* notice *you* more. And this never, ever ends. You never ever "fit in" in Japan. Ever.

Then it becomes a kind of silent violence. *They're hurting you without touching you or saying a word to you, hurting you with their glaring and staring and looking and watching.* Microaggressions. It pisses you off. Even after ten years, I still never completely got used to being stared at all the time. You're that proverbial monkey in a cage at the zoo. You're "famous" but more specifically *notorious* for simply having been born non-Japanese, and that's it. This is one reason why cornball white boys and goofy idiots from anywhere in the world can come to Japan and get play. *You're a movie star.* A strange foreign movie star. Another reason is because Japanese dudes are the clumsiest, most insensitive and socially awkward dudes on earth when it comes to women, I heard this from Japanese women themselves. Many young Japanese men nowadays are turning away from women altogether. They call these dudes in Japan "Herbivores," plant-eating dudes. I'll get to that later.

Then, there are the cultural norms. Japan is a "high context" society. There is nothing casual about life in Japan, at anytime, anywhere. Japanese never let their hair down. Everything is super formalized. There are rules for everything. How to greet, how to look at people, how not to look at people, whom to touch, which is almost no one, whom to address and how to address them. There are different ways to address different people of different hierarchies in Japanese society. The school principal gets a deeper, longer bow than the teacher who just introduced you to him. There are specific words to say every time you enter and leave the teacher's office, *shitsureishimasu*, which loosely means "I'm sorry for entering this room..."

I had to learn all the formalities, and quickly. They let me fuck up a few times, but they also let me know for certain that I'd have to get it, learn it, *do it,* and do it right, each and every time thereafter. There is very little wiggle room in Japan. You've got to be sharp and on point, even if you are a weird foreigner. And then there's time, or better stated, punctuality.

We're lax about punctuality here in America to a degree: often if you're supposed to report for work at ten o'clock you've got a 5, 10, and sometimes even 15 minute window. Not in Japan. Ten o'clock means *exactly ten o'clock.* It's perfectly okay for you to arrive before your scheduled start time but not one minute after. Not one minute. You walk in at 10:01 and the entire office is looking up at the clock and then back down at you silently, and sometimes not so silently, saying *you're late homie, wtf.* Japanese are one of, if not the most, fastidiously time-oriented people on the planet.

Time is the noose around the neck of Japanese society. One of them anyway. But time is also a certain threshold of being "understood" and accepted in Japan. If you can't get the time thing down you've given yourself two strikes without opening your mouth. It's a simple but difficult way to "join the club" in Japan, being on time, every time. Make that a point to remember.

Work hours are also viewed differently in Japan. When your workday is over in America, no one expects you to stay one second longer, you're out the door and so is everyone else. Not in Japan.

Salarymen

Japanese salarymen are forced to stay long, late hours at their jobs to show allegiance to their company and give good 'face'. Not just a couple hours either, but like a whole 'nother workday after. Midnight and beyond. Doing this makes you look good in Japan, regardless of what it is you are actually doing in those after hours. Japanese dudes know very well how to shuffle papers around and appear concerned and look and act like they're on the job, when maybe they are, but most likely they aren't. Japanese have perfected the arts of consternation and busy work when in reality they are dying to drink a beer and greatly looking forward to falling asleep either on the train on the way home from work, or next to the train on the platform.

Japanese salarymen don't have much to look forward to. They burn the candle until the wee hours at the office, stumble home to their unloving and detached wives, then wake back up at the crack of dawn the next day to do the same thing over and over until they die or retire, whichever comes first.

The Japanese daily urban grind is abysmal. There isn't really any such thing in Japan as "starting one's life over," or "second chances", like we allow ourselves in America. There is no reinvention of self nor is there anything akin to "lifetime learning". There is only what you're doing now, what you're supposed to do next, and how efficient you are at doing it. Salarymen are shackled to the system and to their companies and to a dying paradigm that has seen Japan lose its second place ranking among the world's elite economies. There's some shuffling going on with this age-old system as a result of the shifting of the Japanese economy—many former lifelong salarymen aren't guaranteed a lifetime job anymore. You'd think this might result in some sort of entrepreneurial out flux in Japan, people taking their destinies into their own hands and creating a new life out of the old, but I don't see it. The salarymen there are throwing up their hands and surrendering to the dying system. Get into a company. Get married. Have kids. Have your marriage go sexless at about the same time your wife has children. Move out of you and your wife's bedroom and go stag, without the benefits. There are millions of married Japanese couples who are just glorified roommates. Roommates who at one point used to be lovers, marriage partners, but who are now just two people sharing the same domicile and raising children. Realistically, Japanese men have almost zero responsibility when it comes to the raising of the children. They bring home their salaries and hand them over to their wives and then, well, they slowly die. Slog through a torturous life of that for two, three, four, sometimes 5 or 6 decades—all the while dedicating your blood, sweat, and tears to your company, slaving into the deep hours of the evening—only to have your life snuffed out of you after you've become a smelly old Asahi beer–drinking chain smoking *ojisan*. It doesn't always end like this in Japan for Japanese men, but more often than not, it does. It ain't a pretty slog for the average Japanese salaryman. But at least, *the cops there will never shoot him.*

The Plan

Too much time restriction is not the best friend of the slack Jamaican American from Brooklyn. I did my best to show up at least close to eight o'clock every morning. I had to have fresh lessons prepared daily. I developed a routine. I'd teach greetings and sing songs for the first hour or so. I'd teach the alphabet and go through lots of Mother Goose rhymes in the second hour. Then we'd play some run-around activity game, then it was lunch. I'd go to either the ramen shop near my house or to this place where I'd get a bowl of eel, *unagi,* and rice and a cup of green tea, or I'd hit the convenience store and get *onigiri* (rice balls), juice, and a bag of potato chips. Then we'd be back at it. I played all kinds of stupid games. I made up a lot of them on the spot. There was the *Copy My Face* game. I'd make faces and the children would have to copy whatever face I was making. It was a good game actually, because Japanese don't allow themselves to express a very wide range of emotions on their faces. Mostly they just look polite. The kids learned all kinds of screw faces from me and it was funny as hell. We'd all bust out laughing at each other.

We also did a lot of writing because I'm big on writing. We'd spend another hour writing the alphabet, our names, seasons, colors, animals. We learned shapes, months, numbers, adjectives, and nouns.

We'd play games pretending to be animals. We played creative and really fun acting games. Sometimes we went outside to the park across the street and had a sort of outside field trip day. Or if it was raining, because it was going into winter, I'd have them close their eyes and I'd come up off the top of my head with some bizarre story and see if they could "visualize" what I was talking about, and then elicit how they "felt" about it, even though they mostly didn't understand a single word of what I was saying.

My stories usually went something like this: *you're in the forest— it's raining, it's dark, you're cold and hungry. There's some sound in the trees above your head and a river is beside you—there are fish jumping in the river next to you and you can see a few animals—suddenly you see some lights, you get up to see what it is. What is it?*

Then I'd have them open their eyes and tell me what animals they saw or what the light was. I'd ask them if they were scared or nervous or surprised or happy or friendly or worried. I'd have them make faces to match whatever emotion they told me they experienced. I had them draw pictures of the scenes they were seeing in their heads. They couldn't understand a word I said but somehow it went okay. Another game I played was the "remember everything" game. I'd show them a picture from a magazine for a few seconds and then they'd have to close their eyes and tell me everything they had seen on the page. I didn't know what I was doing but the days were going by, the children seemed to be having fun, I was getting paid, eating eel and ramen, and life was pretty decent. That's how it was for a while.

He Said He Taught Jackie Chan

Jack was teaching martial arts. Jack was a proud Chinese and said he had taught Jackie Chan. *Hm. Jack. Jackie Chan.* Whatever. I believed him. Jack was sly and even though he was married he was *about that life.* He always talked about going out and getting drunk and wanting to get some "poosy". He had a bad mouth, was temperamental, opinionated, and acerbic, and I loved listening to him talk. He'd cuss and scream and spit and get drunk and want poosy yet always had these truly brilliant ideas, one after the other. He had ideas about movies and shows and business and travel. He was a strange, drunk, ornery, 21st Century Chinese martial arts expert at odds with the slow *do-everything-by-the-book* traditional Japanese all around him.

Jack's job at Sho Kosugi was teaching the younger kids discipline in the *guise* of Kung Fu, but he was teaching the older kids *real* Kung Fu. No bullshit. His shit was straight-outta-China Shaolin Temple Kung Fu. I watched his class, which was held in the school's gym in the basement after my class regularly because I had nothing better to do. Jack, when he was teaching his Kung Fu classes, was sharp, observant, and demanding. He'd be wearing a black T-shirt, black Kung Fu pants with a white sash and Chinese slippers, and he'd be doing a graceful but deadly Kung Fu ballet all over the gymnasium. I'd just stand off the side watching thinking *this guy taught Jackie Chan.* He was fluid and delicate, sharp and deadly, loud, funny, and emotionally expressive exactly like Jackie Chan is in his movies. Jack may have been drunk most of the time, but at the same time, Jack looked like he could fuck you up if he needed to.

"Man, Trevor, FOCK these Japanese, they so slooooooow. . ." he'd tell me. He'd elongate his last few words every time he spoke, and his voice would rise to a high-pitched crescendo exactly like the Chinese you see in movies. He always wanted to hang out with me, saying "Trevor, I know you are getting a lot of Japanese *poosy,* they like the big black *deeeeeek,* right?" and he'd grab his crotch like a short drunk Chinese Michael Jackson, "when can we hang out so I can get some *poosy* with you maaaaaan?"

We never really hung out like that, because like I said, he always seemed drunk to me and stood a little too close when he spoke, (I think Chinese have a different sense of space than Americans, I mean, there's two billion of them so . . .). Plus, he had horrendous breath, shit smelled like soggy noodles and beer. But still, I liked Jack and appreciated the fact that he was there. He kept my feet on the ground my first few months.

At the school Jack was teaching a tall, slim Japanese kid who spoke almost perfect English because he'd lived in America. He was probably about my same height, but at least twenty pounds lighter than me. Maybe sixteen years old. Maybe seventeen. Tall, slim, handsome Japanese kid with dynamite spinning kicks and excellent control. Jack ran his class through kicks and lunges and punches and flying maneuvers and it was sick. I was watching the real thing in Japan and it blew my mind. It was wild to watch these shy, quiet, unassuming, lithe little Japanese kids doing these amazingly graceful spinning kicks, jumps, forms, and striking techniques. My life at the time started feeling like a movie. So, I started thinking about *making my Japanese life into a movie.*

>Chapter 7

Your Life is Your Own Personal Movie

Cherry Blossom Trail is conceived

Some time ago, I realized something major.
I'm not sure if it happened as a result of my years of meditation, or reading stuff about astral projection, or if it came from my acting in movies and television, but at some point it popped into my head that *you can change your life immediately by changing your behavior,* and you can change your behavior *on the spot* if you're able to see each moment objectively, by projecting yourself either *up above* the reality of what is going on, or by imagining you are watching a movie with yourself in it. However, you must bear in mind, that the movie is reflecting whatever is happening in your real life *right now,* and since you are also the director of your life movie, you control not only the actors in the movie, but of your own character as well. Now you can direct *yourself* to act however you want in any given situation.

Meditation defines this as *awareness,* or *mindfulness*. It's a mind game of slowing down reality and using your third eye to slowly notice what is happening in the right *here* and *now,* without judgement. Becoming mindful allows you to short circuit your own reflex reactions. It gives you space to think and room to breathe *without reaction,* so you can make conscious decisions on how to behave in any given moment. You are pulling the strings of your own puppet which is also "you".

This is liberating and empowering. When I find myself behaving a certain way, I try to simultaneously watch myself behave that way, as if I'm watching the "me" character in my life movie. When I don't like how he (me) is behaving, I simply change, alter or modify my own behavior on the spot in order to effect different results. By changing myself, forces the people around me to change as well. Watch the movie of your life carefully, and if there's a scene where your character is doing something stupid, stop the scene (as the director) and tell yourself (as the actor) what you'd rather he do, and *do that*. It works out marvelously! Most times. Sometimes you want that "you" character in your movie to do some nefarious shit. Don't. *You're the director.* And the actor. *Direct yourself.*

The Transformation OF the Personality: Acting 101

Here's an exercise: When you're in a social situation, act differently than your "real" personality. That is, if you're loud, act quiet, if you're shy, act outgoing, if you're from the north, act like you're from the south, if you're an intellectual, act like a dumbass, et cetera. The point is to act, to pretend, *to be something you're not,* if even just for a few moments, and then take a look at the immediate results you get, and make adjustments accordingly. Make yourself your own personal social experiment. Uploading and downloading different personalities gives you freedom. Freedom to change, adapt, see what works and what doesn't work in your life.

I Started Writing a Movie

I started watching Jack teach martial arts to the kids through a set of different eyes than my own. At some point it became much more than Jack just teaching punches and kicks, it became a scene from a movie and I decided that I would be the director of that movie. The oldest kid in Jack's class was about sixteen or seventeen and was tall, lithe, and sick with the kicks.

I started imagining, *what if this kid were a gang leader?* I started writing skits for the class to perform, with their martial arts. I'd write scenarios for the kids where they'd have to defend their honor against a foreigner. I made myself the foreigner in my own scenes. I studied a little Taekwondo in college and it got me kicking, gave me a chance to test myself against the young Japanese Kung Fu cats. Truth is, I would not want to fuck with them on any given day; in fact, I'd want them on my side.

I did my Taekwondo thing, but Jack's students made me look like I had two left feet. They were performing Chinese ballet while I was struggling to lift my legs off the ground. We would act out scenes with kicks and punches for revenge and love and defense of honor and all that. Each scene would last about two minutes, maybe three at most. Then I'd yell "Cut!" like I was some kind of director. It was exhilarating. Then I started thinking, this would be a *cool movie.*

I injected a female into the scenes. One of the young female students—there were about half a dozen girls around the ages of fifteen or sixteen. I'd put them into the scene and create a sort of Japanese *Romeo and Juliet*-slash-*Warriors* vignette. The young male Japanese students had to clash with me over the honor of their sister/wife/mother/girlfriend. They had to speak a few lines of English I'd written, simple things but a decent test of memory, pronunciation, word usage, vocabulary, emotion, gestures—they had to put it all together. It wasn't easy. We'd get into some sort of climactic emotional confrontation. No one would necessarily lose their honor though. I wrote the scenes so no one would outright win. I kept it fair and equal and Jack enjoyed it.

As those first few months progressed, this is what I did as far as teaching. The songs, games, writing, acting, and emotion exercises; animals, numbers, seasons, fruit, vegetables, shapes, colors, days, months, alphabet, and English basics, phonics and grammar and pronunciation.

And I continued writing those scenes with Jack's class. I kept writing more and more scenes, going deeper and deeper with the characters. I had created a whole cast, a family of upper-society Japanese, the daughter of that family being a young traditional Japanese girl, innocent. She falls in love with the "dirty foreigner," my character, who I named JD, short for Johnny Depp. I had the nickname JD when I lived in Los Angeles. I don't know why. One day my African friend Shekku just started calling me JD and it stuck. I love Johnny Depp, but I don't think I look anything like the dude. Maybe I do. Maybe Shekku thought I did, or maybe it was something else. I don't know really. I dug the moniker JD and it became the name of the main character in my "script".

The other characters in the film idea I was cooking up were a hybrid of the people I had met in my first year or so in Japan. American, Australian, Brazilian, African, and of course Japanese. With the first few months skating by, I'm teaching and creating these scenes, and those scenes eventually became the story for my screenplay, *Cherry Blossom Trail*. What was odder than the script that came out of those scenes, was the *life* that came out of those scenes. Namely, my own life. There's that old adage: *Does art imitate life or does life imitate art?* I think it's both.

In the film, I imagined a foreign man, myself, arriving in a nondescript Japanese city, falling in love with an innocent Japanese girl, causing a rift in her family and causing controversy all through the small Japanese city and in the international circle around the two starcrossed lovers. This is exactly what I did during my time in Japan. Art imitates life or vice versa. I wrote my story. The film asks questions about Japanese racism, and racism in general. Many of the characters are international, all thrown together in a mother society where all of them are suddenly foreigners, while in their countries, they are the majority. The friction created in this mixture, the small group of foreigners amongst the many Japanese, translates to a visual storytelling, a timeless tale of love and tolerance.

In the film, I created my wife, and also created how we would separate, she'd take sole control of the children, ending with the eventual return of the main character, JD (me), going back to his own country. *Art imitates life.* I wrote the script within my first year of living in Japan. I drew out storyboards and shared my idea with Jack. He loved the concept but Jack had his own film ideas. He had plans to start a touring martial arts company, and wanted to work with the Chinese national government to create an international trade of foreign films between China and the rest of the world. This was Jack's goal. *He had taught Jackie Chan.* I was certain of it.

Dazza

Enter another Aussie cat, named Darren Kemp. I met him while I was living at Freebell. He was a funny looking character with a charming personality and a wry smile. We'd spend lots of time talking about our past, about Australia, Vietnam and Thailand, places which Darren loved. Darren was a film buff that fancied himself a writer. He'd tell me about all kinds of different ideas he had for films and I'd listen eagerly while he told me the plot to his latest creation.

Darren was madd proud of his half-Aboriginal background and didn't seem to identify at all with the 'half white' part of his racial make-up. To me, he just looked like a short, dark skinned white dude. He told me his family called him "Dazza." Charming, intelligent, idiosyncratic, down to earth, and easygoing. Darren and I became tight.

We sat in the staircase at Freebell banging out *Cherry Blossom Trail* almost every night for weeks, months. I had the ideas and saw the film in my head, while Darren sat with a pen and a cheesy fiendish grin splashed across his face, transforming my ideas into scenes on a big yellow legal pad. Those nights in that staircase, Darren would roll to-bacco laced joints and we'd fog up the stairwell while imagining scenes and characters like two little kids.

Darren showed me how he was laying out my ideas on paper, and I started to actually *see* my story taking place not only in my head, but also on the yellow notepad in Darren's hand. I'd be standing up gazing into the stairwell, talking wildly about all these fictional characters. There was an evil Japanese Bosozoku motorcycle gang leader Masaki, his father, his father's wife, their daughter-who I fancied as my love interest in the film, the entire Japanese town, not unlike Nagoya, where it all would take place, and all my friends who'd be in the film. Darren wrote my ideas down and added his own, always from a bizarre perspective I would never even have considered.

Darren also created his own little universe of planets and cartoon characters based on all the illegal drugs he had done. He called their leader "Drug God Marihashmeth." People who smoke weed, he called the "Weedish." Darren smoked meth and loved hash, shot speed, sniffed coke, popped pills, drank hard, and loved every minute of it. He'd traveled all throughout Southeast Asia and told me, "Mate, you gotta get to Chiang Mai in *Toi*-land, it's excellent there, mate, you'd love it."

Thing was, Darren had cancer. Some rare cancer that made him ba-sically feel "weak all the time", in his own words. You wouldn't know from talking or hanging out with him though. Even though he was, and had been, on and off chemotherapy for a while, he was still peppy and quick witted. He was a weird gnomish cat actually, but super good-natured and always quick with the smoke. Japan wasn't so cool for him, he was in love with Vietnam. He'd tell me wild stories about prison cells he'd seen the inside of for trafficking expensive watches from Europe and points north into Southeast Asia. He said his best friend was still in jail for that same shit, but that his friend had ten million American dollars stashed somewhere, and that when he got out of jail he and Darren would disappear into the jungles of Vietnam forever. Or maybe Thailand. He said the temples in Chiang Mai were seven hundred years old and that I'd love them. He planned to get back there and drink coconut milk with Vietnamese chicks or whatever they do there. Darren was mostly mild mannered, owing to the weakness I guess, but when he talked about Vietnam, the Ho Chi Minh trail, Thailand, he made it sound like heaven. It was all he could do to barely tolerate Japan. "Too fucking expensive, and the chicks here are tough, mate." His thoughts on Japan. He couldn't wait to get out.

Darren also had these absolutely bizarre memory lapses, kind of like a waking narcolepsy, where suddenly, his eyes would glaze over and he'd go stiff. I've witnessed many times where he would look straight ahead, staring off into space like a lunatic, *while still holding onto his burning cigarette.* Now, here is the crazy thing, if you weren't facing Darren directly, you'd never know he was having a seizure because it was always quiet and sudden. You could conceivably hold entire conversations by yourself, thinking that the fucker was listening to you. So many times I'd be in the middle of talking and suddenly Darren would spaz out and then a minute or so later say, "Sorry, mate, spazzed out there for a minute, what was it you were saying?" and then casually take a drag on his cigarette, looking over at me like *what, man? Spit it out.*

Darren had genius ideas and those times in the staircase at Freebell passing a joint laced with tobacco back and forth between us—were perfect moments. Darren talked lots about leaving Japan. After living with a "French prick," for almost a year, Darren bounced. Said he was headed back to Oz to spend time with his family before taking off for Chiang Mai again. Or Vietnam. He wasn't sure. He needed to hook up with his friend who was in prison first and "get that money." Darren and I vowed to stay in touch and did, sporadically. We'd talk about *Cherry Blossom Trail* and how it could play out. He sent me drawings of his Drug God and highly detailed drawings of the Weedish. They looked like him.

Weird conundrum, imagination. It's our greatest weapon, and our most powerful Achilles heel. Don't fuck with imagination. Or do. Not sure which actually.

>Chapter 8

My First Few Months

Lay of the land

T hose first few months, October and November into December. I was walking around a small area of the city with my CD Walkman bumping Notorious B.I.G., reggae, and some classic rock as well. Jimi, as I mentioned, Zeppelin, Queen, and even some blues. I must have been a sight to see for those eagle-eyed Japanese in Nagoya. A lanky, tall, dreadlocked, Brooklyn kid, strutting in his Pumas and grooving to his headphones. It felt liberating to be in a place where no one knew me, I knew no one, and there weren't very many expectations other than my job and my basic survival. I was *floating . . .* taking the train to the main areas downtown, Sakae, Fushimi, Nagoya station. The city of Nagoya is either the third or fourth largest city in Japan, depending on whom you ask. Nagoya's population is about three million, give or take, which makes it a city almost as big as Chicago. Nagoya is most definitely urban by any standards, but there's this saying that people inside and outside Nagoya say about it, "big city, small town," which means, indeed, Nagoya is a well-populated urban city, but with a small-town mind and very conservative values. This tripped me up a lot during my time in Nagoya, lots of shit they do and think there that just doesn't befit a city with three or four million people. Toyota has its headquarters in Nagoya, they've got a professional baseball team, a famous castle, oh and Nagoyans like *miso* a lot and don't want to be fucked with, either by 'outsiders', 'insiders', or anyone else. That's really about it. Not a tourist destination, not a glamour city.

Nagoya station is the transportation hub of Nagoya. The apartment I moved into after Higashi-ku, Freebell, is located about a quarter mile from Nagoya station. This is where Nagoya's now famous and infamous "Twin Towers" had recently been built. *Two tall semi-skyscrapers connecting all the train lines with a huge underground mall.* Lots of folks told me Nagoya station was the biggest train station in the world. It may be true. It's a massive underground network consisting of hundreds, if not thousands, of shops: restaurants, shoe stores, coffee shops, clothing stores, supermarkets, bakeries, lingerie shops, acres of women's accessories shops, Starbucks, leather shops, art shops . . . I can go on and on. It's mind-boggling. Underground life in Japan is a given, and it's also its own world as well. I learned that Japanese can easily live their entire lives underground.

There is so much shit underground in Japan it is absolutely completely stunning. There are miles upon miles upon miles of underground shopping, dining, bookstores, and shoe stores. There are huge underground supermarkets with rows upon rows upon rows of different kinds of Asian food. Fruits and cakes and spices and paste and sushi and fried shit and all kinds of stuff underground.

There are car dealerships and shit underground. People easily spend the entire day underground in major Japanese urban areas.

They don't have much livable surface land compared to the size of the country, because Japan is a mostly mountainous island archipelago consisting of four main islands. You remember the Godzilla movies. There were always lots of mountains in those movies with steam and smoke surrounded by rice fields and telephone poles and wires. A whole lot of Japan looks exactly like that. Hokkaido, the northernmost island, whose biggest city is *Sapporo*, famous for the beer, but also a winter paradise I've heard, with really pretty girls. There's a big national debate about which island has the prettiest girls. I'd heard Nagoya girls were ugly, but I heard this from Nagoya dudes. I didn't find them ugly. Whatever. How can you judge a whole city on a few girls you come across? I saw, met, and spent time with some really gorgeous Japanese girls.

Honshu is the biggest and the "main" island, and is where Tokyo, Yokohama, Osaka, and Nagoya, Japan's four biggest cities, all reside. There's also Shikoku and Kyushu—both of these are integral to Japan's identity but not so well known or discovered outside Japan. Okinawa is its own little archipelago of islands, but wholly part of Japan. Okinawans sometimes might not consider themselves Japanese in the same way Alaskans or Native Americans may not feel American, but legally, Okinawans are Japanese.

Note to American Cities

Everything, everywhere in Japan is spotless. Always. The streets are clean. The trains are shiny and bright, inside and out, even if they're old. There is no graffiti on Japanese trains. There is NO TRASH WHATSOVER on the tracks. There is nothing on the platforms either, and it's also hard to find a garbage can. So where do they put all their fucking garbage then? They keep it in their bags. Or their pockets. Or somewhere. They don't litter in the subways, or anywhere else for that matter, in Japan. It just isn't done. At first the notion of putting old wrappers and receipts and papers into my pocket until I could find a trash can was anathema to me, but now, and directly as a result of my experience in Japan, it's normal for me to shove my trash into my pocket until I find a trash can, which, thankfully, are everywhere. Kinda paradoxical. Here in the US, there are lots of trash cans everywhere, and tons of trash everywhere, except *inside* the cans. Versus Japan, where its rare to see a trash can but exactly as rare to see trash anywhere.

You can count half a dozen huge ugly wire trash baskets walking a block downtown in any major American city, and in many cases the street or sidewalk itself is filthy.

How *is that*? We've got trash cans on every corner but our streets look like a freaking Hollywood disaster movie. Me, I always seemed to have trash. A can. A wrapper. A cigarette butt. A piece of paper. A banana peel. *Something*. But there was never anywhere to throw my shit away. This was maddening. Eventually, I learned that Japanese either *plan for trash* (can you imagine? "Hmm, later if I eat this piece of gum, I'm going to need to throw the wrapper away, so I've got to bring my own little baggy for trash), or they put their trash in their pockets or whatever they're carrying with them. *They literally plan for trash*. This is a very Japanese trait, to plan down to the minutest detail of any and everything. Regarding trash, one might say it *appears* Japan has solved the problem of trash. *The trash is just not there*. Kudos to them for that.

The Occasional Foreigner

During my walks around town I saw the occasional foreigner. At that time, fall of 2003, Nagoya wasn't swimming with foreigners, but neither was it devoid of them. I hadn't met lots of people those first few months because my work schedule had me arriving at 8 A.M., and leaving at three or four. An average day would consist of me copping food at the *unagi* (eel) shop near my place. There were days that I might go to the gym and then other days I'd just stay home and chill. After a couple of months of this I was getting a little stir-crazy. I was speaking barely any English, except for whatever I was teaching in the classroom. Real communication and expression with other adults had slowed down to a trickle. I couldn't tell anyone how I felt about anything, no in-depth expression, no one to reveal every detail of my thoughts out to, which is how Americans like to think is the best way to live. Always talking, rarely listening, Americans love the sound of their own voices, and I was beginning to miss those voices.

Americans are also goofy about therapy, which I am now in, and which is essentially a peeling back of every layer of every thought and/or feeling you've ever had about anything, which is tantamount to quantifying every molecule of oxygen you breathe. Which, after having lived in Japan for a decade, seems awfully tedious, if not downright fucking maddening. But at that time in Japan, I needed that communication. I was literally running around the city squinting my eyes to see if I could notice a foreigner in the crowd anywhere, and if I did, I'd run up to them and try to strike up a conversation, and invariably they'd somewhat understand because they'd probably gone through the same culture shock I was going through. This run-up-and-talk approach is how I made my first few friends. Was weird, for me and them.

Culture shock is a bitch, and until you experience it, you don't quite know what it is. It's disorienting, jarring, *frightening*. Whatever sense of direction you may have had, no longer works. Your life compass is thrown off across the board, *up* is no longer up and *north* may as well be south. *You're lost.*

Being in Japan those first few months was like being in some kind of suspended animation. It didn't quite feel like my feet were touching the ground most of the time. There was nothing to ground me to Japan, not the food, not the weather, not the people, not the media (especially not the media). You don't realize how addicted and accustomed you are to the constant blaring of radios, televisions, ubiquitous billboards, traffic signs, store signs, newspapers, magazines, signs on mass transportation, flyers, advertisements, posters, et cetera, that you take in on a daily basis. Your brain is constantly reading, listening, processing, computing, thinking, and devouring information to the point where you spend the vast majority of your life an addled mess. No wonder so many people are being diagnosed with ADD or ADHD or whatever it is this year. The lack of all that was as jarring, at first, as the constant bombardment of it. Those first few months, I noticed how silent my world had become, and it was more than a little unsettling. I couldn't read any of the signs, couldn't understand anyone's conversation around me, couldn't read menus in restaurants, couldn't read labels on products in stores, and didn't understand traffic signs. It was like I had suddenly become both literally and socially, illiterate. I couldn't navigate the landscape with my trusty sense of memory, because everything was new, and I had no memory of where I was.

The Media Didn't Help

Japan has its own media of course, and Japanese are subject to their own version of sensory overload, but at the same time, Japanese don't employ the garish media blight that we take for granted in America. At least it didn't seem like it, but that was because I didn't understand any of the messages, nor, why or where they had come from.

But Japanese also love silence, and at least in social interactions, prefer it to the overbearing verbal noise pollution we Americans subject ourselves to. But I couldn't understand a thing.

The lack of all the noise seemed to open up an empty, quiet space in my brain.

This *informational sensory vacuum silence* replaced the crazy cacophony I was totally used to in America. It was beautiful and scary and mysterious and felt totally new. I had turned off my television almost a decade before I arrived in Japan, and now, all other forms of media were being turned off also. I had entered into a world of deeper mental meditation, a more silent place, and it eventually came to be one of my favorite experiences while living in Japan. I miss the Japanese silence, it is absolutely beautiful. (Unless of course that silence is coming from your wife, whom you're begging to answer you, speak to you, tell you something, but that is another story for later in the book.) It was like I had softly floated down to this quiet alien world from outer space and had taken on a role in this world as a teacher of sorts, but was instead being taught. It was both disorienting and liberating at the same time, and over time, the disorientation aspect of it was less and less, and the liberation aspect grew and increased.

More About The School

The staff at the school where I was working was polite enough, but that's about all they were, polite. Which is cool, except I had no one to share anything with, which may have also been cool, if I had someone to share *that* with. And no one seemed to care, really, about what I was going through, the loneliness, the culture shock. This is part of what it is to be in a foreign country, and in particular, one like Japan. For all their vaunted politeness, Japanese people have no time for feelings, *real feelings*. Genuine, real emotions are thoroughly disdained in Japan. Folks don't care to either reveal or be revealed to. Honest emotions are not part of the Japanese repertoire of social interaction. Conversations and social interactions barely scratch the surface in Japan, they just don't do well with people discussing how they really feel about anything, under any circumstance, for whatever reason. This, as I later learned, is what Japanese call *tatemae* and *honne*. These two concepts are the yin and yang of each other, and form the foundation for social interaction in Japan. *Tatemae* is the behavior Japanese display and expect others to display in public, the "outer" behavior, what is socially acceptable, and whether or not it's real or honest or genuine isn't important. What is important is that you're never supposed to reveal your true feelings about anything, at anytime. *Honne* is what you really feel inside, your true feeling about something, your real opinion, which in Japan is almost never asked for, expected, or intended to be heard by the public. The very real and socially acceptable way to behave in Japan is to be completely two-faced at all times, about everything, to everyone. You learn, accept, and practice this in Japan and you prosper socially, which leads to a certain amount of financial reward and social acceptance; you don't learn this, or you consciously decide not to practice it, you'll find yourself alone, and on the outside even more. Japanese are faking it *all, all the time.* Being fake is the way of life in Japan. You just accept this as how it is and work within it. While in Japan, I can't count how many times I was called "pure," which I came to realize meant "naïve," because of my penchant for describing things *as they were* rather than how they should have been, and for answering directly, honestly, genuinely, instead of deflecting and obscuring my truth. This social lubricant, this *tatemae/honne* thing, fucked with me my entire time in Japan. Not being able to say what I really felt, almost ever, the revelation that no one else was ever speaking their real truth, was further alienating. Besides the language barrier, there was also an expression barrier, along with a truth barrier, a revelation barrier, and a listening barrier. When Japanese sense that you're speaking your real interior truth, they don't like it. It makes them uncomfortable. I was greeted with dead-ass silence countless times after simply saying what I really felt, and it added to the loneliness.

I was *super* lonely, and I was missing being able to understand what people were saying, knowing how people really felt about things, being able to express myself *nearly perfectly,* and having that natural camaraderie and friendly repartee that Americans have with each other at my disposal.

I'd like to take a moment here to mention: Despite my Case To Leave America, let's point out that I also feel that Americans are very lucky to have each other in the US, because by and large, Americans are what might be called "super friendly" and "alarmingly optimistic," as well as "disarmingly casual" and almost extraordinarily cheerful *and* helpful. These are qualities and offshoots of American values that Americans themselves take for granted, along with all that other shit I said in the beginning. This is part of what is vexing about America, the best of the best and the absolute worst of the worst too.

Americans are *very* nice people in social situations, and *very* willing to lend a helping hand to a perfect stranger. Americans smile at each other and say "hello" and "good morning" and hold doors open for people and say "sorry" when they bump into you. Americans even stroke each other on the shoulders and arms, and sometimes treat people they just met like family. Americans tell each other intimate details of each other's lives within moments of meeting and often feel like they've become best friends while talking in line at a Starbucks. This is all great, no matter what you've heard, no matter what you believe, no matter where you're from. Other countries' citizens, like Russia's, scowl at each other and think smiling at strangers is some kind of social retardation. Smile wide at some strange Russian man and he'll probably ask you what the fuck is the matter with you.

Japanese aren't as openly harsh as Russians, but they definitely ain't treating you like family at first meeting, or any meeting for that matter, even if you do eventually become family, and they definitely ain't hugging you under *any* circumstances (never touch a Japanese, unless it's your sexual partner, seriously. Just don't touch), and anything resembling friendliness, or what we think of as friendliness, is not very present in Japanese society. I hesitate to oversimplify and say Japanese aren't friendly, but they aren't. Not friendly like what we think of as friendly. They aren't warm people, and they'll readily admit this. They do not do well in environments where they should be warm, jovial, casual, spontaneous, or goofy. Japanese, by and large, are not goofy at all. Unless you meet the occasional goofy Japanese guy, in which case, he's bound to be the supreme most exemplary king goofy dude you've ever seen. But as I said, by and large, Japanese aren't goofy. There's good things about goofy though, in my humble opinion. Japanese game shows, on the other hand, are extraordinarily goofy, like this one show where the contestants put disgusting animals in their mouths and pass them to each other, mouth to mouth. I am not putting a scorpion in my mouth no matter what you pay me. Maybe. Probably. I don't know.

They Do Not Speak English

Americans are idiots. Universal idiots. We go everywhere expecting people from other countries to speak American. What exactly is "American"? Is it a language? I think not.

Americans have very little understanding of how little English is spoken in other countries. Americans, in fact, tend to think that wherever we go, they'll speak English—for us, at least. Chances are, if you're in any of the main Asian countries (China, Korea, Japan), the people will not speak much, if any English, and you can very easily go days, weeks, months, without hearing any English at all. There are signs in English all over Japan, but the thing is, the sign is usually grammatically incorrect, silly, nonsensical, asinine, outright stupid, or just plain ridiculous. The Japanese English signage is poor at best, but naturally, everywhere you look you'll see Japanese Kanji, Katakana, and Hiragana. I didn't make much of an attempt to learn these; I never thought I'd stay long enough for it to be necessary. These letter formations, symbols and figures are extremely intimidating-looking. There are of course many westerners who have cracked the code of the symbols of this most complex language, speaking, reading, writing as well as any Japanese. I had more than a few friends who could read, write, and decipher the language as it is written. I was fascinated by those cats who could do that but I was not one of them. If I'd known I'd stay as long as I did . . . nah, fuck that. I figured I was good with the ABCs. After all, that's what I was there teaching.

Questions you think are simple—"what time is it?"; "where is the subway?"; "what is your name?"—are greeted with absolutely perplexed stares, or a wave of the hand signaling "I don't know what the fuck you are saying, can you please go away?" I was waved off so many times in those first few months, until I learned *do not ask anyone anything on the street they will not know, and if they do they will not answer.* I still asked people on the streets all kinds of shit just to get the reactions or, non-reactions, as it were.

When I first arrived to Nagoya, I didn't see foreigners very often. Once in a while, maybe one or two times a week, I'd see a non-Japanese, non-Asian, western-looking person. It was usually either a white guy or a Russian-looking girl, but at the time I didn't know they were Russian. I'd run up to them, because I literally *needed* to speak to someone. I needed to hear something in unbroken English. *I needed a friend.* It was all too weird. Exhilarating, but weird. I really felt like I was on the other side of the world, and I was. It was another planet, no one I knew and no one who knew me was anywhere within thousands of miles. A deep, wide ocean stood between me and everyone, everything I knew. A completely different language, literally and figuratively, was being spoken all around me and suddenly I was some kind of freak. Everywhere I went, the Japanese people stared at me, but not in a really obvious or disturbing manner, just that *we see you and you are not one of us* kind of stare. I knew they were looking because you can *feel* a dozen pair of eyes locked onto you, but they did their best to try to look the other way. Some people liken it to what it must feel like to be an animal in a cage at the zoo, but I didn't feel it quite like that. I knew I was different. You can't help but know and notice that you are different. And humans enjoy looking at other humans, but they are compelled to look at humans who don't look like them, and in Japan, where almost 99 percent of the population is Japanese, even now, in the twenty-first century, Japanese still stare at non-Japanese westerners in their midst. They can't help it, and they kind of wonder why we don't understand why they are compelled to stare at us. They think to themselves, *Listen Mister Non-Japanese, this is Japan. Look around you. Everyone here is Japanese. But you are not. So of course we're going to look at you. Please try at least to not get angry. We're looking at you as politely as we can. Please do not be offended. There are millions of us and about twelve of you, so, we're looking at you. And you've got strange matted hair down your back. Make no mistake, we are definitely looking directly at YOU. Get used to it.*

I didn't mind all the staring at first, but after about the third or fourth year, third or fourth month for some, it gets to be tiresome. Eventually you know that you are not new anymore, but for the Japanese all around you, you're still the white gorilla in the room, so they're still staring, no matter how long you stay in Japan. This eventually becomes quite a bore and rather agitating and after a while you wonder just what the hell everyone is looking at. You have to control yourself from screaming WHAT THE FUCK ARE YOU LOOKING AT in almost all public places. It can get pretty ugly internally if you don't have a solid foundation of self. The isolation, the objectification, and the lack of any meaningful communication. You can't quite get your bearings, because you don't know where you are. Your bearings are in another country. You're lost, but not just lost, you're madd lost. You've just floated down from outer space and landed on another world. It's earth, but it feels and looks like a different earth. You are Major Tom and your earth is nowhere around. You don't know where anything is, the street names mean nothing. You know how to get to work from your house and back again and that's about it.

The loneliness was heavy, deep, and penetrating. I wanted to talk to anyone, and I often tried. I made a few friends running up to strangers on the street a few times. They looked a little shook as they saw me running towards them, but I think they understood what I was going through. They were friendly enough.

The people at my gig were nice enough too, except for Shane. The two Japanese ladies who'd met me at the airport, Aki and Eiko, were extremely friendly and accommodating. They checked up on me all the time, and since they worked in the office at the school, I saw them practically every day. They took me to buy some household supplies I needed and got me blankets when it got cold, and it got *cold*. The mothers of the children were accommodating as well. Four of them seemed to take an extra liking to me. They invited me to go snowboarding with them during the first winter months of my time there. This was interesting.

No one quite explains what culture shock is, because it's different for everyone, but there are some things that everyone experiences. How you interpret those things, and then how you react to those things, are also your thing. No English anywhere was absolutely unexpected for me.

No one, anywhere, was speaking English. No loud conversations to overhear on the train or in cafés or on the streets. No one speaking their innermost thoughts out loud for the world to hear. No one telling loud stupid jokes or cursing out loud or involving you and the world in their conversations. It was like I was deaf, but could hear everything, and yet understand nothing.

Culture shock winds up being about how you react to your own personal shit, and/or your lack of being as open-minded as you'd like to think you are. It's everything you think you know being challenged by everyone all the time, and then your reaction to having your life compass completely thrown off. It's your own cultural baggage being thrown back at you for you to deal with. It isn't really so much them and they, it's you and yours, or what you *think* is yours anyway. Just like when I had to offload all my physical belongings before I left, and how doing that left me feeling empty, sick, even suicidal, culture shock is a further erosion of your stuff, except your stuff isn't anywhere to be seen, felt, or touched, it's all inside you. You have no idea how much your culture is a part of you until it's nowhere to be seen.

Onsen and Naked Old Japanese Ladies

A few of the mothers of some of the students I was teaching invited me to go snowboarding in Hakuba with them. Hakuba is a famous ski resort town just outside Nagano, which is northeast of Nagoya. They came to my apartment at 8 A.M. and it took us about four hours to drive there. Maki, a slim thirtysomething Japanese mom with a really wide smile, drove. Four other mothers came along, with their five kids in the back of the minivan, and me in the middle between them all. We shared *onigiri* and green tea that the mothers had prepared. They spoke Japanese a lot, I listened, and the kids paid me no extra mind.

We pulled into a parking lot, exited the van, pulled on our ski gear, headed slightly up a snow-covered mountain, boarded a lift, and the next thing I know my black ass was surfing down the side of a snow-covered mountain in the Japanese Alps while hundreds, or thousands, of Japanese winter sports enthusiasts were doing exactly the same thing on mountains and hills all around me. The air was crisp and I could see towns off in the distance while we languidly floated up alongside the mountain in the dangling lifts.

Below me, I could see thousands of tall, skinny trees with snow-covered bare branches sticking off of them. Then there were small snow explosions all around me, down below, off to the west and east. I could hear Japanese voices and the mountains looked like they'd all been placed there for me to see. All of it was covered by a wide canopy of metallic blue sky.

The snowboarding itself was fun. I'd never done it before since snowboarding isn't one of the more popular things to do in either Brooklyn or Los Angeles. Fun, cold, fast, and dangerous, that's how I'd describe snowboarding. Ski goggles and three or four sweaters, there I was whipping up and down the small mountain with a snowboard fastened to my feet. I couldn't get myself used to the board being attached to both my feet—it makes maneuvering and simple movements very difficult but it does make you "one" with the board, which I suppose is the point but which isn't nearly as cool as it sounds. Cold, fast, wind, fall, snow, get up, do it all over again over and over. This is snowboarding.

After a few hours of making a complete idiot of myself and having a great time doing it while the Japanese mothers and their children watched and laughed uncontrollably at how much I *did not improve* all day, I was exhausted, and we called it a day and left to return to Nagoya in the minivan we had driven.

On the way home from the trip, we stopped at a large compound of nondescript buildings for refreshments, to use the bathroom, and to freshen up. I didn't know what to expect, as it was my first trip outside Nagoya since having arrived just a few months ago. We got inside the compound, parked, and we all headed inside the building with me leading the way.

Once inside, there were dozens of Japanese families, children, mothers, fathers, grandmothers and grandfathers, young married couples, et cetera, and of course they were all staring at me. I tried to pretend that I was okay with it so as not to cause any issues with the mothers or their children who had brought me there. I didn't want them feeling bad about me being watched by everyone, everywhere, but it's hard to shrug off a roomful of eyes on you. I had had a blast that day and was still reeling from the rush of the snow and the board and the wind and the air, mountains and sky, and didn't want to let anything get in the way of us all enjoying the day, but man, all those stares bore into your soul and make you feel like you've done something wrong when all you've done was show up.

Once inside the building, I excused myself and took off walking and went looking for a restroom. There was a locker-room area just in front with two young Japanese women manning the entrance, and a huge *tatami* mat area (a type of straw, which is used in many Japanese homes as flooring) where many people were eating at low tables while seated on the floor. I observed and listened, trying hard to be inconspicuous, while young Japanese kids openly pointed at me and laughed out loud, with their parents doing their best to "explain" just what the fuck I was.

I walked around, headed deeper into the building looking for a bathroom, but there were no signs in English saying MEN or WOMEN, and no little stick-figure images anywhere either.

I entered a doorway with a couple of Kanji symbols at the top of the door frame, which lead into what looked like the front of a large bathroom—there was a large mirror on the wall with a row of soft incandescent lights above it and a countertop beneath it. I heard silence. I walked farther into the room and rounded a corner looking for stalls, toilets, but I didn't see any, and didn't see any*one* either, but I did see more lockers, more benches. I kept walking and eventually rounded another corner that opened into a large indoor/outdoor *onsen,* (hot spring), and there in front of me was a vast array of older Japanese women, all totally naked, sitting on the edges of the *onsen,* languishing in the *onsen,* walking around, nude. Fully, totally nude. It was in this moment that I realized, and saw firsthand, that Japanese women do not shave their pubic hair, unlike western women. There were maybe twenty Japanese women in the onsen, most of whom were older, meaning maybe in their 40's or 50's, and a few younger ones too, and every single one of them had hair *down there.*

None of them flinched. Not me, not them. We just looked at each other for what seemed like an eternal moment. All their eyes seemed to lock onto me at the same time and I gingerly stood there, fully clothed, all six-foot-tall black with locks, staring at a gaggle of naked Japanese women. I smiled a stupid small smile and turned around and practically ran out of the room.

They looked at me with curious faces and their chubby but shapely bodies were glistening. This was my first "experience" with a Japanese woman on Japanese soil that involved them sexually, but not really. I guess it was sexual for me, if not them. It stoked my fantasy.

Reeling from this crazy experience, I made my way back to my group, eyes bulged with the image of those naked Japanese women in my mind. I had just seen the most erotic thing I'd ever witnessed in my life, but at the same time it was innocent too, because it was accidental, and nothing had really "happened". Stunned, I returned to the group and didn't know if I should tell the mothers, so I didn't. I didn't think it would be cool saying, "Hey, I accidentally walked into the women's only area of the *onsen* and saw twenty naked Japanese women."

We all rode back to the city and they slept most of the way; me, I kept reliving what I'd just seen over and over again in my head. Highest number of naked women I'd ever seen in my life up to that point and still. Naked Japanese ladies all taking a bath together. Man oh man.

Winter was on its way. The nights were cold and brittle. I asked for more blankets and Aki and Eiko provided them. Cold and lack of English notwithstanding, I was enjoying my Japanese adventure, and it was about to get crazier.

>Chapter 9

YELLOW FEVER

Black passengers in yellow cabs

The *onsen* experience etched into my mind, I was becoming eager to experience something intimate, or at least to get friggin' laid.

Yellow fever is a mostly derogatory term used to describe the sickness/addiction/fetish/affinity non-Asian men who travel to Asia develop for Asian women, and believe me, any non-Japanese who has spent any reasonable amount of time in Japan has yellow fever.

Lots of cats will deny it until their deathbed, they'll say they are there for the culture, the food, the history, the *what the fuck ever*, at the end of the day, most foreign dudes are there for the women.

I have no problem with preference, and I am not mad at the foreign dudes in Japan who are there for the women. If you like Japanese women, Swedish women, Brazilian women, Thai women, white women, Latin women, it doesn't matter to me. I caught the Yellow Fever. I had it like a sonovabitch while I was in Japan. It was my modus operandi, my raison d'etre, my holy grail. Say what you are, own it and be it.

I most likely still have yellow fever to some degree. Place me at a party of assortment and I am inevitably going to be attracted to the Asian woman in the room. Something about their essence, their aura, their grace, their yellow skin, and/or whatever it is they're giving off, and/or *not* giving off too. But I didn't always have yellow fever.

Before I traveled to Japan, I had had a Japanese girlfriend and a Vietnamese girlfriend, but had no particular preference for Asian women. However, one experience left an indelible mark on my mind. As a youth in NYC, I had gone to forty-second street, "The Deuce," and strolled into one of the seedy sex shops that existed there before Disney took over, paid a dollar, and fingered the soft wet pussy of an older Asian woman for about thirty seconds. I've never forgotten that experience. I remember the jet-black, bone-straight pubic hair of this woman jutting straight out off her pubic mound. I remember how wet and gushy her snatch was, I remember her creamy yellowish-white inner thighs spreading open as the booth partition slowly rose in front of me. This may have left some impression on me, but none that I was aware of, until I arrived in Japan. Besides my one previous Asian girlfriend in Los Angeles, before I went to Japan, I had no preference whatsoever for Japanese women. That changed, because *when in Rome, do as the Romans do*, but after having moved back to the US, I still prefer Japanese women. Something about the stillness of their composure is enticing and mysterious. Japanese women have subtle sensuality, they're pliable and sexually receptive. There's an erotic nature about Japanese women that once penetrated, they become rapturously orgasmic. Also, they get *really wet.*

You become addicted to Japan in subtle ways after living there for extended periods of time: the food, the lifestyle, the pace, the work, and the women. *Definitely* the women.

Sex Shops And *Osshibourri*

You hear all kinds of crazy stories about Japanese sex. Japanese porn is weird, tentacles and bizarre games and world records for most number of people fucking in one room, bukkake, Japanese businessmen eating sushi off of naked Japanese girls, and as we know from earlier, a severe case of national pedophilia. You may have heard of sex shops and eager women, perverted train rides and underskirt sex scandals, themed blowjob bars and lusty middle aged JILFs. All the stories are true, and then some.

Truth is, Japanese are on some next shit sexually, *pornographically.* The weirdo thing is, inside relationships, marriages, boyfriend-girlfriend relationships, and more and more of late—outside them too—sex is viewed as taboo and often doesn't even exist. There are millions of marriages in Japan where the husband and wife do not share the same room, let alone the same bed. Men and women in relationships in Japan often estrange themselves from each other due to work and what appears to be the inverted relationship between married Japanese men and women. In those relationships, women assume the leadership position, exerting control over basically everything, from the rearing of children to paying bills to making household decisions regarding education, and beyond. Men are salary appendages, true salarymen, exactly as they are called.

In Japan there's a thriving market for sex outside marriage, and it appears in all forms. There are legal "health clubs" all over the place. Japanese men go there and take their business partners to these sex clubs on the company's dime with impunity. Stories of Japanese men eating sushi off naked Japanese women are absolutely true. There are thick magazines, the size of a fat yellow pages, advertising call girls who will come to your house, apartment, or business, and these magazines are in the *convenience stores.*

Tip of the iceberg. Sex isn't hard to find in Japan, even though the people look like and act like sex is the furthest thing from their mind. Surrounded by all this taciturn, naïve, dark-haired, hidden sexuality, one day I went looking for some ass. And I found some. For sale at a sex shop. Couple blocks from my gig, I went walking. I entered a brightly lit area, lots of Japanese businessmen, women in dresses and high heels, taxis and nightclubs, sex shops and massage parlors. Bright lights, big city, Japanese style.

I saw an entrance with posters of semi-naked women on the walls and decided to enter. The pictures of the semi-nude middle-aged Japanese women on the walls looked like they could have been politicians, mothers, post office workers, or store clerks. I slowly crept down the stairs to an underground location where the pictures beckoned. I was greeted by a shirt and tied Japanese man who emerged from behind a curtain, wearing a tuxedo.

He greets me, "*sumimasen, hai, irashaimasen,*" which roughly translates to "excuse me, yes, you're welcome, come in"—so I enter. The man sits me down and politely offers me some green tea. I accept. He return with a small porcelain cup of steaming Green Tea, along with a leather bound booklet about the size of a magazine. He opens the booklet and reveals several pages of photos of the same type of woman pictured on the posters outside the establishment. He points to a few and offers them to me. I don't know which to choose and I'm slightly terrified but at the same time it feels like Christmas day has come. Literally. I'm happier than a kid in a candy store. I choose one. She's slightly chubby with short brown hair. She looks about 25. He confirms my choice, slaps the photo album shut and tells me "*roku sen yen desu-,*" six thousand yen, about sixty bucks, for half an hour. I gave it to him.

I'm led back into a semi-dark room, authentic Japanese *enka* music softly fills the room like air, piped in via invisible speakers. It feels like I'm in some super erotic forbidden sex oasis. I smell incense. Or cleaning fluid, not sure. There are about eight little cubicles divided amongst the floor space, where the action takes place.

As I'm being led to my cubicle, in two or three of the other cubicles, right there in front of me, there are multiple couples making love, naked as jay birds, engaging in oral sex, manual manipulation, fondling, grunting, sweating, pushing, arching, groping. Each cubicle has a two- or three-foot barrier separating them from the others, but still, all you'd need do is get up on your knees and you can see all the other cubicles and a fair bit of whatever is going on in each of them. Nudity.

Japanese public sex. Dark. Multiples. In all positions. Bodies slapping, sex acts, loud moans and the smells of sex all around you. It's heady.

Japan has blowjob clubs, soaplands, theme rooms, massage parlors and call girls. There are catalogs as thick as the thickest yellow pages you've ever seen, filled front to back with pictures of thousands of Japanese women of all shapes and sizes, brazenly advertising themselves and their sexuality for sale.

I became addicted to this lifestyle almost immediately. The women were, to me, high caliber. I had no idea what level of society they were compared to whatever the "norm" was. I had no idea. It was my wildest fantasies coming true in front of my eyes, for sixty or seventy bucks.

First Pop

Eventually I get to my cubicle. Head reeling. Still hearing the grunts and groans and bodies slapping. While sitting in my little cubicle, in walks my selection carrying a Hello Kitty bag of some sort. She's older than her picture suggests, maybe they took the picture 10 years ago? 20? She's middle-aged, in her 30's at least, but she still has the same haircut as in the photo. She's got a nice layer of soft feminine body fat, she's wearing a bikini.

She kneels in front of me, smiles broadly, and asks, "Anata wa doko karakimashita ka?"—where are you from? I say America, she squeals, "*Sugoi kakuii! America deshou, America ikkitaie*"—words I heard over and over in Japan, — America is *kakuii,* cool, and *sugoi*, great, she wants to go to America.

She reach between my legs in our little space and unbuttons my pants with a huge smile on her face. The sounds seem to get louder, all around me I'm hearing grunting, slapping, moaning, squishing. I'm nervous and ecstatic, feels like I'm about to bust in my pants before she even gets them off, I'm pulsating and *she looks really happy and excited about this, maybe more than I am, but that can't be, can it?*

She takes down my pants and produces a warm, wet oshibourri, a washcloth, and proceeds to wipe down my nether regions, slowly, carefully, she's examining me as she's wiping, like a nurse or a dick inspector.

I can't get any harder than I already am. It hurts actually, like all the blood in my brain has found it's way to my shaft and I'm feeling light-headed but my dick feels like it weighs ten pounds.

She places the oshibourri behind her, produces a tiny condom that she works onto my straining cock. She looks me in my eyes and says "itadaki masu", and gets to gobbling me in her mouth.

She's slurping, moaning, rocking back and forth on my cock, while simultaneously I'm hearing the other bodies around me doing the exact same thing. It's an orgasmic crescendo and it's shockingly erotic. After a few minutes, she stops, reaches into her Hello Kitty bag and produces a long black dildo. I'm baffled, but not really, her eyes pleading, she hands it to me, leans back, pulls off her bikini bottoms revealing maybe the hairiest pussy I'd ever seen in my life to that point. She leans back, spreads her legs, and says "onegaishemasu"- "please do" in Japanese. So I did.

She spread apart her hairy pussy and smiled serenely as I guided the dildo slowly into her snatch. I started slow with small circular motions and pushed it deeper and deeper into her. Eventually I picked up speed and drilled her good with the dildo for about five minutes while her head was thrown back. She rocked and bucked on the dildo, then suddenly she lurches forward shouting "iku...ikuuuuuu", which means *i'm coming* in Japanese. My cock was throbbing through the tiny little condom, so I mounted honey's already wet snatch, pumped a few times, came and collapsed on top of her. I couldn't believe what was happening, or what had just happened. It all seemed to have happened so fast, so *easily,* me walking into the place, choosing the girl, being led to the sex room, meeting the girl, the dildo, the sex, but it felt *oh so right*, like maybe *this was the entire reason I'd come to Japan in the first place.* It was like a crack head's first hit of crack, *Hooked for life.*

Coming from the States, where sex and sexuality are dark, dual-edged double-entendres, and where the sex for sale isn't so up front and open, this entire episode was a crazy real life pornographic adventure, for sixty (60) US dollars.

In Japan I found a culture and tradition of legal sex for sale in places all over town. There were places scattered all over the city where any of-age Japanese man could plop down a few dollars, satiate his need for sex in a completely legal, legit, clean, well-run, regulated establishment, in a very plush location, and then go home to his wife. Sex for sale is a normal part of the culture and society in Japan.

These places weren't in the shopping districts in the middle of town, but they also weren't particularly hidden either. They advertised women of all ages, all types, all sizes, they advertised fetishes. There were stores that re-created a junior high school setting, where the women wore the traditional uniform of the highly sexualized young Japanese schoolgirl. Millions of Japanese men fetishize young Japanese girls between the ages of thirteen or fourteen to seventeen. These are the golden years of a Japanese girl's life.

There are other places constructed to appear like a subway car. Subways across Japan are thought to be places where Japanese men sometimes violate Japanese women. These guys are called *chikan,* perverts. Japanese women have a rehearsed formula for what they are supposed to do when they are confronted by a *chikan*: Scream. Point. Yell, THAT MAN IS TOUCHING ME. HE IS A *CHIKAN!* All in Japanese. This begs the hope that other passengers will then yank him up and hold him for the police, which rarely happens.

Japanese have fetishized the subway grope/chikan phenomenon. They have *fake* subway train cars with women *dressed like* passengers, who are paid to *act like* they are on a real train so the men who are there can touch, grope, and fondle them on the fake train.

They've got soap lands where a Japanese man can pay a hundred bucks or so and have a Japanese woman lather him up with soap, wash his balls and ass, then lather herself up, slather her soapy naked body all over his, then open her legs to him. These places are Japanese tradition. There are blowjob clubs, called "health clubs," scattered all over every major city in Japan.

That first voyage into the world of Japan's sex shops and health clubs threw open the door of addiction for me.

Addiction is a brain disorder characterized by compulsive engagement in rewarding stimuli, despite adverse consequences

For three months thereafter, I tried visiting other shops I'd see around town. I'd pull up on my bicycle, or stroll up casually, like I'd been to each of them before. Almost all of them turned me down. They'd say, "*Nihon-jin dakay*"—Japanese only—smiling and bowing while they shut the door in my face. I must have tried a dozen shops, but not one of them would accommodate me. So, I returned to that same shop. Over and over.

The shop owners became my monthly friends. They'd see me approach, smile, pat me on my back, ask me questions I couldn't really answer, then they'd produce a photo album, or five or six polaroids of the girls who were working at that time. I'd choose the one I liked. The guy on duty would smile, put the photos away, disappear behind the curtain, and come back in a few minutes after having told the girl I chose that I was ready for her. He'd usher me through the din of iniquity, I'd meet the girl from the picture a few minutes later, she'd smile, we'd chat, she'd produce the *oshibourri*, clean me up, and away we'd go. Sometimes I got fat girls, sometimes really skinny middle-aged women, sometimes young super sexy-looking debutante girls, and sometimes girls who just looked *ready*.

I fell in love not only with the experience, but also with *oshibourri.* The moment of cleaning with the warm, clean, wet washcloth became a symbol of the fact that somehow -this act wasn't as dirty as it seemed like it was supposed to be. At every restaurant you go to in Japan, they'll give you *oshibourri,* a small, wet, warm towel to clean your hands with. It's wonderful. And you'll also get the *oshibourri* at the sex shops. It's mandatory. Gotta be clean in Japan. The *oshibourri* helped me to cleanse my mind and wash away any mental residual I had about what I was doing.

And so went the sex stores. I'd spend sometimes twenty or thirty thousand yen a month in there. Sometimes fifty thousand. That's two, three hundred to five hundred bucks a month on a brand-new habit I had just picked up in a country where I'd just arrived. I'd go on the weekends, or holidays—or Thursdays or Mondays. It was crazy fun and I felt like I was on another planet, and who could see what I was doing anyway? I was six thousand miles and an ocean away from anything, anyone, that knew me. I was fucking Martians in outer space.

It was great. I went back to that spot every time I got paid, even if I didn't have to. It was *so erotic* for me. So hot. *So dirty.* The sex industry in Japan had an effect on my morality. There now exists a massive grey area in my brain with regard to the world's oldest profession. I bought pussy in Japan enough to either burn in hell forever, or, to walk past any shame I have associated with it.

No Self Esteem

It isn't that Japanese women, or Japanese men for that matter, have low self-esteem, it's more like they have no self-esteem. But at least for Japanese men, their society is still decidedly patriarchal, therefore as a result Japanese men don't really need self-esteem.

For the women, it's altogether different. There is no pretense of equality between the sexes in Japan, and there is definitely no feminist movement, no discernible one anyway. Whereas American women are constantly being fed the lie that "everyone is beautiful and intelligent", chances are most Japanese women have either never heard the phrase "you're beautiful" directed towards them, or, the last time they heard it, it was something more like "you're kawaii", which of course means "you're cute", which isn't as much a compliment as it is a statement of reassurance, the translation being something along the lines of "you're

Japanese", or, "you're a female". To be cute in Japan is simply another way of fitting into the crowd, if you're a woman and you're not "cute", then you may as well not even be a woman. Self-esteem as a tangible concept essentially doesn't exist in Japan.

Look Who's Talking

Sometimes Japanese people don't understand Japanese. What I mean by this is, there were literally dozens of situations where *I know I was speaking pitch-perfect Japanese*—restaurants, supermarkets, elevators, schools, streets, sex shops, and health clubs—but the Japanese person I was speaking to could not understand or fathom a word I said simply because his brain couldn't process the fact there was a non-Japanese person actually speaking Japanese. For many Japanese, speaking their language is only possible if you are Japanese.

This gets at the heart of what Japanese think about themselves vis-à-vis the entire rest of the world. Every culture thinks itself unique, and indeed, every culture is, bringing to the table different foods, music, clothing, and values, but Japanese think themselves genetically unique, as though they are a different species of human from the rest of the planet. This deeply ingrained thought forms the foundation for what I suppose is "Japanese racism," although, as I said, I don't think Japanese are particularly racist in the way we Westerners view it. Their perspective on what it is to be human, and how to behave accordingly, is set to a different vibration.

Foreigners in Japan, in an act of self-racism, eventually start to discriminate against other foreigners, who are like themselves in being non-Japanese. The competition amongst westerners in Japan for the affection of the Japanese, is astounding.

I suffered more outright racism from non-Japanese than I did from Japanese themselves while I was in Japan. Weird stuff. Non-Japanese posting signs on their businesses, JAPANESE ONLY, when they themselves aren't Japanese.

>Chapter 10

FRIENDS WHOM YOU HATE

"How many of us have them?"

There was this one dude named JP. Those aren't his initials, that's the name he asked everyone to call him—no one actually knew his real name. Took me forever to realize "JP" just meant Japan.

JP looked like he could've been Greek or Scandinavian or Italian, maybe Jewish or even Slavic. He looked like he could've been any one of those nationalities, no one really knew and JP made it seem taboo to ask. The irony was that JP could perfectly mimic all of those accents. This seemed to be a part of JP's modus operandi, for no one to know what his authentic nationality actually was. It was as if JP cast a "don't ask me" spell on us all, so we didn't.

JP was a gypsy, nomad, wanderer, con artist, dirtbag, soul searcher. He ripped off food, clothes, drinks, and men's hygiene products from the convenience stores. He even once showed me where his face was on WANTED posters around Nagoya, *dirty deeds done dirt cheap.* But JP was also a germaphobe. He'd never touch anyone and wiped his hands constantly. But other times he'd have his zipper open on purpose, smelled like old milk.

There was a rumor he posted dick pics on lots of people's Facebook pages but he always magically produced a warm, soft, clean, brand new *oshibourri.* I wondered where he got them all. He may or may not have been homeless, and at the time he had a sixty-five-year-old Japanese grandmotherly figure acting as his 'girlfriend', come to discover she was sponsoring his visa and paying for his apartment so long as he properly serviced her whenever and however she needed.

He'd show up at my apartment at three in the morning sometimes and we'd go to the park and do pull-ups. He came around often for a hot minute but my main girl H hated his guts. Perhaps it was women's intuition because JP was turning me on to a bevy of women including N2, Double M, as well as one of many As. In fact, almost every woman that JP introduced me to ended up in my bed.

JP was a genius at doing different accents and creating fake personalities. For the entire time that I or anyone knew JP, it was as if he was playing a game of *Catch Me If You Can*, in Japan.

Sometimes JP and I would go bike riding in the midnight hour and he'd take us into these hostess clubs where there'd be the most drop-dead gorgeous middle-aged Japanese women I saw during my time in Japan. He somehow knew them all.

Japanese Give the Absolute Worst Hugs In The World

Imagine trying to give a hug to Count Dracula. Instead of embracing a hug and reciprocating, Japanese stiffen up, let their arms hang limp at their sides, and more than likely hate the fact that you're expressing any kind of physical affection whatsoever. To hug a Japanese is to hug a stiff, standing corpse of a human. My advice, don't.

Do not touch a Japanese person. They do not want you touching them in any way, and they damn sure have no plans of ever touching you. This applies to handshakes, pats on the back, or anything involving skin to skin contact. In fact, Japanese have a special name for contact, called "skin-ship," and it means exactly what you think it does: a skin-on-skin form of contact, which is a very "special" form of human contact, devoid and apart from what is "normal" human contact, which is the art of NEVER touching another person for any reason. Touch is fucking important, okay? It's one of the five senses, *you're supposed to use it.*

White "Niggers" In Japan

Here's something odd: White people complain about racism in Japan. A lot. What parallel universe is this? What could be weirder? Like my man Smitty says, "White people complaining about racism will never *not* be ridiculous."

Many, many of my whitey-white friends complained about racism in Japan constantly, as if, well, as if they were black people in America. It was mind-blowing, hilarious, and oddly comforting to hear my white friends from Idaho complaining that they were being discriminated against. I always wanted to say, "Wow. I hear you, brother,".

They were in fact being treated like *niggers*. Not "niggas" with an "a" in which black people use as a term of endearment, and which has no racial overtones. In Japan, "White Privilege" doesn't exist.

*SHH...*Be Quiet

Silence is golden in Japan. *Too golden.* Japanese like to be quiet. Not quiet as in whispering; quiet as in not making a sound. Total silence. They often don't answer you, whether or not they can, but they don't realize this is impolite behavior to most other cultures, especially to Americans, who detest silence.

There were numerous occasions that I thought they actually couldn't hear me, and so I'd yell whatever it was I was saying, thinking this to be the solution, which of course only added to the idea that Americans are loud, obnoxious assholes.

Sometimes, most times, almost all the time, they just would rather be quiet. I witnessed this many times because I was in observation mode. I witnessed many situations where Japanese couples were together, all ages, and I'd sit and watch them speak not a single word nor utter a single sound for hours. Abject silence.

Ask yourself, *who is the weirdo?* The couple who is not speaking to each other for two hours? Or. The cat who has been watching them, equally as silent, for the last two hours?

Don't go yelling anything, anywhere, for any reason, ever. You start shouting someone's name in Japan, "AY YO ERIC!" and you look like a talking gorilla, which essentially you are, of course.

The other side though, is that silence in Japan can be used to inflict pain, and often is. Silence in Japan is used as a weapon. Eternal silence. If a Japanese person, male or female, tells you they will never speak to you again, they won't. It's about honor, but it's also about removing anything from their lives that causes discomfort. Silence can be a deadly weapon. Be wary of it, but learn to embrace it as well. When in Japan, understand that silence is as important as what is being spoken.

Chapter 11

THE MAYOR OF NAGOYA

On Meeting "Dash"

My friend Dash had a profound impact on my life in Japan, at first anyway. I adopted Dash as my first role model in Japan but at the time Dash didn't know how to count money or tell time or give directions in Japanese. He did however, have nine Japanese girlfriends, was pushing a whip, and seemed to know the ins and outs of Nagoya pretty well. I decided to model my life after his, better or worse. Mostly, it turned out to be worse.

One night I'm walking around looking for food and I spot this place 'MOS Burger; I don't know what it was but a burger sounds about right. I stroll in and while in line, I hear a voice say

"Sup my peoples. What you doing in here?"

I turn around and there's a black guy who looks *very much like me*, draped in a three-quarter-length black leather jacket, black leather boots, black jeans, and a black shirt, with a bemused look on his face, staring back at me. This is how I met Dash.

He walked and talked *madd fast*, as if he always had someplace to be, and seemed to know everyone everywhere we went. The clerks at the convenience stores, gas station attendants, girls working behind the counter at fast food places, dudes working in music shops, Dash knew everyone and everyone knew Dash. But he wasn't what you'd call a "nice" guy. He was brusque, abrupt, demanding, and impatient. He always seemed a little annoyed and didn't take kindly to the Japanese people who couldn't understand what he was saying. He'd yell at folks and eyeball anyone who looked at him for even a moment. Dash would go out of his way to make it clear that he was different than they were, which was obvious, being that we were in Japan and he was a black dude wearing a long black leather jacket. His abrasive style didn't bother me much though, he was getting me high and I needed a friend.

Dash became my go-to man for the herb, but he was fanatically paranoid about smoking. I'd walk across Shirakawa Koen to get to his apartment which he shared with his wife and where he had his studio. Dash's wife was a laid back, middle-aged Japanese woman with extremely long, beautiful jet-black hair. She loved classic soul music and her attitude was like a southern black woman, who happened to be Japanese. Dash and I would sit in his studio where he had two drum kits set up, and a huge computer with which he did everything from creating drum beats to duplicating VHS movies to making labels for CDs to producing commercials to giving vocal lessons to sampling tracks to recording. Dash's studio was set up to do absolutely everything. Dash let me know right up front that he was "the man" in Nagoya. He had come to Japan a few years earlier to play drums in a band and had settled into Nagoya. His father was a famous musician himself and Dash never let a moment go by when he wasn't reminding everyone that his father was famous, and therefore, so was he.

I was glad to meet Dash, he took me under his wing and introduced me to lots of what was going on in Nagoya, as well as the fact that he supplied me with the herbs, but like I said, he was paranoid about it. Like, maniacally paranoid. He had this small purple pipe we smoked from. Whenever I came to his studio, he'd pack it up but he never let me actually hold it. He'd put it to my mouth for me, light it, hold it there for a few seconds for me to inhale, then he'd tell me to hold the smoke inside my lungs for exactly ten seconds. If I choked and let out any of the smoke, he'd get pissed, go absolutely ballistic and tell me I was wasting his herb.

"You can't be coming over here wasting my smoke man. If you gon' smoke you hold all that shit in for 10 seconds or you gon' have to find someone else to smoke with" he'd say.

I was thankful either way, even when he was scolding me for leaking a puff or two out of the corners of my mouth. We'd listen to music, he'd show me his numerous laminated backstage passes that read, "I'm with the band". Sometimes his wife would cook something for us, she never really seemed to have much else to do, and then we'd get in his little jeep and drive around town to his various girlfriend's places.

Dash invited me to a club he was working at as the sound engineer, a place called Gary's, where on any given night you'd find an American soul/funk cover band banging out the hits from Earth, Wind and Fire, Kool and the Gang, Lionel Richie, Prince, MJ, and Rick James. You'd also find a fair number of Japanese women all fawning over the black R&B musicians. Dash introduced me to the singer of one of the bands. She was a sister from back home in the US.

She was a *big gurl,* had giant tits and was very friendly to me when Dash introduced me to her. Eventually, she and I ended up in bed together. Dash told me she "needed some D" and said I should "take one for the team," and I didn't know what he was talking about but I ended up doing it because I needed to get laid and she apparently did too. "You don't need no girlfriend here in Japan...," Dash told me, "...*you need whoever is going to help you.*"

Dash and I started hanging tough. After school I'd head to his crib, where he had a monster studio set up. Besides being a drummer, Dash was a technical wiz and had accumulated a heap of electronic studio equipment over the years from doing shows and touring and whatever else. We'd sit in his studio and puff herbs on his little pipe, and he'd show me signed memorabilia and pictures of him with various superstars in the music biz. Dash spoke not one word of Japanese, and didn't give a shit, and I thought this was cool, stupid, and funny all at the same time. I'd ask Dash why he never learned to speak Japanese, why he couldn't tell time in Japanese or count money or anything, and he'd dead seriously ask me, "Why should I change??" I always thought, well, *because you're in Japan man.*

Dash and I produced some songs together but nothing that really sounded good to me. Eventually, Dash intro'd me to another cat 'Bunny', and Bunny and I produced an album's worth of music we called "Mash Up Your Mind", since it was a mash up of a bunch of different styles of music. Bunny lived with his girl too, and had his studio in their apartment, but Bunny wasn't allowed to have foreigners in his apartment, and I later found out Bunny himself wasn't even supposed to be living there. Every time we went to his place to record we both had to sneak up the stairs, and quietly slip inside his place, and keep our recording volume way down low. It was kind of a drag, but I was thankful to be getting the opportunity to do some music. The "Mash Up Your Mind" joint sounded better than the stuff I had been doing with Dash, but still wasn't exactly where I wanted to be musically.

The First "N" and the Botched Threesome

One evening, Dash and I were chilling at his live house. There were two, young Japanese girls standing by the bar.

"Hi, how are you? Can you speak English? What's your names?" I ask. One of them replies in decent English, "I'm H and this is N," and I find out N can barely speak English. The three of us talk for about fifteen minutes and out of nowhere I hear myself saying, "Hey, would you guys like to come back to my apartment? I just moved here from the US and I live pretty close." To which they respond by looking at each other briefly, giggling for a second, packing up their bags, and then following me out. I tell them my place is close, they ask me if I have any food in my apartment, I say no, so they spot a convenience store and stop inside, pick up some *Chu-Hi,* some *onigiri,* some *natto,* and some chocolate.

My apartment was a few blocks away. I had no idea what we were or weren't going to do. I had no food, an old black and white TV, an old CD player and some CDs I had brought, and all my clothes piled up in a corner by the front door. I had a balcony and that *kotatsu* and my futon and my little plastic bathroom and that was it.

We get upstairs, they look around at my place and start putting the food they had bought on my *kotatsu*. It was my first time experiencing the shocking taste and texture of *natto*. Tastes a little like, looks a lot like, smells more like, stale snot, but somehow like many things in Japan which at first seemed completely bizarre, I eventually came to like *natto*. Funny how the same stuff that is at first so unappealing eventually finds its way into your heart. *Are you a teacher?* Yes. *Sugoi! Where are you from?* New York City. *Sugoi! How long have you been in Japan?* Two months. *Sugoi!*

Sugoi means "great," or some variation of great. Everything I said was great. Everything was *sugoi*. Everything is *sugoi* to Japanese girls. The weather is *sugoi*. Your name is *sugoi*. Coffee is *sugoi*. However tall you are or are not is *sugoi*. Wherever you are from is *sugoi*. I was *sugoi*.

We ate. Laughed some. The one who spoke English, H, did almost all the talking. The other one, N, couldn't speak any English at all. But she was smart. She had smart, sensitive eyes, short, dark hair, had an easy smile and laugh, and exuded a certain motherly sexiness. *And she was thick*. The other one had long hair and wore glasses and had more of an "American" look, she seemed like she was trying to be sexy. N, on the other hand, was shy, demure, 100 percent Japanese, and therefore sexy as fuck. They were both in their early 20's.

It got to be late. I suggested the girls stay the night, by this time it was 3 or 4 A.M. I said, "The sun will be up in a few hours and you guys can catch the first train," since subways in Japan don't run twenty-four hours. They shut down just after midnight and restart just around 5 A.M.

I had no idea what they'd think of my suggestion. No idea how they'd answer, I threw it out there and let it hang and . . .

They looked at each other, stared at each other, whispered a few words in Japanese, and H turned to me and said *"daijyobu,"* okay, they'd stay.

Again, I was shocked. Imagine, in America, meeting two women in a club, and within fifteen minutes of meeting them you're on your way to your place with them, and then a few hours after hanging out with them, you've convinced them both to stay the night. Well, it might be normal for you, and if it is, kudos, but that had never happened to me in the US before, and within three months of being in Japan, it was *very much happening.*

We all three climb into my bed, with me in the middle. H is on my right side, N is on my left. Some music is playing on the tiny CD player on the floor next to the bed. We're laying down for about fifteen minutes, all of us pretending to be trying to sleep. I turn to my right and there was H's face staring into mine. We immediately passionately kissing. She's groping at me, grabbing my package and so I reach for her crotch, but, she won't let me touch her pussy, so I'm grabbing for her tits instead, and she's pushing my hand away while at the same time squeezing my bulging cock in her hand. We did this for about ten minutes, while her friend N was acting oblivious to all the action going on right next to her.

It became a frustrating tease, a fun one, but a tease nonetheless, and I felt more than a little funny with her friend lying right beside us. We stop our touch game, and I give up trying to touch her pussy. She release my cock, and we both just stopped. I'm lying there a minute or two. There are two women in my bed whom I just met, one just gave me blue balls, the other is sleeping, or so I thought, and I've got to wake up soon for work. I decide to really try to get some sleep. It must have been 5 A.M. Almost 5 anyway. *Gotta be up in a couple hours for work,* I think to myself.

I turn around facing the opposite direction to my left to really try to get to sleep, but there were N's eyes staring wantonly at me. I look at her and she lunges for my mouth with hers wide open. We start sucking each other's faces and N's legs practically spring open as if to say "she didn't let you get hers but you can have mine, HERE IT IS." I cup my hand over her bush and feverishly finger her, she's gasping, my other hand covers her mouth to keep her quiet, she's biting the palm of my hand, grunting and thrashing, I'm discretely digging her out while her friend lay right next to us. It was nuts. I had no time to contemplate what her friend was thinking. I never thought this was their plan, which in retrospect, I think it was.

We're kissing and groping and rubbing and slurping each other like crazy. Right next to us is her friend who is clearly awake because just minutes before she and I had been having our groping contest.

"Can't you guys go somewhere else and do that?" she finally says, at which point N and I spring up like marionette puppets and I make a beeline to my tiny plastic bathroom with N following close behind, we shut the door, and become wild animals.

I yank off her top, revealing a pair of gorgeous breasts with two of the biggest cinnamon colored nipples I have ever seen in my life. Her nipples are as big as baby carrots, I kid you not. I devour her nipples like a strong hungry homeless man. I then bend down and come face to face with the darkest, hairiest, most divine pussy I'd ever seen. It was wondrous. Her Japanese pussy has a thick patch of jet black pubic hair that stands up straight at a 90 degree angle to the girl's body.

I stand up and she unbuckles my pants, pulls them off and I bend her over the tiny plastic bathtub and pound the living piss out of N for a few furious minutes and then she drops to her knees from exhaustion. I stand her up, turn her around, sit her down facing me on the edge of the small plastic bathtub, throw her legs over my shoulders and bang her face to face while sucking her tits. Uncomfortable. We're making way too much noise anyway, so I decide to pull out. She takes me in her mouth, on the edge of the bathtub, slurping away at my Johnson until I explode on her forehead and in her hair, which she didn't' seem to mind much.

She looks around, finds a washcloth and quietly cleans off my drooping cock. I exit the bathroom leaving her to clean herself up. Her friend is on my balcony now, looking into her cellphone. I fix myself up a little and pour myself some water.

A few minutes later, she comes out, her hair is messy and but her clothes are now like they had been before we went into the bathroom. She walks out onto the balcony, her and her friend have a brief discussion, they come back inside and announce that they're leaving, and I'm perfectly ok with that, but still shocked at what had just taken place.

I get N's text address, and we continued meeting almost monthly for four or five years after that. We'd meet at one of our favorite love motels near Osu Kannon, where we'd spend a few hours watching TV, eating, drinking wine, smoking, and fucking. She always paid for the room, usually about seventy or eighty dollars for three hours. Our routine was always exactly the same, we'd take the elevator up to the 4th floor, enter the room to sounds of other couples making love in the other rooms, we'd take off our shoes, relax a bit, have a glass of wine, smoke a cigarette, then she'd announce she was going to take a shower, which meant it was my time to "get ready."

She'd emerge from the shower dripping wet and stark naked. We'd climb underneath the covers, sometimes not, and I'd marvel at her baby carrot nipples, then we'd lick, suck, and fuck like rabbits for a few hours. Once our time was up, she'd disappear into the subway until our next monthly meeting—and we had this arrangement for five years. Five or six years and I never even knew her last name.

She'd text me once a month, randomly: "*Trevor, do you have time to meet me today? Can we meet at seven?*" She had a long train ride home and never wanted to be in Nagoya past ten. She lived out in the countryside, she said.

It was perfect for me, because after I got married, I couldn't stay out too much later than ten, so once a month or so N mailed me, we'd have our illicit love hotel romp, and then she'd disappear off into the night. She never even wanted me to walk her to the train station, she never asked me if I had a girlfriend or if I was married or anything. We'd exit the love hotel as if we'd never even been there, then part ways with an informal "bye, see you next time," and then we'd both disappear into the darkness. Winter, Summer, Spring, Fall, we continued our relationship like this for those five or six years with no strings attached. Never once did N ask me about our future, N knew when I decided to start a family, but never once did she say one thing about my marriage, my wife or my children. Nothing at all. Her attitude was the less I know about you and the less you know about me the better.

Our monthly trysts reminded me of that saying, *what happens in Vegas stays in Vegas*, except we were in Nagoya. Then one day about six years in, N texts me that she's found a boyfriend, and I never heard from her again. Never. Nothing. Not once. And not since.

Y And the Ramen Shop

The fact that I met N, Y, K, and M, all within my first few months, in retrospect, is perfectly normal. However, while it was happening, I had no idea what I was laying the groundwork for. The mere fact that all these women are only the first of several women I met with either the same names, or names starting with the same letters, is partly the gist of my experience sexually in Japan. *So many women, so many letters.*

I met another Japanese woman at the SKI gym in Higashi Ku shortly after meeting N and H. Her name was Y. I'm doing tricep extensions with light weights in front of the mirror and Y comes sauntering directly up to me, picks up the exact same weight I'm using, and starts doing the exact same exercise I was doing while looking directly at me in the mirror, smiling like a Cheshire cat. I *had* to ask her her name. She says "Y." I say "Nice to meet you." She says nice to meet you too in broken but impressive English. She looks like she could be in her 30's, a little older than H and M, but I can't really tell how old Japanese girls are or aren't. They all look young, unless they don't.

She owns a restaurant, she tells me, right around the corner. A ramen restaurant. Come to discover the restaurant is even closer to my place than the *unagi* place. I start going there every day. I'd get ramen with pork, Karamiso ramen, even though I don't eat pork, with a side bowl of white rice. I drank water with it. When I told her I didn't eat pork she laughed and told me it's *oishii*-delicious, and indeed it was. I could never get her to not put the pork in. "It needs..," she'd tell me. Either way, Y's ramen was delicious.

Y and I hit it off. She's sassy and smart and smiles often, big, wide and easy. She loves to laugh and makes wry observations. She tells me "Japanese people used to be small because we only ate fish and rice, but now, we eat meat and Western fried food, so we're bigger." Makes sense.

She had hella customers in her shop all the time. Winter was coming and there is nothing in the world better than a hot bowl of ramen on a cold winter night in Japan. People would line up for half a block to get a seat in her cramped ramen shop. Waiting as long as an hour to slurp up her family recipe for ramen. Her brother had come up with the recipe, and she'd started her restaurant with him as an investor. Eventually things went sour, she took over, and expanded to two restaurants.

Y and I started seeing each other. Her fancy high-rise apartment was located right across the highway, a few blocks from her restaurant and a few blocks from my place. She'd invite me to her place when she was through with her shift and we'd listen to Hawaiian ukulele music in her ninth floor apartment. Inside, she'd spread blankets floor and we'd always end up making love on her *tatami* mat. More often than not, she'd also have some delicious food prepared for me whenever I'd arrive, fresh baked pumpkin bread, delicious hot soups and fried chicken. Y would allow me to use her computer as long as I wanted. I didn't have my own at the time, and the whole thing was tremendous. It was heavenly being in her apartment with that soft Hawaiian music playing and the smell of whatever delicious food she was cooking and our late night love making sessions on her tatami mats. It felt like Y and I were actually having a relationship.

Her, and her food, and her warm apartment, soothed the culture shock and made the cold winter nights much more bearable, but I wasn't into an exclusive relationship with Y, which eventually caused things to implode. She assumed we were both being exclusive, but I of course, wasn't. I was already having my monthly love motel sessions with N, and there were more to come.

The Bed Is On Fire

Now, I would like to introduce you to k, Short, thick, sexy, stylish, bright, talkative, smiley, fancy-talking K. I met K at a dance club in Sakae. K was younger than N and Y, in her 20's, and in love with hip hop and dancehall reggae. She loved going to clubs to dance her ass off. One night I'm out and spot K in the club dancing by herself, I approached and chatted her up. Soon thereafter, I get her to my place.

That first night with K at my place, left us both naked on my futon. It was winter now, cold, and so I had a thick blanket on the bed, but eventually the blanket became too hot, so in the middle of passion I throw the blanket off, oblivious to where it landed. Holy smoke! The blanket landed on top of one of the two candles I had lit at the foot of the bed. Suddenly, I smell it, but I think to myself, *it must be coming from outside*, so I keep stroking. Then the smoke became a raging fire singeing the shit out of my feet and ankles.

I'm deep inside K and my feet are on fire, but I'm thinking I had accidentally put my foot onto one of the candle flames at the foot of the bed. The addition of the smoke was a little curious, but I was too much into what was going on with K to actually stop, until K finally looks down towards the bottom of the futon and calmly says to me, *"The bed is on fire."*

If you're an egotistical asshole like I am, and you're in bed with a girl strokin' her and she tells you the bed is on fire, you might assume honey is talking about your stroke game. She wasn't. She was talking about the bed.

"WHAT?!" I scream.

I jump on the bed to see the blanket had caught fire and the bed was next. I leap from the bed with my feet as hot as burning coals. My cock and balls flap as I'm hopping on one foot. All the while K is calmly sitting on the bed with her knees pulled up into her chest. I don't quite know what to do and the fire is growing and threatening to catch onto the futon itself. "Put out the fire" K says to me calmly.

I run into my tiny plastic kitchen and fill up a tiny cup with water. I repeat this about a dozen times, back and forth between the kitchen and my room, dumping the water onto the smoldering, charred, burnt blanket.

After a few frantic minutes the fire is finally out. I'm still naked, out of breath, and utterly embarrassed. K had watched the entire episode with her naked knees pulled up to her chest, and when it was all over she calmly says to me, "...come back to bed." Which I did. I composed myself, got back in the sack with K, and we picked up where we left off. K and I 'dated' for a few more months after that, but eventually, she too disappeared.

Something Was On The Rise

Three months in, and I had already answered the call of my vices by finding a sex shop—that would cater to me. N and I were in full swing with our monthly love hotel sessions. I'd banged the black singer whom D introduced me to. Y and I were carrying on something of a 'relationship', and now I was also seeing K. Very heady, very quickly.

I was teaching the kids and getting along with them and getting to know their mothers and eventually the mothers asked me to teach their children after school in a private setting as well. They really appreciated my strict attitude with their sons and my ability to come up with games and my genuine playfulness and exuberance. The truth was I was loving my job, loving my new home, feeling euphoric happiness and freedom I hadn't felt in Los Angeles at all. I felt I had been *released.*

Part II

A Completely New Life

>Chapter 1

THE INTERNATIONAL CENTER

Hook-Up Central

Around the same time I had started going to the gym, I was exploring and learning about the nightlife in Sakae, I had also discovered the Kokusai Center, the International Center. The Kokusai Center is a huge building in the center of town where they hold a library, a Western Union and services for foreigners. They also have a "community bulletin board" where if you wanted to post for private students, or just have conversation exchange with a Japanese person, you could.

This community board was online dating without the online. You put up your picture, some information about yourself, and nine times out of ten you'd have several Japanese women responding to your ad. You could take your pick. The first woman I met on this board was M1. I dated several Japanese women whose names began with the letter *M*, thus the code name M1. She was the first, but not the last. There were numerous *Y*s also, several *A*s, a few *T*s, some *S*s, a couple *H*s, some *R*s, a *C*, some *J*s, some *K*s, some *N*s. There were probably a few other letters also, but I can't remember them all.

M1 was in her early thirties. She dressed stylishly, loved urban culture, liked pretending to be more sophisticated than she was, and had broad shoulders, bigger than average breasts and a crooked smile. You don't see Japanese women with big breasts really often. I remember one day a group of Japanese women were staring at M1 and I asked her why and she said, "I don't know, maybe they're jealous," and I said "jealous of *what*"and she said "maybe they're jealous because mine are bigger than theirs". I asked her how it felt to have bigger breasts than the average Japanese, and she told me it made her feel like "the winner".

We met after she answered that first posting I placed at the International Center and for the first month or so we simply went to Starbucks and we'd just sit and talk. Finally one day I invited her back to my place, and it was on after that. She asked me "why do you always get what you want Trev", without really knowing whether or not I always "got what I want". I didn't know what to say, but we took off from there.

M1 and I dated for a couple months, while at the same time I was still seeing Y, N, and K. M1 took me to see Mary J. Blige in concert and took lots of photos of us doing stuff together and was pretty cool, but she also had a dark undercurrent I couldn't figure out, she cussed often and seemed both angry and admiring of me. She also seemed put off by the fact that she was in her 30's an as yet unmarried.

Eventually, I learned that for Japanese women 30 is a cut off age of sorts. If they're not married by 30, Japanese woman are looked at as sort of has-been. M1 had been scorned before. I'm sure of it, because she allowed her bitterness to bleed into our conversations way too often for me not to notice. However, it didn't bother me much, I knew I wasn't going to marry M1, and acted like it, which made matters worse, fast.

One day M1 is at my place in the early afternoon, and Y, from the Ramen shop comes knocking while M1 and I are in the middle of a noisy sex session. Y usually made herself available late at night after her ramen shop closed, and K never came by without us making plans first, so I hadn't expected anyone to be coming 'round in the afternoon. But Y had decided to surprise me this particular afternoon, and knocked on the door just as M1 was having a loud orgasm. Y is now pounding the door. M1 looks up at me, shocked, still naked. I put my hand over M1's mouth, she pries my hand away angrily. Y bangs louder, screaming, "TRE-Bah I KNOW SOMEONE IS IN THERE WITH YOU!" I never answered the door. Eventually, Y leaves. M1 asks me who it was. A few days' later, Y texts me saying she'd had enough and wanted us to just be friends from then on. Close call. Too close.

Y had been assisting me at my little school with the students from SKI, and when she decided to put the brakes on our relationship, she also quit the school.

I quickly put up another ad at the Kokusai Center for another assistant, and that's when I met the second M, M2. Y and I remained friends, and about a year later she offered me five thousand dollars to get her pregnant, which of course I didn't. But I did start yet another relationship with M2.

Freebell

I had lived through my first winter in Japan and spring was coming. I was seeing 4 or 5 women, if you count Y. I was also frequenting the sex shops as well. I wasn't saving any money and was spending more time on the streets of Nagoya than at my little apartment in Higashi Ku. I was still writing my movie script and had gone back to eating unagi and onigiri since Y and I had split.

At that same time, I was informed by the folks at my gig that I would be reduced to part-time status since the school was losing students. This meant that I had to find my own apartment and pay for it too. You see, the school had decided to cut expenses and my apartment was one of the first things to go. This didn't fare well with me. I was confused about whether I should stay in Japan and look for more work, which I had no idea how to do, or just return to America.

I decided the former, and cut ties completely with SKI. I continued teaching the children through the relationships I had built with their parents, and took on M2 as my full time assistant. I also moved into a new apartment, newer, cleaner, bigger, located in a building just a

short walk from Nagoya station. The apartment was known for en-
couraging non-Japanese to live there, and was called 'Freebell'. Shout
out to TAKA, the manager of Freebell, and his staff. They were cool,
friendly, and helpful, spoke great English, and held a brother down in
times of need, which were often.

Freebell was loud, raucous, and crazy, and lived up to it's namesake,
'Gaijin Ghetto'.

There were constant crawl parties, with young foreigners and Japanese going from apartment to apartment, playing loud music, and
drinking copious amounts of alcohol. It was a college dorm atmosphere, almost like a mini United Nations. There were people from all
over the world living in Freebell.

I developed a crush on one of the Japanese girls working at the
apartment office named Mao, but nothing came of it. Although we had
some really interesting conversations, she was too smart and saw
through me like a window pane.

Meantime, I loved my new one-bedroom apartment at Freebell.
Compared to my Playskool apartment at Higashi-ku, Freebell was
modern, large, and airy, with wood floors and a tatami bedroom. My
apartment was on the twelfth floor and had sliding glass doors that
looked out above the street below. Rent was reasonable, but still I had
to find another job, which I did. I applied for a job as an "ALT", Assistant Language Teacher, working for a dispatch company which
farmed out ESL teachers to elementary, junior high, and high schools
all across Japan. I also still had my part-time gig teaching the students
from SKI with the help of my new assistant M2.

M2

M2, was also in her thirties, but unlike M1, she didn't wear any bitterness on her sleeve. She spoke English with a slight Australian
accent and a delicate and measured voice. M2 was low-key, confident,

and knowledgeable about world affairs. She wasn't into music or dancing or fashion like M1 was, but she also wasn't as pent up.

I 'interviewed' M2 at a café and told her about what I was doing, the students and the school, and offered to pay her 10,000 yen, 100 bucks, per day, per class, if she'd assist me with teaching the class, communicating with the students' mothers, along with paperwork. The classes were once a week, which meant she'd make 400 bucks for the month, for about five or six hours of work. She accepted.

After the interview, I invited her back to my place to talk some more, and there, that first night with M2, with my newfound confidence with Japanese women swelling, we consummated our new relationship, on my new futon, in my new apartment at Freebell.

It was great for a while. M2 and I played games with the students and taught reading and phonics and sang songs and we both fell in love with the students and maybe each other too. We'd give the students a lesson to do and then we'd disappear somewhere and fondle and kiss and play and laugh. We also had deep discussions about Japanese and American politics, history, culture, people, art, and music. We spent most of our free time at my place in Freebell. I was falling for M2, but still had M1, N, and K in my rotation as well. Things were heating up.

Allow Me to Introduce Myself

I met a group of new international friends at Freebell. I had D, who was blazing me at his studio regularly. I had my little private school and my students. I had M1, M2, N, and sometimes K. I was visiting the sex for sale shops regularly and eating unagi and drinking lots of pineapple juice. Japanese don't like cranberry juice, it's hard to find. I digress. I was making money and things had taken on a semblance of a life around me. I had learned some rudimentary Japanese and sort of knew my way around town. I was going out at night to Gary's and ID Bar.

During the days I'd see bands set up playing live music on different corners all over Sakae. They'd set up their equipment and play for hours, sometimes with no one watching, other times several Japanese would gather to hear the band if they were especially good. I'd hang out and watch for hours, dreaming of being able to one day play guitar or sing something with some of the bands.

One of the bands I saw playing regularly featured an absolute killer Japanese guitar player with long hair and a thick mustache. He played a mean blues guitar and I was mesmerized by him and his band. Eventually I got the nerve to speak to him. I told him my idea for fusing blues guitar and hip hop and we started rehearsing together.

We rehearsed classic rock songs from Jimi Hendrix and Led Zeppelin, and then I wrote an original song called "Get Down Make Love," which we played together at an international music festival at Oasis 21 the next year. Our band name was N-Jin, pronounced "engine," and we got as far as performing at the massive Tokyo Design Festa event held twice a year in Tokyo. Eventually he started asking me for money for his entire band to rehearse, which was understandable, but I didn't have the money he was asking for and we fell out.

This was only a part of my musical exploration while I was in Japan. It got better, much better, but the seeds had been sown those first six months of what I wanted to do, what I was *going* to do, while in Japan. I wanted to make music. I wanted to write a film, I wanted to somehow be part of the music scene, and I wanted to write for the local magazine, then called Japanzine. I also wanted to become part of the nightlife going on in Sakae. And, ironically or not, I *really* wanted to *learn* how to be a good English teacher.

By Spring of that next year, I had my small school, my girlfriends and my dirty sex shop habit. I had a small crew of friends, cash in my pocket, my apartment and my job. I was absolutely loving my new life in Japan.

Part III

MARRIAGE, CHILDREN, DIVORCE, HUMILIATION. *A JAPANESE LOVE STORY.*

>Chapter 1

NEUTRON BOMB

Intimacy Implosion

S pring had sprung and those first six months, including the four cold, dark months of winter, were behind me. Japanese spring is an explosion of beauty in the form of the blossoming of the cherry blossoms (*Sakura*) from the third week of March until about the second week of April, depending on which part of Japan you're in. The beauty lasts only a few short weeks, and therefore the *Sakura* embodies an allegory to the cyclical seasons and the shortness and brevity of beauty, youth, and life itself. I was truly stunned to see those beautiful Sakura trees blooming all over Nagoya. Some streets looked like they had been taken right out of a fairytale storybook. The white-pink blossom of the *Sakura* made the trees look like they were set ablaze with white fire. You'd look down the street and it'd look like the tops of the trees were spouting white flames for *blocks*. I'd spend hours walking around the city listening to my music, bumping old-school hip hop while bopping through the city admiring the beautiful *Sakura*.

And so, I named the female lead romantic interest in my film *Sakura*. Sakura would represent everything beautiful, innocent, unjaded, and traditional about Japan.

Yoshimi, they don't believe me. But you won't let those robots defeat me. —The Flaming Lips

Even though I had a number of "friends" by this time, none of them, save D, were close friends. D was cool, but D wasn't trying to hear any of my deepest, most sensitive thoughts about what I was going through. Alienation was beginning to creep up on me.

Even with M1, M2, the monthly sessions with N, K, my students, and my friends, I was still craving deep, meaningful communication, or at least something like it.

Without me knowing it, I was beginning to attach this need for "deep, meaningful communication" with my urge for sex. Every time I wanted to communicate, the thought transposed in my mind to a need for sexual release. The sexual connections I had made allowed me to forget about my need to communicate and share, and instead allowed me to indulge in the momentary carnal physicality of sex. For a while, it replaced, or *supplanted* my need to express and be expressed to. I was developing an addiction along with a fetish, both of which I compartmentalized and chalked up as my just wanting to get laid. Eventually, I convinced myself that I didn't need to express myself, I just needed to *fuck*. Which I did.

While I was getting laid, it never dawned on me how Japanese themselves carry out their own sexual dance with each other. I thought I had some issues, but man, they've *really* got some issues.

The Japanese Sex Problem and the Flight from Human Intimacy

There are record numbers of Japanese women reaching their forties without having produced children, and with no plans to. This combination of attitudes and social trends has been named *sekkusu shinai shokogun*, or celibacy syndrome. Put simply, Japanese people aren't fucking, not each other anyway, and the population is getting older, and old people don't produce babies. The stark reality is that Japan is imploding.

2016 saw Japan have it's lowest birthrate since records began in the 19th century. Less than one million new Japanese babies were born, but about 1.3 million Japanese died that same year, resulting in a loss of over 300 thousand Japanese, contributing to an ongoing decline in population. Experts, Japanese officials, record keepers, all say Japan is experiencing a real "crisis" regarding it's population. The country itself seems to be dying. *The situation is dire.*

Recent talk has escalated about the "Demographic Time Bomb," young Japanese adults both male and female eschewing sex and intimacy altogether, and the dire consequences this will have on the Japanese population over the next few decades. Some estimates say that at the rate Japanese are going, if things continue as they are, by 2040, a little over two decades from now, the population of Japan will decrease by almost twenty million people, which is just about a sixth of their entire population. Imagine predictions existing calling for the US population to drop by fifty million people in the next twenty-five years. This is the situation Japan is facing in *real life* right now. A one-sixth culling of any nation's population over the course of a couple of decades would be disastrous, to put it lightly. It appears, mathematically speaking, that Japan is dying.

For every one person born, 1.3 people die, which is a negative ratio. This is, by all accounts, a dying society. Studies and statistics point to a number of different reasons for this, but the most obvious, and least spoken of, is the simple fact that Japanese don't seem to like each other very much. They aren't dying of disease, they aren't dying due to war, crime, pollution, poison, or anything one can readily point to; what they are dying of is simply lack of human contact, emotion, and intimacy, all of which lead to sex, which leads to more people, which is exactly what they aren't producing enough of.

According to studies, one third of Japanese men and women between sixteen and forty-nine are simply not interested in sex. The same study says almost 40 percent of all Japanese between eighteen and thirty-four years of age have never had sex. Economics and an unstable financial future are trotted out as reasons for this lack of copulation, but in my opinion, again, the reason is deeper, and has to do more with values than money.

Romance, and everything associated with it—love, touch, affection, vulnerability, spontaneity, carefreeness, fun, indulgence, sensuality, passion, excitement, joy, earthiness—none of these very human traits are highly valued in Japan. In fact, the opposite of these are what most Japanese seem to strive to attain: coldness, joylessness, inhibition, repression, fear, hopelessness, cruelty, humiliation. Japanese display a disdain for intimacy of any kind such that they appear to be a nation of androids. Ironically, Japan is the world's leading manufacturer of robots, and as we speak, there are "female" robots on the market which simulate human intimacy in Japan. Need a robot to vacuum your carpet? Japan has those. Need one to hug and kiss? Japan has those too.

Denying physical intimacy to each other and the resulting potential catastrophic drop in population is the totally predictable result of a society that teaches itself that lack of emotion and physical contact is somehow a good thing. The government of Japan has any number of plans in the works to get people fucking—extra vacation days for men, economic incentives, even a "tax on the handsome" was proposed in order to make nerdy Japanese men more attractive to women. This tax would burden handsome Japanese dudes so that less attractive ones would become suddenly more attractive. The idea being, if they've got less tax, they've got more spending money. But the one thing that needs to happen is never discussed, because discussing it would mean Japanese have to take a bold, clear, decisive look at their values and consequently themselves, and boldness, clarity, and decisiveness are three more traits Japanese lack, and seem proud to lack. Japan and Japanese need to take a hard, realistic look at how they treat each other, how they communicate, how they don't, and how love is expressed, and how it isn't. What can you make of a society where no one touches anyone else, and hugging is about as common as talking fish?

Hope as we know it, is another aspect of life that Japanese seem to be devoid of. Rather than hope, in Japan there is *shouganaie*, which is the diametric opposite of hope. *Shouganaie* is the Japanese equivalent of saying "Things are the way they are, and there is nothing that can be done about it." *Shouganaie* is the response you get to any number of questions about why things are the way they are, situations, environments, people places and things, in Japan. Hopelessness is a quiet cancer on the landscape of Japan, and that hopelessness is metastasizing. It isn't bad economics, or earthquakes, or radiation-poisoned sushi that's killing Japan, it's *shouganaie*.

And there I was, in the midst of a ticking population time bomb, wandering amidst this cold, uncommunicative, affectionless, hopeless country, dealing with my culture shock as best I could. I was trotting around looking for something or someone to anchor myself to.

>Chapter 2

MEET THE WIFE

Love galore

I had put up another ad at the International Center asking for a female language exchange partner.

The post read like this:

Hi! I'm from New York City! I want to talk and exchange ideas/culture/language with a down-to-earth, fun, creative, and adventurous woman. I can teach you English, and about my hometown NYC, and you can show me something about Nagoya! Let's enjoy together!

I included my contact information and the first woman to answer the ad would become my future ex-wife. Her name was "A". We first met at the TV Tower in the center of the city. I was tired and dragging ass the day we met, not trying very hard to be impressive when she showed up in tight dark blue jeans. We exchanged the usual "nice to meet you, nice to meet you too," pleasantries. I quickly learned she could barely speak English and I was slightly exasperated by this.

But she was very cute, but not in an overtly sexual way. She looked smart. She had short jet-black hair, big eyes, and pouty lips that swelled into a huge smile filled with white but very imperfect teeth. Her skin was clear and she seemed to shine. She was effervescent and energetic, and she bubbled like soap suds in a bubble bath.

After we spoke for a few minutes, I asked her to turn around so I could see how her ass looked in her jeans, and she did so with a giant smile on her face. She was peppy as hell and eager to do, something, I wasn't entirely sure what. I definitely wasn't thinking *this is going to be my wife one day,* but I did like her immediately. We talked a little and she told me she was leaving town for a couple weeks and would get back in touch with me when she returned, and she did.

We started meeting at cafés and walked around the city getting to know each other. I was new to the city, but it seemed like she was as well. It was exciting and fun to learn about the city together. I was taken aback by her not knowing much about the city though, *why doesn't this girl know anything about this city she was born and raised in?* Come to find out, she hadn't ventured that far beyond her parents' home up near Higashiyama Koen. We went to parks, restaurants, cafés, record shops, we walked around in alleys and side streets, and we talked a lot. Well, I talked a lot, she mostly just listened and smiled and agreed with whatever I said, and was really eager and enthusiastic about me, us, and our times together.

She turned out to be exactly everything that I posted I was looking for—someone down to earth, fun, creative, adventurous. She was bright and funny and I felt really great being with her, and she seemed to enjoy spending time with me as well. She wasn't cold, wasn't angry like M1, wasn't needy like Y, wasn't jaded or aloof like M2. In fact, she wasn't *any* of the things I had gotten myself used to about Japanese people. She was entirely different than every other Japanese person I'd met up to that point. She was open, expressive, warm, receptive, and happy. She was *alive.*

I was teaching her English, and for whatever reason, I didn't have the usual immediate sexual desire to "conquer" her like I'd had with the other women I had met. I sincerely just enjoyed being around her, but slowly, I was falling in love with her. Our moments together seemed to be a genuine connection between us, despite the fact that her English level was low. She was pure and gentle, funny and curious, kind and affectionate. She opened up to me without being able to speak the exact words she wanted to express on many occasions. I could *feel* what she was thinking. She yearned to communicate with me. I could feel she wanted to be closer to me.

We spent lots of time just staring at each other, no words, total silence, just stares, exactly like I became used to seeing young Japanese couples not talking to each other, just staring. It was new and unusual for me, coming from a society that values talking incessantly about everything and anything. However, here's the rub, at the same time, it had become the most satisfying experience I'd ever had with a woman until that point. The staring seemed to allow us both to completely relax and just *be* in each other's presence. The air wasn't being clouded up and discolored with words and sounds and guttural attempts to convey what this "love" feeling we had was. The feeling was both electrifying and soothing at the same time. It felt like I had found this person that I didn't even know, but whom I was *supposed to be looking for*. I felt lucky, like somehow God had blessed me with the best gift ever, a woman I thought was gorgeous to look at (and she was). She wasn't conventionally 'pretty' but to me she was the prettiest thing I'd ever seen. She seemed like an angel.

She had a great singing voice and even though she had no desire to perform professionally, she wasn't shy about singing around me. She had great rhythm too. She loved music, loved to dance, and she loved going to music cafés. She was also an excellent artist, and told me she liked sports, so I bought a pair of small baseball mitts and a Frisbee and we played catch in Shirakawa Kown. And we laughed. A lot. Like schoolchildren. We laughed at the funny parts of movies we watched together, we laughed about people walking in the street, we laughed about the faces we made at each other. She loved to laugh and didn't hold back. This is what I came to appreciate most about her in the beginning. I didn't have to pretend to be cool or macho or smart or anything, and she laughed at everything I said. It felt like I'd somehow found my twin soul living in Japan, in the form of this sexy, young, innocent Japanese girl.

She didn't seem filled with any of the usual self-conscious "I have to be shy" personality I'd come to expect from Japanese women. We'd sit around and make faces at each other. Japanese have an entirely different set of facial expressions than Americans, and she'd copy my exaggerated cartoon faces with so much glee that I couldn't help but laugh out loud at her. She was a comedian.

We'd go to parks and act out scenes from music videos and movies. We would run around and jump on the concrete pylons separating one part of the park from another. We'd race around and act completely like idiots. She'd do whatever I suggested, go wherever I wanted, she became my ride or die.

Eventually, we started going to my apartment and watching movies and videos. I began to notice that when she wasn't around, I was thinking about her constantly. One day while watching True Romance on DVD, I looked at her and said, "...when you're not here, I really miss you," not sure if she understood. To my surprise, she said she felt the same way. It was a warm moment, sweet, reassuring, it didn't feel like what you'd expect, some overwhelming big bang I LOVE YOU type shit, it was small and real and tender, and we both just let it sink in quietly.

From that moment, something, everything, was different. She'd come to my house, we'd talk, laugh, look at each other a lot, and then we ended up making love. After which she'd have to return to her family's house in Higashiyama. The last train in Japan runs only until midnight, and she'd have to catch it to make it back home. This was frustrating. Here I was, a full grown man dating a girl who had to return to her parents' house before midnight. As frustrating as it was, it was also one of the endearing things about her that pulled me in even more. I *knew* she wasn't out running the streets with her friends or other dudes, or anyone, after she left my place. Somehow, I figured I could *trust* her. I also inherently knew she wasn't having male visitors at her parents' house.

Knowing she was in her family's house under the watchful eyes of her parents enhanced the feeling that I'd met someone of quality, someone whose family values and upbringing were worthy of my full attention. It made me feel like I had found something special, like I had a special secret of my own, and that made my feelings for her even more powerful. And though we were having sex, it didn't feel like we were "fucking," it felt like we were creating a bond between each other. It was months before we did anything physical after that first meeting at the TV tower, and we had properly dated for a while. I'd gotten to know her as a person, and I felt she'd gotten to see me for who I was more than the other women I'd met so far in Japan. I wanted to show her different sides of myself, other than me just being "cool" or "sexy" or "kakuii" or whatever. I wanted to draw her in closer to *me,* the person whom I thought myself to be.

We were having a fantastic time, in our own world. I started to think maybe she was the one. She had a good family, had no bad habits I could see, no baggage, no major hang-ups. I started to think of wanting to marry her, but, I had other strings to attend to. Although things with K had ended by the time I met A, I was still seeing N1, M1, and M2.

I knew things with N1 wouldn't progress beyond the love hotel stage. Because she couldn't speak any English whatsoever, and appeared to have no intention on learning English. Besides, we were both too satisfied with our monthly flings. I also knew things with M1 wouldn't go much further because she was developing an attitude and her bitterness was showing through the cracks in her personality. Things with M2 were decent and I needed her for my little private school I was developing, but upon developing my affection for A, my desire to be with M2 waned. I wanted to keep M2 around in case things didn't work with A. I wanted to keep N around in case things didn't work out with M2 and/or A.

One fateful evening. M1 came unannounced to my apartment at Freebell while A was there. I opened the door and saw it was M1 and told her I had company and she wanted to come inside anyway and I didn't let her. A was standing by the stove pretending not to notice that I was talking to M1 outside the door, and I didn't allow M1 to come inside even though she demanded I did. When she left, I never heard from her again and I was relieved. A didn't seem to care one bit that another woman had just shown up at my house, and from that moment on there was a silent acknowledgment between us that now, *she* was my girl, my 'only' girl, except of course for those monthly love hotel episodes with N1, and my ongoing relationship with M2.

New Apartment. New Girl. New Job. New Life.

At the time I was living by myself in Freebell, but I decided I'd look for a roommate to try to save some money. At the Motown Club Gary's, I'd met an Australian girl named Samantha, who was also living in Freebell. She had also placed a "looking for a roommate" ad on the bulletin board of Freebell. I contacted her and told her I wanted to move in immediately and did. She asked me to call her Sam. She was energetic, friendly, and into R&B. She made no secret of the fact that she was into brothers, and at the time, there were more than a couple brothers that were into her. We became great friends right off. She was very chill.

A and I spent lots of time hanging out at the apartment I was sharing with Samantha. "A" cooked dinner for me, folded my laundry and cleaned up whenever she came over. Sam would tell me how stupid A was for doing all this stuff for me when we weren't even married, and I'd tell Sam, "...but she's going to be my wife one day...." Only half serious. It sounded wild coming out of my mouth, but also perfectly reasonable to me at the same time. Sam thought I was crazy for choosing to be with this one young Japanese girl, but I didn't think so. Laughing and joking with A made me feel incredibly comfortable in

Japan. Our moments together were blissful and tender and reassuring and energizing all at the same time.

We did all sorts of things that passed for communication. We made silly faces at each other and developed our own sign language so we could talk in code around both Japanese people and English speakers.

I wasn't desperate for companionship at the time—I had M1, N1, A, the nightclubs, Sam, my international friends, and my job—but still, I was feeling like I needed to move on to *something different.* I wasn't sure if I was "in love" with A or not, but what I do know is that being with her felt very different than being with any other woman in my life had felt before. I started thinking it was my responsibility to take care of her, and make her happy, and fill her life with purpose (which at the time was learning English). I felt we both needed each other. Either way, I have learned it is VERY possible to convince yourself that you are in love, even if you barely know a person and they barely know you. In fact, it's probably the best way to fall in love with someone, without speaking or sharing much more than funny faces.

A and I *were* falling in love. We were meeting a few times a week in the evenings, and I was working at five different schools out in the countryside during the day. I was now a full-time ALT, teaching at two elementary schools and three junior high schools out in a place called Kasugai. I was traveling no less than an hour each way every morning by train. I would then walk a mile or two through rice fields, over small rivers, and along small quiet roads to get to my school(s) every day. Then A and I decided to get married. Seriously.

We started making plans for our future, discussing how many children she'd like to have (three), where she'd like to live (America), and when she'd like to get married (June). All Japanese women want June weddings. The only problem was, she hadn't yet told her parents about me. She had introduced them to me at a dinner meeting, nonchalantly introducing me as her teacher, while we held hands secretly under the table. Again, I felt more than a little stupid being a grown adult and having to pretend that our relationship was strictly teacher-student. A and I discussed the particulars of our marriage. We talked about how we would share our married lives with our children. But how? Her parents thought I was just some weird Black English teacher their daughter was learning English from. It wasn't the best start of a relationship, but it wasn't the worst either.

In Class

The ALT gig was going well. The job responsibilities at the schools were similar to what I had been doing at SKI, teaching the alphabet, vocabulary, playing games, talking about my life in America, and generally just be a benign "brother from another planet." My skills as a teacher were improving and I had developed a sort of curriculum that I used in the classrooms. I printed up pictures of famous places in the US, the Statue Of Liberty, The Grand Canyon, gorgeous images of white sand Florida beaches, and I talked about these. I printed up pictures of famous black Americans, Michael Jackson, Michael Jordan, Martin Luther King, and talked about them and their accomplishments.

I talked about jobs, sports, foods, music, movies. I rarely talked about my time in Hollywood or any of my acting, because I felt that would be overwhelming and confusing. It wasn't until much later into my time in Japan that I started telling anyone I'd been in some movies and on some TV shows. Rather than creating a phony background where I was some kind of superstar, I did exactly the opposite, and dove into my role as a teacher. The kids liked me, I liked them, and I did my best to learn the ways of operation inside the Japanese *shokuinshitsu*, the teacher's office. I had to be at my desk by eight o'clock, listen to the opening remarks by other teachers, then listen to the *kouchou* sensei, the principal, make his remarks about the day ahead. Then I'd arrange and prepare my lesson plans and head to class with the Japanese teacher, and I'd stand up in the front of the classroom in the corner while the Japanese teacher did his lesson, until it was my turn to deliver my 15 minute "English" lesson.

Usually, the students simply stared at me, boggled by whatever I was saying. If I asked for volunteers to answer any of my questions, there were no takers. I was met with dead silence time after time, lesson after lesson. It became unnerving.

Lunchtime, I was expected to eat the Japanese lunch that the school would provide me, *kyushouku,* with the students inside the classroom. During lunch, the students came out of their shells and asked me all kinds of questions about me, and my lunch. They even came around and touched my hair, and the little girls spent lots of time staring and smiling at me. I didn't mind.

I enjoyed their curiosity about me and loved the fact that they called me sensei. This position gave me purpose and responsibility. I was developing character that I had never had in the US. It was humbling and educational.

Evenings, I'm seeing A at my apartment, listening to Elton John while making love with Sam in the next room. It was fantastic.

Deru Kui Wa Utareru, or, The Nail That Sticks Out Gets Hammered Down

There's a Japanese proverb, "*deru kui wa utareru,*" which translates literally as "the nail that sticks up gets hammered down." It's meant to enforce the strict code of homogeneity, or "sameness," of Japanese culture. I, at six foot one, black and with long dreadlocks, was unknowingly, this nail.

Micro-Aggressions

Where at first it had been all politeness and kindness, I also began to notice a few things about the local Japanese that got under my skin. I noticed they didn't sit next to me on the trains, which made me feel like a pariah. Not only do Japanese not want to be different themselves, they also don't want to be associated with anything different either, which would in turn make them different by association. This penchant and biological need to be the same, eventually would become one of the things about Japanese that I came to detest. I began to feel self-conscious about being stared at all the time as well. I kind of figured they'd get used to me, and the stares would eventually stop, but they never did. Ever. Not for the entire time I was there. If you're a non-Japanese in any other city in Japan besides Tokyo, which is a world-class international city, chances are that someone somewhere is staring at you.

My dude Dash had often spoken to me about the Japanese staring at him and his being made to feel like a complete outsider, and how it affected him. At first, I didn't know what he meant, but as time went on, I began to experience the same emotions of isolation and indignation that he had told me about. The difference was that eventually Dash had let these feelings turn into outright anger and hatred for the Japanese—bitterness and vengeance had crept into Dash over time. I got out before these feelings took me over completely, but I definitely experienced them.

Where Do We Go From Here?

The point is to explain how A's parents would eventually feel about their daughter dating, and then marrying, a foreigner. I knew at some point we'd have to let the beans spill that we were planning to get married.

A and I dated for a year and that next summer, 2005, A went to NYC for a few months to study English. That summer, I was still seeing M2 and the summer that A went to NYC, things between me and M2 heated up. Then, I met another Japanese girl at a club, named S, whom I started seeing. S was a hostess at a *kabakura*—a Japanese bar for drunk salarymen. Now, I'm seeing M2, N and I are meeting monthly in the love hotel in Osu, S is driving me around town in her Jeep, and A, the one I think I love, is in NYC studying English.

On the day she left to go to New York, A and I took a train to Nagoya airport. I dropped her off, we said our goodbyes, and on the way back, while on the train by myself, I imagined what I'd do for the three months A was gone. Suddenly, I get a text from my half-Brazilian, half-Japanese friend Marco.

>Chapter 3

A DIRTY THREESOME

The devil inside

Marco's text reads, Hey *Trev, are you free tonight?* I respond, *yeah man, sure, what's up?*

He immediately texts back telling me he wants to bring some girl over to my place and that he wants us to have a threesome with her. Hm.

I text back, *dude, are you serious? Why me? She doesn't even know me.* He tells me that that's the point, *she just wants to have a threesome with another foreigner, it doesn't matter who...*Strange. *Why doesn't it matter*, I text, and he responds, *I'll tell you later.*

Then Marco texts the plan:

I'm gonna bring some champagne, and I'm gonna bring a video camera. The plan is, we'll all drink for a little while, then I'll go to the bathroom, come out, which will be your cue to go to the bathroom, then you'll come out, say you have to do something in your room, then you'll go into your room and set up the camera in your closet while me and her are drinking in your living room. Then you'll come out of your bedroom and say you wanna take a shower. While you're taking a shower, I'll take her into your room and get her started, she'll be drunk by then. Then you can come in and join us. But make sure you set up the camera.

I was queasy about the camera thing. I'm not some kind of exhibitionist. I don't really get down like that. I'm not part of the dick pic, sex tape generation. It's not something I do. Him wanting that camera made me nervous. Plus, him wanting to dick down this woman in my house, why not his house? Why not a hotel? Why me? I knew he had to have other non-Japanese friends he could call. But why me? I guess I had been putting out so much sexual energy that Marco decided I was the one. I was bound to attract exactly the type of crap that Marco was bringing to my doorstep. I had never and haven't since that day, recorded myself having sex.

A Hot, Sweaty, Grunting Threesome

A threesome with two chicks and a dude seems tantalizing, erotic, sensuous, and fantasy-like. A threesome with two *dudes* and a chick is brutal, primal, balls-y and *sweaty.*

I didn't know Marco that well. He had an energetic personality and looked a little like a Japanese, Brazilian Adrien Brody. He was sort of a greasy open-shirt wearing Guido kind of guy, and he had an Australian fiancée when the episode took place.

I waited at the apartment and at exactly seven o'clock, as planned, there was a knock on my door. I was excited and more than a little nervous, "A" had just gotten on an airplane to go to NYC that very afternoon. I'm thinking to myself, *holy shit this shit is really about to go down.*

I open the door and there's Marco with a suit jacket on, holding a bottle of champagne and wearing a knapsack. I shake his hand, *sup brother, sup* he responds with a car salesman, shit-eating grin on his face. The Japanese woman was young, cute, and wearing a business suit. As Marco and the woman pass, she looks at me shyly and whispers *konbonwa* before sliding her shoes off. Marco hands me the knapsack nonchalantly and says, *here's your bag man.*

I take the knapsack into my room and quickly set the camera up at the top of my closet pointing in the direction of my bed. I wasn't sure if it would record what I wasn't sure was going to happen or not, I just set it up. *Her?* I'm thinking. You mean *we're about to bang this fine honey's back out? Together? Tonight? This fine, arm candy, in this dope black suit?* Crazy.

The camera's set up and I return to the living room and Marco and the women are sitting on my couch. Marco looks around at my place, says a few things, "nice place, nice couch, nice view, nice table, nice cups," whatever. The woman is quiet but smiles at everything Marco says in English.

I'm nervously pacing back and forth, and Marco opens the bottle of champagne he'd brought, asks me for some glasses, and pours himself, me, and the woman a glass. Sam's not home. She's out at a club somewhere, and I'm nervous that she might come home and mess up the plan. She doesn't.

We're all drinking and talking, but beyond a few giggles here and there, the woman he brought with him is silent. It's as if she's waiting for something to happen. She looks like she's anticipating something, and every time she looks at me she holds her eyes on mine for just a second longer than normal.

She can't speak English, but I learn she's a Junior High School English teacher, like me. Marco says she likes going to clubs, likes dancing, and obviously she likes drinking. Most Japanese women love drinking. Oh, and she's not married. As planned, Marco excuses himself to go to the bathroom. The woman and I are just looking at each other smiling awkwardly while Marco is in the bathroom.

Finally, he comes out and I say much too loudly to no one and everyone, *well, I'm going to take a shower,* which I'm not sure at this point is the plan. Marco stands up and gestures towards the bathroom with his cup of champagne and says, *yeah man, you do that.* He's smiling. The woman looks a little confused but she keeps sipping her glass of champagne and says nothing. I go into the bathroom and say out loud, again, to no one in particular, *Yup, gonna take me a shower! Pretty good time for a shower huh?* I'm talking *way too much about the shower* and Marco is nodding his head gesturing to me with his glass of champagne, while the woman is sipping her champagne quietly, also looking at me. Both of them seem to be saying *nigga get in the damn shower and let's hurry this thing up.*

I return from the shower six, seven minutes later and they're not in the living room. I walk towards my bedroom and I can hear squishy sounds, muffled sounds of lips smacking, small grunts and groans, etc. I'm nervous. Is this really happening? Right here, right now? I open the door to find Marco stark naked standing over the woman, with his dick on her face. Marco beckons me inside and gives me a look that I knew meant *is the camera set up?* I gesture to him that he's got to somehow turn her around, away from the camera, so I can turn it on. Marco maneuvers her so that she's facing my window, which was the opposite direction of the camera, I reach up, turn it on, and now things get crazy.

Marco turns the girl towards the camera. I pull off my pants. The girl gropes my underwear. I'm not anywhere near erect but watching Marco bang the girl turns me on and in a moment, I am.

Clenched fist in sheets. Marco is angrily banging this honey from behind while she's giving me head.

Marco is sweating his ass off and talking to her in Portuguese, and whatever he is saying doesn't sound pleasant. She's squirming with clenched fists. Marco has a fiendish, demonic aura about him and he's obviously hate-fucking this woman.

The situation got to be nauseating, and I started thinking about A. *Had she gotten to NYC safely? Where was she now? What was she doing? What might she think if she could see what I was doing?*

You ever have an epiphany in the middle of doing something that *this is not the right thing to be doing right now?* My erection disappeared and so did I. I slipped out of the room and left Marco in there for another thirty minutes to do whatever he wanted to do. I took another shower.

Shortly after, Marco comes out shirtless but with his boxer shorts on, dripping sweat, looking spent but satisfied. I tell him, "Dude go put on your pants, man." He smiles and goes back into my room and comes out a moments later with his pants on. Behind him comes the woman wearing her rumpled skirt and blouse, carrying her panty hose in her hands, hair disheveled, looking like she'd just been attacked.

Marco extends his hand, "thanks, man".

The woman looks at me and sheepishly says "*arigatou*," picks up her suit jacket, and the two of them slip on their shoes. Marco opens the door and says "talk to you tomorrow brother, I'll give you a call", then they disappear down the hall. What the fuck did I just do?

I shook my head, wiped my brow and went back into my bedroom, which was hot, and smelled like sex. I pulled down the camera and stopped the recording. I immediately rewound the camera to a random spot on the tape and sat and watched and listened to the images of Marco angrily pounding this woman on my bed, with me on one knee in front of her while she gave me oral sex, and it was disgusting to me. I was ashamed, horrified, and filled with anxiety all at once.

It was surreal. I knew at that moment that *no one* would ever see this video. I knew instantly that I wasn't giving this video, nor making any copies of it, for Marco, or anyone else for that matter. *I felt that it wasn't me on that video.* I had plans for myself, even if I hadn't decided exactly *what* I was planning yet. I wasn't sure what might happen to that video if it got out. I thought if Marco needed it so badly, he must have some kind of plan for it, otherwise I don't think he'd have wanted it that badly. Dude had a *fiancée* after all.

The whole scene was disgusting to me. All I could think about was *what if someone sees this?* I knew it couldn't get out. Within the hour after Marco left I took the video out of the camera and smashed it to pieces by stomping on it behind the apartment building in the parking lot. I was disgusted by it and disgusted with myself.

That night I couldn't sleep from thinking about A in NYC. I felt she somehow had eyes on me and regretted how mightily I had fucked up. I asked myself, *How can this have happened one day after she left to go to New York? Why did I do this?* Dark clouds.

I wondered who exactly the woman was that Marco so badly wanted to videotape, and who had consented to have a threesome with a foreigner she had never seen, let alone met. *Who would do such a thing?*

Chapter 4

HOW CAN YOU MEND A BROKEN HEART, JAPANESE STYLE

Sex, lies and video tape

Marco called me the next day asking about the tape. I told him, *dude, I destroyed it. I just couldn't take a chance on who might see that thing. I trust you, but you never know, I can't take chances, I just got here.* He was pissed.

"WHAT? YOU DID WHAT? You didn't. Tell me you didn't. Tell me you still have that tape. Come on, man, our deal was I bring the girl, you make the recording and give me the tape. Come on, man. I'm coming over, man."

Okay dude, you can come, but there's no tape. I smashed it up and put it in the dumpster. I'm really sorry Marco, but that thing is just too dangerous for me to have out there. I'm sorry.

Marco hangs up and within the hour he's at my place knocking on my door. I let him in and he asks what happened to the tape.

Listen, man, I don't know who that girl is. Shit I barely know <u>you.</u> I got a girl and I got a job and I wanna do something here. I do not want to get busted with my black ass on some damn video tape fucking some woman I don't know. I don't know what might have happened to that tape if it would have gotten out, I know we had a deal, but I couldn't *give you that tape, man, I don't even know what you had planned to do with it. I'm really sorry....*

He sighs a deep sigh and rubs his forehead with his hand, his head hung low, without saying anything for a long time. Then he takes a deep breath, stands up, looks at me and says, "...that girl was my ex-fiancée, man." *Dude, what??*

"She was my ex, from two years ago. I ran into her in ID Bar the other night. She was drunk and crying and I asked her what was wrong. She said her fiancé had cheated on her and left her for another woman. *A foreign woman.* She was all fucked up and said she wanted revenge on him for cheating on her with a foreigner. So she asked me to find another foreigner to fuck her, so she could get back at him."

Karma is a Flaming Boomerang

I had met Marco's fiancée. She was a decent looking Australian girl, I wondered why Marco had decided to marry an Australian in a country full of beautiful, willing Japanese women. *So, was her ex a Japanese dude?* I ask him. "Yeah," he says, "he was". Then he goes on.

"Dude, I was so in love with this woman. You don't even know, man. I worked so hard for her. We dated for a few years and we were just about to get married. But her father didn't like the fact that I'm not 100 percent Japanese. On the day I went to him with her, to ask for permission to marry her, he didn't even look at me. I'm asking him in perfect Japanese for his permission to marry his daughter and he is acting like I'm not even in the room. He was looking at her the whole time I was standing there talking to him. After I asked him if I could marry her, with all smiles to show my respect for him, he looks me up and down for a few seconds, then he looks at her and tells her she is to break up with me right then, in front of him. Her father makes her promise him she'll never see me again, and makes her tell me to my face she'll never see me again, or he says he'll reject her from her family and never speak to her again."

So, she did. She cut Marco off right then and there, and had disappeared from his life, until that night he randomly saw her in Id Bar.

"When I saw her in ID Bar, I didn't know what to feel. I wanted to kill her but I wanted to get revenge on her and her father, for what they did to me. I was heartbroken for a year after she broke up with me. When she told me she wanted to fuck a foreigner, I wanted it to be a black guy, and the only one I know is you. I was gonna send the tape to her father and show him what kind of daughter he has. But now, there's no tape." *Exactly. No tape.*

I was glad I had destroyed the tape, and now, I knew beyond a shadow of a doubt that I had done the right thing.

This was exactly the reason I couldn't have this tape out there. I didn't know this dude very well, and who is or was this "father" he was talking about? Who does he know, who knows him? If he sees some random video of his daughter being banged out by Marco and some black guy, what's he gonna do? No WAY could I risk the possibility of this happening. I was so absolutely relieved that that tape no longer existed. I had no personal beef with anyone in Nagoya, not yet anyway.

Marco and his ex-fiancée, had gone to great lengths to exact revenge on each other and the unknowing Japanese ex-husband to be of the woman involved. And I was shocked. I realized *people in Japan take this revenge thing very seriously.*

I had never heard of anything like this before, and I was a part of it. I had crossed a line. I learned firsthand how important humiliation is to Japanese. How important it is for Japanese women to maintain their 'purity' in the eyes of their fathers, by not marrying foreigners.

"No tape," Marco kept muttering to himself under his breath, like his world had come crashing down. After a while he shook my hand and told me, "Well I've got the memory. At least it happened. Was wild huh? Just like I told you!" and then he left.

I don't much believe in regret, but I guess I'd have to say I regret having taken part in that sordid episode with Marco and his ex-fiancée. What I didn't, and don't regret, is destroying the tape. I felt disgusting and disgusted at myself. I didn't want to have anything to do with Marco after that, in my mind our friendship was over.

I saw him around town with his fiancée a few times, we'd casually say what's up, and then we'd keep it moving. I don't really know if he was pissed about the tape, or felt self-conscious about parading his Australian fiancée around in front of me, me knowing what we'd done. I didn't care much.

After that, as if she knew, "A" started communicating with me less and less while she was in New York. To the point where during her second month in NYC, I had to ask her if we were still a couple, if we still planned to get married like we had discussed, and if she wanted to continue our relationship at all.

She told me she wasn't sure anymore, about anything. She wasn't sure whether she believed in marriage anymore, wasn't sure if she was even still "straight", and wasn't sure if she was going to return to Japan at all. I was dejected. It was during these three months without her, and with the fear of losing her, that I decided I did indeed completely want to marry her. *Don't it always seem to go, that you don't know what you got 'til it's gone?*

When A returned from New York, I steered completely away from Marco, afraid she'd be able to see what I had done in his eyes. Not many hangout spots for the foreigners in Nagoya at that time, we were bound to keep running into each other. It sucked. Every time I saw him it was like me returning to the scene of the crime. I was shook. Eventually he, like so many, just disappeared. Never saw him or his Aussie fiancée anymore. Bad deeds attach themselves to you like apparitions or doppelgangers. Karma.

>Chapter 5

A Returns From New York

Cleaning house

With the Marco episode behind me, I continued seeing M2, continued my monthly love hotel sessions with N1, but my short romance with S flamed out at the end of the summer.

Goodbye To S

One night I caught S making out with a Japanese dude at ID Bar. We had planned to hang out that night but at the last minute she cancelled, saying she felt sick. So, I crept up into Id Bar to see what I could see, and lo and behold what do I see but S up on the 3rd floor in the back of the hip hop room wrapped up in a hot embrace with some young Japanese cat. I stood right next to her and watched them for a while before she even noticed I was there. Then when they unlocked lips and opened their eyes, there I was staring intently at them with a smile. She freaked out, "Daveed, Daveed....", and I walked away with her following me, and the Japanese dude following her.

I turned around and told her, "...dozou, mondai naie dayo, anata wa kare ga ii no? Dakara dozou..." which meant (to me), *go ahead and do your thing, no problem, you like him right?* She pleaded with me to forgive her. I told her we weren't boyfriend and girlfriend, so she could do whatever she wanted. However, seeing someone you're being intimate with kissing someone else is usually a deal breaker, regardless of whatever boundaries you have, or haven't, placed around your relationship. The irony, right?

Besides S's nightclub indiscretion, there was another issue. Every time we had sex, she timed it for exactly six minutes, because she thought if we went longer than 6 minutes she'd get pregnant. No lie.

Imagine every time you have sex, you know you've got to *get it all done* within 360 seconds. I'd literally count down in my head from the moment of insertion. There were more times than not, that I'd have to climb off of her without coming, and without really 'getting into it' to any satisfying degree. I also lost count a few times and tried to finagle my way into a few more seconds.

There were *quite a few times* that I did try to push beyond the six minutes sex curfew. I remember one time she let me do it for 9 minutes, I remember because I started counting up from zero when the six minutes had ended. It was a miracle. When that six minutes ended and she didn't tell me to stop, I thought the world had ended and I'd gone to heaven. It was a surreal moment. For those last three minutes, I was in warp speed with numbers racing through my head like I had just learned to count. I'm seeing digits fly through my head, thinking, *maybe I can freaking count to a million!* 356, 357, 358, 359- but suddenly she wasn't having it and just before I got to 360 she cut me off and told me to stop.

Damn. Madd dry heaves and stutter pumps after that, like a dog humping the air I pull out and my pelvis is twitching uncontrollably for a straight minute after that. I know, because I counted. I get up and go to the bathroom asking myself wtf just happened with numbers ringing in my ears. *177, 178, 179...*

S was not a keeper. Besides which, I didn't like the fact that she worked late at night in these *Kabakuras* with those drunk love-starved Japanese salarymen. The time limit and the image of her making out with that dude in the back of ID made it easy for me to break it off with her. And not a moment too soon, A was on her way back to Japan.

Goodbye To M2

One day, suddenly, my future wife emailed me from New York and told me she'd be back that next week and she asked would I meet her at the airport.

I wasn't sure what to expect. I was excited and nervous at the same time. Excited because I missed her like crazy and wanted to continue with the 'project' of our relationship, nervous because I wasn't sure if she still felt the same about me, and, moreso because by now, M2 and I were deep into a relationship.

M2 was unique. She enjoyed discussing politics and geography and history and challenged me intellectually. Her English was proficient enough so that she could carry on long, detailed conversations about just about anything, and she was adventurous as well. She always complained that Japan was still a 'male dominated' society. She said though she thought Japanese men had lots of 'style', they were also too insensitive and couldn't keep up with her conversationally. She also told me she had entertained the idea of becoming a lesbian (what the fuck is all this lesbian shit about?). I told M2 to try the lesbian move if she wanted to. I told her she'd never be able to get rid of the curiosity unless she actually tried it, and so, she did.

One night she invited one of her close friends to spend the night at her house, someone she had always been slightly attracted to. This friend had spent the night at her house and slept in the same bed with her numerous times. I told her next time she comes over, both of you should drink some sake, get in bed, and see what happens. So she did. She told me her and her friend got drunk, got in bed, and when they were just about to fall asleep, M2 climbed on top of her friend, pulled out her friend's breast, and started sucking it, to which her friend commented, "..eh? nani? Nani shiteru no?" what are you doing? M2 said she thought the question made a lot of sense at the time, and since she couldn't come up with an answer that satisfied her, she had decided the lesbian life wasn't for her.

I eventually told M2 that I had a fiancé, and that that fiancé was in NYC, and that she was coming back soon. I half expected M2 to be pissed, but she wasn't, she coolly told me she wanted to meet A, and I agreed. I wasn't sure why she wanted to meet her but I thought it might be a good idea. I thought if M2 met A, she (M2) would either be willing to amicably segue our relationship away from us having anything intimate to do with each other, or, well, something else, I wasn't sure. I half thought M2 and I could just continue what we were doing, or, if not, I'll still have A. I told M2, "well, you can meet her, I'll introduce you as my assistant and we'll go from there...."

This all may sound a bit crazy but the reality was that, I'd almost given up hope that "A" and I would be together the same way we had been before she went to New York. I thought M2 would be a decent back up for A since I was prepared for A to tell me that she had decided to move back to New York to continue her studies indefinitely.

Perhaps she'd tell me that we'd have to dead our relationship, or that she'd decided she was a lesbian, but whatever it was or wasn't, I was prepared for a giant kiss off from A. I was insecure and my own behavior magnified my insecurity. Justifiably so.

A Officially Returns

She came through the gates, smiled when she saw me, and we took a cab to my apartment. She was as bubbly as ever, but now, after having spent a summer in New York, she was also more down to earth, more sure of herself, more worldly, and all this attracted me to her even more.

The next week, I told M2 that the three of us could meet at Nagoya Station. M2 said "fine". Next week comes and "A" and I head down to Nagoya Station, we're waiting for M2 to arrive. When M2 walks up, A stands up sticks out her hand and excitedly shakes a perplexed looking M2's hand. M2 politely introduces herself as my assistant and we all stroll off to a coffee shop behind Nagoya Station. For an extremely uncomfortable hour, all three of us made small talk about my school, the students, the parents, etc. Well, M2 and I were extremely uncomfortable, but A smiled her wide easy smile and seemed absolutely oblivious to the fact that I had been having an affair with M2. After all, how or why would she know? The entire time, I'm on pins and needles wondering when and if M2 is going to drop the bomb that we have been intimate, but shockingly, she never does. I think it was because A was genuinely such a nice person, so friendly, so pure, that M2 didn't want to hurt her feelings.

Things with M2 cooled way down after that meeting. She was angry that I had actually introduced her to A, (which she had asked for), and I had no more time for her now that A was back. M2 and I stayed "friends" but kept our distance after that, and A became my new assistant, temporarily, at my school.

We picked up exactly where we had left off before A went to New York. Except now, after her experience with freedom and independence in New York, A had decided she couldn't live with her parents anymore. Within a few weeks she had found herself an apartment which she shared with a roommate, and we started spending every night together. Two months later, she's pregnant.

Surprisingly, or not, she was not exactly elated with the news. She wasn't gleeful or particularly celebratory; she seemed perplexed actually, like "how did this happen?" She didn't know how or what or when to tell her parents, after all, they still didn't even know we were a legitimate couple, let alone making marriage plans, and now, she was pregnant. What we did know, was that she was going to have a baby, our baby, and so, we'd have to make some kind of plan.

Should we move back to America and have our child? Should we stay in Japan? When should we tell her parents? How would they react to the news that she had gotten pregnant by her black American English teacher? Would they ostracize her, like Marco's ex-fiancé's father threatened to do to her? Would they accept me, accept 'us', and our marriage, and our baby?

I was determined make this work. I was too glad to have gotten back together with her when she came back from NYC. I had made a decision that this is going to be the woman I am going to marry and we are going to make a family here in Japan. I decided I would do whatever it took to make it work.

Even though I had done so much dirt while she was gone, somehow I still felt she was the one for me, and I was going to make myself the one for her. Her easy laugh, warm manner, expressive character, her independent streak, her family background, her skin and eyes and fucked-up teeth and the way she looked at me and the way I felt with her, it was miraculous to me to have gotten it all back again after that tumultuous summer with Marco, M2, and S. I was not going to lose what I thought at the time was the best thing happening for me. And now she was pregnant.

The incoming responsibility of a child and our relationship which had survived despite the distance made me feel like "A" had come to rescue me from the worst of myself. As soon as "A" left for NYC, that very night, I went back to pure debauchery. Her return and subsequent pregnancy gave me the idea that I could put all that behind me and start again new. She brought out the idea in me that if I could have her, then I myself couldn't be so bad, and that I could once and forever banish the S's and M2's and N's from my life. This meant that all the past bad deeds and vice-laden days of my life could somehow be washed away, just by being next to her. I needed her approval even before I knew I needed her approval. My self-esteem ratings were pretty low. I had begun the dangerous pastime of seeing Japan as my personal playground, with my rules and my win or lose endgame. A, as I saw it, was there to rescue me and to put me right.

Beware mixing all of your self-worth in with the approval of someone, anyone, else. Be especially wary of placing all of your self-worth into the hands and heart of a twenty-three-year-old Japanese girl. Very wary.

Marriage On the Horizon

We debated how and when to tell her parents. We decided to get married that next June, have our child, move forward with our plans to get married, and have two more children.

A is now living with me full time, sharing my room in the apartment with Sam and I. Sam was open-minded about it and seemed to have accepted the fact that we were going to get married. Then one November evening, a rather large and sudden earthquake jolted Nagoya, while me, Sam, and A were chilling in our apartment. It scared the shit out of Sam and I, so much so that Sam decided then and there to leave Japan and move back to Melbourne. One month later, Sam was gone and I immediately found another roommate, also an Australian, but from Brisbane. Rebecca was sassy, nearly 6 feet tall, and took my old room and I moved into the room Sam had left, which was bigger and could accommodate A and I much better than the smaller room I had been in.

Inside our apartment, A's attitude swung from her being elated one day, about us getting married, being pregnant, the prospect of having a family, to her being depressed, catatonic, sluggish, negative and withdrawn the next. I tried to act like I didn't notice it. I figured it was because of the pregnancy.

Unexpected Guest

I had decided to quit the ALT gig when my contract ended that next spring. It was a bit claustrophobic. Two stand out incidents helped me to decide that maybe the ALT gig wasn't for me.

I wear frankincense oil. To me, it smells divine and spiritual. One day I had slathered just a bit too much of it on my body, and the Japanese junior high school students let me know it by shouting "kusiae" over and over at me when I arrived with the smell reeking off my body. "Kusaie" means you stink in Japanese, and I heard a chorus of *kusaie!* over and over at my school.

Another ALT episode involved me being called to the principal's office for doing pushups in the field behind the school. What, no pushups allowed?

Meanwhile, I had gotten a part-time job working at Berlitz, one of these hosh posh, private English schools. One day I was at work teaching one of my adult students and I get a message from the secretary at the front desk that "someone is in the foyer to meet you? "*Who?*"-I ask? "A Japanese woman" the secretary says. "Okay."

I step outside my classroom and A's mother is there. Upon seeing me her eyes widen and she's rubbing her hands together. I approach her gingerly, not knowing exactly what she's doing there, what she wants.

"Yes? *Konnichiwa* Ms. Suzuki-san. *Genki desu ka?* Ah ... *nani?* Dou shita no?" *Is something wrong,* I ask her, *why are you here?* "Ima shigoto shite masu..." I'm *working now.* I'm confused why she's there.

She tells me she's there to see the place where I work, and ostensibly, to see if I *was* working. I tell her *yes, this is my job,* and I point to the secretary, who is also dumbfounded as to why this woman is there. I say, *and that's the secretary,* and the secretary gives A's mother, my future mother in law, a cold stare, telling her all she needed to know without saying a single word.

I play it off, smile, take her to the room where my student is waiting inside, and point at the open book on the table. She seemed to be satisfied with this and finally she leaves.

Back in my lesson, I couldn't focus on what I was teaching. I was infuriated that A's mother had come to my workplace unannounced. I thought it to be the height of disrespect. Would she come to a Japanese dude's workplace? –I thought. No focus, feeling irritated, I ended up making the twentysomething-year-old Japanese student cry because of my sudden attitude change.

I didn't last at Berlitz and went back to being an ALT in the Japanese public education system.

I'm Becoming TV On The Radio

The street life has always been my second home. I guess growing up in New York City and taking the buses and trains has made me a street lifer for life. I'm not afraid to admit that I love seediness, danger, and the lure of adventure that street life offers. I suppose I've got an addictive personality and *what I'm attracted to is vice.*

Nagoya's streets at night in Sakae are a totally different scene than they are by day. Daytime, everything is orderly and behaved, tidy and well kempt, mundane, coordinated, and regimented, exactly like you'd expect Japan to be, everyone doing the same things, walking the same walks, smiling the same smiles, waving the same waves. It's homogenous and clean, exactly like the Japan you expect. The boutiques, flower shops, electronics stores, Starbucks and ramen shops all look professional, polite, and positively pedestrian. The people walk in straight lines towards their destinations, eyes down, and no one throws anything in the street and no one looks at or says anything to anyone else. *Except when they're looking at you.*

By night, though, it's a totally different scene in Nagoya, especially on the weekends. In Sakae, there are three main areas of activity at night: there's Sumiyoshi, the club district, there's Jyoshi-dai-Koji, behind the Chunichi building, home to Ikeda Koen, and there's Nishiki, which is reserved for the more upscale host and hostess bars. By day, Sumiyoshi is in the heart of the shopping district, so there's always traffic, walking or driving. Sumiyoshi is a four- or five-block district of heightened activity and hyper cultural energy. It's where the mix happens in Nagoya. Low-slung but sleek, modern buildings line the streets, lit up like denizens of wanderlust. There are neon pictures of naked Japanese wives splashed ten feet tall on billboards and window signs on four corners. Directly across from this, there are after-hours clubs owned by African cats. Cream was one of these clubs. Weekends, these spots are rammed thick with Africans, Brazilians, brothers from America, and of course dozens of young Japanese girls wanting to get passed around.

Jyoshi-dai-Koji is known as being dangerous. Your average Nagoya Japanese girl is not going to find herself *by herself* anywhere near this area at night. Hookers, pimps, fights, lotsa Filipinos, Brazilians, massage parlors, various late-night restaurants, dance clubs, bars, and notorious Ikeda Koen, known for brazen drug deals right next to the *keisatsu* station (police), located in the middle of the park. I copped a couple of massages in this area as well. The Motown club Gary's is located at the corner of where Jyoshi-dai-Koji starts. Gary's is the *cornerstone* of that area.

Lit up and busy by night, Jyoshi-dai-Koji is a no-man's-land by day. Dull, dreary, and uninhabited, dead. I didn't even like riding my bike through this area during the days. I didn't like Nishiki too much either. Too bright, too many lights, too built up, *too Japanese*. On any street in Nishiki at night, the taxis would be lined up for blocks and blocks looking for customers to take home when the night was over. One of my friends got hit by one of these taxi fucks and almost lost his life. To add insult to injury, the taxi company tried to sue my friend, claiming he'd run a red light and that's why he got hit. Nasty fucks, those old chain-smoking taxi drivers. What a weird scene, a snaking line of parked taxis with their doors open, often, with the drivers sitting in the seat fast asleep.

You're bound to come up on at least one sleeping salaryman sprawled out on the street holding his briefcase, or using it as a pillow, with folks casually stepping over son as if it's normal. And so it is. Drunk, passed out, suit-wearing salarymen laying sprawled with no chalk, out cold on the concrete in the middle of anywhere is a normal thing in Japan, and you'll see lots of it in Nishiki.

There are glamorous hostesses in evening gowns and heels with their hair done up to the moon trying to attract customers to their bars. Half of the hostesses looked at me like I was from Jupiter and the other half looked at me like they wanted to fuck a cat from Jupiter.

The streets in Sakae's club district are packed with a mixed group of nationalities brushing up against each other. Africans, Brazilians, Europeans, Russians, Turks, Indians, Romanians, Australians, Kiwis, a few Americans here and there, and of course, Japanese. It's a heady mixture of flavors and vibes: the hosts, hostesses, DJs, salarymen, dudes, dolled-up decked-out Japanese chicks, different nationalities, taxi drivers, yakuza, foreigners, massage ladies, and me. Folks laying in their vomit, oftentimes young girls passed out on the sidewalk wearing skirts hiked up above their thighs, skinny Japanese legs twisted and bent in pumps splayed out in throw up, fights and scuffles, people laughing, crying, yelling, cruising, posing, and loud music coming out of clubs, jacked-up cars, rumbling motorcycles, gangsters and clangy Mamachari bicycles everywhere. Testosterone and so much snatch you could smell the mixture in the air. Never seen anything like it before or since.

Massagee?

I made friends with a few of the Chinese massage ladies who were hanging on the corner pulling on the sleeves of every other salaryman who walked by. By friends, I mean I'd talk to them, ask them what time it was or how much their services cost. They also became familiar with me because I was DJing in the area and was there so often. Eventually, I became a semi-regular customer of two of them. One was a youngish, tallish chick in her late twenties or early thirties who looked like she should have been someone's *shufu*, housewife. Not ugly, she looked like an Asian Lily Tomlin, but when Lily was young. Her territory was

Sumiyoshi and I could almost always catch her when I was done with my DJ gigs. She'd be standing in front of the Circle K looking for customers, chasing down the drunk salarymen in the area. Generally, the massage ladies weren't polite, weren't pretty, didn't smell real good, and no, they couldn't speak a word of English, nor did they care to. They also didn't give a shit whether you were Japanese, Chinese, American, black, white, or whatever. They only wanted your dough and spent the majority of the time out in the streets, hustling.

None of that stopped me from patronizing them. The thrill of the whole thing was intoxicating to me. The sights, sounds, people, danger, mystique, and total seediness of it just put me over. I'd catch the eye of my Asian, Lily Tomlin regular from across the street, and signal to her that I wanted to go upstairs. She'd nod and then proceed towards her place. I'd follow her on the opposite side of the street, unbeknownst to anyone around us.

Before entering the building, I'd pretend to be on my cell phone, look around to see if anyone was watching, then book it up the stairs as fast as I could. It was all cloak-and-dagger.

I'd go in, slip off my shoes, we'd exchange casual "*genki desu ka?*" with each other, and then she'd lead me back into one of the tiny cubicles. She'd tell me she hadn't seen me for a long time, and ask if I'd returned to America. She went through this exact routine *every single time*.

You can judge. I don't give a shit. I'm not bragging, or asking for reprehension or understanding, or a badge of honor or a scarlet letter, I'm just saying. How do I feel about it? Right now, I'm sitting here wishing I was back there and doing it all over again.

The daytime vista I was witnessing was vastly different from the nighttime world I was immersing myself into. I took advantage of what was made available to me.

I came to crave getting out of the clubs at 2 or 3 A.M., cruising the massage ladies and street girls, being led to a secretive rendezvous of lust, flesh, bodies, and moans.

Chasing Fame

I got submitted for acting work, the few roles for foreigners available in Nagoya. I booked a TV show called *Cyuzaikun Ga Iku,* a comedy about a clueless Japanese cop, in which I played a clueless black dude following around the clueless Japanese cop. My only lines on this show were me repeating the phrase *"nandeyanen?"* which is the Osaka-ben, Osaka dialect, of the word "why", which for whatever reason, every time you say it to a Japanese, it cracks them up. So, hearing a black dude with dreadlocks say it, was especially funny. There was more.

I started doing commercial voice-over work for rice companies, car dealerships, radio stations, and insurance companies. I became the announcer for an international radio show on ZIP FM, Nagoya's most popular radio station, called "Global Voice," wherein on each episode we discussed some issue going on in various international communities. I was interviewed and performed live twice on a show called "Midtown Artist Live" by another radio station in Nagoya which at the time was known as "Radio I". I met a cat from the states named Ali at Gary's who was producing music under the name "Beats That Bump". He produced some music for me, which eventually turned into my song "Anata No Namae Wa Na'an Desu Ka," which means "What's your name." This song became my calling card when my music career started to unfold a couple years later. I'd go to Tokyo, Osaka, and of course right there in Nagoya, and perform this one-of-a-kind hip hop/reggae joint with my chorus in Japanese and the crowd would be rocking. The song even got some radio airplay.

About this time SOFTBANK posters started popping up around Nagoya, featuring a black guy, two Japanese women, and a white dog. At the time, SOFTBANK was the number two cell phone service provider in Japan. I'm walking around feeling myself thinking I'm doing something when I start seeing this brother on posters all over the city advertising the cell phone. This brother was rocking Japan on a whole 'nother level, nationally and large. Come to discover the black guy in the poster was another Brooklynite like myself, named Dante Carver. Dante was also trying to make a name for himself in Japan's film and television industry, and was doing a banging job of it. Seeing Dante on all those posters gave me something to strive for in Japan. It was strange, but also wildly inspirational to see his black face on posters all over Nagoya. Here was this brother from Brooklyn, who didn't look much different than me, on posters all over the country. I told myself *one day that's going to be me.*

Meanwhile, I'm writing my film *Cherry Blossom Trail* in my head while I'm riding around the city learning about the parks and temples and experiencing the nightlife and carrying on my romance with A.

Suddenly, on cue, I was asked to appear on a poster for the *new* Chubu International Airport. Chubu International was built on a man-made island and was set to replace Nagoya Airport as the regional international airport of Aichi prefecture.

When the poster came out it was plastered *all over* the subway stations, stores, coffee shops, and trains in Nagoya. The airport itself, featured a huge thirty-foot poster of me gracing the arrival and departure gates and on the platform for the train to the airport. It was surreal. I had seen Dante in all his black Brooklyn glory gracing posters around the city and imagined it was me, and then suddenly as if *my wish had become my command,* there I was, on posters all over Nagoya as well.

My life was a dream at this point. I was walking on clouds, euphoric at my situation and so glad to have made the decision to come to Japan. It was, to me, the best decision *by far* I had ever made.

>Chapter 6

C.R.E.A.M.

Rises to the top

At night, I'm hitting the clubs like I'm 20 years younger than I actually am, because age doesn't matter if you're a foreigner in Japan, and no one knew the difference anyway. There's no 'time limit' except whatever your visa states, and age ain't nothing but a number. Anytime I told anyone how old I was, and I never lie about my age, they'd freak out and act like I had stepped out of a time machine.

In Sakae, I met a cool Nigerian cat named Tony at ID Bar. He was dripping in gold and diamonds and approached me one night when we were both up in ID about helping him open up a club he was planning to call C.R.E.A.M.—named after the infamous Wu Tang track.

C.R.E.A.M. became the kind of after hour's club where you could catch a cute Japanese girl giving a hand job to an African cat on the steps leading to the roof, which I did.

In fact, all types of shit went down at C.R.E.A.M. Big T, the blond California head-security chief at ID, was sometimes called down to C.R.E.A.M. to handle biz. T loved fighting and went ballistic with his fists almost every weekend, either with the Mafia, the Brazilians, the Russians and Eastern Europeans, or some dumbass Aussie wanting to test an American. Big mistake with T. Dude was as handsome as a movie star but could kick your ass sideways. Brazilians can fight and don't hesitate to throw blows in Japan, maybe anywhere. Them cats love fighting and ain't scared one little bit of brothers. Africans too. Africans can be some of the most mellow, generous, friendly dudes you'd ever want to meet. Cross them, they'll hit you with bottles, jump you and leave you leaking in the street. Frail truce, Africans and Brazilians in Japan. North Korea, South Korea DMZ zone type shit.

Tony, T and I became good friends. Tony and I had crossed paths a number of times at ID Bar. When I arrived in Nagoya, there was one underground after hours hip hop club called *FLAVOR*. Flavor was small, dangerous, and mostly African, and the Japanese girls who dug Africans went there. I have no problem with Africans, except that the African cats in Japan all run around saying they're from New York or LA. They seemed to have their own thing going, so I don't quite understand why they think they have to front like they are from the states, but it is what it is.

Flavor wasn't my spot, and apparently it wasn't Tony's spot either. Tony told me he wanted a more upscale, more international "NYC-type club," so he asked me to help him bring his idea to life. He took me to an empty space in a six-story building in Sumiyoshi and asked me what I thought I could do with the space. I told him where I thought the DJ booth should go, where the couches should sit, and how it should all be set up. He told me when he opened, he wanted me to DJ and a few months later, that's what I was doing. I DJ'd on Thursday nights and called my night "Brooklyn Beat". I spun east coast hip hop and reggae. Couple years later Tony left Japan for good—no one knew for sure where he went or what happened to him, but word was Japanese cops were on the lookout for him.

African dudes in Japan are notorious for pulling scams on Japanese women. They get involved with the woman, get access to their credit cards, then proceed to break the bank. Many Africans can, and do make a great living doing legitimate business in Japan, but many others seem to take the low road just because. This is one reason Japanese women have become wary of dealing with foreigners, black ones especially. I don't condone anyone intentionally stealing from anyone else, and I think dudes whose aim is this are pieces of shit.

Last I heard, Tony was in London, doing what, I have no idea. Rumors fly and people think they know, but what I know is that Tony was a cool cat with a big heart and a gentle, educated demeanor. He was *ahead* of the other African cats I came up on in Japan. *Big up to you, brother,* for giving me my first chance to do something musical in Nagoya.

Prelude To A Festival

I had also devised a mental plan to create some kind of international music festival, owing to the fact that all over Nagoya there were singers, bands, guitar players, et cetera playing their music on the streets. This fascinated me. They were different than the musicians you'd see in America on the streets or in the subways. They seemed more polished and the folks on the streets didn't just pass them by like they do here in the US; they'd actually stop and watch, for hours sometimes, such that it looked like a mini-concert in the street. I loved this.

>Chapter 7

TYING THE KNOT

With All My Strength

June was approaching and "A" and I were planning our marriage. Her family had reluctantly accepted the fact that we were getting married, as a result of the fact that A had told her parents she was pregnant. Things did not go smoothly at first, because during A's pregnancy, her mother had apparently pleaded with her on several occasions to have an abortion, and move back in with her family. To her 'credit', or something like that, A didn't listen.

Despite the fact that her parents weren't feeling me, despite the fact that A couldn't speak much English, despite my roommate Sam telling me over and over how stupid I was for wanting to marry A, despite her going to NYC for three months and me not really having much of an idea of where she was or what she was doing, despite my ongoing relationship with N, the crazy threesome I had had, the fling with S during the summer—despite all that, we got married in a beautiful wedding ceremony at a gorgeous Buddhist temple presided over by an authentic Buddhist Monk, with A visibly pregnant at our wedding.

My mother, my sister, her two-year-old son, my eighty-five-year-old aunt, and my cousin, all flew over to attend the event. I was completed invested, adorned in an authentic *hakama,* which made me look like a black Samurai. My wife-to-be was wearing a *shiromuku,* the Japanese version of the traditional white wedding dress. She looked angelic.

The wedding, was held at a temple called *Hounzan Renkyouji* in Nagoya. I had seven of my best friends there, plus my family. My wife had about twenty or thirty members of her family and friends. It was a beautiful ceremony, carried out entirely in Japanese. I didn't understand the vast majority of what was said and felt like I was in a daze throughout the entire proceeding. However, there I was, draped in my wedding hakama, participating in this exotic ceremony when all I really wanted to do was to marry my wife. After the ceremony, we had a wonderful reception. Ironically, or not, the reception turned out to be at the very restaurant I had envisioned as the setting for my film. It was surreal. We all clinked glasses, a few people gave speeches, and we all became a 'family' on that day.

I had organized an after party at C.R.E.A.M. I invited friends by sending out invitations which I had had professionally printed. I had C.R.E.A.M. decorated with congratulation balloons, streamers the whole nine. At the reception party, I DJ'd.

My friends, my family, my wife's sisters and of course my wife's parents came through. They were visibly uncomfortable inside C.R.E.A.M. They tried to dance with each other while I DJ'd but mostly looked slightly confused. For me, it was surreal DJ'ing in a nightclub with my brand new wife and her parents there. For my wife's parents I'm sure it was equally as surreal to get a glimpse into the life of their new son-in-law.

It was truly beautiful and bizarre. It felt like I was living a dream, me, marrying this beautiful young Japanese girl. Three months after that, we had our son Taiyo.

A Chance Meeting At the Record Store

That September, I encountered H. We met while I was handing out flyers for my Thursday night DJ event at C.R.E.A.M.

I'm in the hip hop section of Tower Records when I notice a thin, young, Japanese woman looking intently at the CDs in the R&B section. She was wearing a flowered dress, with her hair pulled back into a pony tail, sporting thick glasses, looking like quite the nerd. I handed her my flyer and told her I was a DJ at a new club in Sakae. She was extremely shy and not especially attractive at first, but she seemed interested in the club, the music, and me. She looked down at my flyer quizzically, then looked up at me through her thick glasses, smiled shyly, and said "thank you" in English, and then I left.

"A" and I Move Into our New Apartment

Married with my son Taiyo on the way, I had gotten another ALT position with a different dispatch company than the first one. I had decided I'd have to work full time in the junior high schools in order to earn enough money to support my family, and to win over the hearts and minds of A's parents. I had a full plate at the time, working in the schools, then DJing in the clubs and roving the streets at night, writing my film, doing occasional voice-overs. My poster was up all over the city, but it had only paid me a few hundred dollars, and wasn't leading to anything bigger, which is what I'd hoped would happen.

I was slowly developing a small circle of friends, all of whom were non-Japanese. I was still trying to learn the language as best I could, I was still trying to somehow fit in while sticking out like that proverbial nail. I was still gallivanting from one female to another while trying to be the best husband I could be to A. What an oxy-moron.

A and I moved into an apartment in Motoyama, one subway station away from her family in Higashiyama Koen. We put our names in a lottery to be able to get into a government sponsored apartment, essentially Section 8 in Japan. When we were selected to get the apartment, one of the stipulations was that we were obligated to accept the apartment without first being able to inspect it. Rent was lower than usual, and with A not working, we decided to go ahead and accept. For weeks, we were aching to see the apartment. When we were finally allowed to see the apartment, we were both stunned and elated. Our new place was on the third floor of a quaint apartment complex tucked away atop a hill, not too far from the train station at Motoyama. Our place had two bedrooms, one with tatami and one with a nice wood floor. It had one bathroom, a long hallway, a kitchen, living room, and balcony. It was perfect and when A and I saw it, we fell into each other's arms joyful that we had won the lottery.

We lived close to her family, too close. At first, I was elated that we'd live so close to her family. I figured they'd be there to help A whenever she needed them. I also thought they'd provide a comfort zone for whenever she needed to retreat back into her Japanese world. I knew she had her young hands full with me, our marriage, and our son. "A" hadn't been notoriously miserable during her pregnancy with Taiyo, but she wasn't anything like what you'd consider "prepared" for it either, and her parents and sisters were all too eager to help us out. Our lives were full that first year of Taiyo's life. I was teaching, DJing, familiarizing myself with the streets of Nagoya, while "A" was home taking care of Taiyo and our house.

H28 started showing up to my Thursday night DJ affair every week, and soon after that, she started driving me home, and then it wasn't long after that before we started getting intimate. She'd drive me home after my gig, but not before we stopped somewhere to get busy. We'd stop at parks, find empty spaces behind high schools, on wooden benches. We drove behind Higashiyama zoo a few times, in her car, under the full moon, while listening to the monkeys screeching in the park behind us.

I wondered if the monkeys could hear H28 screaming. I'd bend her over the passenger seat, pull up her flower printed dress, yank off her panties and go to town on her small dark twat. By the end, we'd both be quivering in orgasmic exhaustion. Sometimes the best sex is with someone you know you're absolutely not supposed to be with. It was torrid. We'd roll down the windows and I swear all the animals in the zoo must have been able to hear H. She shrieked like it was painful, but I had no choice. I didn't have too much time, so I gave it to H28 hard, fast and furious.

For me, it was purely sexual, but for her, it was much, much more. She was insatiable. It was as if she were an addict, and I was the drug. She was the picture of nerdiness but when her glasses came off and her skirt went up, it was as if she was unleashing years and years of pent up sexual energy. For those furious minutes that we'd spend in her car, or on a bench, or on the grass with a blanket or towel underneath us, H28 freed herself. From *what*? I wasn't sure. I was just in it for the temporary rush of "new", but unbeknownst to me, H28 had decided that I was going to be *hers*. By any means necessary, despite me being happily married, and despite me telling her that over and over.

When I'd come in late, A would already be sleeping with Taiyo in the tatami room. I would quietly take a shower and then go to sleep on the couch, in the living room, by myself. Sometimes "A" joined me, sometimes she didn't.

H28 started buying me clothing and offered to drive me anywhere I needed to go, anytime I needed to go, and essentially became my chauffeur. I told A that I was getting home by way of taxi and she never questioned me.

Circle of Trust

Meanwhile, at home, A had her hands full with Taiyo. Taiyo was a gorgeous baby boy, well-behaved, smart, fun, and cute. I was as excited as any man can be at the birth of my son. I thought to myself, A, and Taiyo were the perfect family, despite our cultural differences.

When A and I were dating, our relationship was kept cloak-and-dagger, clandestine secrecy from her parents. Her parents were extremely taciturn every time I was around, however, once Taiyo was born, A's family came around and completely accepted me into their circle. A's mom set up family portrait sessions with a local photographer, and we all had pictures taken together. Strange images as they were—me, tall, gangly, and dreadlocked, A's parents, her grandmother, and our son Taiyo—we were a family and things were working out well. I even started teaching her parents English once a week, for which they paid me a hundred dollars for. We conducted our lesson in their house, at their dining room table with the whole family watching and listening. They took notes, while trying desperately to learn my language, while I tried desperately to teach it to them.

A's mom, whom I had started calling *Okaasan*, which means "mom" in Japanese, worked really hard to learn whatever she could. She wanted to communicate with me and worked diligently at learning and pronouncing this new language she had never before even attempted. A's father, *otohsan*, "dad" in Japanese, seemed to just be there because his wife wanted him there. At his age, learning a new language was at the bottom of his list of priorities, and it showed. We couldn't communicate beyond just the bare minimal stuff, and we also couldn't bond on drinking beer because I didn't drink, but he too made the effort. Living in the house along with her parents and her two sisters was A's grandmother, who sometimes joined in the lessons, but mostly just played with Taiyo and laughed at everyone else studying this strange language.

Scooter T

We were supposed to be bounding as a family, but here I was, immersed into the nightlife, DJing, boning H28 in her car, collecting phone numbers from various girls, and meeting N1 in various love hotels once a month. I had also met another girl, "Scooter T," whom I named that because of the extra-large pearl white motor scooter she drove. I met T at C.R.E.A.M. while I was DJing one night before H28 showed up. She came up to the DJ booth, took a look at me, screamed "*sugoi!*" and told me she wanted to learn how to DJ. So, I promptly gave her my number and told her I'd teach her. Within a few weeks, Scooter T had bought herself a brand new CDJ system and a few hundred CDs, and we were at her place smashing in the afternoons into evenings before I'd go back home. I'd get off the train at Nagoya station, meet her in Sakae somewhere, she'd scoop me up on her scooter, and we'd vanish into her apartment. For a couple hours, we'd smoke weed from her little glass pipe, listen to the latest R&B/Hip Hop, and fuck each other's brains out. Her finger tips would be black from the hair dye she'd been applying all day at her job as a *biyoushi,* hair stylist.

Scooter T had a deep voice and impeccable sense of style to go along with her gregarious personality and fat white scooter, which she boomed music out of while we cruised the streets of Sakae. There I was, on the back of her scooter, holding her around her waist, helmet strapped with locks flying in the wind, while Lloyd's "Get It Shorty" or Ne-Yo's "Miss Independent" or 50 and the Game's "Hate It Or Love It" boomed out of her speakers. Look at me now, leaned back, head nodding, beaming to myself that *I was the man.* But I wasn't quite 'the man' at all, what I was, was a *married* man.

A Married Man

Traditionally, Japanese women often move back in with their parents immediately after having a child. This allows the grandmother to assist with taking care of the child, and so she could "teach" the granddaughter how to become a proper Japanese mother.

So, the first few months out of the hospital with Taiyo, A moved back home to her parents' house. This was a double edged sword, it gave me 'freedom' to continue my relationships outside of A's watchful eye, but it also felt like I had been abandoned by my wife. Here I was a newly married man with a new Japanese wife and new son, but they weren't home with me. A would sometimes bring Taiyo to our apartment, where I was staying alone, but by nightfall, she'd go back to her parents' in Higashiyama Koen, and then I'd hit the streets. Our communication was beginning to falter. Suddenly, we weren't laughing at or with each other so much anymore, weren't making funny faces, weren't watching movies late into the night. She was preoccupied with feeding and caring for Taiyo, and the shuttling back and forth between our apartment and her parents' place was wearing her out. A rift was beginning to develop between us, silently, but neither of us were consciously aware of it. It seemed like she was slowly "becoming" Japanese again. All the warmth, humor, spontaneity and laughter seemed to vanish. And so did she, literally and figuratively.

We both just felt that *this is the way things are* when you're married, let alone married to someone from a different country, different culture, different language, different ideas, virtually different everything. I was under the impression that things would eventually get better, Taiyo would get a little older, and the *other* A would come back. I thought we'd be laughing, playing, kissing and dating, just like we had before, but that time had come and gone, and I was left with empty nostalgic dreams about a past that would never return.

Our dating time had been euphoric, blissful, exotic, erotic, adventurous, fun, spontaneous, and tender. Our marriage, after Taiyo, became somewhat lifeless, and eventually barren. With her spending nights with her family, it left me mostly alone. It wasn't what I had bargained for in our marriage at all. I was alone the first couple years in Japan, even though I'd had trysts with N, M1, M2, Y, K, H, S, T, and the black band singer. But the truth was that I had fallen head over heels in love with A, or at least I thought I had, and wanted her home with me, with our son, our family.

Things were falling apart and the culture shock and alienation were taking root. I was taking trains where no one would sit next to me, young Japanese dudes in groups were staring at me pointing and laughing, I couldn't understand what was being said about me or not, and I felt completely out of time and place. My wife and family were supposed to help offset those feelings of being an outcast, but that's not how it played out. My wife was *somewhere else* and I was beginning to feel like I hadn't gotten married at all, like I was still on my own in Japan.

Clarissa And The Old Man On The Train

The alienation took on strange forms. One time I was on the train with my Indian friend Clarissa. Clarissa had been giving me meditation lessons in Imaike and we were on our way to her office for a meditation session.

We were in the subway on the train, chatting, about bullshit, the stars, breathing, her meditation practice, and whatever else, in English of course. Some old Japanese businessman-looking cat was giving us the dirty eye our whole conversation. I could see him, but Clarissa had her back to the dude, so she couldn't see him staring at us. She was chatting away, blabbering about her stuff, when suddenly Mister Japanese, Train Language Policeman dude lashed out at Clarissa, "*Densha no naka de, eigo hanasu na—coco Nihon! Wakatta?*"—translated, "this is the train, you shouldn't be speaking English here, this is Japan, understand?" I didn't know it at the time. Clarissa turned around and said "Eh? Nani?"—"what, dude?" He stared her down and then with that cold, hard, grim face only older Japanese men can make, he repeated what he said, "this is the train, you shouldn't be speaking English here, this is Japan . . ." and Clarissa proceeded to tongue-lash dude in Japanese for like five minutes straight, then turned back around and continued speaking to me *louder than before,* after which dude went back to his grim-faced look and his newspaper, and everyone around acted like nothing had happened.

Something Is Missing

I was working hard but work didn't make up for the lack of communication, loneliness, and lack of A's presence in our marriage. Life on the streets didn't either. All the running around, love hotels and hustling made me want to make it work even more with my wife. It was exhausting trying to keep track of all the different women, their personalities and needs. I to make the time to spend with them and then try to find the energy to make it home to deal with A as well.

Beyond the stares and snickers, no one understood me. I hoped my wife would. I had hoped marriage and family life would erase these feelings of alienation, but with an empty house, all these feelings became worse.

Eventually I found myself wanting to call things off with H28. I could see she was developing feelings that I wasn't able to reciprocate. There was something about her behavior that told me she wasn't in it simply for 'fun', she had all the characteristics of obsession, but I wasn't able to quite understand that from the beginning. She was starting to get too attached and she was beginning to be clear that she was buying my affection with her rides home, as well as trinkets and gifts she started giving me. I felt her neediness was a threat to my marriage. When I told her we'd have to stop seeing each other, she volunteered to become my "assistant"—she said whatever ideas I had, she'd help me bring them to fruition.

I said "cool" and tried to put distance between us. However, she became clingier and started texting and calling me sometimes 5 or 6 times a day. She was spending money lavishly and eventually I found it impossible to say "no" to her. She came around when I didn't want her to, and made herself available at any time, for any situation. If it was raining, she'd magically show up to drive me wherever I needed to go. If I was hungry, she'd appear out of nowhere with a delicious homemade 'bento box'. I couldn't find it in myself to tell her outright to *leave me the fuck alone*. I heard D's voice in my head, telling me, *you need to find the woman who is going to help you*, and apparently, H was her. Finally, almost out of desperation to find something to legitimize our 'boss/'assistant' relationship, I pulled out an idea that I had in the back of my mind.

I had thought of doing a music festival, in order to bridge the large gap between the native population of Nagoya, and the plethora of non-Japanese living there. In Japan, Japanese and foreigners seem on occasion to inhabit two totally separate worlds. There are restaurants and clubs and places specifically designed to attract a foreign audience, and then there are the other almost exclusively Japanese places. I didn't want to have to choose between my foreign friends and the Japanese around me. What I wanted to see was a mixing of the two groups. I also thought Nagoya could create a new identity for itself as a vibrant, colorful example of the best of international cultures coming together in Japan. I also eventually planned to take advantage of the Sister City relationship between Nagoya and Los Angeles. I put Nagoya on my back and *I wanted to put Nagoya on the Map*.

Since I had already established myself as a DJ in Nagoya, along the way I was developing an eclectic group of artistic friends. I invited Vinnie Vintage, Camp UG, Ghost Willy, Ali, MC Tendai, Thomas Baurle, a local electronic band named Solskye, Tom Fallon and his acoustic guitar, The Janzen Boys, which was a rock group consisting of a dude from Canada and his two young sons, a Filipino dance troupe sponsored by the Philippine Society of Japan, a Brazilian capoeira group, a killer Japanese rock band, an African reggae singer, a smoking hot Japanese disco band, a group of junior high school aged Japanese cheerleaders, a Japanese conga band which featured a didgeridoo—and a few other cats from Nagoya to perform in my two day 'Springfest', in May. But I hadn't properly put it together in my mind yet. I thought if I had the musicians with me, then no matter what happened, I'd be able to create something if they were willing to come and play. *Build it and they will come*, that was my ethos.

H28 had been on me about the assistant thing so much, it seemed Springfest came into being as a result of the pressure I was feeling from her. H28 helped me locate food vendors for the festival. She orchestrated the usage of electricity and running water with the City Recreation Department at *Shiyakushou*, City Hall. She knew that this had to be done in order for us to properly function in the small portion of Central Park. Normally, this type of business acumen would impress me but all I kept thinking was, *this is the exact location where I first met my wife*.

I slept in the park the night before the festival to make sure the stage was properly set up. We erected a stage, rented a power generator, and I hired a Japanese cat named Nakamura to provide sound. Later, Nakamura would be the go to guy for me, and dozens of other foreign musicians, to record their music at his News 90 music studio out in Biwajima. We rented space to various artisans, jewelry makers, visual artists, clothing designers, and body painters, charging them a small fee to take part in the festival.

H28 and I did all this, while my wife was at home, sometimes, taking care of Taiyo, trying to find her own identity. Other times, she was with her family, which was much more often. It seemed like we weren't a married couple at all. We may has well have been living in a time share apartment. She was there sometimes, mostly when I wasn't. I was there at night, floating in and out of our place in Motoyama, with my gaze fixed on the streets.

Spring Fest was an absolute success, despite it being a rainy, wet two day affair. We covered the stage with a tarp that read "SPRINGFEST NAGOYA" on it. I raffled off a few prizes and played trivia with the audience. The international merchants, food vendors, and craftspeople all made money. Most importantly, the performers were able to express themselves musically to a relatively large and appreciative international crowd. Hundreds of people showed up to watch this festival organized by a black American guy that no one had ever heard of up until that point. It was something Nagoya had never seen before, and H had helped me put it together.

Threes A Crowd

"A" was at the festival with our son Taiyo. A looked wonderful, wearing a long African printed skirt, a grey hoodie, and a pair of blue shell toe Adidas I had bought her. She had great fashion sense and looked like a Japanese gypsy walking around with our hafu son Taiyo.

My wife saw me talking to H. It was the first time the three of us were in the same place, at the same time, and the last. And though my wife saw me talking with H during the festival, she never outright mentioned it, until I felt obliged to tell her that H was my assistant. "Assistant?" she said, "yes", I told her, "I met her at CREAM and she said she wants to learn about the foreign population here in Nagoya...so, she said she wants to help me do whatever I'm doing." A is holding Taiyo at this point. H is watching us from a distance, knows A is my wife, and makes sure she doesn't approach.

During the event, H28 is handling the situation with my wife masterfully. Ultra-professional. While circumventing my wife for the entire festival, H also managed to run the festival like clockwork. She made sure the vendors and the guests were satisfied. She even made sure that the water was running. Hard work is attractive and H28 looked completely stunning. That day in spring, I noticed her. She's wearing super tight blue jeans and a crop top. She's got frosted pink lips and her hair is pulled back tight. She's got on gold hoop earrings.

At some point while the festival was winding down, my wife secretly approached H28, and told her to stay away from me, *us* and our family. She then gestured to our son Taiyo, and told H28 in Japanese,

"That's our son. Please leave us alone. Please leave David alone." I didn't learn of this meeting until years later.

After Springfest, H28 starts spending even more money on me. Since she had been confronted by my wife, she must have felt she had to pull out all the stops, and she did. She had expensive taste and bought me Burberry clothing, Fossil watches, designer hats, jackets, one of a kind Japanese leather belts and wallets. She started hand making things for me too, painting my DJ logo on jackets and hats and shirts. She paid for expensive dinners at Thai, Indian, Brazilian, Turkish and Japanese restaurants.

One day, my wife asked me where I had gotten all this new stuff. I told her, "the store", she asks me, "Which store?" I say, "The Burberry Store", she says, "...where is it?" "Uh....In Osu?"...I stammered. I was wrong. The Burberry isn't in Osu, it's in Sakae. This was evidence that my relationship with H was more than just an assistant/boss relationship. What kind of assistant buys their boss Burberry underwear, new watches? "Why does she buy you something??" A shouted. "I...don't know. Because she wants to?" I said. Stupidly. "Da-veed. You know I don't like her to buy you something. Why she buys?" "A. I don't know. What should I say?"

My wife storms out of the room, and I'm left feeling like the cat's completely out of the bag now. I was just shy of being caught red handed. But, I thought, *she hasn't explicitly seen H and I doing anything together, and for all she knows H did just buy me this stuff because she wanted to, because that is exactly what she did! I didn't ask for any of it.*

What should have happened next, was that I should have bitten the bullet and gone IMMEDIATELY to cut things off with H. Or at the least, not accept any more of the stuff she was buying. The thing was I didn't know how to cut things off with H. I had already asked her several times to stop seeing me, or to find another boyfriend. We had, superficially at least, cut our relationship back, with her now having 'assistant' status. I had told her we couldn't have sex anymore and in truth we hadn't been having sex at that time, for a short while anyway. However. Any possibility of 'learning a lesson' or 'doing the right thing' was immediately dashed to the rocks when I then made these false extrapolations based on current events:

As long as I don't ask for anything from H, I'm not doing anything wrong.
I'm not responsible for what she wants to do for me, or give to me.
I'm just a passive recipient.

This is merely a classic strategy of many foreign men living in Japan who are the beneficiaries of overly generous Japanese women who seem extremely benign, but who have very clear and very definite ulterior motives attached to their seemingly generous behavior.

Some Japanese women will throw money at you, lavish you with trinkets of affection, all in order to gain dominance and control over your life. You think you own them because of how well you're sexing them, but in reality, *they own you* because they're paying for everything, financing your lifestyle, and helping to maintain your *very presence itself*.

Either way, this is how I rationalized the gifts H28 was giving me. But it wasn't just H. There were the others. H28 was spending madd dough, driving me around the city and to and from my gig at CREAM. These acts of kindness usually ended with us having sex in the back seat of her car, either behind the zoo, school, or out in the countryside somewhere in a field. I was sinking deeper and deeper into my relationship with H28. It was like I was a drowning man looking for something to hold onto and H28 was there holding out a long stick for me. Fact is, she *was* 'saving me', while at the same time sucking the life out of my relationship with my wife. She was 'rescuing' me, while I was running from *her*.

And then there was T. The girl who wanted to learn to DJ. Scooter Girl. Scooter T became a sort of respite from H28. *How strange is it to need another sidepiece as a deterrent to your 'main' sidepiece.* H was mostly quiet, almost painfully shy, and socially awkward, T was casual, loose, and fun loving, there was no sense of her wanting anything more than an occasional afternoon fling in her bed. I could relax when I was with her, but still, I knew it wasn't going to last with T, and she knew there wasn't anything permanent there either, so we made the best of it. Even though her apartment was filthy and that dye on her hands made her look dirty, we had a great time listening to music, (eventually she bought herself some DJ equipment and taught herself to mix), and fucking on her bed, which was usually littered with all sorts of shit. It didn't last. Even though I dug it at first, me riding on the back of her screaming scooter through Sakae to get to her place was a little more high profile than I needed to be. I ditched it.

The others had faded into the background of my life. Y had gotten married and had given birth to her own son and was starting her own family. My sessions with N were very low profile and seemed somehow to not really be a part of my life. Hooking up with her was like a vacation *away* from all the drama I was building, but this thing with H was something else entirely. It, and she, had taken on a life all their own.

The Computer Teacher

C was working in one of the junior high schools where I was teaching. She was the computer teacher and career counselor at the school. She was young, thin and coquettish, late 20's, maybe early 30's, tall with twinkly eyes, thick brown hair and a quick, wide smile. She was professional, and looked a little similar to Lisa Kudrow, if Lisa Kudrow were Japanese. I saw C once or twice a week at Sakashita Junior High School. She was always at her desk with her head down, light-brown bangs splashed across her forehead.

One day, we were in the office together. We had just finished having a meeting and the other teachers had left, and only she and I remained. I waited until she looked up from what she was doing and then I winked at her. She looked around startled, almost afraid, wondering if indeed the wink was meant for her.

Japanese cats do not wink at women in Japan, and a wink generally tends to mean *something is in my eye.*

"Anata no namae wa Na'an desu ka?" I said, and immediately a smile crept across my face. My smile owed to the fact, that this greeting was the name of my song which was currently playing on Nagoya radio stations. She didn't know this at the time.

"C", she said, matching my energy. Then said, *"Watashi wa computah no sensei desu".* I'm the Computer teacher, in English.

"*Hai, wakarimashita...*" I replied. It's a common phrase in Japan, it means *I understand. I got it.*

I smiled and walked away. I could sense that C was interested. We started eating lunch together at her desk whenever we had the same work days. She couldn't speak a lick of English, but she was computer smart. She wore business suits almost daily, which I love on a woman. C lived in the countryside with her mom and sister. No boyfriend. Unmarried. C was charming and deceptively intelligent. She was one of many single women, over 30 that I met while I was in Japan.

On our first date we ended up at a place called Asahi Kougen, a beautiful slice of nature located just outside Nagoya. C parked and we followed a trail that led to a big open field surrounded by trees and foliage. At the bottom of the trail there was a covered stage that resembled a band shell.

We found some fabric on the stage, spread it out and ate the delicious Japanese lunch C had packed for us. Shortly after that, C found herself spread out on that piece of fabric, where we made love over and over until nightfall. We were on that stage, being entertained by the blackness of space, the faint moon and shooting stars.

We ended up falling asleep and being awakened by voices, and the clip clop sound of hooves echoing above us. When we looked up we saw several horses with people on their backs trotting around the rim of the depression we were in. We threw on our clothes, headed back to her car, and it started raining. We rolled up the windows, got in the backseat of her mother's sedan, which she'd driven us in, and we made love again. It was one of the most romantic and pleasurable moments of my life.

Shortly after that we went to Adera River. No one else was there that day but it was sweltering hot and this place was the perfect remedy: a crystal clear, naturally flowing, gentle but deep cold-water creek out in the Japanese mountainside. C and I jumped off rocks, walked along the edge of the creek and tiptoed from rock to rock across the water. We ended the day playing *shiritori*. It was a perfect day with a really cool, cute, professional Japanese woman *who couldn't speak a word of English.*

C treated me to numerous adventures outside Nagoya. We spent weekends at tiny bed and breakfast places in the countryside surrounding Nagoya. We researched different types of love hotels and C had no problem driving for a couple hours in order for us to find the most imaginative places we could. We went to one particular love motel whose motif was African Safari, and made love while stuffed lions, tigers, elephants, giraffes, and zebras watched. We shared a common interest in movies and saw dozens together, either at the cinema or on the flat screen television she bought me. C also purchased an expensive electric piano for my son Taiyo, on which she played unimaginable, romantic classical music after every time we made love. However, C couldn't speak any English at all, and this disallowed me from considering getting serious with her, that, and my marriage.

I didn't need her to be able to speak English. I didn't want her to, just as she didn't *want* me to be able to speak Japanese. The communication gap was alluring, but it forced us to keep a certain distance from each other. Unlike H, or even my wife A, C made no attempt to learn my language.

This fact allowed me to compartmentalize my relationship with C into the category of *she can't cause trouble in my marriage because she can't speak any English, therefore I'll never get attached to her, so this will just be another fun fling, however long it lasts.*

This was how I felt about all the women I was seeing outside of my marriage. I didn't take any of them seriously, except H. Somehow I had placed H into a category that I couldn't even explain to myself. She became a sort of *benefactor*. A *homie/lover/friend* with benefits.

Besides H, I never considered that these women were actually *feeling* anything and/or had any actual plans or hopes for anything serious with me. To me, they were just slides, swings, and jungle gyms on my own personal Japanese playground. They existed *for me to enjoy*, or so I thought. When I disappeared back to my married life, I figured they'd just wait emotionlessly for me to pick them up and play with them whenever I was ready. I treated them like *things,* as opposed to humans. They were my *toys.* I was delusional, thinking *they all just want to have some fun,* like I did, regardless of my marriage, regardless of my wife at home, regardless of our newborn son.

C added herself to my coterie of Japanese play things. She really learned more than a few words of English, and always seemed just a bit off-balance, but something was very unique about her personality. She had an artist's soul and a rebellious nature, all while being very bright and informed, super inquisitive and sharp as a tack.

I never *intended* to be so flagrantly unfaithful and opportunistic. Intentions mean *something,* don't they? Things just sort of snowballed and I was caught up in the avalanche. Avalanches are impossible to slow down or stop once they get started.

Once I put the key in the ignition the car took off, speeding 100 miles per hour with my foot glued to the accelerator. I couldn't slow it down if I'd wanted to, *but I didn't want to,* even as my life was becoming a fast moving slow motion car accident.

I was going with the flow while the flow was sucking my marriage out to sea. Fucked-up thing was I still loved my wife like crazy. Or so I thought. Our son, Taiyo, was a beautiful baby boy and my wife was still as physically hot to me as she had ever been, moreso even, now that she'd put on a few pounds after being pregnant. There's no denying how much love can bubble up for a man towards his woman after she gives birth to his child.

But, addiction can ruin even the best of intentions. I was out on the street fucking up my marriage day by day and little by little. "A" had finally moved back in but things were never the same between us again. All the love, all the gentleness, all the smiles and spontaneity had vanished from her face, but I still needed it, and I searched for it outside my marriage daily. I couldn't stop myself from doing my thing out on the streets of Nagoya.

Even if I had wholeheartedly wanted to stop, I don't think I could have, and I *didn't* want to. I had created a wildly sensual and eclectic life for myself apart from my life with my wife. I had sidepieces for my sidepieces and each of them were either giving me money or buying things for me or somehow contributing to my welfare. It had been easy to cut off S, both M's, and T. K and Y had walked away on their own. N was orbiting somewhere way out in space, until our sporadic love hotel sessions, which I wasn't willing to give up quite yet.

But I did want to cut things off with H28. She was getting too close, or trying to, and it was threatening my marriage. Our sexual relationship had ended, but she was still by my side, and now I had replaced H's sexual relationship for C's. *I had to have it.*

H stood by me anyway and told me over and over again that she wanted to help me to do anything I wanted to do. It was her way of staying close to me, of biding her time until I came back around, while weakening and undermining my marriage. I wasn't sure what I was supposed to do or not do, my wife didn't seem to be on my team. My moral barometer was off, because I had convinced myself that *this is Japan, they do it differently here.*

With H constantly in my ears asking me what I wanted to do, I did have some more ideas, and since we'd had a successful Springfest, I decided to try something else that had been on my mind. At the time, there was a popular magazine in Nagoya called *Japanzine*. I had contributed a few articles to it, and I got the notion that I could make a better magazine myself. So, with H's help, I set out to do exactly that.

>Chapter 8

RAN Magazine

Right About Now

I came up with the idea for a magazine and called it, *RAN Magazine*. When I arrived in Nagoya, there were a couple of English-language magazines being published, but they sucked. There was *Avenues,* which tried to be highbrow but was just boring, and there was *Japanzine,* which tried to be lowbrow, but was also boring and extremely white-washed.

I figured with H's help, I'd start my own magazine. I found four guys who went to work on RAN with me. Achim Runnebaum, photographer, Adam Pasion, writer and artist, Jason Gatewood, web host and online editor, and Matt Helminski, ostensibly the layout designer. However, unbeknownst to me at the time, what Matt really wanted to do was be the photographer. But since Achim was already handling those duties, Matt didn't last long, and we replaced him with Adrien Sanborn.

We had a meeting in the Starbucks underneath Oasis 21, and then shortly thereafter we started RAN and the first issue turned out exactly as I had envisioned it. I wanted to have a colorful, street, artistic, funky, informative, and entertaining magazine about life in Japan as told through the eyes of foreigners who knew the street there in Nagoya. The publisher of *Japanzine* was a married dude with children who stayed uptown and didn't know much about what I was witnessing at night in the clubs, on the streets, or everywhere else. I didn't necessarily want to compete with Japanzine, I just wanted to put out what I was seeing, which was missing from the pages of his magazine.

I asked a couple restaurant owners I knew if they'd be willing to advertise, and Chris Zarodkiewicz over at Shooters and Joe Sichi over at Red Rock both jumped on board. Cat named Ray Proper bought a quarter page ad. I asked a Japanese lady who ran a small English school called "My English Room" to buy some space. I asked some Australian cats I knew who were running a relocation company to buy some ads as well; they all agreed, and that was all I needed. H called around and found the cheapest printer we could find. Adrian and I sat down and hammered out a logo and layout design that would benefit the advertisers and showcase the features. Jason set up the website, while Adam drew a bunch of dope-ass illustrations for more aesthetics. Achim took flicks and fired up his environmental column "Greenspot," while I contributed stories and interviews of musicians, local writers, and even the life of a suave, Japanese male gigolo. We also featured pieces about Japanese-foreign relationships, graffiti, nightlife, Japanese culture, street dancing, fashion, and included a guide to what to do, where to eat, and what to see in Sakae.

RAN lit a much-needed fire underneath anyone who was doing anything in Nagoya. Cats lined up to be featured on our pages and advertisers came easy, at first. *Japanzine* changed their format to copy ours, *Avenues* died a quiet death, as did *Radio I,* the only real international radio station in Nagoya, and suddenly *RAN* was the hottest ticket in the city.

H and I drove around in her car and delivered the magazine by hand to two or three dozen locations around Nagoya. *RAN* was real, raw, risqué, and most importantly for me, multiethnic, which was the Nagoya I was a part of. My role as publisher was to decide the theme of each issue, as well as to coordinate and assign features and articles, and most importantly, to find investors and advertisers, and I handled my role with aplomb. *RAN* was one of the best ideas I ever had, and I think one of the best ideas any non-Japanese had ever had to that point, in Nagoya.

That first year, I organized parties and festivals to coincide with the release of the new magazine, to get the word out on the street, to galvanize support for the magazine and our advertisers, but mostly, to just have a good time. *RAN* was a hit out the box. We printed on paper one grade higher than our nearest competitor, and we featured risqué stories and sexual images. We were also the first magazine in Nagoya to feature and embrace local talent and artists as the mainstay of the magazine. We weren't afraid to offend anyone, weren't afraid to push the envelope, but mostly, my idea was to create celebrities out of the artists, musicians, DJs, writers, designers, photographers, and anyone else in Nagoya who was creating. I wanted to give Nagoya some pizzazz, some flash, to go along with its conservative image. We did exactly that *and then some,* for more than six years. I compiled everything I saw, heard, ate, where I shopped and partied. I investigated anything I thought sounded even vaguely interesting to me. I figured, if I think this shit is interesting, someone else might too.

Anata No Namae Wa Na'an Desu Ka?

Around the same time, I hooked up with a drummer from one of the R&B bands that was playing at Gary's, and we recorded a reggae-hip hop flavored song called "Anata No Namae Wa Na'an Desu Ka?".

The words to the tune came to me as a chorus—"*Anata no namae wa na'an desu ka? Tsukiateru hito wa imasen ka? Isshoni odote kurei masu ka? Anata no namae wa na'an desu ka,*" loosely translated as "What's your name? Do you have a lover? Can we dance together? What's your name?"–before I ever heard the drummer dude's beat. Repeating the chorus over and over to myself in my head walking around Sakae, it helped me to learn simple Japanese. When the producer of the song gave me the beat, I filled out the song with a rap and a hit was born. I started performing the song at clubs, parties, and festivals, and word of mouth got as far as Osaka and Tokyo that the cat who was doing that "Anata No" song lived in Nagoya.

Then I met a dude named G Conkarah. Conkarah ("Conqueror" pronounced in Jamaican patois) was a Japanese cat that swore he was Jamaican. Conkarah was a producer who was well known in reggae circles throughout Japan. Somehow he'd heard the tune and put the word out that he wanted to meet me.

Conkarah dressed and spoke like a Jamaican Rasta, "wha'ppen bwoy..." he said that first time we met. Conkarah's Jamaican patois was spot on and perfect.

Soon thereafter he invited me into his studio and we whipped up a full album together, the first of two, which I called *Multi-culti*, owing to the many cultural influences and sounds heard on the album. Radio stations in Nagoya played "Anata No Namae Wa Na'an Desu Ka," and two other songs off the album became popular, "Higher" and "She Says She Loves Me," a song that I wrote based on my relationships with both H and my wife.

By this time, my wife and I were barely communicating. And on the rare occasions that I was at home, my wife and son weren't. She had taken to spending the nights with our son at her family's house in Higashiyama again. We barely saw each other, and whatever little communication we had was usually via text. Not only that, but she had started texting me in Japanese, which made it more difficult for me to understand exactly what she meant. Many times I ended up asking H to translate my wife's texts.

H, on the other hand, was not only now professing her love for me, but she was showing it too. She was behaving much more like a wife than my wife was. She was taking me to the doctor and dentist, she was buying me clothing for the winter, she was driving to and from my shows. She drove me to my gigs in the clubs at night. She was making deals for me with advertisers and printing companies. And when she wasn't doing all of this, she was driving up, down, and across Nagoya to help me deliver my magazine. She seemed to be the one caring for me, while my wife seemed to be slowly disappearing, like a phantom.

Singing In The Rain

I was performing in shows in Tokyo, Osaka, and Nagoya, and H was chaperoning me to each of them. One show called Reggae Explosion, produced by Conkarah, had upwards of two or three thousand people. I was booked to appear as the third or fourth act onstage, on the same ticket as then super-popular reggae artist TKO.

At the show, I was backstage waiting to go on when I heard the keyboard riff that Conkarah created for "She Says She Loves Me". Suddenly, I heard a huge collective scream and the sound of hundreds, thousands, of feet rushing towards the stage. When I came out from behind the speaker column there was a huge throng of beautiful Japanese faces smiling, cheering, dancing, and all wearing the Jamaican colors of red, gold, and green. I performed 3 or 4 songs and it was the most intense, rewarding, thrilling experience I had had in Japan up until that point, and H, not my wife, was there to witness it. It was, and still is, one of the most rewarding, exalting, satisfying feelings I've ever experienced. Unbeknownst to me at the time, H and I were building lifetime memories together, while my wife was, wherever she was.

My wife didn't seem to give a shit about anything I was doing. I was hustling English teaching gigs, plus DJing at night, plus recording music, performing at sold out shows, putting together my magazine, organizing festivals and parties, and she was . . . silent. Invisible. Virtually non-existent, but we were still technically 'married'.

Whenever I saw her, which wasn't often, I'd try to make her laugh, play music I thought she liked, and then I'd ask her if she still loved me, which usually just made her angry. Then I'd ask if she *liked* me, for which I'd also get no answer. I was trying my best to talk to her and tell her about my days and my experiences and she was ignoring me, or more often, looking at me like I was speaking a different language. I guess I was. She understood my English, but didn't understand the language of a lonely foreigner who just happened to also be her husband. I felt small, worthless, like I was more a nuisance to my wife than anything else. It was like we became a couple of frozen popsicles, one blue the other red. The fucked up thing was, *all this made me angry at H.*

Somebody Is To Blame

I absolved myself of the responsibility of what I was doing with H. However, I blamed her for the distance in my marriage that I felt she was responsible for creating. I wanted her to leave me alone. I didn't want her to be a better wife than my wife was being. I wanted her to stay away from me, not buy me shit, not offer to take me places, not worry about my health, not give me money, and not buy me clothing. I didn't want to enjoy her delicious meals and I was often resentful and ornery when she did anything special for me, but she never gave up. I hated that I needed her in order to be successful at what I was doing. I wanted to think I could do it all myself, but I couldn't, she knew it, and took advantage of it. If I'd attempted to get the same success without her, no doubt it would have taken much longer. My relationship with her was friends with benefits *on steroids.*

I wanted her to disappear and just go away, and leave me to my marriage and let me try to work things out with my wife, but she wouldn't, and I didn't have the balls to actually walk way. I asked her to leave me alone many times, but she'd softly argue and ask me why I wanted her to go away. I felt sorry for her, but I also felt damned if I do, damned if I don't. She kept showing up, wanting to be around, asking me what I needed, taking me places, buying me things. She became much more than just a sidepiece.

It felt like I was being pulled between two worlds, except one world, the world with my wife, seemed to be *pushing me away a* whole lot more than it was pulling me in, while simultaneously the other world,

H's world, was pulling me closer and closer, like a giant tractor beam I couldn't escape. H cared about every aspect of my life, except the one that mattered most to me, my family.

She had been benign at first. Generous and willing to be helpful, with an explosive sexual appetite to boot. It's difficult for a man, any man, to walk away from that. She showed me that she wanted to help me with the pursuit of my professional goals in Japan, and didn't express any particular needs or desires that she herself had. She was shrewd and deviously manipulative while at the same time appearing to be innocent and naïve.

She had years of professional Japanese business acumen at her disposal, having worked for one of the biggest Realtors in the country. She knew exactly how and what to say when dealing with advertisers, businesses, the officials at city hall, Japanese English school owners, restaurant owners, whomever.

Whatever ideas I came up with, she immediately translated them into Japanese, and then executed my idea exactly as I had envisioned it. She took my ideas and immediately turned them *our* reality. It was magical sometimes, how I'd come up with something, an idea for an ad, or a show, or an event, or a venue, and she'd know just exactly how I could put myself into the position of actualizing whatever thought I'd had.

It made me dizzy. I got hooked on how willing, ready, and able she was. I started thinking she was better than my wife. I started feeling empowered by how useful and practical H was. I started to make a subtle shift in my emotional outlook on H in particular and Japan more broadly. I started to feel like *maybe I don't need my wife, maybe all I need is H,* and *maybe I can do much more here than just teach English.*

My good fortune in business and entertainment exploded in Nagoya. I had a successful magazine. I had recorded music that was playing on the radio, I was doing shows in different cities, and my picture was in subways across the city and at the airport. I had been on Japanese television and had organized festivals and everyone knew who I was. I was Djing and promoting and helping to jump start a spate of artistic expression that Nagoya had never seen before. Things were going amazingly in the professional arena of my life. I was becoming a brand before I even knew what a brand was. I felt awkwardly 'powerful' in relation to the other foreigners in Nagoya, but simultaneously, my married life was slowly grinding to a halt.

Treat The Disease Not The Symptoms

My wife and I weren't speaking to each other. She was in and out of our apartment in Motoyama, mostly out, and so was I. She demanded I formally learn to speak Japanese, which I thought I was just too stupid to learn, and I told her so. Plus, I thought, *why do I need to learn to speak Japanese?* Her English was serviceable and besides, H was doing everything for me anyway, and anything I couldn't express in Japanese, H could express for me. I didn't tell my wife this of course, but this is what I felt. *Who needs Japanese? I've got a Japanese speaking mouthpiece.*

Eventually, it got to where I'd have to write notes to my wife as our only form of communication. She needed to know how I felt, so I would leave them around the apartment, where I thought she'd find them.

I wrote letters trying to explain how it felt to have Japanese people not sit next to me on the train. I wrote letters explaining how strange it was to have people stare at me everywhere I went. I wrote letters asking her what had happened to us. I wrote to her explaining that I missed her, and wondered with my pen if we could go on a date together. Her only response to my letters, was that they were 'stupid'. Whenever I'd ask her if she'd read my letters, she'd sigh out loud, roll her eyes and tell me the letters were stupid. It hurt like hell and then I'd slink out of our apartment, call or text H to come pick me up, and moments later she'd be at the entrance of (me and my wife's) apartment complex with her car. I'd hop in and she'd take me out to dinner, or shopping, or to a movie, and it made the pain temporarily subside, exactly like a pharmaceutical. I was treating the symptom, not the disease itself, and I'd wonder, *why am I sitting here eating with this girl I don't really like that much, when my wife is...somewhere, and I love her like crazy? What am I doing?* H would notice my discomfort and put her hands on my thighs or my shoulders and attempt to massage me, but it always felt awkward and forced, and I'd ask her to please stop. Then I'd return to my mental dark cloud, *why doesn't my wife care about what I have to say?* There were numerous times I sat in H's car in dead silence wondering just what the fuck I was doing there, so many mixed signals inside my brain, emotional traffic jam.

I began to actually feel *scared*, like I was being pursued by some invisible monster. I created a palpable sense of absolute dread about my marriage, and my own life. I guess I knew on some level that my wife and I were doomed. Although I was creating this superstar brand for myself, I still, somehow I felt my identity was tied up in my marriage to my wife and our son. I didn't know what I'd do if things didn't work out between us, and it never crossed my mind that I could stay in Japan if we were to get divorced. I equated my entire life with the success or failure of my marriage. I wasn't sure if I could return to the US and be successful. Many foreigners who stay in Japan put themselves through this exact syndrome and I had become one of them.

I created a space in my magazine for this very theme, called "Should I Stay Or Should I Go", based on the song of the same name by The Clash.

Decisions, Decisions

It didn't dawn on me, that in the US, there might be opportunities to teach ESL, and even though I had been teaching in Japan, I guess somewhere deep inside I thought it was all a farce. I thought eventually someone was going to expose me as a fraud, a fake, a phony 'English teacher'. In Japan, I had been given a second chance at life and I was now completely *fucking it all up.* How could I even consider going back to the US, while I was destroying everything good in my life in Japan?

I felt like I was between a rock and a hard place. I could either try to save my marriage, which I felt meant I'd have to give up everything else I had worked for, or, I could throw myself into what I was doing outside my marriage, which would inevitably lead to the death of my marriage.

My magazine blew up. RAN was a sensation and invigorated Nagoya like nothing before it. My music also took on a life of its own. I started being requested to do more shows out of town, festivals, events and special appearances. I have no idea how promoters and organizers outside of Nagoya found out about me, but they did, and started requesting I perform at their events. My DJ alias, Maddlove, was blowing up in Nagoya, I was doing club nights and parties, and there was so much attention from women it was crazy. I'd show up to events and girls would crowd around me and act like I was some kind of superstar. Radio stations were requesting me to do voice overs for them and my picture was still splattered all over the subways for my ad for Chubu Airport.

I performed at Tokyo Design Fest in Tokyo, at the WHY NOT festival in Osaka, and at Nagoya's multicultural music festival at OASIS 21. I was absolutely balling, while putting on my friends in Nagoya at the same time.

Father Figure, Can't Figure It Out

My professional life was hot, but my marriage was frozen. I was still seeing H, and also carrying on affairs with three, four, and five women at a time. I barely had time for my wife, who herself was barely at our house. She rarely communicated with me in English, and her family was being unresponsive to my pleas to send my family home.

I went to my wife's family's shop in Higashiyama one day to find out from them why A wasn't coming home anymore. I cornered her father when her mother wasn't around, and asked him in Japanese, "...nande anata no musume wa ie ni kaette ko naie no...?" *why isn't your daughter coming home?* He replied that he had been wondering the same thing. This temporarily bolstered my confidence. I thought *maybe he's on my side,* but if you know anything about Japanese marriages, you know that the woman runs the household like a fascist dictator, and the man is only there to provide funds. A's father may have told *me* what he was really thinking, but he'd *never* tell his wife.

Ostensibly I had gotten married not only because I thought I loved my wife, but also because I thought it was necessary for me to have a Japanese wife in Japan, and, mostly, because I thought having a family would alleviate the penetrating loneliness and alienation I was feeling. That's what family is supposed to do, right? I wanted my own family in Japan to love and protect and be responsible for and to help buffer me against the vicissitudes, peculiarities, and loneliness of modern-day Japan. My sex friends and whatever feelings of 'belonging' they offered were temporary.

I didn't want to become a bitter, angry foreigner like D, and I didn't want to stay frozen outside society either. I was lost, but I wanted to keep my marriage intact. Even though we were essentially estranged from one another, I knew that I still loved my wife, and I *had to do something.*

So, I decided my wife and I should have another baby. I figured another baby would solidify our marriage. I thought it would bring us closer, bring me closer to her family, and reignite the feelings we'd had for each other in the beginning. Plus, this had been our plan from the beginning. I remembered those halcyon days of utter bliss when we were hanging out in my apartment in Freebell, discussing our plans for the future. We had decided we'd make three babies, and at some point, move back to America. I wasn't sure how keen on this idea I still was, but whenever I brought it up, "A" sparked up and seemed interested. In retrospect, I think she just wanted to give us and our family a fresh start, away from the stinking pile of shit that I had turned our marriage into. Thing was, we were still in Japan, and my wife, who once expressed her interest to learn about things non-Japanese, was slowly reverting back into a very traditional Japanese woman, and one who didn't want to speak English at that. So, I thought having another child would cure all this. *Wow.*

My Daughter Asia Jade Comes On

The next year floated on like that. I was doing my events, promoting my magazine as best I could. H was buying me shit, taking me places and massaging my thighs and shoulders in her car. On weekends, C and I went on outings and awkwardly tried to communicate, and ended up having exhausting sex. My wife was barely home, or maybe I was barely home, but whatever was or wasn't happening, we weren't communicating. We were growing further and further apart, so I thought it'd be a grand idea to get her pregnant again. So I did.

I figured having TWO children might slow me down and force me to take account of what I wasn't doing in my role as A's husband.

I couldn't keep it secret from H that I had gotten my wife pregnant. It felt perfectly preposterous to me that I should have to keep it secret to begin with, but the truth is I was worried at how H would react when I told her that my wife was pregnant again. I felt indignant at the prospect of having to "come clean" to H about having a second child *with my own wife.* She's my wife, I thought, *why am I treating H like I'm having an affair behind her back with my own wife?* It was ludicrous. My whole world was turning upside down like the streets in Leonardo DiCaprio's *Inception* flick. How could I feel guilty about telling my sidepiece that I was going to have a child with my wife? Yet, this is exactly how I felt, and it fanned the flames of resentment I already had for H. H reacted almost exactly like I thought she would. She was devastated, which made me feel angrier towards her.

"Why are you having another baby..." she asked incredulously.

"...Why Trevor? You want *another* baby with the woman who doesn't help you? Oh my god..." This infuriated me more.

Why do I have to explain why I've decided to have another child? How does it affect you that I'm moving forward with my marriage? Why are you sad that I'm having a child? It's my freaking life! I can do what I want! It did not go over well.

H reacted like I had taken away her future, like I'd kicked her in her stomach. I found myself having to console her. *Fucking crazy.*

Here I am in Japan, married to a Japanese woman, with a son, *about to have a another child with my wife*, which should be a cause for celebration, *but instead I'm here consoling my sidepiece* over the fact that I've decided to have another child with my wife. *This is not how I expected life to be.*

The whole thing was egregiously *absurd*, and sent shock waves of mixed feelings reverberating through me. It made me want to hate H, for forcing me to feel bad about what I had hoped was a great decision, albeit one that my wife herself didn't seem all too thrilled about. It also made me feel somehow closer to H at the same time, not only because it felt like she was somehow part of my 'family', but also because I had to console her for the first time in our relationship.

In that moment, H opened up to me about her abusive alcoholic father, who was currently suffering from terminal cancer. She told me through tears that her father had been given not too much longer to live by the family doctor. She also said that her father had been emotionally and physically abusive to her and her mother when she was younger. She said he'd been a loud, insensitive, violent alcoholic during all of her childhood, and that as a young girl she wondered over and over why her mother never left him. She recalled night after night of lying awake crying in her dark bedroom and listening to her father berate and badger her mother, smashing dishes and throwing things around the house. H's family owned their own small pottery business out in the Gifu countryside.

H said, time has allowed her to feel a sense of pride for her mother for enduring her father's violent alcoholic outbursts. She said she'd learned a lot from her mother about how to endure, how to be loyal, how to isolate and compartmentalize her feelings about anything and everything. She told me she'd lay in her bed in her room listening to her father ranting to her mother, and she'd imagine being somewhere else, anywhere else. She told me music gave her an outlet to escape the reality of her abusive household and that she was determined to be exactly like her mother, but not have a life anything like her mother had had.

Then she told me that she'd stay with me no matter what. These are words my wife had never said, and rather than making me feel better, it terrified me.

What do I have to do to get rid of her, I thought, *and how can I get my wife back?*

I was in over my head, emotionally drowning, as it were. I was having multiple affairs while struggling to balance all of the projects I had going on.

Drowning would be an apt metaphor for what came next.

>Chapter 9

WHITE WATER RAFTING

Merrily Merrily Merrily Merrily I Think I'm Going to Die

One in 250,000 people die white-water rafting every year. And I almost became one of them.

You ever drown? Or almost drowned?

Have you ever felt yourself sinking under water, gasping for a few non-existent breaths while gulping in mouthfuls of water, air having left your lungs either moments or long ago, you can't tell and it doesn't matter anyway, leaving you, feeling like your lungs are a pair of dehydrated raisins, arms and legs flailing madly in the cold wet darkness, while your head feels like a hand grenade that is going to explode any second?

And everything is happening in slow motion, but you're panicked and frantic and it isn't happening in slow motion, it's all happening rather quickly...

Another minute or two and you're dead...

Sinking underwater against your will is a lonely, fucked-up, nightmarish feeling. It chokes you up, frightens you, and causes your eyeballs to pop out of your head. The experience forces you to expend vast amounts of energy you desperately do not have any of to begin with, grasping at nothing, while you not so slowly fall deeper towards you know not what.

Drowning is the worst way to go.

It just plain sucks.

One very rainy Sunday morning in June, the crew of foreigners I was hanging out with decided to go rafting. My wife was just about seven months pregnant at the time. Asia, my daughter, was due to arrive into the physical realm that August, one month before Taiyo's birthday. Even with the maelstrom of drama I had created, even with "A" being rarely at home, even with all the affairs I was having, I had found the time, and the energy to impregnate my wife again. I was still wildly attracted to her, and chances are if we'd stayed married, we'd have half a dozen children by now.

At the banks of the river, there were about twenty of us, three rafts full, and each raft held exactly seven people. I'll never forget. Ever. I'm not really a "swimmy" type dude. I mean, I don't go around jumping into fucking pools and shit. We didn't have rivers or creeks where I grew up. Swimming was barely even mentioned as a *word,* let alone as an actual option of something to do where I grew up. Swimming was some exotic activity white people did.

I went to the beach lots when I was in Jamaica, and when I lived in Florida. Now that I'm older, I realize I never really was much of a beach person, but I didn't know that then. When you're a kid and your family is going on a beach trip you get excited by default, *we're going to the beach!* -not knowing whether you really like any of it. The sand, the sun, the heat, and of course, the ocean. It all seems too fucking random to me, dangerous and unknown. Waves and sharks and the deep blue sea. Too many variables. But I guess I'm a risk-taker.

My wife was home with Taiyo, seven months pregnant and not very happy. She was not very talkative, and seemed angry that I had put her in this condition, especially since she was already skeptical about whether or not I was being faithful to her. I wasn't being faithful and it was getting harder and harder to fake it. We both knew that she was going to return to her parents' house after she had given birth to our next child. Her being home was temporary, she just wanted to give birth already. We had tacitly decided to work things out, so when she had our next child, it would be smooth sailing from there out. *Jesus was I naïve.*

I gave her a kiss while she was sleeping early that morning and told her I'd be back later that evening. She hadn't expressed any feelings one way or another about my plan to go rafting. It wasn't surprising. There wasn't really anything there between us. I was doing whatever I wanted to and she was essentially just going with the flow. I left at 5 A.M. to catch the first train down to Nagoya station to meet with the other guys and girls. Three carloads of foreigners headed to Nagara Gawa to *raft* down that bitch. I had no idea what rafting actually meant.

We stopped at a convenience store on the way and the leader of the group, Christian, an Australian cat, gave us directions as if he was some famous camp director or counselor. He showed a slight concern for the weather, which I now know was a warning.

Christian said he'd expected the rain to have let up by now and this should have been enough for me to go home. He explained that it had been raining for the entire week and casually joked about it. None of us thought twice about the rain, after all, aside from earthquakes, *nothing life threatening ever happens in Japan.* My two best buddies at the time, twins by the names of D and D had brought some weed to smoke. So we rolled it up and smoked behind the conbini until the three of us were nicely lit. The majority of the other foreigners loaded up on chu hi's and beer. Stupid foreigners.

We disembark from our cars and eventually make it down to the river. Where we were standing looked placid and peaceful, but it was, in fact, still raining. Not a torrential downpour but not a light drizzle either. It was a steady rainfall that made the air between the river and trees more than slightly opaque. And there was fog. There's always fog in Japan, it's just mysterious like that. Fact is it had been raining for almost 10 days straight and the river was probably 2 to 3 feet higher than usual. Maybe 4 and 5 feet in some places. June is rainy season in Japan but nobody tells you that on a rafting trip.

Christian, our guide, explains that the river is "a little higher than normal" and "a little rougher" than normal. This meant nothing to any of us, because none of us had any idea either how *high* or how *rough* the river was *normally*. Plus, the twins and I were high, and most of the other foreigners were buzzing from their Chu Hi's.

We're all wearing life jackets, long sleeve thermal shirts or sweatshirts with hoodies, t shirts underneath, helmets, long jeans, and boots. Our clothing was heavy and I momentarily thought to myself *damn nigga, if you go into the water your ass is gonna sink,* but since that's what Christian had told us to wear, that's what we all were wearing. I quickly erased that idea because it immediately brought me down off my high, and I wanted to be high.

The trip had been planned for a couple of weeks. It was too late to cancel I guess, we were there at the river and everyone was amped about the expedition, the idea of cancelling never even materialized. After a really, *really* long "orientation" given on the banks of the river by Christian, we all climbed into our rafts, with each raft having it's own "professional tour guide" as the anchor of the raft. It was his job to keep us safe, to lead and steer us as we made our way along the river and over the rapids. I was thinking this was going to last an hour or so and it was going to be fun and kinda wild, like a water roller coaster or some such shit. We all pile into our rafts. In mine, there's me, the twins, B, a cat named Fred, an Australian dude named Paul, and our guide, or 'captain', and a tall muscular American dude named Roger. Rog looked capable.

We're still on the banks of the river and I'm looking for seat belts. Or straps. Or Velcro. Or *some shit* to tie us into the raft. Roger sees me looking around in the raft and asks me what I'm looking for. "Where's the fucking seat belt, man?" He laughs his ass off. "Dude, if you were strapped to this thing and we went over you'd drown, bro." *Oh yeah, that's right.* If you get into a car accident, you don't want to be thrown from the car, thus seatbelts. If you get into a rafting accident, you *do* want to be thrown from the raft so you can maneuver yourself without a heavy-ass raft strapped to your waist. That might not be a great thing floating down a river. A little disconcerting, but whatever, what do I know?

We push off from the edge of the river. For about thirty seconds, the river is relatively calm and slow, then we round a corner that is jutting out into the river and covered with trees and suddenly the river opens up into what looks and sounds like Niagara Falls to me. My high immediately disappeared and was replaced with complete awe and terror. The momentousness of the situation suddenly dawns on me and before we know it the river is raging all around us. We're barreling over the water, with the rain coming down in sheets and we can barely see a thing in front of us.

Rog starts yelling "Left! Left!" which means that the guys on the right side of the boat are supposed to stick their oars in and push so that the raft itself can go left. However, we're confused and the guys on the left is paddling instead of the guys on the right, and we're now headed directly towards what looked to me, again, like Niagara Falls. I'm thinking, "Holy shi...", and within a few seconds we're at the waterfall.

Time seemed to stop. Silence. Then in a giant whoosh, we go over the waterfall. The front of the raft comes crashing down on a wave, the raft flips over and I see Rog go careening over me. Silence. I'm now underwater. Less than a minute into this damn river we're all overboard.

Now, let me say, I didn't know what the fuck had just happened. All I knew was that suddenly I was underwater, under the raft, which had flipped on top of us, and I couldn't see anything, and I'm sinking, and it's cold and dark and wet and I'm moving forward at the same time while under the water and I'm sinking.

I'm flailing my arms, sucking in water and trying to swim towards up, but I don't really know exactly which way up is because the raft is on top of me and I can't see. I'm flailing my arms and my boots feel like they're made of lead. I'm panicking, using all the breath I have, *I can't wrap my head around what the fuck is happening.*

As I'm sinking deeper underneath the blackness of the raft I started thinking, *no way, man. No way is this happening today. No way am I drowning out here in this fucking river in Japan. A is home with Taiyo and pregnant with Asia and I won't get to see Asia born and A's gonna be really fucking pissed that I died today...*And then I felt something hard and sharp tear across my shin. *What the fuck is that scraping my leg? Fuck, it's cold.*

I'm sinking, yes, even with the fucking life jacket. I don't know how or why. I just was. Sinking and it's dark and I'm petrified and terrified and I couldn't breathe—and then I thought *Fuck this, man, swim your fucking black ass to the top of this river right the fuck now.* And I did.

Somehow I made it above the river and could see that I was floating downstream really fast. I couldn't see anyone and then B, the same cat who thought to become a pedophile, pops his head above the water a few feet away from me. We both desperately attempt to grab the raft floating a few feet in front of us.

After what felt like an eternity, we somehow managed to grab hold. I'm thinking, *thank you god, thank you god, thank you god!* But it's over, the raft is upside-down and our legs are dangling underneath it. I'm facing the opposite direction from where the raft is traveling, still gasping for air while still moving down the rapid-ass river.

B is on the other side of the raft and I scream to him, "WHAT THE FUCK, MAN! YOU ALL RIGHT?" I'm holding onto the edge of the raft with all my might and he says, "Yeah, mate, I'm foine, wheh's everybaudy else?" I look around and suddenly behind us Rog pops his head out of the water and he's literally screaming, "Help me! Help me!" and he's reaching out to us while going under at the same time. B looks back at me and says, "We've gotta flip it oh-vah," and I scream, "HOW MAN?!" I've got my back facing the direction we're traveling. I'm thinking, *if we try to flip this thing over, there's a chance of me sinking into the fucking river again* and I don't want to do that. B shouts, "Kick it from underneath! Let's kick toge-thah!" So we start kicking from underneath the water and the raft somehow flips over. The raft is dragging us almost helplessly downstream and then under the water I feel another sharp rip at my thigh.

I scream out in pain and as a knee jerk reaction, I cling tighter to the raft. My will to live has increased by the moment. I get a good grip on the edge of the raft, grab one of the ropes and heave myself over with all my might. B does the same, and we both come tumbling into the raft together.

I'm exhausted, cold, wet and I still can't quite understand what's going on. The raft is still floating downstream and I'm thinking, *holy shit, holy shit, holy shit dude, what the fuck just happened and why are you not dead? Weren't you just dying? You gotta get outta this raft RIGHT NOW and get your ass onto the earth and calm the fuck down.*

Suddenly, Rog's head bobs back up and down, he's reaching out, screaming "HELP ME!" but there are no oars. Then I see the other people who were in the raft with us. The twins and Paul are floating downstream in the water, but there's no sign of Fred. One of the twins is maybe 40 feet ahead of us and he's holding onto one of the oars with his feet up in front of him. His back is facing downstream, exactly like Christian had told us to do. His twin brother is floating about 20 feet away from the raft on the other side of the river. I still don't see Fred and just then, like a god from the afterlife, Fred suddenly emerges holding an oar. He swims up to the raft, clambers in, and sticks out the oar for Rog to grab onto. Rog climbs inside, looking like a tall shaggy, shivering, wet dog. Rog is petrified, he's in shock. Paul and the twins continue floating downstream.

Eventually, we were able to maneuver the raft over to Paul and the twins. They are rescued. As a battered but unified group we steer the raft towards the river's edge.

I climb out of the raft shaking. *Did I really almost die?* I wasn't sure. I walk up the banks of the river to higher ground and fall to my knees, and then I notice my jeans are ripped at the knee and the flesh of my skin on top of my kneecap is all torn up and bloody. My thigh on my other leg is also torn and bleeding.

All I can think at this point is *I didn't die, I didn't die, what the fuck, what the fuck.* Then I start thinking, *Thank God I don't have to tell A that I died today. Thank you God. Thank you God. She won't be mad at me when she finds out I died, because I didn't die.*

Suddenly Christian's raft pulls up to the banks of the river and he asks us all if we want to continue, reassuring us that "that was the roughest part of the river," and everyone except yours truly climbs back into the raft and continues down the river. Fuck that.

I opt to sit in the back of Christian's station wagon with his wife and his newborn son. I'm sitting there, sopping wet, and thinking *I gotta go home.* After the near-death experience, the group celebrates with a barbeque near a small bridge that spans the river. Everyone is laughing, high fiving and drinking. Then out of nowhere B, with his crazy ass, decides to dive off the bridge into the river. Australians are fucking crazy. Later we drive back to Nagoya and I'm sitting quietly in the back of the car with my knee burning, thinking to myself, *Seriously, man, you almost died?*

We return to Nagoya and everyone piles out of the car at Nagoya Station. We say our goodbyes and then I head into the subway and hop the train, looking and feeling like I'd been attacked by a bear. The Japanese people are staring at me, this tall, disheveled, dreadlocked black guy, and all I'm thinking is *thank god for all of y'all.*

I get off the train at Motoyama station and walk the long walk up the hill towards my apartment, put the key in the door, walk inside, slip off my shoes, and walk towards the kitchen, where A is cooking. She takes a look at me, looks at my ripped pants and asks "dou shita", *what happened?*

I tell her that I almost drowned. She nods, looks disapprovingly at me, then return to what she was doing and that was the end of it, for her.

White Water Aftermath

The rafting incident brought everything that I'd been doing prior too close to home. I had come closer to death than I ever had in my life before that moment. It made me temporarily take stock of what I was doing, but as an addict, behavior is very hard to change. I wanted, needed, searched for, and found more willing women than I knew what to do with. *The more you get, the more you want.* I wanted a lot to begin with, and I was getting more than I ever bargained for and *it took over me. It was like a monster, and it scared me.*

What did I expect? I was running around, DJing, putting on events, spreading myself all over the city, spending time in H's car driving to and from midnight performances miles out of town, and creeping into my house sometimes at 7 A.M. Sometimes my wife was there, more than not she was not.

I was slipping in and out of love hotels and going to women's apartments and still occasionally hitting up the sex shops and massage ladies, and it was never enough. I was craven. All this, while my wife was either hanging out with her family or cooped up at home with our son, pregnant with our next child and trying her best to be a wife. After all, she was a newly married, young Japanese woman caught up in the sordid lifestyle of her middle-aged, black American/Jamaican "husband".

Bizarrely, selfishly, *stupidly,* at the time I felt slightly betrayed by *her.* Since she wasn't home much, I felt it *entitled* me to be out doing my dirt. *I* was feeling betrayed, while I was out doing all the betraying.

There Is A Light

Things weren't going especially well during those last months of my wife's pregnancy with Asia, and the rafting episode was portentous of things to come. I thought things might change somehow after the rafting experience, but they didn't. As the days counted down for my wife to give birth to our daughter, I saw her less and less. Sometimes she paid quick visits to our apartment, but these were only peppered in between the days and weeks she was spending at her parents' place, which led us to grow even further apart, which led to less communication. Eventually, my wife and I became almost completely estranged from each other. I don't know why I thought another child would make our situation better. But I did.

For about a second everything seemed like it was going to work out. When Asia Jade made her entrance in late July, one month after my near drowning, she was born a month prematurely. I received a text from my wife, saying the doctors had decided to induce labor, but I was too "busy" to go to the hospital to see her. By the time I went to visit my wife and Asia in the hospital, Asia looked sickly, she was tiny and her eyes looked jaundiced and weak. Newborns never look exactly "beautiful" but Asia looked especially raw, like she wasn't really "ready" to come out yet. She was *really tiny*, but my wife seemed more relieved than anything, for the pregnancy to be over. It was as though she hadn't just given birth to her own child, but rather, like she'd just seen someone else give birth, and she behaved like she was simply relieved the whole thing was finished.

I was confused and worried about our new daughter, but, I thought since she didn't seem too bothered by Asia's condition, then I shouldn't be either. A week or so later, my wife left the hospital and promptly moved back to her family's house. Somehow, I still thought everything would work itself out. I figured with two children now, a boy and a girl, my wife would come around and we'd live happily ever after. It didn't quite work out that way.

Now, with two grandchildren, A's mother took complete control of them, as well as A's mind. Unbeknownst to me, my family was in jeopardy. However, I was too preoccupied with my projects, other women, and work to notice that my marriage was desperately on the rocks. I convinced myself that everything would eventually work out, despite the fact that I hadn't changed my behavior. Even after the rafting incident, even after my daughter being born unhealthy, even after all this, still no change. Now, my wife was almost never home, but we still had our little two-bedroom apartment, I was making money, our children were now healthy, and the bills were getting paid.

But here is the rub, I was use to my wife not being home. Instead of being stung by her absence, I embraced it. Instead of allowing the loneliness and silence to bother me, I took a look at my life, my magazine, my music, my parties, clubs and festivals, and I dove headfirst into all of it. I was determined to make *something* work.

>Chapter 10

Club Maverick

I become a club promotor

In between teaching, DJing and supervising my magazine staff of five, I had plenty on my hands. *RAN* Magazine had grown exponentially by this time—we were printing thirty-six glossy, heavy-weighted pages, bimonthly and had an online presence, that could compete with any magazine company in the world. My name was also getting out for organizing and promoting numerous events around town. My moniker DJ Maddlove, was becoming more important to me than myself, or my marriage.

I had no time for being a husband to A, but I was doing my best to be daddy to Taiyo and Asia. I loved both of them like crazy and they loved me back. I'd visit A's family's house and go upstairs and play with Taiyo and Asia. We kept up with the English lessons I was giving their family, but it seemed like a show than a real lesson. I was antsy whenever I was in their house, it felt foreign and forced. So, I'd rush through the lessons so I could return to the streets. Once I was out, I would fly through Sakae like a bull in a China shop.

I Heard You've Been Asking About Me

Summer was ending and my son's 3rd birthday was approaching. At this time, his sister was only a few months old. One day, "A" brought Asia home from her family's house and I noticed that Asia's eyes had cleared up. I held Asia in my arms and she was looking directly at me for the very first time, *seeing me*, and I was elated.

"A" had *kind of* moved back into our apartment but was still waking up every day and heading out to her family's place. "A" would leave, only to return in the evening to put the babies to bed and then fall out herself. She had no time or energy for me, and most of my time and energy was being expended out in the streets of Nagoya.

I heard through the grapevine that some woman had been asking around town for me. Turns out she was the owner and manager of a Japanese-only nightclub located in Fushimi called JMAXX, which at the time was playing techno only, with no non-Japanese customers, and was dying a slow death. JMAXX hadn't jumped on the hip hop/reggae/R&B bandwagon like all the other clubs and was losing customers. Most of the foreign population in Nagoya had never even heard of it, even though it was only two blocks away from ID, C.R.E.A.M., Emporium, Steps, and all of the other clubs that catered to mixed crowds.

Apparently, prior to my arrival to Nagoya, JMAXX had had a "black music night," but some Africans had gotten into a fight, and the management decided from that point not to allow foreigners in anymore.

Five years later the manager of that club was looking for *me* to be the miracle worker to resuscitate her dying venue. Irony.

According to the rumor, the manager had decided to revitalize the club to appeal to a diverse crowd. She knew about the huge crowds that ID Bar and CREAM were bringing in, and had decided to turn her club into an international spot. This meant switching up the format from techno to hip hop, and of course she'd now have to allow in all foreigners in including Africans. Why not cash in on some of the international yen that was passing hands nightly in Sakae? She'd heard I was the one who could save her dying venue, owing to the success of my magazine, and my ability to pull both Japanese and non-Japanese to my events.

So, H set up the meeting between Ms Isobe, myself, and my wife.

I wanted my wife to meet Ms. Isobe because I didn't want to cause any more curiosity in her mind about who I was working with and where I was. I figured it might score me a couple points with my marriage. I wanted my wife to the think, to feel, that not only was I being sought after by a club owner, but I was also *introducing you to her* so there's no mystery in this particular situation. I also felt that I needed someone I could completely trust with me, someone who had me, and my family's best interests. That person was my wife.

Despite our not having particularly open channels of communication at this time, I convinced A to leave the children with her family, and we take the subway down into Fushimi. It's the first time we've been together anywhere without our children, since we'd had them. It feels like a date that's going bad. We're not communicating with each other at all.

We walk the two or three blocks to the club without saying anything to each other, and I realize this is the first time my wife and I have ventured out of the Motoyama/Higashiyama area for months. She's still exceptionally beautiful to me, and even though she's just recently given birth to our daughter, she looks thin, lithe, athletic and stylish. She's wearing a pair of jeans I bought her and black leather boots. She looks *hot.*

We enter the club and walk down a long flight of stairs. The club is literally located underground. It's a huge old-school disco style club, huge by Japanese standards anyway. It's about as big as a medium sized American supermarket, which is gigantic for a club in Japan. But, as I said, it's old, *really old,* like something you'd see in Saturday Night Fever. There's a big old disco ball hanging from the ceiling, it's missing more than a few of its tiny mirrors, and it's absolutely gigantic, like it could have been one of the first ones ever made. There are grey-ish, gold lame curtains on the walls, some with spider webs. There are old wooden tables and chairs scattered randomly. Along one of the walls there were about half a dozen booths with ripped leather seats and sunken cushions.

There are floor to ceiling dirty cracked mirrors in some places, bizarre plastic mannequins in others. There's a giant dance floor in the middle, surrounded by roman looking columns. At the front of the dance floor, there's the most decrepit looking DJ booth I'd ever seen. There was a pair of turntables that looked like they hadn't been used in 20 years. The whole place was in need of a paint job and a total make-over. Clubs never look good when the lights are on, but this place almost didn't look real. It was a relic of a time long gone by. *No wonder no one comes here,* I thought.

After walking around the club a bit, my wife and I end up standing near the bar not talking to each other. I don't quite know what to say. Here we are in a club, waiting on some woman to show up, to discuss what, I wasn't really sure.

The silence is thick and the air is stale inside the club. My wife and I are waiting, silently, for what seems like an inordinately long amount of time. Just as I'm beginning to think *fuck this,* Ms. Isobe saunters up smiling, bows, sticks out her hand, and greets us. She's in her 40's. Her hair is pulled back and she's wearing long pants, a simple buttoned up top and glasses. She looks like she could be attractive but I can't really tell. She smiles professionally and leads us to a back room with glittery gold beads hanging from the ceiling, like those you'd see in a 70's porn movie. I notice Ms. Isobe, looks and appears like what H would look like if H were 10 or 12 years older.

Together, my wife and I sit in one of the old booths with Ms. Isobe seated across from us. She asks me what I think of her club, which honestly looks like a mockup of an old beaten up disco from the 70's, rather than a modern dance club, but I tell her I'm impressed with its size. My wife is translating but appears to have absolutely zero interest in the entire affair. She doesn't want to be there.

Ms. Isobe tells my wife she wants me to help turn her club into an international nightspot, and wants me to manage and promote the club, hire new DJs, create some high-profile international events, bring in some *gaijin* security, and find an entirely new bilingual bar staff to work the bar. Essentially, she wants a total re-branding of her nightspot and she wants me to do it. Quickly.

She offers me two hundred thousand yen monthly, about $2000. My duties will be to work at the club on Saturdays, from 10pm until 2pm. Her salary offer includes the time I'll be spending outside the club doing promotions, looking for DJs, doing research, handing out flyers, etc. This is great, who can't use an extra 2K a month? At the time it was a stellar offer, and I accept through my wife. Isobe-san tells me she wants to get started immediately. Ms. Isobe expressed that she wants to have the first event one month from now. I tell her it's possible, but I'll need to meet her staff first, and actually see what's what in the club. I didn't even know if the DJ booth worked. *I didn't even know if she had a staff.*

She asks me specifically what I'd do to change the club itself. I immediately tell her the gold beads have to go. I tell her the booths had rips and tears in the leather seats and they made the club look cheap and old. I tell her the flaky gold painting on the walls looks dingy and suggest changing the color of the inside of the club. I ask her if the huge disco ball was really necessary, and if there's any way to improve the looks of the DJ booth. She's giving me the impression that the changes I'm suggesting are really possible, that she just might paint the place, fix the DJ booth, and somehow modernize the club, before we have our grand reopening in one month.

We stand up, Isobe-san shake's my wife's hand and bows politely, robotically, and says, arigatou gozaimasu to my wife, then shake my hand, and in the exact same tone says arigatou gozaimasu to me. Then she interrupts herself mid-sentence, saying she's been thinking of changing the name of the club, and would I please give some thought to a new name as well. I was surprised, and elated. I thought *whoa man, you're going to have an opportunity to name this place too??*

Ms. Isobe, my wife and I stand looking at each other in awkward silence, no one saying anything, and after a moment I decide *well I guess that's it.* We all bow a few times at each other again, and my wife and I turn to leave. Bowing is like smiling in Japan.

When we get upstairs, my wife turns to me, looks at me, bows slightly in my direction and says "omedetou gozaimasu", which means "congratulations", in Japanese. I was slightly startled and told her "thank you", then she turned away without saying anything else and took off, leaving me standing there wondering if I should go with her or…She didn't look back. She clearly didn't want me to follow her. She didn't want to be with me, and she didn't want me to be with her. I felt sad, but at the same time excited about the opportunity to create something at this new club. It felt triumphant actually, like the culmination of everything creative that I'd done to that point while I was in Japan. I was now going to be the Manager/Promoter/"Producer", of my own club.

For weeks before, A had been telling me she needs a car. Now, here was an opportunity for me to buy her a car within a few months. It was right on time, since we now had two children and I didn't want her either taking the train, or riding her bicycle with two children in tow.

I was proud that I was making enough money to sustain our household without my wife having to work. I had *never* envisioned being able to do this in my life, it wasn't even an option. My history and environment had taught me that it was an *absolute necessity* for both parents to work, and in my mind there was no choice but for my wife to work: This is how I had been conditioned to think. Brainwashed. *Hoodwinked.*

In Japan, I was the only breadwinner in my family. I was buying the food, paying the bills, providing dough for whatever little outings we had, and still holding onto enough cash for my own "extracurricular" activities. I was taking care of my family like the white dudes on TV I saw growing up.

I thought to myself, *nigga you are the man.* All my hard work with the magazine, DJing, events, promoting, and just being visible in the scene of Nagoya was about to pay off.

I was about to become the producer of a nightclub just outside the main nightlife district, with a hefty little salary to boot. I had a beautiful new daughter to compliment my beautiful wife and son, my regular gig teaching, my successful projects, plus my extracurricular activities with H, N and the love motels.

I was living on the edge and balling like a rock star, but unbeknownst to me, my life was just about to unravel.

I felt empowered and emboldened by the fact that I was making all the money and paying all the bills. It wasn't that I felt superior to my wife, comparisons weren't necessary. What it was, was that I felt that I had surpassed my own expectations for my life. I had been broke nearly my whole life up until this point. I had never made more than 3 thousand dollars in one month, except for residuals I had made on a Chevrolet Neon commercial I'd shot in LA years before, but those residuals had long dried up.

Before Japan, I never had enough money to buy anyone much of anything, let alone pay bills for anyone else. But here I was paying *all* the bills, and still having enough money to buy appliances for our apartment, clothing for my wife and children. I kept the refrigerator stocked with food, and still managed to keep money in our savings account. I felt like I was *winning*, even while I was losing—my family that is.

Come September, Taiyo has his second birthday, and things are going decently. Except for a massive amount of promotion, I hadn't properly started working at the club yet. Eventually, I arranged a huge opening night for the end of the month, complete with live performances from a sick-ass electronic *shamisen* player named Okita, a couple rappers I knew from town, an acoustic band, pole dancers, Nagoya celebrity DJs, plus myself on the decks. I had invited everyone who'd shown up for Springfest and it looked like we were going to have a massive opening night. Things were actually going pretty smoothly, my wife had temporarily returned home, and I had shifted my relationship with H away from anything sexual to a more business-like situation; she was now my "assistant," and she was happy to be just that, or so I thought.

Ms. Isobe Means Business

Ms. Isobe turned out to be an all business, no joke middle-aged Japanese woman. After that first meeting with my wife, she never smiled, never had anything pleasant to say, and never took any of my advice as to how to increase business at her club. She always looked like she had a stick up her ass, was always bespectacled, was always dressed in proper business attire. She had attitude to spare and H bristled at having to work underneath Isobe. She didn't show it, but I could tell. After that first meeting between Isobe, myself, and my wife, I had asked H to take over translation duties because my wife was too busy with Taiyo and Asia. I conveniently didn't tell my wife that H was going to take over, I simply just didn't mention anything at all about it.

We set out to re-launch the club in late September, the week after Taiyo's birthday. For whatever reason, Ms. Isobe had decided to re-name the club, Maverick. She didn't care for any of the names H and I had come up with. The only thing she cared for was the tagline I came up with, "The Next Nightclub Experience", in which she still uses to this day.

H and I were so busy with promotions and gathering the artists that neither of us had time to visit the club until the night before the grand opening was set to take place. We'd both thought that Ms. Isobe had at least heeded some of the changes I had suggested, but when we showed up to make sure things were ready for the grand opening, the club was exactly the same as it had been on the first night I went there. Nothing had changed. The spider webs were still there, the rips in the leather seats, the cracked windows, the huge disco ball, the dingy gold curtains, the ridiculous gold beads, everything. The old wooden furniture was still all in the exact same place it had been the night we had had our first discussion. In fact, it seemed like no one had been inside the club since that night. H and I were absolutely flabbergasted, but by now, it was too late to think about why nothing had been changed.

Over seven hundred people turned out for opening night, and it was, by any standard, a humongous, smashing success, and I was ecstatic to be able to add another feather to my already heavily feathered cap. Festivals, events, music, modeling, a magazine, voice-overs, a bevy of Japanese mistresses, a wife and two beautiful children, and now, club manager/promoter. I thought to myself, *Nigga, you are winning.* And I was, kinda.

Ms. Isobe Doesn't Hear Me

For the next month, A was back home much more often. I had successfully navigated my relationship with H away from anything sexual or intimate. H was now my full-fledged, indisputable assistant. She was doing my translations, making business calls for *RAN,* arranging meetings with potential advertisers, working at the club on Saturday nights and helping to promote. After those Saturday nights working at the club H would drive me back home, to Motoyama. My wife was home with the babies, Asia was a newborn, and I was still out in the streets.

October rolled around and "A" starts digging in deeper about the fact that she needs a car. I figured I'd save some dough for a few months and buy her something used. November comes and I'd saved about four grand and I had my eye on a small white Toyota station wagon. The numbers at Maverick had dropped precipitously since opening night. Not blaming anyone, but Ms. Isobe wasn't listening to any of my advice. I'd told her to hire at least one bartender who could speak English, so the foreign customers would feel more welcome. She didn't. Told her to make a schedule of her special events so the employees knew what was happening on any given night. Didn't do that either. Told her to put a sign on the corners nearest the club, since the club was literally underground and a bit removed from what was happening in either Fushimi or Sakae. Didn't do that either. I asked her to make flyers that I could give out and she said they were too expensive.

"How are you promoting the club?" I asked her.

"Website," she said.

"How do you expect to get foreign customers in here with a Japanese-only website?" She hadn't thought of that.

We were not getting on well, but still, she expected numbers like she had seen on that opening night.

Middle of November, Ms. Isobe tells me she's cutting my salary in half, with no forewarning and no real explanation. We had no contract, no signed forms, nothing except a verbal agreement, and now that verbal agreement was broken. My salary dropped from two hundred thousand yen per month, to one hundred thousand yen. She had paid me once, for the month of October, and was now telling me she wasn't paying me what she had promised. I was heated but accepted it. *Fuck it*, I figured, I'm basically DJing 4 nights a month, had placed a couple half page ads in RAN, and was promoting the club on my Facebook page. I figured it was still worth it for the grand a month.

Ms. Isobe continued to not take any of my advice. She had put me "in charge" of the DJs, and I'd brought in Ghost Willy to spin, but within a few weeks she was telling me we were playing too much black music, and that she wanted to have her old techno DJs blended into the rotation. "Aren't you trying to develop a more mixed crowd? Hip hop and reggae are what young Japanese want to hear..." I told her. She said she wanted to try to bring back some of her old customers, and thought they wouldn't like so much black music. She was still stuck in a moment from the club's glory days that had long since disappeared. She still wanted droves of Japanese to come to her club and line dance to blaring, soul-less techno music. I had no choice but to accept her DJs, but it was tragic. On the nights that we did have a crowd, as soon as her DJ got on the tables, the crowd would disappear.

She also held fast to her idea that flyers were "too expensive", so there was nothing tangible for me to promote with. There was nothing on the website announcing the changeover from a Japanese only venue, to the one Ms. Isobe had envisioned when she first reached out to find me. It became obvious that Ms. Isobe had no intent to accept any of my suggestions. I began to wonder what I was doing there.

Fuck it. *Take the money and run.* I kept going. Did all kinds of stupid crazy promotions, "Obama Night," "Brooklyn Night," "Dancehall and Calypso Night", "Red White and Blue night". I brought in my man Hoss Funk for "Freaks Come Out At Night" night. I tried to bring in Nagoya "celebrity" DJs. There was a second room in the club and I made that room the electronic music room. Ms. Isobe hired pole dancers and created drink specials. We tried everything. I did my best to make Maverick pop, despite her unwillingness to cooperate *and* despite her salary cut but it just wasn't happening. The location was weird and Ms. Isobe just wasn't cooperating. Besides, I myself wasn't feeling the whole *old-club-becomes-new-club-while-still-being-old-club* thing, and with ID Bar and C.R.E.A.M. just up the street, it just wasn't happening. The club, and my promotion of it, was failing. *I was failing,* but I wanted to make good on buying my wife a car. She wanted one, and it was my responsibility to provide whatever she wanted.

>Chapter 11

THE CAR

She drives me crazy

In the beginning of December, I buy my wife a car and have it delivered. I came home one afternoon with the car keys, hoping to surprise her. I enter our apartment while she's tending to our babies. I stand in front of her for a few seconds, long enough to get her attention. As soon as a look of curiosity cloaked her face, I flashed the keys and asked, "What do you think these are for?"
Instead of elation, she gives me a shocked, open-mouthed, deer in the headlights look.

"*Kuruma?*" she says, "...a car..?" I respond with a big smile on my face, "Sou dayo, kuruma desu!" "Yes, it's a car!" I'm expecting her to be excited, happy, something. Instead her look of shock quickly changes to one of concern and she says to me, "Daveed, what are we going to do about rent? Do you have enough money for rent?" and Rent?!

"Yes I do, but why are you worried about rent?" I snap back. "You said you wanted a car, so I bought you a car! Didn't you say you wanted a car? Don't you want to see it?" Silence. She's looking around the apartment as if she's searching for something, then she says, "Daveed, what about *rent?* How much did the car cost?"

By this time, I'm beginning to get pissed. More accurately, I'm offended by the fact that not only does she not seem the least bit interested in this car which she'd been asking me for, and which was now sitting in the parking lot of our driveway, but she seemed suddenly much more interested in our rent, which we hadn't had any problems paying since having moved into the place two years before.

She's staring at me, waiting for my response about her rent question. Her stare is burrowing its way into my brain, into my heart. It was the first time she had properly looked at me in maybe 2 years, but it wasn't a look of approval, of gratitude, of love, it was a look that said to me *you've done something stupid Trevor.*

"A, why are you worried about rent? I always pay rent! Don't worry about rent right now, I bought you a car.", I say. I hold up the keys again and shake them close to her face, trying hard to hide the fact that I can't believe she's showing absolutely no interest in this car I'd just worked and saved for, for the last two months. Instead, she looks at the keys as though I'm dangling a cockroach in my hand. She looks back at me and says condescendingly, "*Da-veed,* why you say don't worry about rent, we have to worry about rent *Da-veed,* what will we do if we can't pay rent?" I flipped.

"CAN YOU STOP WORRYING ABOUT THE RENT FOR A MINUTE PLEASE? I ALWAYS PAY RENT AND IF I DON'T HAVE ENOUGH FOR RENT I'LL WORK SOME MORE AND I'LL PAY THE RENT JUST LIKE I ALWAYS DO! OKAY? I DON'T UNDERSTAND WHY YOU ARE SO WORRIED ABOUT RENT ALL OF A SUDDEN! SINCE WHEN HAVE I NOT BEEN ABLE TO PAY RENT? I'M BUSTING MY ASS TRYING TO GIVE YOU WHATEVER YOU WANT AND YOU DON'T GIVE A SHIT! YOU DON'T CARE ABOUT A FUCKING THING I'M TRYING TO DO AROUND HERE DO YOU?" She gets up and walks out of the room. I follow behind her.

"THIS IS SOME BULLSHIT!" I continue. "I TRY TO GIVE YOU ANYTHING YOU WANT! I'M WORKING 2 AND 3 AND 4 JOBS TO KEEP THIS HOUSE UP AND YOU'RE NEVER FUCKING HOME ANYWAY! AND NOW I'VE BOUGHT YOU THIS CAR YOU'VE BEEN ASKING FOR AND YOU CAN'T EVEN SAY THANK YOU? YOU DON'T EVEN WANT TO SEE IT? FUCK YOU!" Mistake.

She gathers up the babies, takes the keys from me and heads out. I don't know exactly what to do. I'm standing in our apartment and eventually I head downstairs and the "new" used car I'd bought for her is gone.

For the next three months, she's back at her family's house again. Maybe once a week, if that often, she'd come home to our place and pick up clothes for the babies, but that was it. We were effectively separated for all intents and purposes. She was driving around in the car I'd bought her, staying at her family's house, and I was doing my thing trying to put some life into the club. Still, even with her gone, I bought all kinds of stuff I thought "we" needed for our place. I bought track lights, a microwave, another television, and stuff for the babies, etc. I was still doing what I thought I was "supposed" to do as her husband, as a father but that *car* started to feel more like a curse than like a blessing.

>Chapter 12

New York State Of Mind

Lower East Side blues

My relationship with Ms. Isobe was going south and the club was taking an absolute dive. One afternoon Ms. Isobe tells me she's going to have to cut my salary again, down from a hundred thousand yen a month to fifty thousand yen and I simply wasn't having it. I had grown to despise her. She hadn't cooperated with any of my suggestions to improve the numbers at the club but now she wanted to cut my salary, again. I received the news from H, since by now H and Ms. Isobe had established communication apart from me. I told H with no hesitation to tell her to go fuck herself. She'd already cut my salary once, and now she wanted to cut it down to a quarter of what she'd promised me? Plus, I was still doing the same amount of work I'd been doing based on the original offer? *Oh hell no.*

I told H to tell Isobe that I didn't want the job anymore, that I'd quit, and was no longer interested in working for the club. When H informed Ms. Isobe that I wasn't going to accept the salary cut and that I was going to quit instead, she told H that if I didn't take the salary cut and if I didn't continue doing the gig, she'd prosecute me. I laughed my ass off and told H to tell her to do whatever she wanted but that my days at Maverick were effectively over.

I decided I needed to get out of Japan for a minute, to clear my head and try to figure out what my next move was going to be. I was still in sporadic contact with my wife. She wasn't coming to the apartment at all and we were now basically just texting each other again. "How are you and the babies?" "Fine," she'd reply and that was it. No details, nothing personal. I wasn't seeing her, wasn't feeling her.

I informed my wife that Ms. Isobe had cut my salary and that I had decided to quit the club and that Ms. Isobe had threatened to "prosecute" me, but my wife had no response. I told her I was planning on taking a vacation out of the country to think about what to do about Maverick. No response.

I bought a ticket to New York, told H my plan and immediately after H bought a ticket of her own. I didn't ask her to come with me, but I also didn't ask her not to. Somehow I knew she'd end up in New York with me. She asked me where I was staying, and I had no real idea, I figured I'd hook up with old friends, maybe stay in my man Tony's apartment in Chinatown, stay with family, something. I hadn't given it much real thought so, she said she'd get us a sublet anywhere I wanted in the city. By this time she wasn't letting me do anything on my own. I had allowed H to infiltrate every aspect of my life, and even though we weren't having sex, she was still my surrogate wife.

I flew to New York, spent one night in Tony's place in Chinatown, and H showed up at Kennedy the day after. We spent the next six days on First Avenue in the Lower East Side in a wood-floored apartment with a big queen sized bed and an old television. We made time traversing south Manhattan and Brooklyn. H was making it clear that she wanted to be with me and was willing to do anything to make that a reality. Here she was, after all, in New York, with me, with us in a sublet that she was footing the bill for, while my wife was in Japan with our two children.

Even after the car episode, the lonely nights in our apartment, the cold responses and silent treatment, I still loved my wife. H was no comparison to my wife for me, even though she was doing everything my wife either wouldn't or couldn't' do. Even though my wife had gone cold, that place that she had touched inside of me years earlier was still smoldering. Being in New York reminded me of my own childhood, and these memories made me sentimental about how beautiful and perfect my wife had seemed to me when we were dating. I felt like even though things between us were no good, it was supposed to be *her* there in New York with me, and not H. I resented H for being there. If it wasn't my wife, then I wanted to be in my hometown *by myself,* hang out in clubs, walk around in the Village, visit family, do whatever. But there she was, tagging along like a stray cat. I hadn't asked her to come with me, so *why is she here?* I asked myself. She wanted us to hold hands and pretend we were a couple but I didn't want to pretend what I didn't feel. She didn't care. She was in her own dreamland. She was in New York, it was spring, and she was ecstatic. She bought all our food, paid for our room and transportation, and took us to see Rock Of Ages on Broadway. We took a double level tour bus uptown, and downtown to the South Street Seaport. We rode the Circle Line and visited ground zero. We ate cheesecake, hamburgers, falafels and I took her to Two Boots pizza in Alphabet City. We bought midnight snacks from a 24 hour bodega on First Avenue where the Arabic dude at the cash register told me "your wife is beautiful", without knowing that my wife was in Japan. Despite this, we actually had a really nice time despite my mixed emotions. I wondered what my wife was doing in Japan. I wondered if she knew I was in New York with H. I imagined her driving around with our babies in the car that I'd bought her, and wondered if she'd visited our apartment at all while I was gone.

Meanwhile, I'm in New York with H. I didn't want to want her, but I needed her. She wanted romance, excitement, and sex, and I, though we were having what appeared to be a great time, I was feeling overwhelmingly guilty about her being there. I felt emasculated due to needing her in my own city, away from Japan, but H didn't seem to mind at all. Every night, once we'd return to our place in the village, we'd climb into bed, and she'd start touching me. I could feel her hot breath kissing on my neck, and all it did was turn me off. On our last night, I gave in and we had sex. It wasn't much good to me, rote and mechanical, but H didn't care. She'd gotten what she wanted.

Couldn't she feel that I wasn't interested in her sexually? How could she not know? Afterwards, I rolled over and stayed awake all night feeling like my wife had watched the entire thing. I just knew that somehow, she knew I was in New York with H, and it terrified me. It made me feel that my marriage was completely over. It made me even angrier at H.

We flew back together and barely spoke on the airplane. The tension was incredible. She wanted a boyfriend experience while in New York and I wanted time away from my issues in Japan. Neither of us had gotten exactly what we had gone to New York seeking.

The Prelude To The End

A week after we returned to Japan, H arranged another, but very different meeting between Ms. Isobe, myself and my wife. The week in New York had given me a chance to think more deeply about my relationship with Ms. Isobe and Maverick. I had decided unequivocally to quit. I was perplexed at why Ms. Isobe had requested my wife be there instead of H. For five months, it had been myself and H elbow to elbow, shoulder to shoulder, dealing with Ms. Isobe, but suddenly Ms. Isobe wanted to deal with my wife? *Why?*

H deferred to Ms. Isobe, like a proper assistant should, but unbeknownst to me, they were secretly at war. Their personalities were very similar, but Ms. Isobe had a few years on H. The two of them seemed to be in a competition with each other for who could be more mechanical than the other. Whenever they spoke with each other, it was like watching a jousting match between two sexy Japanese female robots wearing business suits.

Either way, I had developed an infatuation with the stereotype of the strong, sexy, worldly, independent Japanese businesswoman precisely because so few of them existed, and now, I was caught between two of them. My wife, on the other hand, was a different stereotype altogether. In my mind, she was a combination of the traditional Japanese woman who stays at home cooking rice, and the young, energetic but innocent Japanese concubine she seemed to be when we met. The truth was, my wife was neither of these. She had outgrown her "innocent" phase long ago, as a result of having had our two children, but she had also turned back into somewhat of a traditional Japanese wife, the kind that doesn't talk to her husband, doesn't express any vestige of affection towards him, and essentially thinks he's a human wallet. She had also lost the energetic energy she'd had when we first met. The truth was, I wasn't sure who she was anymore.

It was definitely weird that Isobe wanted my wife at the meeting and not H, probably exactly because Isobe knew H was strong and smart, and my wife, well, she was someone Ms. Isobe figured she could have her way with. But H, man, H always translated what I said directly, without the frills, because I told her to. She never backed down from Ms. Isobe, while always being diplomatic and carrying herself with the utmost feminine class. No woman I met while I was in Japan carried herself with the self-assuredness, strength of character, and grace H had. She had built it up in herself as a result of all those years of watching her father abuse her mother. She was determined to be the author of her own story. She read books and knew what was in the international news. She had invented herself rather than allowing Japanese society to dictate who or how, or what she'd be. She was stealthy and professional and *so fucking on it.* She was there every night at Maverick until the very last person had left and then she'd go outside and wait in her car around the corner for me, and Ms. Isobe knew it. I think it got underneath Ms. Isobe's skin that H was such a staunch ally of mine. Even if H wasn't always exactly visible in the club, she was there. She was smarter than Ms. Isobe and did everything she could to protect *me,* and so, Ms. Isobe was scheming something on H. She wanted H out of the picture and planned to use my wife to make that happen, but I had no idea at the time. I should have known something was up.

>Chapter 13

Isobe Stabs Me In My Heart

Then the twist...

I didn't want to go to any fucking meeting. I just wanted to be done with Maverick and Ms. Isobe. I was making a quarter the money she had originally promised me, and I was barely five months into the job. Ms. Isobe had never listened to anything I asked her to do and walked around scowling. She asked my guests weird questions and scoffed at the few foreigners who came to her place. She seemed like she didn't want them, us, there at all, but without us, there would have been no one in her club.

Her bartenders couldn't speak a word of English and neither could her staff, but she was hoping to entertain an "international" crowd. *How?* That, plus the place still looked like an old disco. The underground location was hard to find, plus Ms. Isobe wouldn't spring for a sign. H and I had printed our own flyers with our own money but still, no more than a smattering of people had been showing up.

The meeting was arranged to take place at a coffee shop just across the street from Maverick. I had convinced my wife to come by telling her that Ms. Isobe wanted to prosecute me for wanting to quit the job. My wife reluctantly agreed to meet me at the Kinko's across the street, where we'd rendezvous and then head to the coffee shop. When she arrives my wife says to me, "meeting no basho wa doko desu ka?" *where is the meeting.* I gesture towards the Komeda, "asoko", I say, over there. I notice she's still wearing her wedding ring. I'm momentarily elated.

We head to the Komeda, located about a half block cattycorner from Maverick. When we arrive, it's mostly empty and dark, aside from two people. Outside it's daylight, but inside it may as well be night time. There's an older Japanese salaryman sipping coffee by himself in one of the booths closest to the register. Soft non-descript café music is piping from concealed speakers while one female employee feigns to look busy behind the counter.

I see Ms. Isobe and another woman sitting in another booth on the opposite side of the Komeda. I gesture to my wife to walk in front of me towards the booth where Ms. Isobe is sitting. Ms. Isobe stands up as we approach and bows and says "Konnichiwah. Genki Desu Ka? Sasshibourri da ne!" *good afternoon, are you good? It's been a long time,* to my wife. This is standard Japanese small talk. My wife responds with a small perfunctory bow of her own, "Konnichiwah. Genki desu. Sasshibourri da ne..." *good afternoon I'm fine, yes, it's been a while.* My wife doesn't look exactly happy to be there, but she is, and I'm proud of that. For whatever reason, I felt stronger with my wife there than I think I'd have felt if H had been there.

Isobe introduces the other woman as her assistant, and then we all sit down. My wife slides into the booth and I slide in after her. Ms. Isobe then sits down next to her assistant. *And it's on.*

The meeting starts relatively innocently. Isobe explains to my wife in Japanese why my salary has been cut. This is the first time the two of them have seen each other since our first meeting five or six months before. My wife is listening intently and seems to be empathizing with whatever Isobe is saying. I can't make out most of it because Isobe is talking extra fast, or so it seems. I'm sitting next to my wife who has taken keen interest in whatever Isobe is saying, and I'm thinking about *her,* how beautiful she looks, how straight her posture is, how clean her skin looks, and I'm intermittently glancing at her wedding ring, marveling to myself that we're still married, after all this shit, we're still married. The fact that she is still wearing her wedding ring is heartening and emboldening. *Maybe we can make it through this shit,* I'm thinking, *maybe she really doesn't know I went to New York with H.*

I sit up straight to match my wife's posture, and Ms. Isobe is droning on and on about the club and what we might have been able to do to salvage it. She starts telling my wife she's disappointed in the club, in me, that I hadn't delivered what she expected. She all but said that the club wasn't meeting her expectations solely because of me. She goes on and on, I could only decipher about thirty percent of what she was saying, and my wife wasn't translating a single word, she's just listening. From what I can make out, Ms. Isobe was dogging me. She's telling my wife all sorts of straight-up bullshit, and not mentioning anything about any of the ideas I'd shared with her, the requests I'd made for her to improve the club. The weird thing is that for whatever reason, Ms. Isobe didn't want me to quit, and that was why we were here. She was dragging my name through the dirt, but doing so while at the same time wanting to get my wife to convince me not to quit. Or so I thought. Either way, I'm heated. *You slimy bitch,* I'm thinking, *you cannot keep me at your bullshit club and then tell me you are going to prosecute me.*

Ms. Isobe stops talking finally, and there's a long silent pause. I'm not sure if it's my turn, or if it will ever be my turn. My head is down and when I realize no one is speaking I look up and everyone, including my wife, is looking at me. I wait momentarily for my wife to translate, but she doesn't. She's just looking at me waiting for me to respond to whatever Ms. Isobe has just said. *She's not on my side,* I think to myself. *She looks like my wife* but she's just another Japanese woman. "Ms. Isobe", I start out slowly, then I turn to my wife and say, "yaku shite kudasai ne", *please translate,* to which she coldly and absently replies "un", which basically means "okay" in Japanese. She's staring at me intently, it's the first time she's looked so directly at me in more than a year. Maybe two. Except for when I bought her the car.

I turn to Ms. Isobe, "Ms. Isobe, I asked you several times to hire an English-speaking bartender, you never did and still haven't. I asked you to put up signs, I asked you to make your staff aware of our events, I asked you to advertise, you didn't do any of that, but you DID cut my salary two times. I'm making a quarter of what you promised me . . ." My voice is rising, I'm bringing it directly to Ms. Isobe. I continue, "I don't know why you don't let me just quit the job. You're not helping me to do anything, and I don't know if you want to be successful."

I turn to look at my wife, waiting for her to translate what I'd said. It dawns on me that whatever it was Ms. Isobe had said, my wife completely agreed with *her*. She no longer had my back, and I think to myself *what a mistake you've made asking her to be here dude.*

Then Isobe starts talking about H. She's saying H's name, saying (in Japanese), "H does most of the work and H is a great assistant and H always works hard . . ." but, she says H has been absent for the last week, exactly during the week when I was absent. She says she was nervous about what may have happened to H. She tells my wife that she had called H's job the week before to discuss the situation of my wanting to quit but she says H's job tells her that she was in New York City on vacation for a week. And then she falls silent, looks at me coyly, and smiles. *Wait, what just happened? Did this bitch just tell my wife H was on vacation in New York last week, the same time I was there? Is that what she just said? Really?!* Really.

My wife is looking at me, eyes wide, and mouth open. She gets up, doesn't say a word, pushes past me, and walks out the door. I look at my wife walking out and then I look at Ms. Isobe and she's looking at me wryly, as if to say, *What? Is something wrong?* I get up to chase my wife, but first, I return a glare to Ms. Isobe. I've never wanted to strangle someone as much as I wanted to right then. I couldn't believe what had just happened.

I shoot outside. My wife is quickly rounding the corner. I run up right behind her. I can see she was struggling with her wedding ring, she wanted to take it off *right now.* I grab her arm, turn her around, but before I could say anything she's screaming, "YOU WENT TO NEW YORK WITH HER?! ARE YOU CRAZY? ARE YOU CRAZY?" at the top of her lungs, right there on the street. Japanese people do not yell in the street, ever, but there was my wife, yelling her ass off, right at *me,* while struggling with the ring on her ring finger. I guess she was right, I guess I was crazy.

I try to grab her arm, she's struggling with the ring. She gets it off and throws it across the street. It wasn't a casual toss either, she threw that ring like she meant it. I run and retrieve it. She's walking towards her car. The car I bought her. I chase her. She gets in and drives off. I'm left standing there in shock, looking down at her wedding ring in the palm of my hand. I don't know if I should go back inside and confront Ms. Isobe, try to follow my wife, or jump in front of an oncoming bus.

I return to the café and Ms. Isobe and her assistant are still sitting there, chatting nonchalantly as if nothing had happened. When they notice me, a sinister grin creeps across Ms. Isobe face. I wanted to go over and strangle her. But I couldn't, I was thinking about my wife, so I turned and left. I hop the subway. Home.

"A" isn't there, of course she isn't. She hadn't been there and she still wasn't. Our apartment suddenly felt like a small ghost town. Everything was so still and quiet. Taiyo and Asia weren't there. They hadn't been there very often recently. I stood in the doorway of our apartment wondering what I should do, what had just happened. It was pretty much all out in the open now. Suddenly. My wife now had concrete evidence about my ongoing relationship with H, but at the same time she didn't know exactly what had or hadn't happened in New York. There was still a chance. She still hadn't spoken up about what she either wanted to do or didn't want to do as far as our relationship. She had taken off the ring, which is hugely symbolic, but it didn't mean we weren't married anymore. But, she was staying at her family's place and being silent and she'd just found out I had essentially taken a vacation with the very woman she had told to leave her and her family alone. I was sure our marriage was over. But it wasn't. Yet.

>Chapter 14

PURGATORY

Don't shit where you sleep

Over the course of the next few months, I actually continued working at Maverick. Don't ask me why. Habit? Money? Stupidity? Ms. Isobe wasn't in the club much anyway, it was mostly her assistant, the bartenders, security, me, H, and the smattering of guests. Fuck it. I figured, my wife hadn't been acting like a wife for a year or more anyway, and even though she'd just tossed her wedding ring out into the street, what had changed really? Not much.

She didn't return home and didn't expressly make any demands on me after finding out H had been in New York the same time I was. Things between us just continued to silently deteriorate. We continued not seeing each other and she continued not responding to my text messages. However, on the few occasions when she did respond, she'd text something in *hiragana* or *katakana,* neither of which I could read, and she knew it. Our communication had evaporated and our relationship flat lined.

She even got a job. She started working in the bakery, in the bread section of a popular Japanese department store. I tried to come by her job a few times, tried to see if I could get her to talk to me, but she'd just tell me to leave and ignore me. She literally would walk to the back of the store, where I wasn't allowed, and stay there until I left. She instructed her coworkers to tell me to leave whenever I showed up. I was worried about the cops, worried about all kinds of shit, but still, I rolled through her store several times but she just wasn't trying to hear me.

So I kept working. I don't know exactly what compelled me to continue working at Maverick, and continue seeing H. Perhaps it was the little money I was making, or the fact that I wanted Maverick to be successful somehow. Or perhaps it was the routine, or the addiction to the projects that H and I were working on. Or perhaps it was a need for my relationship to continue with H, even though with each day spent together we put more distance between myself and my family. Or, it could have been the need to keep busy, or the addiction to the nightlife—I don't quite know, but I continued—with everything. The magazine, music, Maverick...all of it.

Nothing Is What It Appears To Be

With gritted teeth and clenched fists, I continued to show up every Saturday night to work. H and I continued to come up with themes, ideas and plans in order to revive the club. I bought more music, hired DJs and brought in exciting acts. This along with heavy promotion, the club picked up sporadically, but not significantly.

Each night, H was there to chauffeur me home. I never had the balls to invite H into my place, even though I knew "A" wasn't there. It seemed like the ultimate disrespect to me, to have H inside my apartment where my wife, I and our kids had called home. I never even allowed her to enter the building. She dropped me off and I went up the stairs to the empty apartment with all my belongings, and the ghosts of my children and wife.

With my family seemingly gone, I threw myself into Maverick. Small groups of guys and girls from Gifu had found out about Maverick, and they came almost every Saturday. Maverick had followers from before I took over Saturday nights as promoter, and sometimes they showed up, not sure what to expect.

R23 – I Should Have Left Her Dancing

One such semi-regular was a young Japanese woman. Her name was R23. She was innocent looking and loved to dance. I always put myself last in the rotation of DJs, because I wanted to rock them with heavy hip hop, then soothe them with killer lover's rock reggae. R23 always stayed and danced to the very last song, but she was always with two or three other Japanese guys, and they were pretty cool looking. The three of them would dance all night, and it looked like maybe both of the guys were taking turns being R's boyfriend. What did I know, maybe that was the case. Either way, R23 liked to dance a lot and she'd dance until the very last song every time she came.

She looked like she was in her early twenties. Had a punk rock hair-cut. She always wore giant loopy earrings and dark eye-shadow. Looked like a cuter, thicker, cleaner, preppier, sexier, Japanese Joan Jett. She wore a big purple leather belt buckle around her red skirt.

One night I decide to talk to her. Her two Japanese boyfriends are by the bar and she's softly dancing by herself on the dance floor. Orchestral Maneuvers In The Dark's "If You Leave" is playing. I fucking kid you not. I find out she's 23. R23. She's from Gifu, same as H. Her English is pretty good.

R23 is dancing in little circles around me while we're talking. H is outside somewhere. *Somewhere.* I'm watching R23 dance. My wife hadn't been home for months. H is waiting in the car for me around the corner, like she always did. Ms. Isobe is lurking in her trousers and her silk shirt and her bifocals with her hair pulled back in a bun. R23 is eyeing me. Her skirt is sashaying up and caressing her thighs. She's full on dancing as the song builds to a crescendo. Club is ending. H was outside waiting for me. My Kenyan man Ghost Willy is hanging around, he's still DJing for me at Maverick.

R23 is staring. I tell her, "Wait here." She says okay. I rush over to Ghost. "Yo, Ghost, I'ma try to kick it with honey over here, but my girl is waiting upstairs for me, so you and I gotta leave together like we're getting into something. Once we get around the corner, I'ma jet, aight?" Ghost says, "I got you, Maddlove." Cool.

H has the car across the street warm and waiting. I run over to her window and tell her that Ghost and I are gonna go check out some after-hours spot in Sakae. She says okay. I tell her I'll get at her tomorrow. She asks me if I wanted her to wait for me. I say "no, go ahead, I'm good, I'll get home by taxi." She asks me again if she can wait for me. Again, I say "no, really, you can go, I'll be fine..." she reluctantly, sadly says okay and leaves. *She always did whatever I asked, she waited however long I needed, and she went home whenever I needed space, but she never disappeared. She was always there, regardless.*

I run back over to where Ghost is waiting and we round the corner, just to make it all look authentic. Once we got about a quarter of the way up the block, I looked back to make sure H was gone—and she was. I pound Ghost down and split back around the corner, back into the club, and down the stairs where R was waiting. She was alone. Her dudes had vanished.

I ask her how was she getting back to Gifu tonight, now that the trains had stopped running. She wasn't sure. I ask where her dudes were, she says they've left. I hear myself saying, "You wanna come with me?" I hear her saying, "Okay." I see myself grab her arm and lead her up out of the club. I watch myself hail a cab. I see my arm guide her into the back of the cab and see myself climb in after her. I hear myself giving the cab driver directions, in Japanese, to my—my wife's and my family's apartment, up in Motoyama. I feel my heart beating and my skin getting warm. The taxi is slowly chugging up Higashiyama Dori and I'm lunging at R23 and we're kissing and groping in the backseat of the cab. I'm grabbing at her thighs and pushing up her skirt and she's into it and I notice the cabbie is watching us in the rearview and we're barely moving. Our eyes meet in his mirror and I flash him a *motherfucker you better stop watching and drive* look and he presses on the gas.

We're in the backseat of the taxi and it feels to me like our tongues are lashing at each other. Yellow street lights pass over us intermittently as we slowly climb the hill going up towards Motoyama. After a few moments of me trying to swallow her face, I realize her kiss is actually very tender. She's not sticking her tongue in my mouth, she's actually got her lips barely parted and her tongue is more like a turtle's head. She's darting it in and out, as if she's tasting me, rather than kissing me. We catch eyes at a red light and she giggles. I smile. *Seems like she's having fun*. It's late, or early, depending on your perspective. The cab windows are all fogged up. She's got a pair of big, puffy pink nipples and they're catching light in the backseat. Then suddenly a voice enters my head:

Why is this girl's left tit in your mouth, in the backseat of this cab that is headed to the very place where you want your wife to be? What if your wife decided this is the night she was going to come back home? That's what you really want, isn't it? Are you really gonna bring this strange girl into your wife's home? Your family's home? This is bad.

And then in a flash we are in front of my apartment. I pay the cabbie and R23 and I step out into the quiet parking lot. It's late, 3 or 4 A.M., my sense of time was all messed up. The apartment buildings around us are absolutely dark and silent. I felt like those windows, in those apartment buildings were staring down at us in that parking lot. Massive dark structures, watching our every move.

Cool, still, quiet Japanese twilight air. More still than usual. R23 and I are standing there talking a while. About pure bullshit. I was sure my wife was going to pull up right then. R23 is staring at me wantonly but I'm terrified to actually bring her upstairs. But there we are. *What else am I gonna do? Call another cab to pick her up after talking to her for fifteen minutes in the parking lot? No, son, you're not doing that. Can't really stand out here in the parking lot too much longer either. Everyone in this apartment complex knows who you are man, you can't be seen. Dude, you have only one choice. Complete what you've started, bring her upstairs.*

We walk up the three flights of stairs to my apartment. The gravel on the old concrete stairs is shifting underneath our feet, I've never noticed how loud it was until now. The metal banisters are creaking every time we touch them. I'm walking slowly up the stairs, practically tip toeing and R23 is following suit behind me.

We're upstairs, I quickly stick the key in the keyhole, push open the door and allow her to pass me to enter. Once inside, the apartment is absolutely still, dark, and foreboding. It's eerie. Taiyo's shoes are at the door when we walk in. This is not the scenario one wants when one is trying to get some ass. It should be at least slightly conducive to romance and/or sexual pleasure; it should not be a terrifying death walk that makes your teeth rattle.

We're inside and I'm sorta just standing there looking at R23, then past R23 into my dark apartment, and it's very, very quiet. We're both just standing in the dark and R23 is looking at me and finally asks, "Is someone here?" "No. No one is here. Just us." The door to the bedroom where "A" kept her clothes and the babies' clothes and stuff was shut. The dresser with their clothes was still in there. Their blankets were still in there. Toys and books and baby stuff and A's clothes, it was all still in there. Asia's bassinet, it was in there.

I guess I'm here with a mission, I tell myself. *Here we are, brother, do what you came to do.*

We walk past the kitchen and head into the little tatami living room. I slide open the wooden doors and pull out the futon and blankets that I'd been sleeping on alone, without my wife, for the last half a year. I lay them out on the floor and R23 says she wants to go to the bathroom first. "Sure, down the hall, first door on the left." When she returned, I was already sprawled out on the futon. I wanted to get to whatever was about to happen, and get it over with as soon as possible. But still, there was this feeling.

I took her hand and gently pulled her onto me. We kissed and she gave me more of her tongue than she had in the taxi. With her on top of me, I reached between us and put my hand into her panties. She arched her back so I could get at her pussy. She actually went into a push up stance, with her heels spread apart and her hands shoulder width apart on the futon.

I leaned up and curved my finger and started stroking her very wet pussy. Her panties were wet too, I guess from the taxi. She came out of her clothes really quickly. First, we did it on the futon, then we moved to the couch. It was strikingly erotic and *so very bad.* Sharp moans, shudders, and shakes on the futon. It suddenly became *very wet* between her legs and underneath us. I didn't want to get the futon wet and smelling like sex, so we moved to the easy to clean, pleather couch.

She was loud and I became very paranoid, so eventually I just stopped. The sin factor of the moment hung heavy in the room and a thick, dank sex cloud dripped off the walls. We were in my family's house. It was all blurry. We returned to the futon and laid there quietly. Our clothes were strewn all over the small room. I wondered what this strange naked girl was doing in my apartment, just lying there peacefully, stark naked, in my wife's house. She closes her eyes and maybe she falls asleep for a few minutes. I'm staring up at the ceiling wondering what to do. Wondering what I had just done.

We lay there a while and soon I notice that the sun is coming up. It's very quiet, soft rays of golden sunlight stream through the window. I get myself up and start getting dressed. R23 is stirring, naked on the *tatami* in front of me. She looks up at me and I'm just about fully dressed. She slowly drags herself up, wipes her eyes, looks around and finally gathers her clothing. She reaches for her panties as I gather up her dress and hand her, her purple belt. I'm standing impatiently over her. She's kneeling on the *tatami,* pulling her shirt over her shoulders, putting on her panties with her back turned to me, buckling the big purple belt buckle she had on around her red skirt. I'm silently thinking *please hurry, please hurry, please hurry,* when suddenly the unthinkable happened.

Caught In The Act

Is that the key I'm hearing in the door? God. Please no. She's the only person with a key besides me! This can't be happening! What time is it? Why is she coming here at this time? On a Sunday? At seven A.M.? She hasn't been here for weeks, Months! What is she doing here NOW? Why is my wife about to see me in our apartment with some strange girl who is on her knees buckling her belt buckle? Why is she still buck- ling her belt buckle? How long can that take? What am I going to . . .

I run over to stall my wife at the front door. I'm thinking, maybe R23 would self-combust or teleport herself, or jump out the fucking window or something. The door swings open and it's my wife. It's 7 A.M. I'm fully dressed. My wife looks at me momentarily, then she walks past me into the living room, where R23 is still on her knees, struggling with her goddamn belt buckle.

Upon seeing R23 on her knees trying to clamp the fucking belt buckle, my wife lunges at her and I instinctively grab my wife just as she's about to tiger swipe R23. I'm holding my wife back and she's lash- ing out like an animal at R23, who seems bemused by the proceedings taking place before her. Her disposition was as if it weren't really hap- pening, or, like it was a movie taking place in three dimensions right before her eyes.

"WHAT THE FUCK ARE YOU DOING? GO! GO! GO! NOW!" I scream at R23. She's moving in slow motion, finally clamps on her fucking buckle, grabs her purse, straightens her skirt, and tiptoes around my flailing wife and I. My wife tries desperately to grab R's hair or dress or whatever. R is still looking bemusedly at my wife and I. Why is she so puzzled while taking her time to leave? I'm screaming "HURRY UP, GET OUT, GO!" and finally she vanishes down the stairs.

I'm still holding my wife and she's still struggling, telling me to get off her. When I think R is completely gone, I finally release my wife. Immediately, she faces me and says "*Saiaku! Saiaku! Sai te!*" over and over again. She looks possessed, like an evil apparition. Enraged and venomous.

"You're the worst!" she shouts, over and over, "you're the worst!" You're the worst. *I am the worst.*

I'm trying to grab her wrists, trying to put my arm around her waist, *"*Baby wait, please let me, let me explain . . ."But I have nothing to explain. Momentarily, there seems to be an eye in her emotional hurricane. Suddenly, for a moment, she's still, just looking at me with her huge, pretty eyes welling up to tears. She wanted me to say something, something smart, something consoling, something . . . just something, but all I could think to say was "Why are you here now? I don't understand why you came here today, why today, A?"

Her eyes cloud over again. Her lips curl up again. Her body stiffens up again. I hadn't said the right thing. She backs away from me, spitting that *saiaku* barb at me like a venomous snake. I have no idea what I was planning to try to say. My wife runs out the door and I'm left standing there wondering what to do. Idiot.

I bolt after her like a douchebag. "Please, A, please wait . . ." She turns around in the stairwell and hiss at me like a snake. She points directly at me, like she's casting some kind of spell, and for a moment it seems like I can't move, I'm frozen on the top step. She slowly backs down the last few steps, then she slips around the corner, into her car, and takes off.

The spell breaks after she disappears and it quickly washes over me that my wife has just caught me red-handed with another woman who was getting dressed in our house. Had she walked in just a few minutes before, she might have walked in on her husband and some strange naked Japanese woman laying on the same futon we'd been sleeping on since we got married. *This is it. My marriage is washed.*

What's Wrong?

The whispering morning breeze, the chirping of a few birds, the beating of my own heart and the heavy sound made when one's spirit is crushed is what I'm hearing right now. I hop on my bike and book it to Higashiyama Dori where my wife's parents live.

Once I arrive at her parent's house, I jump off the bike, kick the kickstand and barge into the bottom floor of my wife's family's barber shop business. It's maybe just a little after 7am. *Otosan,* my wife's father, my father-in-law, my children's grandfather, is inside sweeping and cleaning up the shop, getting ready for a brisk Sunday business. "*Ohayo,*" he says, surprised to see me when I stumble inside. I'm sweating from bicycling all the way to his place from Motoyama. I'd thought maybe I could somehow arrive before my wife and head her off.

"Ohayo otosan, genki desu ka?" —*Good morning, are you happy?* I've got to say something, but I can't quite say *good morning father in law, I just got caught cheating with another woman in me and your daughter's house.* He looks me up and down with concern, I'm sweating profusely and wearing the same clothes I'd had on all night at the club. He crinkles his eyebrows,

"*Dabeed wa, nani? Dou shita Dabeed? Dou shita no?*" He's asking what's happened, and I can't answer.

It's not even 8am, I'm sweating and just barged into his house, he knows something's up. Finally he asks

"*A wa . . . daijyobu desu ka?*" David, what happened? Where's A? Is she okay?

"*Hai. Kanoujo daiyjobu...Tabun. Wakaranaie. Gomen Otosan. Sumimasen jikan ga.*" I stammer. I'm looking at the clock.

"*A coco y naie desu ka?*" Yes, maybe she's okay, I don't know. I'm sorry, sorry for the early time, A isn't here?

"*Naie, Naie, coco jya naie . . . dou shita no Dabeed,*" his eyes widen and he's more serious now, demanding I tell him what's going on. I'm standing there panting, looking at my father in law in his barbershop.

It's way too early on a 'normal' Sunday morning, and his black son-in-law is standing in his barber shop sweating, panting, eyes bulging, trembling in fear. He has no idea that his daughter had just caught me with another woman in our apartment two miles down the road.

How many lives are you gonna fuck up, man? Can't just concentrate on fucking up your own life? Gotta fuck up other people's lives too?

My wife bursts in. Crazy Train.

Death Throes

"GET OUT OF HERE! WHY ARE YOU HERE? GET OUT GET OUT
GET OUT!"

My wife is yelling at me in English. Her father is stunned and has no idea what's going on or what he should say or do. Neither do I. She's coming towards me, teeth gritted together, yelling through her teeth. Her father is alarmed and she's flailing her arms, coming at me with the same energy that only moments ago, she was trying to get at R23 with. I'm literally afraid.

"A, dou shita?" Her father is asking his daughter what happened. Silence. She's glaring at me. I'm literally shaking, trying my best to muster up a look of apology, sincerity, regret, hope, and familiarity, all mixed together. I don't know what to say, feel, or do. Too late for an apology. Way too late for anything like that. Her glare seems to last a lifetime, but momentarily there's a flicker of that same moment of expectation she had given me at our front door before she bolted. I didn't know then, but I know now that there was a tiny glimmer of her yearning for me to say something good, but I didn't know what good there was to say. I said . . . nothing.

"GET OUT!" she screams, thunderclouds rolling back into her eyes. I give her one last pathetic, silent "I'm sorry I did this but...where have you been anyway?" look. Her father, my father in law, *otohsan*, is standing there with a broom in his hand, perplexed, concerned for his daughter, defiant upon hearing A tell me to get out. They're both staring at me, *what should I do now?* I turn and leave.

I pedal home, long blocks between Higashiyama Dori and Motoyama. Downhill, then up a steep hill. Then up the even steeper hill leading to our apartment building. I had to push my bike to make it up the hill. No energy. I return home.

Return To The Scene Of The Crime

Inside, the apartment is silent but there is evidence everywhere. The futon is still spread out on the floor, with a huge wet stain on it, exactly as it was when R23 was sprawled out on it. The same as when my wife charged into the room and saw her there putting on her stupid belt buckle. The entire room has a quasi-murder scene feel to it, eerily silent. I peer down at the futon going over the scene in my head. Everything was exactly as I'd left it. A bizarre image of myself and R23 laying there outlined in chalk flashes into my mind. Two dead bodies intertwined on my wet futon.

I quickly scan the place and palpable terror grips my being. I rush through a cleanup and call my brother in Florida. My breathing is irregular. My chest is heaving, my hands are shaking and I can't keep myself standing in one place. It was eight in the morning in Japan and I had no idea what time it was in the States. I hadn't called my brother in God knows how long, but I needed to talk to him *right now.* He picks up, groggy, it's after midnight where he is.

"Yo, I think I just fucked up my marriage out here." I'm breathing fast and heavy while I pace the crime scene.

Therapy is desperately needed. I repeat my heinous indiscretions to my brother. I needed him, I needed his words but all I could *see* was my own, it was as if I was in a drug induced state. I couldn't feel my face, I couldn't hear my words, I could only feel my heart. I needed my brother to fix this, *Say something...*

"Wait, wait...what?" My baby brother assess the brazen stupidity of my actions.

"Dude, she hasn't been back here for like three months yo." I tell him.

Rationalization. Humans are not rational beings, humans are *rationalizing* beings. I marched on with my bullshit.

"So where is she now?" my brother asks.

I suddenly hear the key enter the door. *No, it can't be.* I was both elated and terrified. Petrified almost.

"I gotta go, it's her man. I'll hit you back." Right before I got off the phone with my baby brother I heard him say,

"Trev, just come home..."

My wife walks in, completely different than she had been moments before. She's calmer, composed, steely, almost serene. She softly shuts the door behind her and we're standing face-to-face in the tiny foyer of our apartment. She takes a moment to look me directly in my eyes and then calmly says to me in Japanese,

"*Nimotsu wo motte ie kara deteite. Kyo kara watashi tachi wa tanindesu. Ima kara, watashi no ryoshin ga kuru kara. Deteite kudasai.*" Take your things and get out of this house. We are strangers from now on. My parents are coming here soon. Please get out.

She then steps aside and casts her eyes down to the ground as if to say, "There's the door." I'm confused, but not really. I knew what was happening, but couldn't process it. Why was she so calm? Why were her parents coming here? What should I do?

It had never dawned on me that all that time she had been spending at her parents' house, her parents had been working on her, trying to convince her to leave me, get rid of me, divorce me, and now, she had tangible reason to do so. I'm standing there still wondering why in the name of God did you come home today? Why today? Why this morning, of all mornings? Then the notion that maybe I was set up creeps into my brain. But who could know? Who *would* know? "A" had developed a friendship of sorts with the neighbors who lived directly across from us on the third floor. *Was it them?*

I'm searching the ground around her feet for answers. I'm sure she can sense my confusion. I look back up at her and our eyes meet and my mind is swirling, but hers isn't. She's 100 percent sure, there's no anger in her face, no malice, no hatred, what there is, is resolve. The only thing written on her face is her desire that I leave. *Now.*

I look around and spy my backpack, pick it up, and silently walk into the room in the back of the apartment where I had kept my things. All my shit is scattered haphazardly back there. I scoop up some underwear and socks. I grab my toothbrush and some other bullshit from the bathroom. I don't quite know what to do or where I'm going, but I'm trying to walk a line between cocky and apologetic. There is no such line.

It's 8 A.M. on a Sunday morning in Nagoya, Japan, and I'm being thrown out of my house by my wife after she's caught me in our bed with another woman. This wasn't about hearsay, or cryptic texts, or mysterious phone numbers or phone calls, not about rumors, misplaced trinkets, odd behavior, nothing so vague. No. She walked into our apartment and found another woman dressing herself in our living room. I was busted.

I swear I hear Shaggy and Ric Roc singing *it wasn't me* in my head—momentarily I have the strange idea to tell her that it wasn't me, but there's nothing funny or cute or sexy about that song at the moment. It *was* me. It was *all me. How in the fuck* had I done this? Again, a flood of thoughts race through my mind: *Where am I going to go? What am I going to do? What should I do? Is there anything to do?*

I've got my bike, my backpack, some clothes, a little bathroom bullshit and that was it...and oh, I had my girlfriends—there was H standing by waiting in the wings for her turn. There was N, with whom I was still having my monthly, maybe bi-monthly love hotel body fluid swaps. There was C who, no matter how many lessons I gave her, still couldn't put together a decent sentence in English. There was T with her white motor scooter. There was R23, who had just been an accomplice to the beginnings of my ending, and who, yes, did continue to see me after. There was another long and lanky R who I was having sporadic one-offs with, I mean . . . man, *how many were there really?*

I had my backpack and A is still standing inside the foyer. I slip on my shoes and there's another moment of silence. She wasn't looking at me, she was peering inside the apartment, looking like she was working out in her mind how she'd change things once I was gone. I try to reach for her shoulder, but she jerks away, looks at me, and quietly but confidently says "Sayonara, *Daveed*." That was it.

When Japanese say sayonara, it doesn't mean *see you later*. It doesn't mean "hey, we'll catch up" or "see you soon" or "take care" or "bye bye for now". Sayonara means goodbye forever, or at the least, goodbye until I don't know when. It means this chapter of our lives is over, and there may never be another chapter.

I smile weakly as I cruise past my wife and out the door. I give her a whiny, pathetic "I'm sorry". She looks away and closes the door behind me. I'm mentally, and somewhat physically crippled but still I manage to toddle down the stairs.

Where Is Your God?

Tomes have been written about the submissive quality of the Japanese woman. It's part of their allure. Yeah, sure, all well and good. However, what isn't as well known is the tenacity they have, and the lifelong *will and conviction* to punish and forever banish you from any portion of their hearts for any wrong you may have committed. I committed *lots and lots* of wrongs. They will continue to keep you in their minds, but only as the person that they must maintain a lifelong active hatred for. They will never forgive you, nor will they ever forget. They may "get over" whatever you've done, but you will never be "friends" or anything like it. It is just not Japanese to do so. Forgiveness is weakness, it is a foreign characteristic found in childish, sappy, romantic, Hollywood movies. Forgiveness is not a virtue in Japan, as it is in most western countries. Forgiveness is some foreign bullshit to Japanese. Christians try their best to be forgiving but *ain't no Christian God living in Japan.*

SORRY I DID THAT SHIT

Two societies collide

Realistically, the truth was that I *was* sorry, but not sorry for the right things. I was sorry that things had to end the way they were ending, but they weren't quite ending yet. I felt horrible for putting A's parents through what they were bound to go through. Felt horrible for being exactly what A's mom had feared. I was sorry for the shame and trouble and confusion and dirt. But I wasn't quite sorry about my behavior. I was still feeling justified in doing what I was doing, partly because A hadn't been around much, partly because I was still holding onto that stupid "I'm a foreigner and I'm only doing what all foreigners do here" shtick. Stupid.

From jump, it had been me versus A's mom. Her mom never really took a shining to me, but it wasn't about me personally, it was more about whatever dreams her mom had had about her marrying a Japanese guy, and I wasn't that guy.

Have I already mentioned the times she came by our apartment to tell A to abort our first child when I wasn't there? I think I've already mentioned her coming to my job to investigate whether or not I *had* a job. How about the times she made me stand outside in the cold or rain before answering the door for our English lessons or when picking up Taiyo and Asia. She was always polite, never rude, but never welcomed me, never treated me exactly like family. What she had done, was watch me, calculatingly waiting for her moment to spring into action and execute her plan to rid her daughter, and her life, of me.

Humans Are Not Rational, Humans Rationalize.

I wasn't married to A's mom, I was married to A, but her mom was always lurking just beyond the shadows. It hadn't quite registered what a stretch it was for her parents to accept that their first-born daughter had gone outside the normal scope of things and married a foreigner. A black foreigner at that. Like most people who "don't quite fit in" for whatever reason, all I saw and felt was distance, estrangement, like a red-headed stepchild, and it made me bitter. I went about my way thinking, *Why don't they just accept me for me?* And all that bullshit. All foreigners go through that in Japan. We want to be treated the same but the truth is we aren't the same. We don't think like they do, don't act like they do, don't react like they do. We're outsiders through and through and they know it, but we act like it's our birthright to be "let inside" because of our fancy notions about equality and freedom and all that. Right now there's some white dude from Nebraska complaining somewhere in Japan about Japanese racism, and like my good friend Alan Smithee says, "*That* shit will NEVER not be patently absurd.", white people complaining about racism in Japan. Funny.

Would You Be Happy To Find Out That Your Child Wanted To Marry A Martian?

I was that Martian. And now, I was on the outside, where I belonged. Heading down those steps I felt a combination of emotions: release, fear, despair, liberation, confusion, self-pity, paranoia. I felt like the whole Japanese world had burst through the door that morning to find me and R23 kneeling down on that futon. I felt like everyone in Japan was suddenly made aware of what a total jackass I was and had been for so long. I felt like all of Japan was screaming at me, "See, we knew it! You've got no scruples, no honor, no morals, and you can't keep your fucking dick in your pants either! Fucking foreigner."

But I also felt uncaged. I felt like all the internal spasms I had put myself through to try to be a decent husband were now suddenly gone. I felt unshackled. I felt oddly liberated. Our marriage had deteriorated to one of those loveless marriages you hear about so often in Japan. I felt like I had just arrived in Japan, all over again. I never saw A cry. Maybe she didn't. Maybe she just felt relieved, like I did, that she didn't have to go through the painful motions of being married to *the foreigner* anymore. I hadn't considered how torn she must have been throughout our marriage, torn between her husband, her society, her family, her traditions, and her*self*. I had never given any of this one thought. Selfish. Stupid. Asshole. *Sai te.* The worst.

Sitting here now writing this, I can feel those same emotions I felt when A discovered R23 and I in our living room, but without the liberation, without the release, without any of the "good shit" I felt on that day. Now, I only feel the fear, the paranoia, the dread, like a low, dark specter creeping up my spine, and those feelings have stayed with me like dark residue in a pot pipe.

I slowly walked to my bike thinking *What now, Trev, what now?*

Out Into the Wild Again

I wondered who to call, where to go, what to do, what to say, what to feel. I called a friend, Mark Lavers, a good Canadian dude who I had asked to write a couple articles for *RAN*. I asked him if I could come over and talk. It was early Sunday morning, who needs to talk about what on an early Sunday morning?

I arrive at his place in Issha and share my story. He listens and somehow feels sympathy for me, despite my actions, despite my behavior, despite my dirt. I tell him everything and unload. There are lots of foreign dudes in Japan who get caught up in the exact same bullshit

I had been doing. Divorced dudes living a fabricated past where they convince themselves somehow that it wasn't their fault. I knew many of them, and I always smugly thought, *I'll never be like that guy.* Yet, there I was, *that exact guy.*

I ask Mark if I could crash at his pad until I figure things out. Mark's place is small, he's got two bedrooms, one of which he uses for his classes and another which is a storage room for all his stuff. He's got a small kitchen and a small living room. He's single for all intents and purposes, a recovering alcoholic who has rebuilt his mind and body. He's in his late 50's, maybe even 60's, but his body is rock hard from his obsession with going to the gym. It's helped him recover and focus on being healthy he tells me. Everyone's got a story.

I stayed in Mark's empty, extra bedroom for a couple months. It wasn't really "empty" by any means, with boxes, books, equipment and clothing scattered all over the place. No bed, I curl under old blankets and sheets on the wooden floor. Every night, I'm wondering, *how in the fuck did you get here Trevor.* All my stuff is still in my old apartment, my wife's apartment.

Every night Mark and I would sit and talk about our situations in Japan. How lonely it could be at times, how much we missed our family. Mark was wonderfully present in all our conversations and never patronizing. He listened intently and indulged me in my philosophical bullshit about freedom, sex, and marriage, whatever. He never once made me feel bad about what had happened, never once made me out to be the bad guy, nor did he ever make me feel as though I owed my wife anything at all. He always spoke with wisdom, clarity, and a certain fatherly gentleness. He was therapy for me without me really knowing it, and those months I stayed at his place allowed me to not spiral down into a self-hating, self-destructive maelstrom.

I was remorseful, but made no attempts to fix things with my wife. The feeling of liberation won out over the remorse, at first anyway. I continued doing what I was doing, but now, more recklessly.

Now, I had to tell H that my wife had thrown me out, but I couldn't tell her exactly why. I assumed she'd suspect it was because of our relationship, and I let it rest there. I couldn't say my wife threw me out because I brought another woman, not you, into our apartment. However, I also couldn't say she threw me out because of you. The truth was she had thrown me out because of me, and this is what I told H.

Ostensibly though, it had been about our relationship, in the case that our relationship was a sort of a metaphor for all the other relationships I'd been having. It didn't really matter who my wife had caught me with that Sunday morning, but I couldn't tell H that I'd been caught with another girl, because at this point, H was my default girlfriend. She was paying for everything, taking me everywhere, buying me clothes, answering my mail, helping me with *RAN* and my events—she was, and had been, doing everything a wife is supposed to do, and *I was cheating on her as well.*

I could have fallen further. I know and knew lots of cats who had disintegrated into drug users, criminals, went homeless, and completely fell off the wagon when what happened to me had happened to them. I couldn't be one of those guys. I chose to rise. Sort of.

Another Move

I couldn't stay at Mark's place too long. Too cluttered, too far away, too foreign. I felt I was getting in his way and even though he was always kind and always welcoming, a man needs his space. Having some cat who is going through a break up with his wife isn't quite the most positive situation.

Mark always showed boundless kindness and consideration to me. We hashed out the whys and wherefores of the failures of so many international marriages night after night. He indulged my self-pity, my musings and ruminations, and he even allowed me to have guests. H came by a few times, C did too, but it was very uncomfortable in that tiny, cluttered room on the hard wood floor. I guess I hadn't learned.

My staff and I held weekly meetings about *RAN* in his living room, he allowed me to eat his food and offered me sage advice. He never once looked down on me and was nothing but a friend. He, himself was a recovering alcoholic with a couple of sons—one was a problem child, the other, not so much. He was also a divorcée, out playing the field in the rocky waters of Nagoya's over-forty set. We maintain a great friendship to this day, but I had to get out—the floor was becoming too cold, too hard, and the clutter of that room seemed to creep up on me in the middle of the night. H, C, *RAN*, DJing and teaching all provided ample distraction to the reality of what had happened and what was happening. I was a cheating husband who had gotten caught, found out, thrown out, and now sleeping on the cold wooden floor of an ex-alcoholic's, living on the outskirts of some city in Japan. It was as bad as it seemed.

Hypnosis/Mild Psychosis

I needed *something* to help me get past what was happening. I asked another friend, a cool cat, rock-n-roll guitar player named Tom Baurle, if he'd hypnotize me. He'd told me he was a certified hypnotist and had offered to put me under before. I called him on it. Tom had played with his band in my Springfest event and seemed like a really down to earth dude. I went to his place, a big old house in Kakuozan, just down the street from Motoyama, where he had been house-sitting for years. The couple who owned the house had gotten too old to climb up the steps and couldn't keep up the house the way it needed to be kept up, so they'd offered it to Tom to live in indefinitely.

I showed up at his house one evening and he told me to sit down on the couch. There were no swinging clocks or clinking tea cups like in the movie "Get Out", but he did ask me to sit down and relax as much as I could, close my eyes, and he counted down from ten, then I was under. It was the weirdest thing. The whole time he's counting down I'm thinking *what is this? I don't feel shit* and then at zero, my mind went blank, and it felt like I had no power to resist whatever he asked. He asks me what I want most out of life.

"Success," I say.

"What kind of success?" he asks.

"Success with my music, success with my magazine, a life of prosperity and peace," I tell him. He asks me why I want success.

My mind goes black for a moment and then I feel tears welling up in my eyes, but I'm not sure why. Then I start thinking about my own dad, who had died about 8 or 9 years earlier. He tells me it's okay and the tears stop and he tells me I'm going to get my success and says something about seeing me wearing a nice white suit and having people throw accolades my way, counts back down to zero and tells me I'm now "awake".

After, he tells me old emotions tend to come up unbidden, and that maybe I was going through remorse about my marriage failing, maybe that's why I had started crying. I hoped so. I still hadn't properly let it register that I was alone again. I tell him I've been sleeping on Mark's floor out in Issha, and that it wasn't the most comfortable setup. He offers me the upstairs bedroom to his place. I immediately accept. I return to Mark's place and tell him I'm moving on. I tell him thanks for everything, he wishes me luck and I head out to Tom's place in Kakuozan. I stayed with Mark for about 4 months.

Asia's Birthday Surprise

At this point, my wife and I are still married, but I hadn't properly spoken to her since the day she'd found me at our place with R23. We were, however, on sporadic texting terms. Asia's birthday was approaching and I begged my wife to allow me to have a little birthday party for her at the local Mister Donuts in Motoyama. She had been decreasing communication little by little but I hadn't noticed it much, too steeped in my own comings and goings. When we had the 'party', I showed up with cake and a few gifts for both my daughter and my son. I didn't want to only bring something for Asia, I figured Taiyo wouldn't understand that this was Asia's day, and since they weren't seeing me much anymore, I didn't want to mess things up between him and I.

I arrived at the Mister Donuts before A, and went to the back and set up my little party. I had the cake, some balloons, the gifts, a card, and bought some donuts. A short while later, my estranged wife arrived with the kids and they were both elated and curious about the balloons and cakes. "It's Asia's birthday", I said, and we sang happy birthday. But "A" didn't. She didn't even sit with us. She chose to sit in an empty booth away from us while Taiyo, Asia and I had our little party.

I tried my best to make it seem 'normal', even while their mother was sitting about 10 feet away, staring at me, the cake and them, stone faced, not saying a word. It was one of the most uncomfortable situations I've ever experienced in my life. I let Asia and Taiyo dig into the cake with their hands and they had cake all over their faces, their clothes, everywhere. I loved it. It was one of the tenderest moments of my existence in Japan, and also one of the heaviest moments of my life.

When it was over, or, when my wife had decided it was over, she scooped up Asia and Taiyo without saying a word to me. Asia grabbed a balloon, I stood up waving at my children, and then she walked outside to her car with the babies, got inside, and drove off. I was left there in Mister Donuts alone with some uneaten cake, balloons, and half eaten donuts. I sat there a moment while the other Japanese customers looked at me. One old woman seemed to know what was going on. We smiled weakly at each other, I cleaned up, and left.

>Chapter 16

Divorce At My In-Laws

Breaking up is hard to do

I had to work. I was still DJing, was building *RAN* magazine, and had my various girlfriends to attend to. H stood by faithfully, picking me up and driving me around, both of us acting like not much had happened. Things between us weren't really any different than they had been before I moved out of my place in Motoyama. Sexually, we weren't really getting it on much—I had convinced myself internally that she was the cause of my divorce, but I still needed her, and this was vexing to me. But even without anything physical or intimate going on between us, there she was, being a better wife than A had ever even attempted to be.

I moved into Tom's and that godsend of an upstairs bedroom. The room had a big *real* queen-sized bed in it, on a frame and everything, no futon. There was a window with a ledge that led to the roof, which I could open up and go outside and smoke on. There was a small TV with a VCR attached to it as well. I watched documentaries about Bob Dylan on it. At this point, I was buying herbs and getting high more and more, despite the fact that the herb was low quality "stress" weed and super expensive.

One day towards the end of the summer my wife texts me asking me to meet her at her family's house. I hadn't actually been inside her family's house since the day she had caught me with R23, and even then, I had only been downstairs in the shop, not in the actual house.

There are two main strata of Japanese society: outside, and inside. I was most definitely *outside*. Tatemae/Honne, Omote/Ura, Soto/Uchi, these two concepts which can be translated loosely to mean outside, inside, front, back, in/out, play themselves out as the backbone of how Japanese people comport themselves on a daily basis in their society. The word *soto* can also be said as "gai", which is half the word "gaijin", which of course, means "outsider". When you find yourself on the outside of society in Japan, it's pretty much impossible to get inside. That's the life of a foreigner in Japan, no matter how long he or she stays, he'll never become Japanese. No matter what he does, or doesn't do.

For my wife and her family, unbeknownst to me at the time, I had been forever banished outside. During the moments, which were many, that my wife had been spending with her family over the course of the last year, her family, and especially her mother, had been re-socializing her. During our dating time, A had taken on noticeably un-Japanese traits. Her time with me and her time in NYC definitely opened her mind up in ways the average Japanese woman simply is unaccustomed to experiencing. Her family was taking care of that.

A and I decided that I could see the children on weekends while she was staying with her family full time. I had no idea how generous she was being and even thought that she was somehow *obligated* to let me see them as often as she did. Even when I'd come to pick up my children, both of A's parents did their best to offer me a healthy dose of impenetrable *tatemae honne*—they'd never say exactly what they felt, but their actions, the way they spoke to me, the way I was immediately relegated to the small front portion of the shop every time I came to either pick up or drop off Taiyo and Asia told me all they themselves never would. In Japan, actions speak much louder than words, and sometimes, most times, there are no words, there are only actions. Silence as a weapon. Again. I was back outside of their lives, like a dog who had behaved badly inside the house. Kicked out the back door and banished to the "outside". In Japan, if you're not on the inside, then you practically don't exist.

I hadn't seen A much in the preceding six months. I was seeing our children, three or four times a month on weekends. A, had arranged with her family to drop them off at their shop in Higashiyama. I'd arrive around 10 or 11 am, they'd already be dressed and ready to go, but my wife was nowhere to be seen. She wasn't showing her face at all, but I didn't think too much of it.

When I read the text asking me to meet her at her family's house, I half thought maybe we'd reconcile. I thought maybe her family might have encouraged her to give it one more chance—we did, after all, have two beautiful biracial children we'd created together. I figured mercy, forgiveness, nostalgia and love everlasting and all—or some—of that may have worked in my favor, and that I'd perhaps be greeted at their house with smiles, hugs and love. I was wrong.

Breathe

I arrive at my wife's family's front door that evening around seven. A answers the doorbell by swinging the door open so wildly I thought it might pop off the hinges in her hand. She has fire in her eyes. She looks really pretty to me as usual but the first thing she says to me is "WHO HAVE YOU BEEN SEEING?" She's screaming with her eyes fixed unwaveringly at mine. I'm surprised at this question because the last time I heard her voice, she was calmly telling me to get my things and move out.

I honestly thought she didn't care who I was seeing. I don't quite know why I thought that, or maybe I do. She hadn't given me any indication that she was even the slightest bit upset by the fact that we weren't together. I had tried to text her many times, tried to make some kind of approach, phone calls, gifts for the babies and I tried explaining to her that there wasn't any real "reason" for us to be enemies. I had even made the mistake of asking her once how long her "attitude" would last, and she told me forever. I said it here before, beware the wrath of a scorned Japanese woman. An American woman might slash your tires or throw your shit out the window, or have a restraining order placed on you, but chances are you'll have some kind of communication with her. A Japanese woman will absolutely vanish in every way from your life. She'll "change her mind" such that you never existed in the first place. It seemed to me that my wife was in this mode, closing the door on my existence. At this point, I had told myself that I was fine with our 'break up'. I guess I figured at some point in the future, we'd address the future of our relationship. That 'some point' in the future was tonight.

I fixed my mouth to say something but before I could answer, my son Taiyo runs up behind her and peaks out from behind her and says "Hi, Daddy!" in perfect English. I hadn't seen him in a while so I bent down to scoop him up but A stepped in front of Taiyo, blocking me, and without breaking her gaze said again, this time slower, "WHO. HAS. BEEN. COMING. TO. YOUR. HOUSE?" and directly in my face this time. Taiyo is standing there.

I'm confused. *How does she know I've been seeing anyone?* My mind scans through my current life immediately in a quick blur of events. H driving me around. M's tits on the porch. N at the love motel. C making bread in Tom's kitchen. Cradling R23 on the rare night she stayed throughout the night. All these images breezing by right beneath my eyeballs while I stood directly in front of A, whom I hadn't properly talked to for months. I was sure she could see what I was seeing in my mind's eye, but at the same time, I thought nervously to myself, *she doesn't know any of the girls I've been seeing and none of my friends know who I've been seeing besides H, and everyone already knows about H because I've been parading her all over the place promoting my magazine.*

Besides, H hadn't been coming to my new spot that much anyway. In the wake of my being kicked out of the apartment, even though H was supporting me, helping me, *carrying me* essentially, still, I was angry with her. Imagine my insolence. I was angry with the very person who was showing me any love whatsoever—blaming her for what I'd gotten myself into. I felt justified at the time because when I found out my wife had approached H at Springfest and told her to leave me and our family alone, H hadn't done it. This allowed me think it was less my fault and more H's fault, which is only half true. Still, I let myself off the hook somewhat since H was halfway responsible, even though it hadn't been H that my wife caught me in our place with. Still, I wasn't quite feeling H. Knowing my wife had asked H to leave me alone when H hadn't even given me permission to fully open my heart to her.

At least R23 didn't know I had a wife. But H did. There were countless moments with H where right in the middle of whatever we might be doing, I'd have sudden hot flashes of deep resentment for her.

I wasn't strong enough to end our relationship, but damn, my wife came to you and asked you to back off and you still didn't? This thought crashed around inside my head constantly.

H had not backed off, but instead had poured it on even more. She bought me clothes. Took me to the doctor. I had insane allergies called "kafunshou", pollen allergy, in Japan and H had taken me to the doctor to get laser surgery in my nostrils. Crazy experience. Picture a skinny old Japanese doctor burning the insides of your nose away with what looks like a smoldering iron. I had cavities and H used her dental insurance to make sure my teeth were healthy. She paid for a colonoscopy, health checks, eye-exams and took care of my taxes. She took me to us to see Cirque Du Soleil and lavished me with clothes, jewelry, shoes, shows, dinners, movies, whatever I wanted she gave me and whatever I couldn't think of, she thought of for me. H and I were driving through the city brazenly flaunting our relationship, while I was still married to A. It was a fact that I could never really get over, and which ultimately brought our house of cards crashing to the ground years later.

Still, there in that moment at the front door, with Taiyo hiding between my wife's legs, I knew A wasn't asking about H. No, *she knew something else.*

"No one, A..." I stammered, lying and unsure of my footing, trying to feign being casual by looking at Taiyo instead of her. I knew if A knew beyond a shadow of a doubt that I'd been with other women besides just H that our marriage had absolutely no chance of surviving. Judging by the looks of things, at this moment though, it didn't look good either way. At TB's crib, I had H *and* the new M, and C, and N, and R23 all coming around, and I'd only been there for what, six weeks? Nuts.

"Why are you asking me that?", I continued pathetically, trying to reach for Taiyo's hair, but by now, he sensed his mother's anger and was standing defiantly by her side, scowling at me, protecting her, defending his mother, showing his solidarity with her. Like a fool I tried to reach out to A, but she swatted my hands away violently and glared at me. Taiyo reached out instinctively at my pants leg and I thought he wanted to touch me or hold me or... but no, he was growling at me and his teeth were bared and he was trying to rip my pants or take me down, he was punching at my leg, *trying to hurt me.* My own three-year-old son was trying to kick my ass for hurting his mom, *ain't this a bitch?* I was shocked, proud, taken aback, nervous, filled with glee to be seeing both of them, and petrified all in one moment.

My wife's eyes are fixed on mine.

"MY FRIEND SAID THEY SAW YOU TAKING SOME GIRLS TO YOUR HOUSE."

I didn't even know she knew where I was staying. What friend? Apparently she did.

"A, I don't know what you're talking about..." Feeble, pleading almost.

"YES YOU DO. *SAITE.* TONIGHT WE FINISH!" She turns around and storms up the stairs. I'm standing just inside the foyer of her house, not sure what to do. Leave? Follow? I hadn't been upstairs in the Suzukis' house for half a year. Things had not started out well.

"*KITTE!*" she says angrily.

"Come!" I resolvedly kick off my shoes, confused but secretly thrilled to be able to go upstairs. I figure I'd get to see Taiyo and Asia, show some love, bat my eyelashes, and walk out with a reconciliation deal. No haps.

As I slowly climb the steps, I'm wondering what's about to happen. I'm actually becoming wildly paranoid, I wonder *maybe they're going to kill me.* A cold shockwave of emotion shoots down through my chest like an icicle lightning bolt.

I didn't think *they themselves* would kill me, because then they'd be murderers and that'd be stupid for them to do, but the idea that maybe there were three or four big Yakuza guys up there waiting to break my neck or slice off my head or disembowel me crept through my mind. So much so that I dallied momentarily on a step forcing A to tell me to "*HAYAKU.*" Hurry up.

I enter the kitchen area which for all intense and purposes was also the dining room. Everyone is seated somberly throughout the room. My wife's two younger sisters, Ayumi and Atsuko, her mother, father, and her grandmother, all staring sadly, if not sternly, right at me. Taiyo and Asia play innocently, yet noisily, running in and out of the room. I'd gone from zero to hero, and back to zero again.

"A" positions herself behind her mother, who is sitting at the head of the table. A is standing in front of the fridge between the sink and the table; her mother, sitting directly below her, is looking at me somberly and gestures to me to sit. A is shooting hot daggers into my heart with her eyes. She's *freshly* angry, this is not residual anger about what had happened months before at all. *What did I do? What did I do?* I keep thinking over and over. *She can't know. She can't know.* She's staring directly at me and my eyes are darting around furtively, I'm nervous, she *can't* know. "I KNOW!" she screams.

I swear to god. Her scream startles the shit out of me, and I damn near jump out of my seat. *W.T.F. is happening, man?*

"My friend said she saw you bring many girls to your house. You don't care what you are doing. You still doing same things. I WANT A DIVORCE!" she screams. She's absolutely livid.

"Divorce? What do you mean A? Who am I seeing? I'm not....I mean, what about Taiyo and Asia?"

"WHAT *ABOUT* THEM? THERE THEY ARE. SEE? YOU SEE?" she gestures at Taiyo and Asia who are now also looking at me, unsure, but they know something is definitely not right and their Dad is in the hot seat. "YOU DON'T CARE ABOUT THEM. YOU ONLY CARE YOUR-SELF. DISGUSTING! I HATE YOU!" She looks like she actually wants to *kill me*. I'm literally scared. I look at her feebly, open my mouth, but nothing comes out. A is panting, livid, enraged, fuming, she looks like she's working herself up into a frenzy. If she were a cartoon there'd be black smoke coming out of her ears. Her fists are balled. *She looks like she wants to knock my lights out.*

"I TOLD YOUR ASSISTANT TO LEAVE US ALONE, BUT YOU KEPT SEEING HER AND STILL NOW TOO *DA-VEED*," she says, both an-grily and accusingly. My head is hanging like a guilty dog.

"YOU BRING TWO OR THREE OR MORE DIFFERENT GIRL TO YOUR NEW HOUSE. I KNOW. DON'T TELL LIE. *USOUTSUKI. SAI TE! SAYAKU!* I HATE YOU! I WANT A DIVORCE! " She explodes again. I have nothing to add, subtract, or divide. I knew I couldn't win. I didn't even know what "winning" might be. All I knew was that *she knows, man, she just knows. She knows* <u>everything</u>. *But how?*

"*DA-VEED*. WHY YOU DON'T SAY SOMETHING. YOU DON'T HAVE SOMETHING TO SAY?"

Her entire family is looking at me. Taiyo and Asia are by now qui-etly observing from the back room. Her grandmother is looking over at me in a semi-confused state. A's mother and father are seated next to each other waiting for my response. Her father now seems thor-oughly on their side, it's me against all of them. No allies in this room whatsoever. A's sisters are standing on either side of my wife, consol-ing her while tears are streaming down her contorted face. I'm on the spot, *all eyes on me,* I want to console my wife but I dare not try to touch her.

Eternity passes in a moment. What should I say? What *could* I say? I'm busted. Caught red-handed. *How had she known I was bringing women to TB's place?* Her "friends" had been watching my every move, that's how. Who they are I have no idea, but they know where I live, what time I come home, what time I leave, who comes to visit me, what train stations I'm using, everything. I'm slightly, but only momentarily proud of the fact that she cares enough to have her "friends" watch me. I'd thought at this point, that I was a complete afterthought for her. Knowing she was actually still jealous lifted my spirits for a moment until . . .

"I WANT A DIVORCE! RIGHT NOW!" She screams, at which point her mother unfolds the divorce papers, which had been heretofore concealed in her lap. I notice A's name was already on them: *She's signed them already,* I think to myself. Splinters in my heart. There's an empty line directly underneath her signature where my signature belongs. I'm staring at the empty line. Signing this document would effectively dissolve our three-year marriage. Wow. *This is it. This is really it,* I think to myself. It's happening *right about now.*

I look down at the paper. A's mother smooths out the folded documents and magically produces a pen in her hand. The pen is coming towards me, slowly. The empty space on the document is huge, reverberating in my eyeballs. Taiyo and Asia are oblivious as to what is taking place, other than to see that their mother is enraged at their father and the family is gathered to watch. I look at my wife one last pleading "Are you sure?" time, but she doesn't hesitate,

"SIGN!" she bellows, pointing at the document. The whole family has gathered to divorce me.

I take the pen from her mother's hand. I'm holding the pen and I lower my head with sad acknowledgment. *After this I'm a divorced man.* I look at A's mom one more time, she looks confident and concerned, resolve etched onto her face. A's father looks shell-shocked and angry, his face says *Motherfucker, we could be drinking beers together right now, but instead you got us all going through this shit.* I can't blame him. It was me, my fault, for having put him, his wife, his family, and especially his daughter through this most embarrassing situation. This was exactly what he didn't want, what none of them wanted, and here it was happening. I may as well have been Satan in their dining room.

I had no choice, or so I thought at the time. No one told me that I had to sign. I scrawl my name onto the empty line, and lean back into my chair, looking around. No one is "happy", somehow I'd expected they'd be relieved, satisfied, something, but they weren't. No one moved a muscle, except my wife's mother. She smiled politely and quickly took the divorce documents away from me, got up, and left the room. "NOW GO!" my wife screams, bursting into tears.

I look around at Taiyo and Asia, who had since stopped playing and upon whose faces the knowledge that their mother and I were no longer married seemed to have registered. I slowly rise to my feet and shuffle out, back downstairs, accompanied by no one, back out onto Higashiyama Dori, which suddenly seems like an entirely new location. A new street I'd never been on before. A sadder, grayer, and *completely foreign place.*

I took a deep breath. *I'm divorced. What should I do?* No second chances. No second chances. *No. Second. Chances.*

Dream On

It's taken me two years to write those last four pages. I have recurring dreams where we're all together: me, my ex-wife, and our two children. Vivid, emotional, soothing dreams that feel exactly *like it's really happening.* In those dreams I'm walking on air with some residual happy contentment. I'm talking to my son and my daughter, and laughing with my beautiful wife. I've had maybe two or three dozen dreams about them over the course of the time since I've returned to the US. Those dreams are the closest I've come to my ex-wife and our children in the five-plus years I've returned to American soil. If there were a way to make myself have those dreams, I'd go to that channel every night. What does that say about my psyche? For all the bluster and bravado, *have I ever really gotten over losing my wife and children in Japan?*

I never properly apologized to either my wife, or to her family, or our children. I thought she didn't want to hear it, but even if someone doesn't want to hear your apology, that doesn't excuse your responsibility for doing it.

I wish I could talk to my wife. It might be that my greatest dream is to have a sit down with her and tell her I'm so very sorry for not being able to be who she wanted me to be, and who I wanted myself to be. I myself am broken and dysfunctional and I brought my broken pieces and dysfunction with me to Japan and handed them to my wife. Sorta hoping her and our family would be able to glue the pieces of me back together again. But she hadn't even been in the room when I was broken into those pieces. *Hell, she hadn't even been in the same country.* It wasn't her fault. I wasn't man enough to be the man she needed me to be, even if I wrongly thought that man should have been Japanese. It was *me* she had chosen, not some Japanese dude, and me who fucked it up. She knew what she was getting herself into, as it relates to her society and her family, *but she chose me anyway.* I'm so sorry to have broken her heart. I'm so sorry for putting my wife and her family through all that negative stress and garbage. I'm so sorry for having been exactly what they didn't want me to be, and for doing exactly what they didn't want me to do. I'm ashamed of how I had a great opportunity to create a real international *Future Love Paradise*, like I had printed on our wedding invitations. I walk with an inner scar that won't ever go away, because I was in way over my head. My intentions may have been good, but the train had left the station and the final destination had been decided long before my good intentions came into being. *I played myself.* I apologize to my two gorgeous children for inflicting the pain of divorce on them. They are innocent and they were innocent. They only wanted to have a loving mother and a loving father who would care for them and protect them and be there for them. I apologize to them for being a dad who they only remember bits of pieces of, rather than a dad who they can look up into his face and say *hey Dad* to.

For a long time I tried to hate my wife. I tried to tell myself *if she had done this or that and been this way or that way and listened to me, things would have been different.* But it's not my decision how other people "are", that's for them to decide. *I am the boss of no one but myself and I was a shitty boss of myself.* The release of the self-created grudge against my wife has helped me to heal. It sucks walking around every day with an acute grudge on anyone, for whatever reason. *Hate makes us sick.*

>Chapter 17

DIVORCE, DELUSIONS AND DEBAUCHERY

Lost

The actual ramifications of what divorce meant took a long time to actually sink in. In some ways, for me, it still hasn't completely sunk in—what I did to my marriage, how it all ended, the smoldering ruins behind me, and the fact that just a few years after marrying in Japan, I was a divorced man. No one sets out to become divorced, unless they're masochists. Divorce hurts like hell and is a confusing, perplexing, emotionally wrenching ordeal that takes months and years to settle into your system. It's a parasite that slowly takes over your body until you're able to adjust to its presence in your life. It's exactly like the death of a loved one except *no one's died,* unless you count the relationship as a living, breathing entity, which I do. I didn't want to stay in a place of mourning and grieving, so I tried to block what had happened out of my mind by focusing on my magazine.

I was having meetings with the *RAN* staff at the Oasis 21 Starbucks. We charted how we were going to splash the magazine onto Nagoya, making plans for marketing and discussing ideas for stories.

Delusions

The reality is that the immediate aftermath of the divorce paper signing at my wife's family's house was anti-climactic. We had already been separated for at least 6 months, and the actual signing of the paperwork was just a formality. However, I still had the keys to "our" apartment. One afternoon, about a week after the melodrama at my wife's family's house, I went to the apartment to drop off some clothes and books for Taiyo and Asia. My team and I had just published an issue of RAN, which I had a copy of with me, and I had planned to leave it on the kitchen table for my wife to see. I was proud of RAN, and I wanted my wife to be proud too.

I hadn't expected to see her there. The last time we'd both been in the apartment at the same time was when she had caught me with R23 on that fateful early Sunday morning. I slipped my key inside the lock, stepped inside, and the apartment was silent except for the sound of water running in the kitchen. Taiyo and Asia weren't home, probably at their grandparents. Nervously, I kicked off my shoes and walked into the kitchen to find my wife, now *ex*-wife, standing with her back to me at the sink quietly washing dishes.

"Konnichiwa..." I said feebly, but she didn't respond, not even a flinch. It was as if I wasn't there at all. She stood silently washing and rinsing cups and bowls and plastic containers, while I stood behind her. I placed the bag of babies' stuff I had brought onto the floor, took off my backpack, reached inside, pulled out the shiny new issue of RAN and took a step closer. I could see her shoulders visibly tense up as I came nearer.

"Hey, I just published this...", I said, holding the magazine up, hoping she'd turn around to see, but she continued washing the dishes as if she were alone in the apartment. As if I didn't exist.

"You don't want to see?" I pleaded. No response. Having published a magazine in a foreign country was, at the time, just about the biggest accomplishment of my life, but she didn't care. The dishes had all her attention. I placed the magazine onto the kitchen table and said, "...hey, I bought some stuff for the babies..." hoping she'd look, but she still didn't turn around, and continued washing, and rinsing, and washing, and rinsing. I looked around a bit, then walked back towards the silent front door, put my shoes on, and silently exited the apartment to the sound of dishes being washed and water running in the kitchen sink.

The rejection depressed me and made me feel even more inadequate than before. I thought this was a big deal, this magazine I'd created and made. Even in the aftermath of our split, I somehow figured the magazine, *this accomplishment,* might get her attention. I hadn't hoped it would spark a reconciliation, but I had hoped for *something.* I wanted to see her smile, or see her being proud of something I'd done, or have her say "good job," or something like it. I thought hearing her say that would alleviate some of the guilt I was feeling about destroying our marriage. I thought it might make me feel somehow worthy of her again, even just a little. And yet, there was nothing. No response. No "good job," no nothing. *Why should she give a shit about a magazine?* I was tripping.

I suppose the reality of what was going on was still just a mysterious fog inside my mind. I was trying to create some kind of weird "friendship" between us by buying things for the apartment. We were divorced, but I somehow thought we could remain friends, like the media tells us to in the West. We're bombarded with images and stories and the weird notion that staying friends with someone you've just given your heart to and had it stomped on by is the most "healthy" way to end a relationship. They don't play that "stay friends" shit in Japan *at all.* It's anathema. They usually either completely cut off contact with ex-husbands/wives or, more likely, become lifelong enemies, and why not? *You've really disappointed me and hurt me and I fucking hate you for it, I do not want to be your friend.* It makes so much more sense than our phony "let's stay friends" ideal, but I didn't know that at the time. I was still brainwashed into thinking A would eventually come around, maybe even soon, and we'd be laughing and maybe even hanging out together and, in fact, we did, for a while. Sort of. We went to a pizza place a few times down in Kakuozan, close to Tom's place where I was staying. I thought these moments would bring us closer together, and "A" would see that we could be friends. I thought she'd remember how funny I was, that I could still make her laugh and see how fatherly I was with our babies, and she'd be "cool" with me, even though we were divorced.

But how do you remain friends with someone who tore your heart out and stomped on it? After a few weird months of trying her best to be my friend, A cut our friendship off completely. Those fall months of 2009 I still had a working key to our apartment. I'd come by in the day, unannounced and vacuum, fold stuff and wash dishes she'd left in the sink. I bought light fixtures and appliances and brought them to the apartment and left them there for her to find, thinking, hoping, wishing something might snap and she might, what, come around? I wasn't even sure if I wanted her to come around, I just didn't want her angry at me for my having done what I'd done. Ego.

She told me one day she didn't want to be my friend anymore. She said she had wanted me to be her *husband* and since I'd fucked that up she didn't want me to be *anything* for her, or to her. She killed our friendship right there on the spot one day in that pizzeria and it forevermore infuriated me. I thought I had worked hard and tried to be supportive as a husband when things were going well between us, right? Hadn't I? I'd bought her a car and clothes and paid virtually all of our bills while we were together, that didn't mean shit anymore? I had taken her on trips to America and worked hard at trying to have her family respect me, and us, while we had been married. I had tolerated the Japanese schools and stares and weird culture shock and everything else, right? That stuff didn't mean *anything to her* anymore? That's not right. I couldn't figure it out really. *Why didn't she want to be friends anymore?* This was the ringing rhetorical question in my head. So what, I'm nothing to you? But yes, that was exactly what she wanted me to be. Nothing. Nothing I had done before mattered, and definitely not some stupid English magazine or any microwave. But still, there I was thinking, *I made a magazine! Here in Japan! I bought you a car and paid all your bills and bought all your clothes!* Why doesn't my wife care about any of that? I still referred to her as my wife, both inside my head and to anyone who asked. It seemed she didn't care about me, us, anymore at all. *Why?* Stupid question.

Despite my wife's indifference, and my selfish bitterness *about* that, I was becoming a rock star in Nagoya. *RAN* was growing, becoming "famous," and because of that, so was I. My events were the talk of the town and I was being offered celebrity DJ status at other events and clubs. People were looking forward to each issue of *RAN* hitting the streets and everyone wanted to be involved. Doors opened to me as far as business and professional relationships. Shout-outs for life to Chris Zarodkiewicz for supporting *RAN* from day one and seeing my vision. Likewise to the staff of heads who jumped it off: Achim, J7, Adam Pasion, our first editor Matt Helminski, and our reigning uber-designer Adrien Sanborn.

>Chapter 18

ARE YOU SOMEWHERE FEELING LONELY?

M3 has an abortion

I was living it up at TB's. Having different girls come over. H, C, and R23 were all making their rounds in my bed. I was divorced and, fuck it, why not just let it all hang out. I was smoking weed and having my run of TB's place. He's a cool dude and I was snacking on his Doritos in the middle of the night, high as hell with munchies. *This ain't so bad,* I thought, *this divorce stuff. I can still see my children, have a little contact with A, and do whatever I want basically.* I gave myself another chance.

One day I'm at this restaurant in Sumiyoshi that was owned by this Turkish character named JJ. Cool enough guy, he'd let me eat free and had placed a couple ads in my magazine. He talked a lot, was married—and divorced—with kids of his own. He was like a young Turkish Ralph Kramden kind of guy, big belly and square head. He always complained about *Japanese this and Japanese that,* but he had a good sense of humor to go along with his big gut and his sly wit.

Her Name Is M3, She's A Photographer

One day, we're at his place and we're chatting about bullshit, divorce, Japanese women, etcetera, when in walks a very cute but serious looking 20-something Japanese girl. She comes inside and she's actually not only cute, but somehow she's also super sultry looking. Her mouth is tucked into a pouty pucker and her eyes look placid and mature. She's got a mane of thick curly reddish brown hair and she's wearing blue jeans with no belt and a halter top that just covers her belly button. She seems confident, but unpretentious, but also sophisticated. *She's very sexy.*

JJ says hello, and she says hello back with a twinge of an Australian accent? JJ introduces her to me, her name is M. *Another M.* JJ tells me she's a photographer, and says maybe I can "use" her with my magazine. She's interested, and she and I chat a bit with JJ. She's curious about my magazine. She tells me she wants to take some pictures for the magazine, and then she proceeds to show me some of the images she's shot on her cell phone. They're interesting. She apparently likes taking pictures of everyday items—salt shakers, coffee cups, flowers, chairs, subway platforms, rain—but she takes the photos at super close up range, so that the image in the foreground is in sharp focus, but there's always something just out of focus in the background. Her Japanese-Australian accent is intoxicating. There's an attraction between us, our conversation is smooth and unforced, we can both feel it, but I'm wondering, *is this one of JJ's girls?* She could very well have been. I don't tread on another man's territory, but her accent has me reeling; plus, *she's got a very big, very round ass. Maybe the biggest, roundest ass I've seen on a young Japanese girl so far.*

I don't want to be presumptuous so I play the background and let JJ take over the conversation. He and the girl chat a bit more and I'm tucked into the background, watching, listening to see if I could catch a glimpse of something that might let me know if they're together. Yeah, I know JJ is married, but so what? *This is Japan.*

I hear her tell JJ she's going to Central Park. She gets up, says goodbye, and goes outside and hops on her bike and pedals off. A few minutes later I tell JJ I've got to bounce. I go outside, jump on my bike, and I'm headed to Central Park.

I catch up with M on her bike. When I see her, she's standing up pedaling on her bike. For whatever reason, seeing a woman standing up and pedaling on a bicycle is very sexy to me.

I ride up next to her, "hey, so you're a photographer huh? What else do you take pictures of?" I ask. She demurs. "I can't tell you . . ." she says. Naturally, this piques my curiosity. "You can't tell me or you *won't* tell me?" "Both," she says. This became part of the dialogue in my movie *Cherry Blossom Trail,* where the Japanese vixen Naomi tells JD she can't tell him her name, on account that her boyfriend is the leader of the local *Bosozoku* motorcycle gang, and he hates *gaijin.* I tell her I'd like to talk to her some more about my magazine and her pictures. I ask her for her keitai number. She gives it to me. I text her later that night and ask her if she'll please show me more of her pictures. She says sure, she'd love to. I invite her to TB's house that night, and she agrees. I meet her at Kakuozan station that evening around seven. I catch her as she's walking up the stairs of the subway, and she's even prettier, thicker, *finer,* than I remember. She's wearing tight white jeans and a flowery top exposing her midriff. *Bang.* We walk back towards Tom's place, about a mile away from the station.

Back at Tom's, in my room, there's a window overlooking a tiny balcony that leads out onto the roof. We climb outside and talk a while, smoked a few cigarettes, look at the sky, with Bob Dylan's "Hey Mister Tambourine Man" playing on the VCR player in the background. It gets late and she misses the train. If a Japanese woman misses the train, it means she wants something from you, they know exactly what time the trains run and they never just "miss" the train. If she does, it means she wants to stay with you.

She asks me if she could stay. *Sure.* I climb back inside the window and she follows me. The dark skies of Kakuozan are yellowed with the fuzz of the streetlights on Tom's street. My room is quiet, except for Dylan singing "Lay Lady Lay" softly on the small television. We hadn't touched each other. We're listening to Dylan sing "Lay Lady Lay". I take off my pants and shirt and climb into bed. I have no idea what she's going to do. She's looking at me while I'm laid up against the wall on my bed in my underwear. Then she unbuckles her jeans at her waist and shimmies out of her tight white jeans and exposes her thick thighs flowing down from her plain white panties. *Here we go.*

She asks me for a T-shirt, I produce one. She then takes off her flowery blouse and bra with no shame whatsoever. Her gorgeous globes are now fully visible in the moonlight, and her legs, midriff, and panties appears cinematic in the light from the television. *This can't really be happening this easily, can it?* But of course, it was. She kneels onto the edge of the bed, falls on top of me and we start kissing.

Stop! We didn't have sex that night. We kissed a while and I touched her breasts and when I tried to push it further she said she "wasn't ready" and I was cool with that. The next day we meet at the aquarium at Nagoya Port. She's wearing a pretty blue dress and it makes her red hair look like fire on her head. She's got on lipstick and high heeled shoes and she's positively radiant. It's like she's never been on a date before in her life.

M3 and I start dating heavily. I'm turned on by her intellect, her photography, her accent, her thick ass. We smash in her apartment and at Tom's. One night we get so wild with it we break her folding bed in her studio apartment. I was thrusting so hard, I ended up bending the metal legs and the frame supporting the bed.

Her apartment is small and minimalist, but extremely cozy. M3 is confident and comfortable with herself in a way H isn't. She's more natural and 'softer'. More than a few times I had H bring me there to see M3. H never exactly knew where she was taking me, she was just always happy to have me in her car.

M is young and laughs out loud like my ex-wife and has that Australian accent and that fat ass. Sometimes we'd sit and do absolutely nothing besides stare at each other, motionless, in her apartment. Then we'd eat some small food she prepared, then we'd make love on her tiny single-person metal-framed cot. She lived in an area I hadn't known before I met her. She's open and cool, sensitive and artistic.

The photos that she'd told me she couldn't show me, turn out to be nude photos of women. M3 is a part time photographer of the women who work in the health clubs and sex shops of Nagoya. The photographs I'd seen when I'd visited my sex shops may well have been taken by her. I find it wildly erotic that her job is to take pictures of naked women. I ask her if it might be possible for her to set up an interview with me and one of the sex workers for my magazine, which she does. So one night, me, M3, and the sex worker, who was a painfully "normal" 26 year old Japanese woman, meet after the woman gets off work. We have the interview in a Denny's, which gets filled up with various sex workers, hosts, hostesses, and other patrons of the night from Nagoya's underground world of sex for sale. She had agreed to the interview as long as I promised not to show her face in the magazine. It was M's job to be discreet with the photos, this was going to be M's first official contribution to RAN.

One night, M3 confides in me that she doesn't really "feel Japanese", but that she's also very proud to be Japanese. I ask her why she doesn't feel Japanese. She tells me that her male bosses at her nude photography job don't respect her. She says more often than not she doesn't understand what they want her to do, and what they don't want her to do. I ask her what she means, like, is it their Japanese? She says it isn't their Japanese exactly because she's Japanese and she can understand their words, but, she says, she can't understand their meaning. She tells me in Japan, it's very important to be able to "read the air", and tells me that Japanese have something called nissin densin, which means that they can understand each other without speaking. She said that their hearts and minds can communicate without words, but that she can't understand what they are saying through their nissin densin. M3 said she's had this problem her whole life, which makes her feel like an outsider in her own country. This is monumentally interesting to me at the time. I'd never met a Japanese person male or female, before or after, who told me that they couldn't understand other Japanese. Being Japanese is so important to Japanese that if one doesn't feel like they are Japanese, then they are essentially nothing. *She feels like an outsider, just like me.* This revelation gave me the idea that maybe M3 and I were somehow destined. I briefly considered deading things between H and me, because I felt closer to M3, but I didn't, because I felt I had too much to lose if I gave up H.

These Negatives Can't Make a Positive Picture

Then one day a few months into our relationship, I receive a text from M3, saying she needs to "speak to me urgently." I text back, "about what?" She tells me we'll talk about it when we meet.

We meet a few hours later at a Saizeriya restaurant in Osu. She greets me somberly and leads me to the back and her solemn face and stern attitude tell me something is wrong. We sit down and I ask her what's wrong, but she isn't answering. Our waiter comes over and asks what we'd like and she says water, so I say water too. The waiter returns with two glasses of water. I'm asking her what's wrong and she's still not speaking, only staring at me. Finally, she tells me she's pregnant. I'm shocked. I feel faint. I ask her, "Are you sure?" She practically screams "OF COURSE I'M SURE." I tell her to calm down and she's not having it. "What are you going to do?" She asks me. "What am I going to do?" *I'm not going to do anything,* I'm thinking.

I tell her we, *she*, has to get an abortion. Her solemn face turns into a scowl. She's heated. She says to me, "That's it? That's what you think? Only that? Abortion? What if I don't want to have an abortion?" I tell her I can't have any more children, I tell her I can barely see the two I already have in Japan. I tell her there's no way I can become a father to another child right now, especially with a woman I just met. I'm thinking entirely of what I can and can't do, and how this the resolution of this situation needs to happen for my life to be uninterrupted. *I am the king of pain.*

She's fuming. Our waiter returns and asks if we're ready to order, I pick up the menu and start looking at the choices.

"WHAT ARE YOU DOING? I JUST TOLD YOU I'M PREGNANT
AND YOU'RE GOING TO EAT?" She grabs the menu from my hand.

Well, it's a restaurant, I'm thinking, *and I'm hungry, and why did
you have us meet here if you didn't want to eat anyway?* I say this last
part out loud. She becomes furious and storms out. The waiter is
standing there looking at me in anticipation.

"Sumimasen, gomen nasai," I say, and I get up and follow M3 out.

We're outside and she's walking away. I grab her arm and finally
ask her what *she* wants to do. She tells me she doesn't know, but says
since I've already told her what I want her to do, she says she has no
choice. She says she isn't ready to have a baby on her own, so she
guesses that was what we'll do, have an abortion. This is what we decided to do outside of that restaurant, even though she says, she
doesn't "believe" in abortions. She's not happy about it. Neither am I.
Storm clouds swirl above. *Massive fuck up.* What was I thinking while
I was pounding her on her tiny metal bed? The pull-out method is not
foolproof, *especially for fools.* She turned and disappeared.

I didn't hear from her for a few days. Then one day she calls me and
tells me she's made an appointment to have the procedure on a Saturday. Saturdays are the days I see my children, I tell her. She says
Saturday is the only day she can go, and that she was going, and that I
was going with her, and that was that. I tell her I *can't* go, while thinking mostly that I didn't want to go.

I tried to rationalize, choosing not to see my children because I had
gotten someone pregnant and had to accompany that someone to ostensibly *destroy* another one of my children, though unborn. I couldn't
imagine myself giving up a day with my own live and in the flesh children to take a girl I barely knew to have an abortion. Mind fuck.
Heinously insensitive. She tells me if I don't go with her she'll tell everyone I know and that she knows that I got her pregnant, and she
threatens to go to my ex-wife and her family as well. I tell her, "Go
ahead and do whatever you want, I'll give you money for the abortion
but I can't go with you." False bravado. She says, "Okay, I will," then

hangs up on me. I'm shook. Worried. Nervous. Afraid. Petrified. What if she does go to A's family? *What have you done now Mr. Asshole?*

Paranoia Sucks

A week or two passes. No word from her about . . . anything. She isn't answering my texts or calls. I'm frantic. Did she have the abortion? *Has she already started putting me on blast around the city? Who knows what's going on? Anyone? Everyone? Are the cops going to come scoop me up one day for getting this young Japanese girl pregnant? Can they? Will they? Would they? Does she know the Japanese mafia? Is she the Japanese mafia? Has she told JJ? And is he rounding up his Turkish crew to come find me and kick my black American ass? He runs with a lot of Eastern European cats and they're all looking for an excuse to kick a nigga's ass in Japan anyway.* Man, I'm telling you, paranoia fucking sucks.

How Do You Mend a Broken Heart? I Don't Have a Clue

One day I decide to just go to her apartment, to see what was what. I get there and she opens the door crying, holding her belly. I try to hug her and she's not having it. She stiffens up and turns her head away from me, "*Yada! Dame!*" she screams, exactly like my wife used to say when she was angry. *Flashbacks.* I'm standing there looking at her in the doorway and she has her head down, her eyes are red and puffy, she's wearing pajamas, and it looks like she hasn't been outside in days. We're standing a foot apart for what seems like hours until I shut the door. No words pass. Just me, looking at her, and her sobbing quietly holding her stomach while fat tears splash on the ground below.

Finally, I pull her in to hug her and she collapses into my arms, sobbing loudly, saying "ittaie, ittaie", over and over again. She's still clutching at her stomach, *it hurts, it hurts.* I tell her over and over "I'm sorry, I'm sorry, I'm sorry," as she's steadily sobbing into my shirt. Finally we release, and I hand her an envelope with one hundred thousand yen. She takes the envelope, stands there with her head down for a moment, then she opens the door. I turn around and leave.

That next Saturday, I'm with Taiyo and Asia. A heavy pall is cast over the day. I'm doing my best to enjoy the day with them, all the while imagining M3 lying on a cold table having her insides vacuumed out. I feel disgusting, disgusted with myself. How could I have done this? I felt God shaking his head in deep disapproval. My children are running around in the park while I'm watching them, emotionally miles away, sitting on a Japanese park bench.

The next day, I call M3 to see how she is. "It hurts," she says, her voice small and frail. I'm empty for more words, and she probably doesn't want any more of my words anyway. I ask her if she'd like me to visit, she says no. I'm at a loss as to what to do.

But you didn't do anything, I tell myself. *You had sex with her and got her pregnant and made her have an abortion by herself while you played with your children in the park. What a fucking asshole you are, man. What a fucking asshole you are.*

After a few weeks, M3 no longer answers my texts or calls. I don't dare go visit her at her apartment, once again, I'm too afraid of the consequences—I don't want to visit the scene of the crime, unlike most criminals.

I was beginning to think that I was somehow different, 'special', because of my magazine and music and events and all that other bullshit. I cheated on my wife, got divorced and lost my family. I was sleeping in someone else's house and bringing women to my room and eating my host's Doritos and cookies and smoking weed upstairs and acting like a complete degenerate. I had lost what I thought was *a really good girl.* But H was still there, very much by my side, despite my own self. *Is this my life?*

Gut spill

Every once in a while, I crash.

I wonder what the fuck I'm doing here all over again.

And all the flesh and freedom is no consolation.

I imagine back to how it was before all this happened.

We talked about getting married and having babies.

It would be beautiful, all "mixed" and exotic, we'd give them fancy exotic names.

We'd all live together. She'd enjoy being mom, I'd enjoy being dad.

I never figured she'd tell me to stop doing half the things I was doing, ALL the things I LIKE doing.

I hadn't planned on her wanting me home at her time, whatever time is hers.

She'd start with the constantly feeling sick thing, she already has, I'd have to turn around my life and cater to her.

What was I thinking?

Have another child?

All with three other ones vying for my attention?

What was I thinking?

You get tired of them all no matter how beautiful, however big tits, whatever.

That's why you fuck so many of them. It's because the "distance" between you is at its smallest, sort of, when you're pushing your cock into them. In that moment, it doesn't really matter what either of you is "thinking", what matters is what you're feeling, because you can't understand what they're thinking anyway, so why should it matter, and they'll never tell you what they're really "feeling". Right?

Right.

Otherwise, you're a fucking monster. And so is she.

In a few months/days/weeks, whatever, it'll return to exactly how it was before you knew each other, and that means you'll never speak to her, she'll never speak to you, instead of growing "closer" you'll grow apart until that moment when she'll disappear and never return and then she'll become a mirage and you won't believe it but it'll be oh so true and it'll make you wonder just what the fuck you thought was going on all those times she swallowed your cum or let you fuck her in the ass and she fucking jumped and squirmed with delight at every move you made and every sound you made, but now, the bitch doesn't return your mails and would just as soon forget you ever existed and doesn't even acknowledge anywhere inside her that she ever spoke English.

"Eigo." –English, in Japanese.

Whatever.

The weeks turned into winter. Christmas came and went. The ATMs were all closed. Fucking Japan.

Taro, Dan, Ebony, Chikayo, Me: T.A.O.W.

The Art of War

Despite and perhaps as a result of my own heinousness, I was still DJing, making moves, doing things. When you're one of about four black DJs in a smallish town in Japan, your name gets around. I got booked as a DJ at a New Year's Eve party up in Hakuba in winter of 2009 going into 2010. Hakuba is a famous Japanese winter sports resort where folks go to snowboard, ski, snow Jet Ski, and do all things wintery. I don't.

It was a cool little setup, a big old traditional-style Japanese rooming house, a bunch of bedrooms with lots of different nationalities staying there over the weekend. I met a hot Nordic chick there, made some friends, old and new.

There were several DJs booked for the New Year's Eve event, I was one of them, and a couple cats named Taro and Dan, known at the time as Solskye were also booked as DJs. Taro and Dan were part of a scene I hadn't infiltrated yet, the electronic music scene. The three of us struck up a quick friendship and decided to start working on a musical project together.

Taro, the alpha male of the pair, half-black, half-Japanese is Washington, DC, born and bred. Taro is a charming cat with deep musical skill, plays Japanese *Shamisen* like a true master and produces sick electro dance beats with dashes of *shakuhachi* bliss. And his partner, Dan, is a new-age spiritualist dude from Virginia, he's "Robin" to Taro's Batman.

The three of us killed our DJ sets at the New Year's Eve party. I spun R&B/Hip Hop classics and club bangers from eighties dance rock and new wave, B52's "Rock Lobster" and Nelly's "Dilemma". They spun dubstep and electro, they were amazing. The three of us spent the first day of 2010 snowed in, discussing plans for our collaboration when we return to Nagoya. I was excited to have a new project. I was hoping this new project would distract me from how I was feeling about not being able to see Taiyo and Asia that Christmas and New Year's. To add to the void of my children, I was still gutted from the abortion experience with M3.

I decided to call the project "The Art Of War," since I'd heard of the famous book on the strategy of war, written by Sun Tzu. Never read it, but heard it was a treatise on how to win in military conflict, which could be extrapolated and applied in other situations in life. I thought the name could reflect conflict of any kind, and since I was deep in conflict with my wife, her family, parts of Japanese culture, as well as parts of myself, I thought the name was symbolic of struggle within relationships. Little did I know at the time how art can reflect life and vice versa.

Be extra careful how you name things and what you call things— words have energy, and projects and people take on the power of the energy behind their names.

When I returned to Nagoya after the Hakuba trip, I was charged, and so were Taro and Dan. I recruited Tzuru, the Japanese singer with whom I'd performed "Anata No Namae Wa Na'an Desu Ka," and who had done vocals for my "Multi Culti" project. Taro and Dan recruited Chikayo, who was Dan's girl at the time, and we immediately started writing songs and headed to Nakamura's News 90 studio out near Biwajima station to record. Dan bought a sick electronic drum kit which he couldn't play, but that didn't matter. We were about to take over Nagoya. For a minute.

We Will Surround You

TAOW was a crazy outfit from jump. I don't know how I imagined it into existence, but I did. Like I said, in Japan, I lost my fear, and whatever I thought of trying, I tried, and most of the shit I was doing was *completely popping*. Cats were lined up to work with me. Recording music, organizing festivals, DJ-ing parties, publishing my magazine, photography sessions, personalized clothing made by H, maddlovely indeed. My DJ name "MADDLOVE" became synonymous with great music and a great time. *I'm getting my thing in action.* When I thought up TAOW, I had no idea what would pop off from it, I just knew it would be sick. And it was.

We were to be international, intergalactic, musical superheroes. A more hardcore, international electronic version of Fleetwood Mac. A darker, Asian-tinged version of the Black Eyed Peas. Spiritual Musical Prodigy. A fusion of hip hop and electronic, laced with reggae and international vibes. We were ready to rule the fucking world.

Taro was the producer, his beats were hard. But they're also soulful, melodic, hungry, dark, and fast. He's able to insert emotion into a minimalist musical landscape somehow. It sounds like poetry without words. I wanted to add something specific to his beats. I had been writing poetry for years, dating back to when I was living in Crown Heights in Brooklyn USA, way before it became a gentrified haven for hipsters and yoga.

I brought my philosophical pseudo-reggae raps and blended them with Taro's souled- out space beats. His deep voice and traditional Japanese shakuhachi added yet another dimension to the music. Harmony, strength, power, wisdom, these were our foundations. You can check out our album entitled *The Way* on Bandcamp, just type in 'The Art Of War," and we're the first band you'll see.

Bitter Sweet

In early January of 2010, Haiti suffered a catastrophic earthquake. I had a friendship with a gorgeous Haitian woman named Dee Fev at the time. Before her, I hadn't had many Haitian close friends.

Me, Dee, and the staff of *RAN* held a huge charity event at the Nagoya Hard Rock Café. It was a super success and one of the best, most unique events Nagoya has ever had. The event sold out and the Hard Rock ran out of liquor. People were lined up to get inside, and Japanese passersby wondered why the Hard Rock suddenly had a long line down the block. It was a local star studded event in Nagoya.

I recruited several local bands, DJs, singers and rappers. We put on a stellar show, plus we raised a lot of money for Haiti. This event went down in Nagoya history as the first and only event to ever cause a liquor sellout in the Hard Rock. When the bartender told me they'd run out of liquor, I could see why, the place was packed to the rafters, every table was 5 and 6 people deep, no standing room at the bar, with people clamoring to get inside the little DJ booth we made by putting a couple chairs around a table to block it off.

RAN was bubbling, we were three issues in but I still hadn't completely wrapped my head around the fact that I was now divorced, my family was missing in action, or I was.

Burning the Way

I'm breezing through the city of Nagoya with my dreadlocks flying, listening to Taro's enigmatic music in my headphones. I'm cruising through temples, sloped hills, deserted parks, down the alleys of Sakae, Imaike and then back into the residential areas behind Kakuozan.

Lyrical ideas and concepts flowed like air during these moments, which matched perfectly with Taro's mysteriously magnetic music.

We're recording songs at Nakamura's News 90 music studio. Dan, the drummer, is learning to play drums on his electronic kit. Chikayo strikingly pretty Japanese woman, in her late 20's is blessing Taro's beats with enormously beautiful piano/keyboard/synthesizer riffs. Tzuru, the beautiful Jazz, Soul singer, and I had a short lived fling during the recording of my Multi Culti project. The song, *First Kiss* is about our (mostly) unrequited love affair. We allowed, or shall I say, *she* allowed two romantic "incidents" to occur between us, but then told me she didn't want our relationship to get in the way of the music we were making. She basically said "Trevor it's me or the music…" and I chose the music. It was a good decision on my part because with two couples already in the band, we'd have ended up like Fleetwood Mac, which might not have been such a bad thing. *Three couples* in one band? Nah. Fuck that shit.

All of us were rehearsing, writing songs, hanging out. I wanted to fuck Tzuru, but that phase of our life was done and we were making music now. Taro was a cool cat to be around, measured and polite mostly. Dan had a west coast gypsy spiritual vibe thing happening, which I felt I needed to be around. Made me feel closer to Jimi [Hendricks]. Chikayo, Dan's lady, gave off a friendly, intelligent vibe herself. Tzuru was fine and her voice was soulful and she could really sing. Then there was me. I had pulled us all together, introduced the team to Nakamura's studio, and I was writing the lyrics to Taro's music. *Something was happening…*

At this point, I'm texting my wife a few times weekly to get some information about our children, to hear something from her, to stay in touch, to … *whatever,* but she's not responding. New year, new things I guess. She'd vacated our relationship completely. It sucked. I had thought we could remain friends, or that things might be different by this time, but how? It *sucked.* I underestimated how far my wife, ex-wife, would push me outside of her life.

Tears at Nakamura's Studio

Our new band was holed up at Nakamura's Studio, where we recorded, "Sorry", a song I'd written for my ex-wife. The profound lyrics of the song, were words that I was unable to say to her. If I may –

I had a girl/made the girl my life/loved the girl so much/I made the girl my wife/I did my best/tried to treat the girl right/so I worked all day/and gave her loving at night..
I apologize/for all of my lies/and all of the times/when you looked into my eyes/and I left you alone/inside our home/with two babies in your arms/and I'm somewhere in the zone
-went the lyrics.

There's onigiri, potato chips, cans of Chu Hi, and Japanese music magazines strewn all over Nakamura's coffee table. I'm in the vocal booth while the others are all watching me spill my guts to my wife. Tzuru and I had just ended our quick romance and the whole divorce episode with my wife comes rushing in, like it felt when my raft went over at Nagara River.

I'm really missing you/Just want to hold you/and like I told you...

Taro is watching intently from one corner of the couch, while Tzuru is sitting at the other end of the couch looking directly at me. Dan is feeding Chikayo potato chips and Nakamura is softly nodding his head to my lyrics.

That song. Those words. I pull off my headphones and don't say anything to anyone. Walk down the steps, slip on my sneakers and head outside to the parking lot. I round the corner towards the back of Nakamura's studio, walk along the gravel covered lot and the rocks sound like heavy static underneath my feet. Once I'm in an area where I think no one can see me, I pull out a cigarette and pull it to my lips to light it. Suddenly, I'm crying. Tears are pooling up in my eyes and my throat feels tight and I'm looking around with the cigarette smoke curling up towards my eyes, wondering *why am I standing here crying outside in Nakamura's parking lot.*

Inside, this new band, these great musicians, *a new crew of friends,* are all chilling on a couch having a great time enjoying our triumphant moment of creation, but outside, here I am crying like a bitch because *I really miss my wife and I don't know what I'm doing.* I was just married wasn't I? I had a family and a wife and kids and a house. *I'm not supposed to be single.* I didn't mean to fuck things up with my wife.

The tears continue while I'm puffing on a cigarette and looking up into the sky feeling stupid. Finally, I decide *I shouldn't be out here crying.*

Panic Attack

The release flooded me out. Anxiety. Weird solipsism. Inner kaleidoscope tunnel. Heavy breathing. Japan? Children? Marriage? Divorce. Teach. Magazine. Songs. Studio. *Now.* Panic. Full on panic attack in Nakamura's parking lot. No one knew what was going on because they were all upstairs recording, drinking *Chu-His* and eating stale *onigiri.* I'm outside and my throat is closing around my breath and I think I'm choking. My heart is racing, my head is spinning, and *why do I feel so scared?*

The world is a vortex and my eyesight is closing in on the corners. My vision is getting blurry and dark and darker ... and ... then I think of Taiyo and Asia, and it all slows down. Something suddenly gets a grip of me.

I'd see them soon. I thought,

I have to make lunch for them, tell them when to cross the street, put on Asia's shoes, hold Taiyo's hand, they need me.

I come back around. My eyesight returns to view and my breathing slows down.

They've gotta keep seeing me, I thought.

I've gotta do whatever it takes to make that happen. I have to keep seeing them and they have to keep seeing me. I can't fall apart.

Tom Kicks Me Out

Tom had asked me several times not to smoke in the house, but I didn't listen. Whenever he'd leave, I'd flame up on the windowsill ledge. Then I'd go into the little room adjacent to mine that Tom kept as his office, and watch porn on his computer. One day, apparently after burning, I accidentally left a little pile of herbs on the desk.

"Tom, look!" a pile of herb silently screams Tom's name.

I returned home later that night to find a note from Tom sitting on the kitchen counter:

I told you not to smoke weed in the house, but you did anyway. You left your weed on my computer table. You've got no respect for my house so I want you to get THE FUCK OUT OF HERE as soon as possible! I don't care where you go or how you get there, you've got until the weekend to clear out. No second chances. You're lucky I don't break your fucking face...AND DON'T EAT MY FUCKING DORITOS!
—TB

No second chances. No second chances. No. Second. Chances. Just like that, I was not only divorced, but now I was homeless again.

Standing there in my room, holding Tom's note, it suddenly occurred to me how different my life was right then from how it had been just six months before. Six months ago, I thought, I was married, and had a home, even if my marriage wasn't going great, I had a wife and children. Even if they were rarely at our apartment, we lived together. But now all that seemed like a dream.

I thought about how different things were from when I arrived to Japan some six years ago. My mind ran across images of getting off the airplane, that first ride into Nagoya from Chubu airport with Aki and Eiko.

I recalled having absolutely no intentions on finding a wife, getting married, having children, or any of it. Hell, I'd had no intentions of staying longer than a year. Is this my life? Is this my life? I asked myself over and over again, looking up into the ceiling of the room in Tom's crib, hoping there'd be a huge "NO IT ISN'T!" emanating from the heavens. I'd close my eyes and reappear in my old apartment. A and the babies would walk in laughing and I'd laugh too, even more than them.

I shook myself out of the stupor and realized, *Nigga, you gotta find someplace to go.* Like right now. I didn't want to call Mark again because it seemed to me that would be going backwards, and I didn't want to drag him back into my sordid life. I didn't want to contact H right away either. Although I knew I'd have to eventually tell H that I had to leave Tom's place, I didn't want her to know that I was kicked out for smoking weed. That would have pissed H off and right then she was the best thing going in my life. I wanted to do this on my own, as best I could.

I acted quickly, searching my contacts in my phone. I figured there'd surely be some name that'd pop up that I could call or text for help. I scrolled through the As. Lots of Japanese girls' names, but no one that could help me. The Bs next. Not many Bs. Tom was on this list and he was kicking me out of his place. It seemed surreal. Why am I looking for a place to live when I have an apartment and a family and . . . but I didn't. Cognitive dissonance.

I went on. The Cs were comprised of C, another few Japanese girls and my mom whose name is Constance. Then the Ds. As I scrolled through the Ds, I came across this dude named Deiter, a tall red-headed Australian cat who had once told me he had been studying Aikido under this Japanese Grand Master who also happened to be a Real-Estate Agent. Deiter said that the Grand Master/Agent owned property in Fujigaoka, the last stop on the Higashiyama Line. I had taken the Higashiyama Line to the second to last stop to Hongo, where I'd had lessons, but I had never gone all the way to the end. No need to. It was far outside Nagoya, the boondocks, as it were. And it was destined to be the next stop on my journey.

Fujigaoka

I remembered Deiter mentioning the real-estate dude because it seemed weird to me that an Aikido master could also be dabbling in real estate, but I wasn't sure why it seemed weird. I call Deiter, he answers and I ask him if his Aikido sensei might have a place I could stay. Deiter says I'd have to join the Aikido class because anyone who lived in any of his Master's rental properties had to also take his classes. There were no exceptions. Deiter asked would I like to come to a class that very night to meet the sensei and of course, I said yes.

I take the Higashiyama line to its end. Last stop. Fujigaoka. I'm thinking to myself, *not only had I been banished outside of my wife's family, not only had I been kicked out of Tom's place, but now, here I am at the very last stop on this train.* It felt like the whole city had put me out to pasture.

Meet Master Furukawa

Off the train, I make my way to the dojo based on Deiter's directions. When I arrive at the dojo, there are a few students taking off their shoes outside on the sidewalk. Deiter is nowhere in sight and the students all sort of look at me quizzically. They're all wearing Aikido uniforms, but I'm wearing sweats. Suddenly Deiter strolls up smiling broadly, extends his hand and says, "G'day mate!" Deiter looks regal and powerful in his uniform, and I'm here on his mercy so *nigga, no Crocodile Dundee thoughts, just be cool and gracious* I tell myself. Deiter pulls me in for a hug and introduces me to an older, distinguished-looking, short Japanese man with a full head of black hair and thick-rimmed glasses, the sensei, Master Furukawa. Outside the dojo, Master Furukawa is talking to a woman who turns out to be his wife. She also takes the class, and like most Japanese wives, handles all the accounting for the family business.

Master Furukawa looks at me bemusedly. Deiter explains in Japanese that I'm there to join the class and also that I'm looking for an apartment. Deiter slips this in—it became obvious to me that the apartment was supposed to be an afterthought, what was important here was the Aikido, not my need for an apartment. Master Furukawa looks me up and down, nods his head, says something to his wife in Japanese, and Deiter turns to me and says, "You're in, mate. Master says you can move into the apartment in a couple of *dize,* he wants to have it cleaned fuh-rst. You have to stahht class the *saime* week you move in though. Rent is thirty thousand a month and the lessons are thirty thousand as well, including the uniform. You'll be paying the woife here." He gestures to Master Furukawa's wife, who nods politely. "Noice, mate, you got a ploice to live!" Deiter exclaimed. *Noice* indeed.

A few days? Where would I stay those few days? Tom had said I had to be out immediately, and had threatened me with a knuckle sandwich. Even though Tom was about a decade older than me, I was still shook that he made the threat. He was stocky and talked lots about his martial arts training and *shit, what the fuck did I know? He just might do it,* I thought. Either way, I knew I had to return to his place and ask if I could stay a few more days until I moved into Master's place in Fujigaoka. So I did. I return and ask Tom if I could crash just a few days but he puts his fist in my face and says "Hell no, get your shit and get the fuck out right now!" He stares me down, and then follows me while I go upstairs to get my shit together.

At this point, I had no choice but to return to Mark's cluttered room and the hard floor in Issha. Back to a few days of abject loneliness and soul introspection on how I'd fucked my life up. But somehow I had found a place to live. *Bullet dodged.*

>Chapter 20

FIVE STAGES

Maybe more

They say men go through five stages of grief after a divorce: denial, anger, bargaining, depression, and finally resignation. I was *deep* in the denial phase for those first few months, and my heady lifestyle contributed to it. Too much movement, too much activity, too much stimulation, total change—it was all happening too fast and too close together for me to be able to properly process what was happening. It was as if the events of my life mimicked Chinese firecrackers exploding one after the other, while some morbid Chinese Dragon danced macabre, as I stood there watching my life explode. *Pop!* There goes my marriage. *Pop!* Gotta find someplace to live. *Pop!* Gotta find someplace *else* to live. *Pop!* You're pregnant? *Pop!* Your magazine is coming out. *Pop!* Where are your kids? *Pop!* What the fuck is Aikido? *Pop!* Fujigaoka? *Wtf is that?* My decision-making ability was corrupted, my mind was shaken and stirred, my emotions were tumultuous, and I felt emotionally nauseous. Alternately, like some dead animal carcass smushed by crossing traffic in the middle of the road. Dead inside, but on fire too.

Plus there were all the various women who were a part of my life in some way at that time, including H, who was burrowing herself deeper into my skin like a leech. Or a tick. She was not so subtly making her presence felt, especially in the immediate aftermath of my divorce. She was the Red Cross after my personal earthquake, and I grew more and more dependent on her. It poisoned me and nearly crippled me. She would not leave me alone. She showed up wherever I was, unbidden, and slung open the passenger door to her little Toyota. She paid for everything, everywhere, all the time, without the least hint of feeling anything whatsoever about doing it. She came to my house every night, unless I had someone there. She made lavish dinners: pineapple chicken, breaded chicken, *niku jaga,* soups, and huge overflowing salads. She called me five and six times a day, then another three or four times to apologize for having called those other six times. *She told me over and over that she was "smart" and I believed her.* She was all smiles, all the time and offered herself whole to me however I'd take her. She took me to the doctor, dentist, shopping, had my taxes prepared for me, helped me with my children, translated my many business meetings with advertisers and promoters who wanted me to either perform or DJ, or both. She facilitated meetings with restaurant owners and researched the lowest priced printers for me to use for *RAN.* She drove me around to all our distribution points every month faithfully, no matter the hour. There were times we were delivering *RAN* in the dead of a cold winter's night, her pulling up to the curb at the front of Elephant's Nest, or Red Rock, or MYBar, or wherever, and me lugging hundreds of magazines up flights of steps, for hours, once or twice a month. She was booking me in shows and driving me to these shows in the pouring rain, in snowstorms; whatever the weather, H was there.

But I was losing. Or, more specifically, I had already lost. My family was gone. I saw my children sporadically. I found it harder and harder to concentrate on work. My confidence was withering. Even though H was doing all she could to help me, she wasn't, and I wasn't doing much to help myself. H was rescuing me, but at the same time, I was becoming more and more dependent on her, in every way, psychologically, mentally, emotionally, physically, financially.

She enabled me. She created logos and brand images. She even designed elaborate costumes for my band, The Art Of War. Amazing right? She drove me to rehearsals and drove my friends home if they needed a ride. She waited for me at dawn when I'd get off work from any venue I was performing or working at. She once slapped me in the face because she saw me give a fan a kiss on the cheek at my ROCK THIS TOWN benefit show at Nagoya's Hard Rock Café.

On The Surface

There were my various part-time English teaching jobs to maintain, there was my ongoing and noxious club life to maintain—it all was too much and I was absolutely in over my head. *Denial.* To my friends and fans, it appeared as if I was on the winning side, but my insides were completely rotting away.

One night, I tried to deliver some toys for the children to A's apartment, but she wouldn't open the door. She didn't acknowledge my being there even though I pounded on the door and screamed, "A. I just want to give the babies some stuff I bought for them." No response. Nothing.

Later that evening H and I sat in her car, parked alongside Shirakawa Park. We're talking about my ex-wife, her family, and our babies. And I just lost it. I broke down in tears in the passenger seat of H's car with H sitting next to me. Again. Blubbering like a neglected baby.

And then, I promptly discovered Spice.

Scary Spice

Liquid nitrogen, brain freeze. Coal furnace, lung barbeque. Dragon's breath, throat torch. Eyeball spiral, vision distortion. There's being high, and then there's being *really fucked up.*

Spice is synthetic marijuana. It's a mixture of "herbs"—exactly *which* herbs you don't know, scary enough—which are then sprayed, or soaked in man-made chemical compounds, including, but not limited to, ammonia. The resulting concoction is an android version of cannabis, a *cannabinoid*. It attacks your brain's nervous system connectors like those tentacle robot monsters in *The Matrix*. It's toxic as fuck and sucks your soul away. Quickly.

Spice is listed on the package as "not for smoking," the chemicals reproduce the effect of THC on pleasure receptors in the brain. Except that the human brain has limits on how much THC those receptors can handle, and when they've had enough, they simply turn off, which is why few people overdose on marijuana. No matter how much weed you smoke, your brain receptors are only going to process a certain amount of that natural THC, so you can only get so high off weed, which is a good thing. However, the man-made cannabinoids in spice seem to override, or turn off, the THC safety valve in your brain, and thereby flood those receptors with the fake and noxious THC chemical compound, which you've put to fire, and which sometimes does extreme damage. *Very quickly*. There have been reported cases of spice smokers dying after exactly one smoking session. Apparently the cannabinoids, which trigger the hallucinogenic highs, sometimes cause shock and paralysis of normal brain functions, as well as respiratory failure. The cat who invented spice, a dude named John W. Huffman, himself said, "People who smoke spice are idiots." *Really.*

Almost from the moment I moved into that apartment in Fujigaoka I started smoking this shit called spice. I discovered it one night at a spot called Herb Harbor, which, ironically or not, was located just up the stairs from that very first sex shop I'd visited six or seven years earlier. Every time I'd ride my bike through Sakae on my nightly runs in and out of the area, I'd see the neon sign, and wonder, *What the fuck is an Herb Harbor?* One night I had the balls to walk up the flight of stairs to check it out.

Inside, it's brightly lit. Plush wraparound burgundy velour couch in the corner and a flat-screen TV playing hip hop videos in another corner. A couple of Japanese salarymen slumped over face-first, knocked out cold on the glass counter. Zombies. Displayed underneath the counter were dozens of the brightly colored, little packets of different kinds of spice. Some with pictures of Bob Marley, others with foreboding pictures of skulls and crossbones, dynamite, flowers, eyeballs, crocodiles, purple clouds and bonfires. They had names like *Luau Love, Demon, Dose, Meltdown, Mad Hit, Moon Rocks, Skull Krush, Joker, Nerve Fire, Freedom, Kronic, Bizarro, Chatterling*, and worse. The packaging, however, made the shit look downright enticing, at least to me, in the mental state I was in.

Behind the counter there's a tattooed-up blond, punk-rocked-out-looking Japanese Suicide chick with permanently sloped eyelids and jagged teeth. "What do you need?" she slurs the first time I came in, in English. Come to find out, there are more than a handful of foreigners who had come to rely on this place, and its product to get them through whatever they needed getting through. She offers me a hit right then and there, inside the store. *Whoa,* the rush is immediate and shocking.

Imagine a cold kerosene torch being shot through the canals of your brain. Imagine a flaming freight train thundering its way along your nerve endings. Imagine a burning hot-coal furnace being lit on fire inside your skullcap. Imagine your cerebral cortex feeling temporarily glazed over and barbequed like red-hot, charcoal briquettes with your head being the grill. Then feeling your mind hollow out temporarily, then your chest, lungs, and stomach feeling like they'd all been scraped from the inside out with an ice shaver, leaving you emotionally gutted and truly wasted, but not in any good way. Imagine your senses being fricasseed and blitzkrieged by a cold blue flame. This is what the high of spice felt like. A dive-bombing of your brain. A shot of burning gasoline sizzling your dome piece. And for almost the entire time while living in Fujigaoka, I became addicted to it. It becomes me.

One day I'm in the Aikido class wearing sweats, while everyone else is wearing their cool looking uniforms. I'm on the mat and Deiter is grabbing my wrists and crunching them between his huge Australian hands. I'm figuratively and literally flying as Deiter flings my spiced-up, black ass to the ground. Master Furukawa is laughing at me, and so is everyone else, taking their cues from him.

I Almost Died. Again.

Spice became my after-work, before-work, afternoon, evening, and late-night secret spice vice. Larry and I would cruise the streets of Sakae just before dark, cop from Herb Harbor, then smoke ourselves into a frenzy, so much so that we'd almost black out and have to stop in our tracks to let the high settle in. We had to allow our brains and racing hearts to calm down enough for us to continue moving. We smoked spice while watching stupid old British sitcoms on his beat up Apple computer while eating chicken soup he made.

Before it got too late, I'd hop the last train up to Fujigaoka, walk home to my little one bedroom, take a shower, smoke some more spice, and go to sleep.

I Can't Breathe

H had booked me to perform at a school benefit for orphans. The show was to be held at a high school somewhere. The night before, instead of putting together my set list and practicing, I had decided to get high with Larry. We smoked all night, and in between, we chain-smoked his Marlboro Reds.

Australian Larry and I were hanging out a lot at my new spot in Fujigaoka. His dark aesthetic and wicked sense of humor was keeping me afloat. But the next morning I when awoke, Larry was gone. I'm in my underwear, sweating like a racehorse, heart beating like 120 BPM. My chest is pounding and I'm reeling in my tiny living room thinking,

Oh shit, I'm breathing really fast, oh shit, oh shit, oh shit, what the fuck?

Then I start having an anxiety attack, because I couldn't breathe. The world starts closing in. It feels like I have vertigo, everything starts spinning and I can't stand up straight and I fall onto my black pleather couch. My vision is getting narrow and weaker by the second. I break out into a cold sweat, and then I remember about the performance scheduled for later that evening, and this makes everything *much* worse. Holy shit. *How am I going to perform?* My heart beats even faster, so fast I could feel the muscles of my heart pounding. My heart literally felt like it was going to rip itself to shreds.

Again, I start thinking about Taiyo and Asia, but this time it doesn't help me. I'm even more panicked. *Where are my children? What have I done? Why am I here in Fujigaoka?* I'm having another full-on panic attack, but this time I'm feeling the after effects of a night of smoking Spice and about a dozen Marlboro Reds.

I race across the hall, and bang on my neighbor's door. I hadn't met this neighbor, and didn't even know if he, or she, was there. An Asian cat opens the door, but he's not Japanese. I'm panting, standing there in my underwear, and he's startled.

"Yes, may I help you?" he says in English.

"Hey, I'm sorry to bother you..." I gasp.

"I think I'm dying, can you help me?"

He invites me into his place, which is an exact replica of my apartment, but with different stuff. Turns out he's from the Philippines, and he tells me he was a doctor in his country. *Thank God.* I'm standing there in my underwear and tank top sweating like a pig, panting, eyes bulging.

"Man, you gotta help me! I just moved in next door. I have a show tonight, but I can't catch my breath and my heart is beating like a freaking piston. I don't know what to do..."

My chest is heaving and I'm clutching at my chest while pacing back and forth in his kitchen.

"Calm down "he says evenly, "have a seat."

I sit at his tiny kitchen table.

"Did you take drugs?" he asked.

"Yeah I smoked some sp-sp-spice," I stammer.

"What's spice?" he asks.

"Man, come on, dude, it's some synthetic marijuana shit, man, I don't know what the fuck it is!"

I'm feeling absolutely *wild*. My heart is beating faster, I stand up again and start pacing back and forth in his apartment. Suddenly I feel hot and I peel off my tank top.

"I gotta call my Mom, she's a nurse, she'll know what I should do," I say.

"Okay," he says,

"Do you want to use my phone?"

"Yes. Please."

He disappears into his bathroom and returns with his phone. I call my Mom. She answers, thank God.

"Mom, my heart is beating really fast, and I can't catch my breath, I've got a show tonight, Mom, and I don't know what to do," I tell her.

"What happened, dear?" she says in her soft Jamaican accent, concerned.

"Mom, I smoked some spice last night with my friend, and now I'm all messed up. I think I'm having a heart attack, Mom, what should I do?"

"Spice?" she says slowly, "*Spice,* Trevah? Yuh seh yuh smoke *spice?* What kinda spice yuh smoke, Trevah?"

Then I hear her saying to my stupid sister in the background,

"Day-dreh," (my sister's name is DIEDRE but my Mom pronounces it "Day-dreh" for her own reasons)

"What is spice? Trev say 'im smoke spice.'"

Then she gets back on the phone with me, and I hear my sister in the background asking my mom,

"...Cinnamon? Like nutmeg? Wow. THAT'S STUPID."

My heart is pounding and I'm breathing like my chest is going to explode, and my skin feels like it's peeling off, and my head is getting heavier and heavier and lighter and lighter at the same time-and my chest is pumping a million miles an hour and my eyes are bulging and I don't know what to do and it feels like I'm about to incinerate and explode simultaneously, and I can't catch my breath.

Then I hear my mom on the phone saying,

"...wha' you seh, Trev? Spice? Which kinda spice yuh smoke, Trev? Mi nevah really know spice c'yan smoke before now, nutmeg spice? Dem 'av different spice yuh c'yan smoke in Japan—ee Trev? . . . Trev yuh al'right?"

She's speaking slowly, confused, but concerned. She's asking me about nutmeg. My heart is about to shoot out of my chest onto this guy's kitchen table. I know it. But suddenly I'm pissed and I say loudly, directly, and firmly into the phone:

"YES, MOM, SPICE. SPICE, MOM. OKAY? I SMOKED SOME SPICE WITH MY FRIEND LARRY LAST NIGHT AND I HAVE A SHOW TONIGHT AND I CAN'T GO BECAUSE MY HEART IS BEATING OUT OF MY CHEST AND I'M SWEATING AND I CAN'T CATCH MY BREATH AND I DON'T KNOW WHAT TO DO, MOM. OKAY? PLEASE MOM. CAN YOU PLEASE JUST TELL ME WHAT I SHOULD DO, MOM? AND TELL DIEDRE TO SHUT UP. OKAY? PLEASE MOM. JUST TELL ME WHAT TO DO."

And I hear my sister laughing in the background saying,

"Turmeric might be good to smoke. . ."

And I want to kill both of them, but the whole episode of my Mom not understanding what I'm going through, and me having to get clear headed enough to explain to her, and her asking about nutmeg, and my sister laughing, somehow worked together to calm me down. It took my mind off my immediate situation. It made me think of home.

By this time, the Filipino cat hands me a pill and some water.

"Take this," he says.

"It'll calm you down."

I throw the pill into my mouth like it's a Tic Tac, and gulp down the water. I can hear my Mom on the phone still talking to my sister,

"'Im seh 'im smoke spice . . . what is spice, Day-dreh? Yuh know what is spice?", and I hear my sister in the background,

"No, Mom, I don't know what spice is. Like, spice for meat you mean? Or like nutmeg? That kind of spice?"

My Mom returns to the phone,

"Trevah, what kinda spice? Like . . . nutmeg spice? Or, black peppah? Like that? Yuh c'yan smoke nutmeg, Trev?" and my sister is laughing in the background, and I'm pissed that they don't understand, and then I notice my heart has slowed down considerably. Everything is relatively normal again, except that I'm sitting in this dude's apartment in my underwear with my shirt off.

I stayed awhile at the Filipino dude's place and calmed all the way down. He told me he'd been working at a hospital that belonged to my Aikido sensei, and that this is how he'd gotten his apartment. He tells me his family is still living in the Philippines, and that he's saving money to either go back there or to have his family move to Japan. I thank him graciously before returning to my apartment. Once inside, I look in the mirror and my face is drawn and my eyes are red. I thank God for my life.

I ended up going to the show at the school, no rehearsal and no practice. I performed two songs and the children seemed to love it. They called me the next year and asked me to do it again.

The crazy thing was, this episode wasn't enough for me to quit smoking spice. I kept at it for the entire time I lived there in Fujigaoka.

Don't Stand So Close To Me

One night after Aikido, which were generally "classes" where Deiter wrung my wrists like they were wet washcloths, he and I head to some bar he knows about which was located close to the station. He's wearing his Aikido gear, and I'm dressed in my sweats. Australians love to drink. We arrive at the bar, and Deiter strides up to the counter in his Aikido uniform and orders a beer. I don't drink, so I get some pineapple juice. We're chilling, shooting the shit, Deiter is telling me about his broken heart, he tells me a Japanese woman he'd been dating had trampled on his feelings, then vanished from his life suddenly. Familiar.

There's a clamor at the door behind us and I turn around to see four young Japanese girls entering the bar. They all look like hip hop dancers, wearing sneakers, hoodies, jean jackets, tight jeans, and colorful T-shirts. One of them looks familiar to me. Deiter immediately starts clumsily chatting the girls up. He's asking where they live and the familiar-looking one is looking at me *hard* with huge curious eyes. These girls couldn't have been more than twenty, twenty-one, if that old. More like eighteen or nineteen, I'm thinking.

Deiter introduces me as "David," which is the name all my students in Japan know me as (have I already mentioned that "Trevor" was WAY too hard for anyone to pronounce in Japan? I learned quickly that I did NOT like being called "TOH-RAY-BAH," so I had them all call me by my middle name). When the familiar one with the large eyes hears my name, she runs up and stands directly in front of me squealing,

"Da-veed Sensei! I knew it was you! Do you remember me? I was your student at ------------ chugako, remember? I'm S."

We're standing about six inches apart, and she's smiling widely and her eyes are practically bulging out of her eye sockets. I'm looking at her wondering *where does she know me from*? Suddenly, her face comes into focus in my mind, and she's sitting at the back of a classroom, wearing thick white socks and penny loafers, smiling at me quietly while I'm teaching her and her class English in a non-descript, Japanese junior high school, maybe five years prior. Recognizing her now, I look her up and down and say,

"Wow, you're really grown up. How old are you now?" I'm actually nervous, but not sure why.

"*Ni ju ni*," she says—twenty-two.

Nerves.

"Really? What are you doing here now?"

"*Coco chikaku ni sun de imasu*"—I live near here.

"Oh, really?" I smile nervously.

I notice she's moved even closer to me, her smile looks huge, like it almost hurts her face. She is standing between my legs now, and I can smell her perfume. I'm becoming flustered. She's standing between my legs, smiling like a Cheshire cat, directly in my face like I'm her Christmas present or something.

I'm sipping my pineapple juice and Deiter is standing on the other side of her making faces at me. Her friends have all floated away to a pool table located on the opposite side of the bar. They're watching me and my former Junior High School student, with their own huge smiles. It's awkward, but I can feel *something is going to go down.*

"*Anata wa ima mo sensei desu ka?*" she asks—are you still a teacher?

"Tokidoki", I reply in Japanese, sometimes.

"Demo saiking watashi wa DJ desu", but recently I'm DJ-ing too.

Her eyes bulge and she leans closer and puts her hands on my thighs. *How could her smile get any wider? It's already practically cracking her face.* It's like she's seeing Santa Claus in person for the first time.

"DJ?! Daveed DJ desu ka??"

She gives me that long, incredulous, rising "ehhh?" sound Japanese love so much, especially girls. She yells to her friends, "*Kare wa mae wa watashino sensei deshita . . . demo ima wa DJ desu.*"

A chorus of "ehhh? Ehhh? Ehhhhhhhhhhhhhh?" from her friends as they all come and crowd around me. Deiter is nursing his beer at the bar in his Aikido uniform with a "fuck me, mate" look on his face.

"Yes, I'm a DJ", I say, confidently.

"Ehhh? *Daveed sensei wa DJ doko desu ka?*"—Really? Where do you DJ?

"Well, I just moved here, so I DJ at my apartment mostly, just practice, but there are a couple clubs in Sakae that I DJ at too."

"*Ei-ay de?*"—at your house? She asks, eyes bulging somehow wider, inching ever so close to me.

"Yes," I say, then I hear myself asking,

"Do you and your friends want to come to my house and hear me DJ?"

She says "yes" emphatically, I turn to Deiter and say I'm leaving,

"Where ya goin' mate? The party just started!"

I tell him the girls want to come back to my place and here me DJ and he says,

"Have at it, I'm beat and I have classes tomorrow."

I shake his hand and fifteen minutes later the girls and I are at my apartment.

I'm now DJ'ing for a party of four. I'm spinning old-school R&B on my Pioneer CDJs, smoking a spice joint, and they're all whooping it up, dancing in my tiny living room. They're eating stuff they'd bought at the *conbini* on the way to my place, making noise and acting like my house is a straight-up club. Alternately, they're flopping down on my couch, then standing up and dancing again. My dude J calls and says he's in the neighborhood, wants to drop by.

"Dude, hurry the f up," I say.

"There are four fine young chicks in my apartment, they're all fucked up, and I'm by myself."

Fifteen minutes later, J is at my door. The girls are relaxing, on the couch and floor. Everyone's feeling nice and drunk by now. Things have calmed down a bit, and it's after midnight, which means no more trains anywhere. One of the girls says she can walk home since she lives close, and she bounces. We're all in my living room, Biggie Smalls' "One More Chance" is in my CDJ. I'm high, J and the other three girls are in my living room. The girls are giggling and talking softly with each other on the floor, while J and I are sitting on my couch wondering what's going to pop off. *How's this going to go down?* I was thinking.

Suddenly, my ex-student stands up and takes her friends outside and they have a short powwow on my porch. J and I are looking at each other. I ask J what he thinks is going to happen, he doesn't really give a shit. He never really gave a shit about much besides computer shit. Me, I'm a bit more optimistic. When Japanese girls are drunk and have these powwows, things can easily go either way—they'll either come back and say, "Sorry, we have to leave RIGHT NOW"and just be out, or they'll all be down for whatever, and then it's on.

They were down for whatever. At least my ex-student was. Suddenly, my front door bursts open and my ex-student asks me if she can talk to me in my room.

'Sure," I said.

We disappear behind my sliding door and she says,

"Can I sleep with you?"

This type of thing is far more common in Japan than anyone outside of Japan realizes. Still though, this girl used to sit in my English class in the back of my classroom as an 8th grader, something about it seemed at least, weird.

This can't be happening, I think to myself, there were so many "this can't be happening moments", *but of course, it is happening dude. Of COURSE your ex-student wants to sleep with you, man. You were her teacher and now you're a cool DJ and she's just met you at a bar and introduced you to her friends, which makes her cool, and now you're all at your apartment. They've all been drinking and dancing to your music and drinking some more and you're the coolest thing they've seen in a long time, probably. It doesn't matter that you just got divorced and almost killed yourself smoking spice. This young pretty girl wants to sleep with you and that's just fine.*

"Sure you can sleep with me" I say.

She smiles her impossibly huge, wide smile again, hugs me, says "*arigatou,*" like I was doing her a huge favor, and exits my room. I'm stunned and dumbfounded, but not *too* stunned and dumbfounded. I smile a little smile to myself and unfurl my futon, spread my sheet and comforter over it, place my two pillows side by side, and change into my long johns.

I peek outside my room to see J on my couch looking at his iPhone, my ex-student and her friends are outside on the porch chatting. I whisper to J,

"I think she's staying, man, in my room."

"Well, there's that then," he says dryly, and returns to his iPhone.

I shake my head and retreated back into the room. A few minutes later she returns, slides the door to my room closed behind her, asks me to give her something to sleep in, and she slips off her jeans and stands there in her panties watching me while I'm reaching into the top of my closet for something to give her.

I hand her a pair of my white long johns, which she sits on my futon to pull onto her legs, and she looks much better in them than I do. I hand her a black Jimi Hendrix T-shirt and she takes off her shirt and bra without the least bit of self-consciousness, revealing a pair of tits that looked like they belonged on a mature Japanese woman, not a 22 year old Japanese girl. They're much bigger and fuller than I had imagined. They were almost *too big* for her skinny frame—full and kind of droopy, with big pink areolas. The whole moment of her changing clothes happened in slow motion, and she wasn't the least bit shy. In fact, I was more self-conscious of the moment than she was. Much more. She had a look on her face like she was about to ride her favorite roller coaster. I had a look on my face like *I was the coaster.*

We begin kissing and immediately peel off the clothes we had *just* put on moments before. She climbs on top of me, lifts up her leg and carefully places my dick at the opening of her pussy. Once inside, she slides up and down a few slow times, looking at me smiling. We did that for a bit, then I leaned up and cradled her in my arms. I improved my position where I'm now on top. Balls deep, I proceed with long slow thrusts until her quivering thighs wrap around my body.

It was really good, but the entire time, I'm thinking, *I wonder if she was thinking about this when I was teaching her at school?* Which led to, *I wonder if there were* more *students who thought about this when I was teaching them at school?* Which led to, *there had to have been more, why just this one?* Which then led to, *Oh my god, there's probably hundreds, thousands, maybe hundreds of thousands of students here in Japan who fantasize about banging their teachers.* Which led back to, *and that's exactly what I'm doing right now.*

We didn't even try to sleep after. When we were finished, I put on my long johns, slide the door to my living room open, to find J on the couch still looking at his iPhone. The other two girls are passed out on the floor, huddled close together in the fetal position underneath an Indian blanket I kept folded on my couch. I go into the bathroom, clean up a bit, look in the mirror, and say out loud to myself, but under my breath, "Dude, what in the fuck are you doing?" Then I return to my room and we do it again. This time, I take her while she's on her knees. Her head is down and I've got her wrists in my hands banging away.

How could I not do this? How could this have gone down any other way than exactly how it's going down?

By the time our second session was over, it's maybe 3 or 4 A.M. We both rolled over on either side of the futon, exhausted, and tried to sleep for a couple hours, but it was less like sleep and more like uncomfortable fidgeting and twitching. Her trying to put her head on my chest, me trying to get my arm underneath her neck, her trying to curl up beside me, me trying to move her hair out of my face, it just wasn't right. So we did it again. Three times.

She had the energy I guess, but in fact I did *not*. It was a fluke. I don't know how it happened. I felt like I was *supposed* to be able to deliver. Like I had to live up to whatever fantasy I thought she *may* have had—whether or not she actually did have a fantasy was irrelevant. I created the fantasy I thought she had had for myself to be able to feel like this wasn't something I had instigated. But who cares who instigated it? There we were . . . and this third time, however, was anticlimactic, literally and figuratively.

This time, instead of actually ejaculating, I just pulled out and dry-heaved—nothing' left—. Painful. She gets up, asks if she can have a towel, wraps herself, heads to the bathroom, showers quickly, comes back into my room, throws on her clothes, stands at my sliding door, and says,

"*Zenbu arigatou Da-Veed.* Sugoi tanoshikatta." Thanks for every-thing David. This was really fun.

She then bows, in the most formal manner imaginable. I bow back a little and say,

"*Doitashimasite, S*", *you're welcome.*

She beams that crazy smile, as though she'd just won a cheerlead-ing tournament or something. She turns and steps into the living room, waves, and slides the door shut behind her.

I laid on my futon for a while, fingers locked behind my head, star-ing up at the ceiling, not quite knowing what to do or how to feel. I didn't want to go out into my apartment and face her and her friends; I felt that would just be too much tension and weirdness to bear. So I didn't.

Total Recall

Who was whose fantasy? Was it mine, or was it hers? Had I imag-ined her into existence, or had she? Bizarre.

I'm lying there thinking, *dude, you just fucked your former stu-dent,* and replaying the events of the last few hours over in my head. *The Aikido class. The bar. Them walking into the bar. Deiter with that "fuck me" look on his face. Her standing too damn close to me. Us all walking to my apartment. Me DJing, her wearing my T-shirt and long johns. Her squealing underneath me.*

Then I hear the door to my apartment open and close. They left. And I lay there some more. I never heard from or saw her again after that night. She disappeared into the mist. And it was normal. I felt a lot less triumphant, or whatever, than I expected.

I felt more or less confused, empty, and like I'd done *something else* wrong, something I should feel ashamed of. Instead of feeling great about what had happened, I felt...ashamed? It felt, somehow, like my ex-wife had actually seen what I'd just done. Like she'd watched the whole affair, and that moreover, she was chastising me in my head for my bad behavior. I heard her voice in my head saying, "Da-veed! ARE YOU SEEERIOUS? WHAT ARE YOU DOING?" like she used to say whenever I'd done anything she didn't like. I heard her voice growing louder and louder in my head. I felt worse and worse about what had just happened. I pulled the comforter up right underneath my eyes, like they do in horror movies when the slasher/murderer/stalker/killer/psychopath is right outside their door. I couldn't shake the feeling that A was watching me, right then and right there. I was literally shaking, thinking to myself, *Oh my god, A knows what I've done.*

Even though we were now divorced. Even though she didn't even know where I lived, and probably didn't care either. It just felt . . . weird. I wasn't sure if I was supposed to feel proud of myself for having fucked a girl who used to sit in the back of one of my previous junior high school English classes, or feel like a lecherous *gaijin* preying on young ex-students, or like a cheating asshole husband, which I wasn't anymore, but I still felt like one.

You don't have 20/20 vision in every moment of your life, and the ability to retrospect is a luxury of having lived through things. The weirdness of the episode with my ex-student, the shame and discomfort I felt, combined itself into a murky, dark, anxious, paranoid, depression-filled miasma. This feeling became my default "normal" emotional reset going forward.

I'm Being Watched Through a Crystal Ball

The months in Fujigaoka bored on into Winter 2010. Colder than cold. Far away from civilization, the feeling of having been banished from society grew. The self-imposed banishment made me feel angry, bitter, depressed, and lonely. I felt stupid for feeling paranoid, but that didn't stop me from feeling it. Now, I felt paranoid and stupid, a worthless failure that was being watched by my ex-wife through a crystal ball somewhere. My marriage was a memory, something I had "done," not something I was doing anymore. I felt I had let everyone down: myself, my wife, her family, and my kids. I felt I'd let down the whole foreign community in Japan who were there giving international marriage their best shot. I felt I'd become exactly what Japanese suspect about foreigners, especially black males. I felt I'd fucked up my life because I couldn't keep my dick in my pants, and every time I went anywhere, I felt like everyone was looking at me knowing I'd done just that.

I tried to convince myself that I'd done the best I could in my marriage, but I knew I hadn't. I was confused and dejected and felt sorry for myself and was angry at myself. Part of what kept me going was that I was seeing Taiyo and Asia on the weekends—not every weekend, but most.

Charity Helps

April 2010, a rig leased by oil company BP, explodes in the Gulf of Mexico-the worst marine oil spill in history. A huge, gooey black mess spread over the waters of the Gulf, and it catches on fire. It feels synonymous with my life. I decide my magazine will do a fund-raiser. H does some research and discovers the US-government-sponsored National Wildlife Federation Fund. We contact them and tell them about *RAN* and that we're a Japan-based English magazine and that we're planning to have a benefit fund-raiser. In July, we hold *RAN* Unplugged at the Hard Rock Café. The National Wildlife Federation sent us a certificate. We called our event *RAN*Unplugged because it was all acoustic. It was another Hard Rock success. Folks like Brian Cullen,

Dave Dycus, James Bloke, and Tom Fallon played sick emotional sets while seated on a stool, accompanied by a guitar. I love charity work.

>Chapter 21

THE BABIES

The good times are killing me

The babies and I spent those months when I was living at Fujigaoka going all over the place. My spot was too small to really accommodate them, no room for them to run around inside, so we went out instead.

It was super fun, for me, and for them too. Taiyo was five, Asia was three, and they were still both babies. They played with each other like best friends instead of older brother/baby sister. Taiyo is always talking to Asia, asking her questions in Japanese, tackling and teasing her. He gently pushes her around but always manage to offer her something to look at, play with, or to discover.

Asia is quiet, serene and inquisitive, and she likes electronics. Taiyo likes to draw and has crazy artistic talent. There's Asia screaming out, chasing Taiyo and smashing his face with her little hands. There's Taiyo laughing like a little goofball, giggling and falling all over himself and flailing his arms in Asia's direction. Asia is fiercely trying to smush Taiyo's face with all her might, she's dead serious. Taiyo is laughing. I'm watching, but doing my thing too. It's always like this, it's annoying and necessary and impossibly cute all at the same time. Unless they're sleeping. At some point during the day Asia takes a nap every time I see her. She's needs to sleep during the day and just zonks out at some point.

Taiyo has a full head of thick, almost completely straight black hair, which grows into big, fat curls when his hair grows out. He's a handsome caramel-colored Japanese boy. Taiyo Ja'el. Taiyo is the Japanese word for *The Sun*, I wanted to give him a cool, macho-sounding, but unique name. I hadn't met anyone else named Taiyo, but I'd met cats with other similar names. Taro for one, Takashi, Takeshi, there are plenty of boy names to choose from beginning with 'T', but as soon as I thought of Taiyo it had stuck in my brain. Everyone in my family had immediately fallen in love with him. We brought him over to the US just before he turned one. However, at that age, he already knew how to bow and say *"itadakimasu,"* the Japanese equivalent of "grace," before eating. Taiyo likes to eat.

Asia's hair is in soft, wispy curls, her big eyes and quietly serene attitude is friendly, open, and warm. When the three of us are on the subway, she likes to strike up conversations with old ladies about their bag, or their dress, or their hair, or whatever. Old Japanese women love playing with Asia, and she loves talking to them. Taiyo likes standing and hanging onto the pole so he has a good view of the posters and art all around him on the train. He's always looking at the posters and pictures and images around him. He loves trains. His favorite book is Thomas the train. He's always attentive and alert.

These are my children and I was loving the opportunity to just *be with them*. My Japanese was improving. I had about the same level of Japanese skills as my daughter, but not as well as Taiyo. I had to make a serious effort to understand whatever he was talking about and maybe 75 percent of the time I could understand him. It wasn't frustrating though, because I knew it wasn't going to be like that forever. I knew my Japanese was going to continue to improve, and I also knew that I'd be teaching Taiyo and Asia Jade how to speak English. The fact is, I already was. I spoke in English to them almost 100 percent of the time. Whenever we'd walk, which we did a lot in Nagoya, I would point at things and say what they were in English. "Motorcycle", "Bus", "Restaurant", "Family", and they're repeating whatever I say, hearing it spoken with a native English accent.

I learned to make a serious effort to listen as well as to speak. Therefore, I kneel down to my son's speaking level, and look directly into his eyes *every time* he wants to talk to me about anything. I want him to see me looking directly into his eyes, I want him to feel comfortable looking at his dad, and I want to be at his level instead of him looking up at me looming high up above him. I could hear him better from his level, he could see my face, and it left less of a chance for either of us not to understand the other.

Anytime Asia wants to speak, I pull her into me. She doesn't say much, she's shy and sparing with her words. So whenever she feels compelled enough to actually speak, I need to listen with 100 percent focus, I want no distractions. Plus, it was an excuse to be able to hug her close to me. I love feeling her breath and hearing her voice and seeing her use her words, and the soft innocence of her up close to me. She makes me aware of how much bigger and stronger I am than her, which also makes me aware of how careful I've got to be with her.

I'm Absolutely In Love with These Two Kids

We're taking the subway to museums, parks, temples, shopping centers, game centers, malls, restaurants, toy stores, shoe stores, supermarkets, magazine shops, and clothing stores. We're at Oasis 21, Tokyu Hands, Toys"R"Us, Matsuzakaya, Shirakawa Koen, McDonalds, MosBurger, La Chic, Meijo Koen, Osu Kannon, Nagoya station, and all points along Hirokoji Dori. Up and down Chikusa and all through Motoyama, up to Higashiyama Zoo and back down to Fushimi. I'm taking Taiyo to a Tomika toy car event, located in a huge tent inside the park across from the zoo. We're in and out of the new science museum down at Fushimi. Along the way we're stopping to watch street artists do their thing on the streets while the three of us are bopping through Sakae.

Taiyo has his face smashed up against the glass at the aquarium at Nagoya Port. Taiyo's throwing stuff at the monkeys in Monkey Park in Inuyama, while Asia is trying to imitate how they walk, all by herself, oblivious to who might be watching. There are tons of different people, festivals, and art fairs all along the streets as we're walking. I feel absolutely proud to be with my two cool and fun children walking the streets of Nagoya. We're going swimming down at Utsumi Beach, playing soccer at Shirakawa Koen, going to hamburger shops, eating pizza, and visiting my friends. I took them to Larry's underground apartment cavern and we played in the park up the street from his house. We went to my friend Yoko's house and had pool parties with her kids in Yoko's pool on the roof of her house. I'm teaching Taiyo how to tie his shoes and showing him the cars and buildings and people and trees, counting numbers and pointing out letters and colors and sounds to Asia. When it's too cold or raining, we're inside my small apartment watching *Toy Story* over and over, and it was great every time. Taiyo loves Buzz Lightyear and Asia loves the slinky dog. The three of us are all laughing and eating chicken, potatoes and vegetables that I'd made. Sometimes H is there, and she's very helpful with them, but doesn't try to be their mother. Asia's asking H questions and Taiyo is curiously polite, but keeps his distance from her.

My kids are both growing up right in front of my eyes and I'm right there, next to them and despite the fact that things with me and their mother were spoiled, at least they were there, with me. I was thankful for that, at least.

My cold war with my wife, ex-wife, raged on. Taiyo and Asia, and their grandparents, are in the middle of it. I'm picking the kids up at the Suzuki's barber shop, showing up at the scheduled time. My ex and I are barely communicating, almost nothing.

For now, our communication was stilted and difficult, but at least I was hearing from her semi-regularly. It was oddly comforting. *At least she's out there somewhere,* I'm telling myself, but it's cold—it feels like there's an old abandoned lot in the middle of my soul. My life feels like my own personal September 11th, a huge burnt hole in my soul with smoke rising from the ashes of my own life.

I'm getting short, terse texts from my ex-wife, devoid of any real recognition of me, us, or our co-parenthood of Taiyo and Asia. It's angering and frustrating and saddening and hurtful all at the same time. I wasn't sure how to feel actually, but the warmth of Taiyo and Asia gave me reason to keep going. Japan wasn't *totally* done for me. Not yet.

In December, right before Christmas, I receive a letter from the Nagoya Family Court saying my wife has decided to cut off my weekly visits with Taiyo and Asia. No forewarning from her, just the letter, and things changed irrevocably after that. The letter stipulates that A has decided, for "personal reasons," to force us into "mediation" with the Family Court, whereupon the family court would decide how my future relationship with my children would bear itself out.

Shock to my system. My relationship with Taiyo and Asia is my mainstay, my essential raison d'etre of my presence in Japan, and now, *was my wife trying to take the children from me completely?* According to the letter, I'm not allowed to see Taiyo and Asia until the family court proceedings are complete, which wouldn't happen until next year. Needless to say my New Year's was a piece of shit. Instead of celebrating, I'm wondering if I'll ever see my children again.

>Chapter 22

New Year

More problems

Things with H are touch and go. It's hard for me to be with her. At this point, I had lost my wife and was about to lose my children. All things lost in the fire, had nothing really to do with H, but it had everything to do with H. At least that's how I felt. I still held on to the idea that my divorce was 50 percent her fault. Still though, I'm accepting all her gifts, driving around in her car, she's throwing cash around like it's nothing. I suppose she was using me too. Pimping my dependence. Throwing cash at my stripper ass and I was dancing for her.

Shitty situation, but it somehow helped me to deflect responsibility for my actions. It also disallowed me from developing real feelings for her, even though we were going on five years into our "relationship." To me, she was still just my assistant, the same way she had been through the Maverick ordeal, the same way she had been in helping me start *RAN*. However, for her, it was a full-fledged relationship, even though I barely concealed the fact that I was seeing other women.

It's All About TAOW Baby!

My band, TAOW had its first live show in September at RADIX. It's sold-out. There's mayhem outside the club with people wondering who and what this new band was all about. I'm walking around outside watching the line of people and everyone's madd excited, like they're about to witness a superstar international act. That's what we wanted to be, and that's what we gave them. I'm prowling the stage spitting the lyrics to "New Spirit Soldier" while Taro is blessing the audience with his spiritual Shakuhachi. We end the show with me wearing a spacesuit while performing our song "Standing On The Sun", and the wall to wall throng of people in the audience is ecstatic. We are absolutely killing it, and it's all blowing up much faster than any of us expected.

Meanwhile, I'm still going to Aikido classes a couple times a week, however, Deiter tells me the sensei doesn't like that I'm not coming regularly. The only reason I'm even able to live in the apartment is that I 'm taking these Aikido classes, but now that I'm not going to class regularly, the Master is pissed and asking questions, and Deiter is his mouthpiece.

Deiter is telling me his reputation is on the line, and that I'm fucking with his reputation with the Master. Japanese are very serious about agreements. I should have known. I wasn't thinking much about that, too busy with all the other stuff going on, my kids, my magazine, my women.

I Meet Another A

I suppose it's okay to give this woman a real name. We'll say her name is Ayaka. I met her at Shooters one night. She thought I was funny, and a few days later she hit me up on Facebook. We eventually started seeing each other. Ayaka was *very pretty*, but had terrible fashion sense. One day, Ayaka tells me she's really interested in going to New York, and that she'll pay for our tickets and a room if I'll "tour" her around New York for a week. I felt I needed a break from Japan at the time, so I agreed.

We decide to take the trip together, but decide not to fly together. I figured we couldn't fly together, because there'd be no way I could explain to H why she couldn't take me to the airport. I tell H I needed to see my family in NYC, but I'm not obligated to tell her anything actually. My own feelings about my responsibilities to H are confused.

I tell Ayaka that I'll arrive one day before her to 'set up' our living arrangements. This way she'll be immediately comfortable when she arrives. Slick.

I decide to sublet an empty, one bedroom from an older Japanese woman whom I'd thought would be absent during our stay. I was wrong. She stayed in a second room the entire time we were there, and seemed to never leave her apartment. Whatever time we came in, she was awake, walking around in a neck to ankle robe and slippers. She looked like a Japanese Morticia Adams. We're in New York and things are cool. Until...

I'm Kicked Out of My Apartment While Several Aikido Dudes Watch

One afternoon while Ayaka and I are walking around the Lower East Side, I receive a text from Deiter in Japan.

Mate. Where the fuck are ya? You better get back to class quick. Master Furukawa is pissed that you're not in class and he wants you out of his place as soon as possible. Call me when you get this.

So I immediately call. Deiter tells me the Master doesn't want me in his apartment, if I'm not in his Aikido class. He's made up his mind and I've got to get out. Soon. *Immediately.* Fuck. Here we go again.

I return to Nagoya and immediately call Master Furukawa. He tells me I have to vacate the apartment within a week. There's no point in asking him anything, or begging, or coming up with excuses, or asking for an extension, nothing. There's nothing you can do when a Japanese person has made up his or her mind. It's a done deal.

I had no time to spend with Ayaka once we returned. I kept seeing her but the intensity of our relationship wore off. I enjoyed hanging out with her but our time together was becoming more of a distraction from the other things swirling around in my life at the time. Eventually we stopped seeing each other partially because I had no time, and partially because she started seeing this French cat whom I had introduced her to. Whatever. I had to find a new place to live. In a week.

Naturally, I tell H about my dilemma, and she and I go into furious *find-another-new-apartment-right-now* mode. An artist friend of mine named Rob tells me about an area called Fukiage, which I'd never been to and had only barely heard of. (Rob eventually designed the front cover of this book.) H and I head over to the apartment Rob told us about and there's one 2LDK apartment for seventy thousand yen a month. LDK stands for *living, dining,* and *kitchen.* 2 means I've got two bedrooms.

We meet the landlord, a grandfatherly Japanese man walking with a cane. He's leery of me, but H smooth-talks him into letting me move in later that same week. He's cool with it, and tells me he needs to clean the apartment.

On the seventh day, exactly one week after Master Furukawa had told me I had to be out, H and I are making trips back and forth between my new place in Fukiage and the Fujigaoka pad, shuttling the last of my stuff to the new apartment. On the third visit back to the Fujigaoka place, there are six dudes from the Aikido class wearing black suits standing in my parking lot, looking quite serious. Japanese are the best in the world at the stone face, and these dudes' faces looked like granite. I recognize all of them immediately, they're the black belts from Master Furukawa's dojo. They're there to make sure I completely evacuate the apartment on the exact day Master Furukawa has dictated. Furukawa's thugs.

They're staring dispassionately at me while I'm carrying boxes back and forth to H's car. My mind flashes back to the dojo, where these same dudes had tossed me around effortlessly and laughed at me when I was writhing in pain on the dojo mat. I'm thinking, *how in the fuck did it get to the point where I'm being escorted out of my apartment by a bunch of Aikido black belts in suits?*

You never know where you'll end up. You never know how you'll get there, you can't know who you'll meet along the way until you meet them.

>Chapter 23

Last Stand At Fukiage

Almost desperate

When I moved into my apartment near Fukiage station, I had no idea it would be the last place I'd call home in Japan. All I knew at the time was *I need a place I could rely on not being suddenly thrown out of.* A place of my own, even though I'd thought my place at Fugigaoka was that. It wasn't. Truth is, in retrospect, I knew I wouldn't last long out in Fugigaoka. *Where the hell am I? I gotta get outta here.* These were the thoughts I kept thinking up in Fugigaoka. It was too far out, took too long to get to, and I felt like I was at the edge of space. Think about something long enough and eventually it comes to fruition, sometimes in ways you can't predict, bad or good. Plus, those spice episodes had left burnt edges on the mental images of my Fugigaoka Polaroids.

So, at the end of February 2011, I was exhausted and determined to have another go at it all. The cold, bleak, grey, dour Japanese Winter was just about to come to an end. *Spring is coming*, I thought, *better must come.* I couldn't let the situation and circumstances defeat me.

Somehow I'd made it through more than seven years of life on the streets of Nagoya, Japan. Scrapes, bruises, mental phantasms, emotional tremors, and the comings and goings of insanity, depression, extreme anger and acute loneliness covered my body, mind, and soul. Drugs, divorce, loneliness, culture shock, alienation—these were my badges of honor and scars of battle, having made it past the seven-year mark. Divorce behind me, more humiliation was afoot. Had I known, I might have turned a different corner.

Fukiage station is a relatively quiet nexus not too far from Sakae. I could ride my bike to where my ex-wife is living in 16 minutes and 18 minutes to her family's place in Higashiyama Koen. Fact is, I live right down the street from their place, which is located directly across the street from the zoo. Fukiage is almost directly in the middle of all the places that are important to me. Sakae, Fushimi, Tsurumai Koen, Maranouchi, they're all biking distance.

I knew the area like the back of my hand. I timed my rides. Many times. *Every time.* I bought myself a dope brand-new dual-use mountain/city bike at this bike shop up near my old-school Little Village. I'd race around up and down through Imaike, Sakae, Chikusa, down to Fushimi, back up through Osu, and back into Fukiage. Sometimes I'd swoop back through Imaike, cruising with my arms in the air and my hands up, standing up on the pedals like some kind of idiot-on-a-bicycle night warrior, flying like crazy on my bike at 4 A.M. I loved these solo missions through the dark, back streets of Kakuoazan, in the rain or whatever, pumping my legs quietly with looming temples up above and dark quiet streets up ahead.

Night Rider

I made dozens of silent midnight bike rides up to Motoyama where my ex-wife lived with the children. In the parking lot, I leaned on my parked bike while smoking Seven Stars cigarettes back to back. I would look up at their third-floor apartment like a midnight stalker. Sometimes I swear I saw shadows of my family, swear I heard them talking and playing and laughing. But the really weird truth was, I wasn't sure if my ex-wife even lived there anymore. The car I'd bought her wasn't parked in the parking lot, so how could I know? I was petrified to go knock on the door, so I'd just lean up on my bike and look. Sometimes I made the ride *just because* it made me feel closer to them.

Other times, it was just the freedom to be able to hop on my bike and cruise, like folks do with their cars. *Joy riding* without the joy.

Still, I made the ride on my bicycle dozens of times, throughout the seasons of those last two years. Winter, Spring, Summer and Fall, I crept on my bike to see what was what with my babies Taiyo and Asia.

A Safe Place

There is a massive Tenri Kyo temple directly across the street from my place in Fukiage. The place looks like a combination of a modern, yet traditional Japanese temple and a military fortress. I hear the sounds of meditation and prayer waft through my second-floor apartment at Fukiage nightly. Sometimes, I'd stretch out on my beat-up, broken-down pleather couch and take in the sounds. I'd light candles and incense and zone out blissfully. The temple, the sounds, the distance from Sakae and Motoyama/Higashiyama—made me feel somehow safe, like I'd finally found my spot in Nagoya. After seven years, with all that had happened, this temple being right across the street from my house seemed fitting. There were guards outside every night. Two of them on all sides of the temple. It was eerie and yet comforting. It was my home.

There's a twenty-four-hour GEOS just around the corner from my Fukiage spot. I'm in there renting flicks for me and C, whenever she's over, or for H and I whenever she's over. At the time, Denzel Washington's *Flight* was a film that signaled a change in my thinking. I watched that film over and over, seeing myself in the cockpit instead of Denzel. There is a scene in the movie where Denzel clips the spire on a church and crash-lands in slow motion. He wakes up in the hospital all bandaged up, lucky to be alive. Now he's on the brink of losing his career due to extremely bad judgement calls—that's what I felt like. Glad to be alive, but oh so regretful of the choices I'd made up to that point. But I can't allow those choices to stop me from persevering, progressing, *doing, creating, making.*

Then suddenly a really fucking huge earthquake and tsunami hits Japan.

>Chapter 24

I FEEL THE EARTH MOVE
UNDER MY FEET

The Great East Japan Earthquake

I t was almost spring, 2011. I'm living in my cozy, large (comparably) 2 LDK apartment in Fukiage. My apartment has a balcony that sits right above an Indian restaurant. I've been here for a month or so. Things are starting out decently at Fukiage.

By early 2011, I had experienced some sixty earthquakes in Japan. Sixty is a moderate estimate. It may well have been six hundred. Somewhere in Japan, every day, the earth is moving, be it ever so slightly as to go essentially unnoticed, or be it larger, sudden jolts wherein the ground beneath you suddenly gives way, no warning, and everything is shaking. There are 1,500 estimated earthquakes that hit Japan yearly. Let that sink in. Five per day.

Something about living on an island perched on the shaky edge of a shelf steels the populace against reacting with alarm every time an earthquake occurs. It's like rain to them, mostly. Unless a quake is major, Japanese folks generally ignore it, so I learned to do that as well. Until March 11th.

March 11, was Japan's September 11, delivered to them in the form of a natural disaster. Christchurch, New Zealand, no stranger to earthquakes itself, had suffered a major earthquake on February 22, 2011. The 6.2 earthquake, not huge by any standard, had turned the ground beneath Christchurch into liquid, and the aftermath was dangerous. *RAN* responded by quickly organizing another benefit show at a rock club named Taurus in Shin Sakae. Same folks who had been supporting *RAN* from day one, were planned to be a part of the charity event. These were my dudes in Japan, stalwart guys ready to lend a hand with some rock and blues. *My guys.*

On the scheduled day of the Christchurch event, I'm lying on my couch, parallel to my balcony door that seemingly protects me from the world outside. The giant temple is quiet and the street is one story below me. It's early afternoon and my sliding glass doors are open. A barely noticeable breeze is wafting into my place, and cars and trucks are passing below, creating a small wind draft. Every time a truck drives by, I can feel and hear the wind moving ever so slightly. Nothing unusual.

Suddenly the air outside begins to sound louder, as if a giant vacuum cleaner has just been turned on outside, off in the distance. I can feel and hear something "sucking" or "pushing" the air. I don't pay too much attention to it, figuring it's the trucks, or the traffic. Plus, I'm desperately trying to cop a few ZZZs before the event later that night. Then I feel soft undulating waves moving the couch, no, wait, it's moving *the whole apartment*, the whole building, and I realize it isn't trucks, or the wind, it's an earthquake.

I sit up quickly, brace myself on the couch and look up at the light fixture which is swaying softly back and forth. Earthquake for sure. When earthquakes happen, you never know how long they will last, or how much damage they will do. You have to essentially wait until it's over, hoping it'll be over soon. The longer it lasts, the more damage it can do. I'm sitting on my couch and the apartment and ground underneath me are softly moving like the waves inside of a water bed.

It seems like it's lasting a really long time. Two minutes? Three? Four? Big earthquakes do massive damage in less than 30 seconds. Less than 10. It feels like I've been sitting on my couch with the earth

swaying back and forth for *five fucking minutes.* A five-minute earthquake would be devastating. It's lasting too long, and it's just rolling,
not jarring. This tells me that maybe it's further away. Most earthquakes are a quick jolt, but this is different. There's no jolting, no
sudden movement or shift, just this soft undulating swaying motion,
for five minutes. That's what it felt like while I was sitting up on my
couch looking around.

Finally, the swaying stops. No damage anywhere, things on the
streets look normal. Hmmm. I jump up, put on my clothes and head
out the door with some promotional paraphernalia, stuffed into my
backpack. I head out on my bike towards Taurus in Shin Sakae. *Weird,*
I'm thinking, *we just had an earthquake and I'm going to a charity
event that I've organized for victims of an earthquake.*

I'm the first person from my staff there. None of the musicians
have arrived yet. I spot the manager of the place outside as I'm locking
my bike. "*Ji shing da ne,*" he says to me, "...earthquake right?" "Yeah," I
say, "*sugoi ne.*" I head up to the fifth floor on the elevator. I get inside
the tiny club and the sound guy is there behind the mixing booth. It's
just he and I. It's eerily quiet. Eventually the musicians start to arrive.
Tom is first.

"Hey, you know Fukushima is getting hit by tidal waves?" he says.
"What? Are you serious?" I ask him.

"Yeah, the earthquake caused tidal waves and they're coming
ashore right now..."

Fucking tidal waves? This is Japan, earthquakes are kind of "okay",
but *tidal waves?*

"Are you serious?" I ask him, shocked. A sharp wave of fear shoots
down my spine.

"Yeah man, the earthquake was huge..." he says, "...a bunch of people are dead, maybe thousands...."

"*Whaaaaat?! Thousands??*" Holy shit. I didn't know any of the details of what had happened until that moment. I heard in parts of
Japan, the ground moved so much that it made it difficult for people

to stand. In parts of Japan, where I was able to ride my bike, others literally watched the ground crack underneath their feet. Unreal.

I immediately ask the sound guy if he's got a TV or radio or something so we can listen to reports. We come to discover that a massive 9.0 earthquake, one of the top five earthquakes ever recorded by humans, has struck the coast of eastern Japan, and tidal waves had begun rolling in. Thousands of people were already dead, no one knew exactly how many yet. The skyscrapers in Tokyo had been rocking and rolling like crazy, and people were screaming and crying and running for their lives while aftershocks happened one after the other.

People across the country had already begun rescue efforts. Surreal television videos of wave after wave crashing against the shores of Tohoku showed devastation that seemed like it was a disaster movie. Cars being pushed up against each other. Boats crashing on top of each other. Nightmarish videos of waves of water carrying refrigerators, cars, debris, and all manner of stuff deep inland. I'm watching this, thinking, *there are people in there.* One Tsunami survivor best described his experience as being in a washing machine full of bricks, wood, glass, razor blades, concrete and strap metal. I didn't have that experience, but many did.

The damage wasn't nearly over. Fires raged in Tohoku. Moving fires sitting on top of debris that was floating inland on the filthy waves of water that was rushing in from the ocean. The ocean itself covered the land. Houses, cars, boats, refrigerators, toilets, couches, animals, knives, gas, oil, wood, garbage, dirt—all of it was floating in the millions of tons of ocean water that was flowing into Tohoku, and it was on fire. But that wasn't it.

The nuclear reactor at Fukushima was, and still is, sitting right on the edge of the ocean. The ground shook and the ocean crashed in and *the shits broke*, the reactors that is. Tons of radioactive poisonous water gushed into the ocean. No one knew, and it seems no one still knows, how much of the ocean was, and still is, poisoned by the reactor breach. There's really only one ocean, and it gets circulated around the entire planet. All the oceans are affected by each other. Some maps of that radioactive shit make it look like the waters of the entire planet had been affected.

TEPCO, Tokyo Electric Power Company, covers up their cover-ups, and no one seems to know what to do. It's as if there were no plans for what to do if something like this happened. Video showing skyscrapers in Tokyo swaying back and forth like Jenga buildings *with people still inside* are on the TV screen. The whole mass transportation apparatus in Tokyo comes to a screeching halt. Normally staid Japanese are terrified. Millions of people in Tokyo are stranded and end up walking home. Some for miles. Store shelves go bare, water off, power off, towns become completely black as fires rage hundreds of miles north in Tohoku. There is no phone service and no internet service which prevent loved ones from checking on each other. More videos from within skyscrapers, supermarkets, and apartments surface, and it's almost unbelievable. Shelves, cubicles, stairwells, tables, and furniture are seen shaking violently back and forth, with stuff flying off of them as if Godzilla himself was stomping through the city. And then there were the voices of horrified Japanese shrieking "Kowaie!", "Yabaie!", "Abunaie!" *I'm afraid, be careful, it's dangerous.* Understatements.

Trains, escalators, houses and buildings all shaking like a bomb, or a million bombs had exploded. The shockwaves reach as far north as Hokkaido and down through almost all of the main island of Honshu. It's discovered that the ocean floor rose up *thirty feet* from where it had been before the earthquake, and the entire archipelago of Japan had moved a couple inches from where it had been before the quake.

I and others, all pitched in to box up supplies to those in need. We load the items on trucks headed for Tohoku. Chris Glenn, superhero that he is, gets in a helicopter and reports damage, saves lives, and shuttles much needed goods to the survivors up in Tohoku. Everyone in Nagoya, and beyond, pitches in to help. It's as if the country is under siege.

To their credit, Japanese line up neatly and quietly for hours in order to get rations and supplies. Imagine if a 9.0 earthquake hit LA. Or New York. Imagine the chaos. The comparatively orderly manner in which Japanese reacted to the quake made me feel proud, even though I wasn't Japanese.

Folks arrive to our event and although they're present in the physical form, everyone looks like they've just seen a ghost. You could tell in their eyes that this wasn't normal even for the Japanese. Shocked faces and nervous energy. I considered cancelling the event, but we went on to have it anyway, and changed the focus of it from Christchurch to our neighbors up in Tohoku. Folks didn't quite know what to do, what to say, but the show went on and all the performers played their sets with manic energy. After the event we all went home and watched the disaster on our computers and television screens. I remember watching the news and seeing a mother lay lifeless on top of her small son. Her final offering for her child came in the form of love, valor and protection. That unspeakable image will forever remain in my heart and mind. Sad. Armageddon had come to Japan.

March 11ᵗʰ Aftermath

Since the earthquake, tsunami, and resulting nuclear catastrophe, Japan has closed down most of its nuclear reactors. Only three remain, with controversy over whether those three should be in operation.

In the wake of the earthquake, hundreds, if not thousands of foreigners packed up and left Japan. I found myself contemplating leaving too, but then found myself thinking,

Where would I go? Back to California? New York? Back to the struggle for a nonexistent American dream? Back to cops wanting to shoot me? Back to overt racism, bad food, and high crime?

Controversy erupted within the foreign community over loyalty, but loyalty to what? Or whom? Who were we supposed to be loyal to? Japan? It wasn't my country. Japanese? They weren't my people, and I wasn't even sure if they wanted me in their country or not. Other foreigners who decided to stay voiced outright hatred for those who had left, or were considering leaving. It was bizarre. *Should I stay or should I go?* These questions all brought me back to my children, Taiyo and Asia. *Was I ready to leave them?* No. Not nearly. Not yet anyway. I stayed.

Even though I decided to stay, the seed had been planted. How long *should* I stay in Japan? Was I making a difference here? Would anyone care whether I stayed or not? What if another massive earthquake hits? *How many more years should I stay?* Three? Five? Ten? The folks I knew who had been in Japan that long didn't seem happy. They were either bitter, angry, lonely, borderline insane, or all of the above. I started to wonder if maybe I was becoming one of them. The country had been shook and me with it. Things would never be the same.

That earthquake and tsunami and resulting nuclear disaster crashed into Japan like a million-ton shock wave, and Japan is still feeling the aftershocks. There were daily news reports of the ground underneath Fukushima being irrevocably damaged, poisoned with the leaked radiation. News stories abounded about how the disaster poisoned the world's oceans, and even today radiation levels near the fallen reactor are at higher levels than they were in the days immediately following the disaster. Robots sent in to do radiation level checks *died*. What does it sound like for a robot to die? *How* does a robot die?

Cleanup was predicted to take decades, yet, miraculously roads, bridges, buildings and their infrastructure repaired rather quickly. However, despite the effort to makeover the massive impact, the earthquake had essentially given Japan a permanent black eye.

Sadly, government agencies began courting foreigners, offering huge cash incentives for anyone who would go into the area and help with the cleanup. They wanted to use us as guinea pigs. I was approached on the street by someone to go. *Nah man, I ain't got a death wish*, thank you. But more than a few people did go. I don't know what happened to them.

Japan has never recovered from that quake, and it's quite possible they will never fully recover. The effects of radiation will extend far into the unforeseeable future. What's clear is that on that day, Japan became a scorched, drenched, inundated, polluted, poisoned, and unstable country. No one knows how safe it is or isn't, or if it will ever really be safe again in certain parts. There isn't another country on earth quite like Japan, and there has never been a disaster quite like the one that struck Japan on March 11, 2011. Over 200 billion dollars in damage. 5000 aftershocks in the 12 months after the mega quake. A crippled, and still leaking, nuclear power plant perched at the ocean's edge. 20 thousand people dead. Crushed, drowned, burned, suffocated. Sad.

>Chapter 25

My Own Personal
Aftershock

I lose my kids

Less than a week later, I'm wearing a too-tight suit with my locks braided tightly on top of my head, sitting in a room at the family court in Nagoya enduring a torrid mediation, fighting for my rights and ability to be able to see my children.

I had thought, mistakenly, that somehow the immediacy and threat of life being snuffed out instantly by an earthquake and/or tsunami might somehow make things better between my family and me. I thought my wife, ex-wife would call and ask me if I was alright. I thought maybe she'd even want to reconcile, or at least allow me to see our children more. None of that happened.

That second week of March I had to appear at the mediation to determine if, and how, I might be able to keep seeing Taiyo and Asia Jade. It turned out to be one of the most humiliating moments of my life. 9 A.M. on the dot. There I am on the fourth floor of the Nagoya Family Courthouse, in my too-small silver suit, black shirt, purple and blue tie, my hair in cornrows, looking like a broke Jamaican pimp. I use the word not as a term of endearment or locker room talk delivered to a guy who knows how to get what he wants from women, not that kind of pimp, but a real life street pimp.

I hired a "translator," but by the end of the fucking mediation I wasn't sure if I'd hired a double agent or what. That's why I keep putting shit in quotes, because in Japan nothing is ever what it seems. I asked around to some friends if they knew anyone who might know a decent translator who might also be a paralegal, who I could bring with me to the hearing, knowing I'd need someone to translate what was being said to me, and what I needed to say during the conciliation proceedings.

This New York cat Mark Bailey, who had been trying to kick-start an online radio station, and who had been asking me to host a show on his erstwhile station, introduced me to his partner Dennis, a trench coat–wearing fast-talking, fast-walking, chain-smoking British dude, who then introduced me to his wife, who became my translator.

Dennis' wife was a middle-aged Japanese woman with whom Dennis had been having issues regarding their own children, information I didn't know until after my mediation. We met at her office in Fushimi and she seemed nice enough, never once mentioned Dennis, and before I left asked me if I was available to teach English classes, which I thought was odd, seeing as how her husband was a native English speaker himself. "Maybe after the mediation we can talk about that," I told her. I didn't want to discuss classes. I wanted to be able to keep seeing my children, that's what I was there for. I should have taken into account that every middle-aged Japanese woman has a streak of hatred for men inside her. Every one. But I didn't. My bad.

I had no idea what a "mediation" actually was, nor how to conduct myself in one. I wasn't sure what it was going to feel like to be in the same room with my ex-wife after not having properly talked to her for over a year and a half. I hadn't even seen her in the last 6 months. Or was it a year? I had forgotten.

The Mediation

My translator is seated next to me, wearing a dark sweater, a skirt, stockings, and heavy black shoes. She looked like a middle-aged Japanese librarian. They all look like that. We barely knew each other, and she wasn't at all invested in me seeing my children. She's just there to collect whatever dough I promised her, four thousand yen per hour, and facilitate whatever goes down as best she could. That's what I thought.

I'm uncomfortable in my tight silver suit. The mediation room is small and cramped and I'm sweating and leaning forward a little too much in my chair, trying to make out what the "mediators" are saying. My dull black pleather shoes are a little too small and the heels are worn down, I had been walking on the corners of the shoes, flat footed. My head is burning from the tightness of the cornrows and I'm nervous. My translator is sitting to my left and we're both sitting on a pair of old, dirty, uncomfortable, plastic lawn chairs that look like they'd been bought 40 years before. There are six of us in the room. The four mediators on one side of a table, and myself and my translator seated across from them in our two plastic chairs. I notice there aren't any more chairs, there's barely any room for anyone else in the room. Then I realize my ex-wife isn't going to be in there with us.

I have no idea where she is. *Is she even here?* I ask my translator to ask where she is, and they tell her that she is here, but in another room. The mediation is going to be separate, we won't be seeing each other at all. *Wtf?* I'm in one room and she was in another. *Where?* I have no idea. I ask if I can go to the bathroom, hoping I might be able to catch a glimpse of my ex in order to say, *what?* I have no idea. We're here now.

The mediation lasts three hours. For those hours, the mediators stare at me and *seem* to listen to me and watch me rant and rave, frothing at the mouth about how they are my children too, and how I should be allowed to see them as much as I want. I'm livid, pointing and gesturing, standing up sometimes, standing over them, and raising my voice about my "rights" as a father. If someone ever wrote a book about "Everything *Not* to do in a Mediation 101", everything I was doing would be in that book.

The "mediators" are silently listening to me, or are they? They're looking at me alright, or are they looking through me? Every once in a while they'd solemnly nod their heads, stand up in unison, slightly bow, and then quietly file out of the room. They would go to wherever my ex-wife was—*I had no idea where she was*—and they'd tell her, hopefully, some semblance of what I said, but in fact I had no idea what they were or weren't telling her. I wasn't allowed to follow them and had no ears in her mediation room.

Three female mediators, one male. All Japanese. Late forties, fifties, one was definitely in her early sixties at least. *Middle-aged.* Middle-aged Japanese are some of the most obstinate people on earth. They're deeply embedded in the system of Japan and it's difficult to talk them down. The one dude looks like an older Japanese version of Mr. Bean, but with a mustache. He's wearing a brown plaid tweed dinner jacket. The women are all wearing light-colored sweaters with little frills around their collars buttoned all the way to the top. They look like the type to hit your knuckles with a ruler at school. They all look very serious and stern.

They've got papers and pencils in front of them, they're taking notes during the mediation, writing in Kanji, or Hiragana, or Katakana, or all three—I couldn't read what they were writing. They're alternately looking up at me, then back down at what they're writing, dispassionately. Actually, it seems like they are embarrassed for me, like *poor foreigner, look what you've gotten yourself into, don't you know this is Japan? You'll never make it out alive.* The oldest woman seems like she can barely stand to look at me at all, she's got her head buried in her papers for almost the entire time, just writing.

"Do you have children? You?! You?!" I'm screaming and pointing, challenging the "mediators". It's not going how I'd planned. My translator looks embarrassed to be "supporting" me. I had no plan—shit, I had no idea. I didn't think it'd actually be a fight and deposition for me to prove why I should be able to continue to see my own children. I'm furious.

"THEY'RE MY CHILDREN AS MUCH AS THEY ARE HERS!" I'm screaming when they tell me that my ex-wife doesn't want me to see them anymore. *No, they are not your children*, is what the mediator androids seem to be thinking, that or *it doesn't matter.*

Hague Convention Came Late For Me

Until recently, just a few years ago, there was no legal way a foreign man could see his children if they had been kidnapped by the mother. Thousands of children have been wrongfully ripped from their homes, mostly American homes, and scurrilously taken back to Japan by mothers claiming varying degrees of distress. Thousands more have been isolated away from their fathers, Japanese or otherwise, right inside Japan. Fathers who lived just up the street from the children, like I did, who could never see their children. Finally, after pressure from the entire rest of the world, Japan, became signatory to the Hague Convention in November 2013, but this wouldn't happen until I'd already left.

Japan also doesn't recognize the concept of "dual custody." In ninety-nine percent of divorce cases, women are awarded custody almost by default, and men have to either just turn and walk away, or hope for decent mediation. Foreign men, however, almost never get decent mediation. Mine, in retrospect, was decent, but *wasn't* while I was going through it. Hague is in place now, but is Japan abiding by it? Have you heard of any half-Japanese children being returned to their original country of residence in the case of an obvious kidnapping by a Japanese mother? I'll wait.

I'm Tom Cruise

I'm pleading, being *way too emotional* with the mediators. Japanese hate overt displays of emotion. Makes them uncomfortable and afraid. I was a black lunatic in a tight silver suit with a purple tie and worn-down shoes yelling at them with my eyes bulging and my arms waving. What was I doing? I was way over the top. "I love my kids! They love me! You don't know anything about me! Where is my wife? Why isn't she in here?! I didn't do anything to her! I DEMAND to see my kids every weekend!" I'm slamming my fist onto the table like I'm Tom Cruise in the court scene in A Few Good Men. But it wasn't a movie. It was my life.

I feel like a total fucking idiot, and the mediators are looking at me like *what a total fucking idiot.* It was as if they were watching a movie, and I was the main character who was losing his mind right in front of them. W*ho the fuck is this black guy in this tight grey suit with the purple tie? And the fucking cornrows? Why is he screaming at us?*

They're all sitting perfectly still with poker faces. Stone-faced Japanese. This must have been the funniest thing they'd seen in a long time, but they couldn't laugh, not out loud anyway. Hilarious. Watching this black guy in his small silver suit, begging them to let him see his children every weekend! BWA HA HA HA HA HA HA! What a fucking joke. I must have made for a good story for them to tell their families or friends. *Some nutty black foreigner screamed at us today about seeing his children, can you believe it?*

I'm shaking the notes and letters I brought with me in their faces. I had had C and a few friends write letters in favor of my character. Jokes on paper is what they were.

They file out for about forty minutes, during which time my translator and I aren't saying a word to each other. She didn't seem to want to talk to me and I was fucking furious and had nothing to say to her anyway. She had spent the entire session apologizing for my outbursts, apologizing for our presence, apologizing for having to be there to ask for me to be able to see the children, and essentially apologizing for *putting them* through the mediation.

I came to discover, my translator isn't saying what I'm telling her to say at all. I've got letters from friends saying what a great dad I am. I've got pictures and video of me, Taiyo and Asia in museums and parks and restaurants and department stores, but the "mediators" don't care. I'm flipping pages and reading passages out of the letters and holding up pictures. I'm explaining how much fun my children and I have whenever we're together. I'm telling the mediators how necessary it is for them to be able to spend time with their father, their foreign, black father—but the "mediators" aren't flinching, and my translator is still apologizing for us being there. She's barely looking at my evidence herself. *She and the mediators seem to be agreeing on things. What the holy f is going on?*

After three grueling hours of back and forth, the only real "reason" the mediators could offer me as to why I couldn't see my children anymore was that my ex-wife had told them that she was "stressed". My ex-wife told them that I was stressing her, but they couldn't provide me with any specific examples of this stress.

After having left the room to go talk to my ex-wife 3 or 4 times during the 3 hour session, the four mediators file into the room solemnly to tell me that my ex has decided to let me see my children once a month. They sit down, and the lone male mediator clasps his hands, and says to me slowly, haltingly, as if he doesn't believe it himself, "*Sumimasen, Kanojo wa stress ga ippaie aru.*"—she's got a lot of stress. My translator is nodding her head approvingly, as if to say, *yes, yes, I have stress too.* That's it. No further explanation. *That's fucking it, man?! "Stress?" That's all?*

I can completely understand what he is saying and I don't need my translator to translate, but she does anyway. She looks at me and condescendingly says,

"He says your wife has a lot of stress." *Okay.*

I think I heard that, but WHAT KIND OF STRESS? WHAT DOES HER STRESS HAVE TO DO WITH ME? I'M NOT GIVING HER ANY STRESS! I DON'T TALK TO HER! WHAT STRESS DOES SHE HAVE? I'm yelling at my translator, she's visibly uncomfortable, maybe even afraid. I'm standing up again, towering over them, angry, yelling. No answer. The dude tells me I can return in a month and ask to have our situation altered. You mean I have to go through this again? They tell me if I "behave" for a month, she might change her mind. I'm legally allowed another mediation session, he says, to try to get a different result. I'm livid again. Indignant. *Ghetto*.

"GOOD! I'LL BE BACK NEXT MONTH. THOSE ARE MY CHIL-DREN TOO. WHY SHOULD SHE GET TO DECIDE EVERYTHING?"

I'm throwing a temper tantrum like a petulant kid. A tall, black, pimp-looking kid with cornrows in a tight silver suit and purple tie.

I leave the courthouse furious. Once outside, I reach into my wallet and flip 12 thousand yen into the translator's open hand and take off in the other direction towards the train station without saying a word. Once I reach the train station, before I head down into the subway, I light up a Seven Stars black and puff the smoke into the March afternoon sky. Dejected. *I lost*, I'm thinking to myself, *I fucking lost*.

I'm angrier than I think I've ever been. My blood is boiling. I want to fight someone. I head downstairs and hop on the train, fuming all the way back home. My legs are spread wide on the subway. Man spread from hell, glaring at all the Japanese around me and off into the distance. *I hate these people*, I'm thinking. *I hate these people*. My lips are curled down in disgust and my eyes are slivers.

In Risa I Trust

Risa. Middle-aged Japanese woman I met working at one of the *shougako* schools where I was teaching. She was living with her husband, but told me they hadn't spoken to each other for over five years.

So bizarre, and so perfectly Japanese. A couple with two young children, in a sexless marriage, sleeping in separate rooms, not speaking to each other for years, and carrying this charade on indefinitely. I was repulsed by and attracted to Risa simultaneously. Upbeat, great attitude, sexy body, long, cascading brown hair, slim waist. She had two children of her own, I felt a kinship with her, her relationship was in a shithole after all, and so was mine. I felt we were slightly fated to meet. We became fast friends and fast lovers.

I had been working part time at an elementary school at the time, and Risa was one of the teachers at the school. Risa made me feel welcome. So, after just a few weeks, I asked her to be my mediator at the next mediation. Risa and I had become friends, so I felt she might be compassionate to my situation. Well, at least I knew her.

The Mediation Part Two

I'm confident. Somewhat. This time, the mediators already knew me, already knew what my ex-wife wanted. Risa and I are seated in the old plastic lawn chairs when they file in and ask me,

"What do you want to change from last time?"

"Well...," I try to say calmly, again feeling the pinch of my silver suit,

"It's just that, I think I'm a great dad for Taiyo and Asia, and I would really like to see them more than once a month. It doesn't have to be every weekend, but I'd like to see them every other weekend, if possible, so, instead of once a month, I'd like to see them twice a month, if that's possible." As mildly, as calmly, as evenly and unemotionally as I could say it, I said it.

I figured even if I wasn't directly speaking their language, at least I wasn't performing a show for them like I had last time. Risa had coached me to be less confrontational and more appealing, more apologetic, less threatening. *None of it worked.*

The mediators spent ten minutes—five reintroducing themselves, the case, our whereabouts, the date and all that shit. Then another five more minutes listening to me say the above, in various ways. They rob me of my soul before shuffling their asses out the room. Ten minutes later they return, and said,

"Your wife has not changed her decision from the last mediation. Therefore, you are able to see your children once a month, on the last Saturday of every month, for six hours, unsupervised. You will make arrangements with your wife to pick up your children, but you are not allowed to have any other contact or communication with your wife for any other reason. If you do, she can stop the visits with your children. Do you understand?"

Here we are. Exactly one month later, the exact same situation played itself out, in the exact same room, with the exact same four mediators, except this time, in miniature. What took three hours to decide during that first mediation, was settled and affirmed in thirty minutes this second go around. Why had I trusted Risa any more than the first middle-aged Japanese librarian woman?

I look at Risa and she quickly translates what they'd said, and I feel my stomach drop. Suddenly I feel empty, like I hadn't eaten for days. And I'm hot. Not hot as in angry hot, but more like hot as if I were in a sauna. My head also felt light, or more specifically, heavy. Or both, somehow, as if I had just smoked some kind of emotional spice. My vision was blurry. I could feel my hands balling up into fists, contracting and loosening, over and over again. *I lost again.* This couldn't be. *I must be a loser because losers lose, and I keep losing.*

Risa tells them that I've agreed to the terms. I turn away and want to throw up. Or yell. My mouth feels dry. The suit is itching my skin and it feels like I'm developing an all over body rash right then and there. *I must be about to catch fire. I'm burning up.* The suit feels like a silver straitjacket. *I want to punch the wall.* I sign some papers, Risa and I walk out solemnly, and thus it began. *She wins. Again.*

I was dejected. I couldn't figure out what exactly she'd won, but there was a definite sense of loss on my part. I no longer had the same weekly access, even though sometimes it wasn't exactly weekly, to my babies.

I exited the building with a general but very palpable feeling of deep hatred for Japanese, but I didn't want to live in the hatred. I knew cats who lived their lives every single moment in Japan with that hatred worn brazenly upon their shoulders every waking moment of every day. They made their own lives, and the lives of people around them, miserable. I didn't want that for myself. Or anyone around me, especially my babies. *My half Japanese babies.*

I was vexed to the extreme with my wife but I didn't want to be mad at her either. I was just super frustrated and couldn't quite see how "good" I actually had it. There are thousands of other men, both foreigners and Japanese, in Japan who *never* get to see their children. Truth is, there are millions of men the world over who cannot see their children, have not seen their children, have no way of seeing their children, but want *oh so desperately* to somehow be involved in their lives. My one six hour visit per month was actually generous by Japanese family court standards, but I didn't know it at the time.

The bitterness and hate and anger welling up inside me was poisoning me, but I didn't want to indulge those emotions because I knew they were destructive and could do me no good, but I couldn't calm myself down. I was conflicted. It suddenly felt like "me against them", me being me, and them being, Japanese people in general and my ex-wife and her family in particular. It felt like I was, and had been engaged in a war for some time, but one that I hadn't recognized until right then. An acute alienation set in, *I'm a loser in Japan,* but at least I'd still be able to see Taiyo and Asia. This was comforting. I lost, but I could still see my babies.

They can still see me, I'm not completely out of their lives. All I've got to do is communicate with "A" monthly, pay a monthly fee to A, and I can see the children. I can do this.

Unrequited Love

Risa and I became lovers momentarily, but it didn't last long. She brought her two children, a boy and a girl who were a little older than Taiyo and Asia, and the six of us went out a few times. In getting to know Risa, I discovered that she and her husband had been engaged in a classic sexless/loveless Japanese marriage. I asked her to write a piece for RAN describing how her life had come to this point.

Happier Times: A Japanese Love story
By Risa Chujo

I am a forty-year-old Japanese woman, living in a three-story house with a big yard and big parking space for five cars, in the suburb of Nagoya, with husband, an eleven-year-old daughter, and a seven-year-old son. I have been married for thirteen years. I am a housewife and have been teaching English to little children and to adults for fourteen years . . . it sounds nice, doesn't it? Well, it must be. . . My husband works hard six days a week and earns our living enough, luckily I have my own lesson room in my house, and my children are healthy and enjoy their school lives. We should be happy . . . ostensibly, but the reality is . . . not really. What is the happy family like for you? How should the ideal relationship between husband and wife be?

Encounter with Husband

I spent four years to go to college in the US. I enjoyed the life with my friends there, far away from my family and friends in Japan. I had some close friends, shared the house/life/thoughts, cared and supported each other. At that time, I had some boyfriends, but I was too young and neither they, nor I could afford to turn these relationships into marriage. In 1994, at twenty-four years old, I returned to Japan, and then started working as an English teacher at a language school. In the very first class I had, he was there—he is my husband, one year older. He was just one of the students. I worked very hard to become a good teacher and saw him twice a week in the lessons. He was a punctual, hard-working student though he was not a quick learner. He had a purpose/goal to learn English, which was to do farm staying in NZ. I wanted him to have opportunities to see and learn something different and unknown in the world just as I got the chances in the US, so I supported him to make it true somehow. After his trip, we became closer, not as a student and a teacher, and started dating as a man and a woman. I believe it was six months later after we first met. Another half year later, he moved out of his parents' house, and I visited him at his new place frequently. Soon, I moved in and quickly realized that I wanted to marry someone and have a baby them. At that time he was reliable and sophisticated for me because he started working at the age of eighteen and knew better about the system of the society. On the other hand, I was ignorant, Americanized, and selfish, but I tried hard to be his someone special and ideal; finished work and went home early to make time to share with him, did the house work and prepared dinner for him before going to work, and tried to accept his taste and interests even though they were not mine really. I believed it could be possible for me to accept anything about him if only I had a big LOVE for him. About one year later he asked to marry me, surely I accepted, and we got married in September 1997—I was twenty-seven. It was just the age to marry for the women of those days. More came to have higher educational backgrounds and careers. Also it's getting common for them to continue working after getting married, and certainly I did.

Marriage Life

I think my husband is a very old typical Japanese man. Though he didn't show/express LOVE so much, I felt his love, which was not the Romantic one I really expected though. He was nice, cared about me, and spoke well of me especially in front of his parents. Luckily they have been very kind to me and liked me a lot. When I first met them, I felt sort of surprised they had the different family background, characters, lifestyle and rules from mine. From them he learned the men should; work and earn for family, not cook and do the housework, not talk while having meals, and not give a hand to raise children. In January 1999, our first daughter was born. All responsibility for raising and education were dumped on me just as it used to be common at his/my mother's generation. Also I didn't want to depend on anybody, even my husband and our parents, for everything because they could do, so I believed I could do myself. Probably I wanted to be regarded myself as a mother/person. All my interests and energy were shifting to my little angel gradually. Of course so my love was. As having more days and time spent with her in a small world, I started to think how I should live as a person and what I can/should give/tell her as a mother. I started teaching English to little children with her in the living room in April 2000, to have the place for learning/enjoying/socializing through English. He is/was the man of few words, but he understood and supported my work at home. His life is basically the same as before, it has been well-regulated life even after our children's births. However my life and roles have been changing a lot over time. Our first son was born in February 2003. Basically he was healthy, but until he became six, he would have asthma attacks and I often had to drive him to the hospital even at midnight, when I had a fever of 38 degrees/lack of sleep. I was always stressed out and worn out for everything; teaching for long hours every evening, raising children, housework and yard work, being sociable in kindergarten/ school/neighborhood/mothers' society etc. . . . . I just wanted my husband to share anything each of us faced on, communicate with words warmly/sincerely, without saying silly Japanese jokes. He likes enjoying his time for himself, not having interests to others, not like being involved someone's trouble. Now, every moment, each day, I realize we each have different tastes. Three years have passed since I gave up communicating with him. My future and his future . . . No one knows what's happening in the future. However it is clear in my mind that I feel difficult to continue the present uncommunicative relationship. Also he seems to call off the fake relationship we keep. He and I are looking towards the different ways. Thanks for my children's support and understanding, I can step forward to make each of us shape his/her own future. Recently, I feel that I am the daughter of my mother. Probably I will take the same way as she did live and raise without husband's help. I'm not sure that is the best way each of us will take—maybe not . . . it is not the only solution, it would be the best if we could communicate/understand/care/support/encourage/notice with love, trust, respect . . . and compromise. Even if you are Japanese or non-Japanese, you should keep in mind that you will have some possibilities to confront with invisible/unpredictable/understandable reality to share the life with someone in your long life when you think of marriage—Love is blind. Husband and Wife should be the best partners and friends in a family, to take a journey of life, "Marriage".

The Bitch I chose to Hate

After reading the piece Risa wrote, I ended our brief affair. I couldn't bring myself to be sleeping with another man's wife, let alone a man's wife who had decided that her husband wasn't worth talking to. Beyond ending our brief affair, even though Risa had helped me with my mediation, I found it hard to even be friends with her. I just couldn't understand how a woman, any woman, could financially rely on her husband, but couldn't find the decency to communicate with him for any reason. Plus, that article, those words somehow eerily sounded like it could've been the very voice of my ex-wife, if she had a voice. In another time or of a similar life, she too could think, feel and react the same way as Risa. After that article, I saw Risa as my wife reincarnated. I felt as if she was the ghost of my wife, the part that I didn't like or care to know.

Vanishing Act

For a few months after that second mediation, things were decent. I picked up Taiyo and Asia at A's parents' house, rarely, if ever seeing my ex-wife at all. I'd text her, she'd tell me to pick up the kids at 11 A.M.

I'd go to her parents' house, she wouldn't be there, the grandmother would hand the kids over, and the three of us would go walking down Higashiyama Dori. We would read signs, count numbers on doors and mailboxes, point out cars, colors, bicycles, and stop to smell the flowers. We would also spend a lot of time playing in the park. Taiyo almost always found a flower along the road to give to his baby sister. It was magnificent to me each and every time.

My ex-wife made herself invisible. She told me to pick up the babies at 11am on the last Saturday of every month, and then, when that Saturday came, I never saw her. She was nowhere to be found. Ever.

K Papa

Then one day after an afternoon spent in Sakae, Taiyo, Asia and myself are walking back to the grandparents' house. Taiyo is walking slowly behind, lollygagging, I'm holding Asia, and suddenly I heard Taiyo behind me saying out loud,

"*Kono kuruma K PAPA no kuruma ni nitteru, ne Asia?*"

"That Looks Like K Papa's Car, huh Asia?" I shudder. *Who the fuck is K Papa?*

I'm walking about 20 feet ahead of Taiyo and I stop in my tracks, eyes bulging brow furrowed to the max, but trying to maintain composure so as not to startle Taiyo. I swing my head around and casually look at him and ask,

"...what did you say, Taiyo? Whose car looks like what car?"

He sheepishly looks up at me, sad-faced, knowing he'd said something he wasn't "supposed" to, and he's not exactly sure how to get out of it. I'm walking towards him slowly, holding Asia, staring directly into his eyes. He says it again, sadly, but with his head down, knowing he has to, since *I'm his father, he's got to do what I'm telling him to do.*

"*Kono kuruma K PAPA no kuruma ni nitteru.*"

He waits for my reaction, as the three of us find ourselves standing in front of a brand-new shiny silver chromed-out Mercedes Benz G Class *dope as fuck* SUV. Heart race. Again. Tired of that shit.

Who in the fuck is K PAPA? And why is my son calling some motherfucker "PAPA"? And the nigga is driving a G Class Benz truck?!

This is really what's happening right now? I could feel the adrenaline shooting out of my adrenal glands. Asia was in my arms. *She's cute.* The three of us are standing there looking at this car, Asia is in my arms and she's playing with my hair like she always does.

I need information, but I can't stand here and grill Taiyo with the emotions I'm feeling right now, I think to myself, *I have to keep it casual.* We start walking towards their grandparents' place. I take some of the bass out of my voice, look down at Taiyo, smile, and say, in as non-threatening a manner as I can,

"Taiyo, K Papa wa . . . dare desu ka?" *Who is K Papa, Taiyo?*

"*Mama no tomodachi,*" he says Mommy's friend. *Hmm.*

"*K Papa wa don na kanji no hito? Kare no kao wa . . . dou?*" I'm gesturing with my hands over my face. I'm asking him, *what does K PAPA look like? What does his face look like?* Taiyo says,

"*Chotto daddy ni nitteru.*" He looks similar to daddy.

To me? She's dating a brother? Electric shocks travel up my spine, my flesh heats up immediately all over my body. I don't know if I'd have felt any different if I'd found out she was seeing a Japanese cat. Or a white cat. Or an Indian cat. Or whomever. One more question.

"Taiyo, K Papa wa doko ni kare su'n de imasu ka?" *Where does he live?*

"*Mama toh,*" he says quickly. With mommy.

Ho-lee fuck. Not only was my wife, err, ex-wife, dating some black dude driving a Mercedes, but they were living together too. I felt nauseous. Thoughts traveled light speed through my brain.

A is dating some motherfucker that looks like me? He's black? And they're living together? My ex-wife, some motherfucker, and my children? And that's his fucking car? She's already completely replaced me, within the span of a year and a half after getting divorced. And they live together. *I thought someone told me it was difficult for Japanese women to find a dude in Japan when they have children?* What. The. Fuck.

Ain't that a bitch? I'll be damned. All that stupid shit men say and think when their little grasp on "manhood," or what they think it is, is confronted—acute momentary ego overload syndrome, AMEOS. I had it bad; however, in the moment, I didn't quite know *what else to say.* The fact is, I was afraid to say any more, as if every word Taiyo revealed to me was ripping away another layer of my confidence and puffed-up self-pride. *I was afraid to ask my five-year-old son questions,* because I was afraid of his truth and what it would reveal about me. I wanted to ask Taiyo more questions, but I was too bewildered, too shocked, too confused, too angry, too heated, absolutely riddled with indignation, and too scared. Ego strangles reason. I was choked up emotionally.

We walked on in silence and before I could actually think of anything to say, we'd arrived in front of the Suzuki shop. We're at the front door. I gently put Asia down and ring the doorbell, staring down the street at the Mercedes truck, furious and confused. Taiyo is fidgeting nervously, looking up at me while I'm looking down the street at the Mercedes truck. Suddenly, the door swings open and *Okaasan* greets me with her usual half smile.

"*Genki?*" she says.

I peer at her in the doorway, Asia runs inside, and Taiyo is still fidgeting outside at the door, like he has something to say to me. Or maybe not.

Okaasan, my former mother-in-law whom I wasn't sure what to call anymore, continues,

"*Kyou wa nani shita no?*" What did you do today?

"Uh . . ." I stammered,

"*kyou wa, shirakawa koen ikemashita.*" We went to Shirakawa Koen.

I look at A's mother, then I purposely look down the street, squinting my eyes at the Benz, then back to okaasan, then back to the Benz, squinting, then back at okaasan, hoping she'll notice and ask me what I'm looking at. She doesn't say a word. Taiyo is standing between us, looking up at me, wondering what I'd say, I guess.

Okaasan finally notices me looking down the street, and just as she turns to walk inside, she says,

"...*nani?*" What is it?

"*Nani mo naie,*" I say. Nothing.

"*Kyou arigatou Okaasan*", I say, *thank you for today.*

I bend down low to kiss Taiyo on his cheek,

"...see you next time buddy..."

"...bye daddy..." he says.

I straighten up, bow slightly to his grandmother, and walk away in the direction of the Benz.

Passing the truck, I look it over. I don't want Okaasan to know I know something, that is, if she's watching me. Damn. *It looks new all right.* Silver with black trim, chrome rims, clean, with that Mercedes Benz *I got money* feel to it. *Fuck. Is A dating some nigga who is driving this shit?* I had to know the answer. *Right then. Even if it fucking kills me.*

The worst thing that can happen to a nigga whose ex-wife is fucking some other cat, is if that other cat has more money than you. Even worse is if he has *a lot* more money than you. I nonchalantly stroll one block past the truck, slip around the corner, and hide behind the edge of a building. I'm determined to wait there for however long it takes to see who comes out of their shop, and if that *who* owns this Mercedes Benz truck. It didn't take long.

About twenty minutes of eternity later, Taiyo come blasting out the front door, with Asia trailing behind him, followed by a shortish-looking Japanese cat wearing sunglasses and jeans with the cuffs rolled up. *Okaasan* is with them, carrying backpacks and some other stuff.

They're walking *directly towards me.* I'm sure they can see me, because I can see them, *but they can't,* because they're not thinking that I'm standing at the corner of this building watching them. Taiyo is skipping merrily along and Asia is running behind him, and all of them, including the short Japanese Roy Scheider motherfucker with the mustache and goatee, are headed directly for . . . the fucking Mercedes. *Turns out he's not black.*

Why this made me feel somehow better, I'm not sure. Fact is, my ex-wife's parents wouldn't have allowed A to date another black guy, or most likely any foreigner whatsoever. She had been thoroughly re-socialized by this point.

The short Japanese Roy Scheider dude opens the back passenger door, Taiyo jumps in and Okaasan helps Asia in behind him. He closes the door, walks to the driver's side, gets in, cranks the ignition, puts the truck in gear, and I watch as he drives off with my children playing in the backseat of his truck...Gutted. Humiliation times a hundred. Shock and dismay. *God Smack.*

I bury my face in my hands and stand there shaking my head back and forth, trying to make sense of what has just happened, and what I should do about it. But what *could* I do? What was there for me to do? All I had left to do was to go home.

H Before I

H had been by my side for five years at this point. She had gone through my divorce with me. She had helped me find places to live, fed me, bought me clothing, and helped me with my magazine. She had taken me to the doctor, the dentist, and had taken care of my legal and financial responsibilities with the state as well. She'd helped me to find my new apartment at Fukiage and she was as supportive as she could be. She'd cooked countless delicious meals and paid for everything, everywhere we went, every single time, without raising an eyebrow. She took me to Cirque Du Soleil two times, went with me, Taiyo and Asia to Monkey Park, and made costumes and personalized clothing for me, my brand, my band. She'd facilitated every aspect of *RAN* magazine, from contacting printers and negotiating prices, to speaking with advertisers and advising me on what not to print. Larry had taken nude shots of some cigarette girls and I wanted to print them but she told me it would alienate readers and potential Japanese advertisers. I printed the images anyway but not without a huge blowout with H. She cared deeply about my brand, me, and everything I was doing. We were meeting with art colleges and manufacturing companies, we had Heineken buying our back cover, we were anticipating approaching Toyota and Sony. We compromised on the Larry piece, which you can see as *RAN* Issue Number 6, August 2010. Larry's nudes are there, but not the best ("worst"—according to H). I love Larry and always will. Nude photographer.

I opened up to H about seeing my ex-wife's new boyfriend, husband, "friend," or whatever he was. I told her I'd seen him pick up the babies and drive off with them, most likely towards A's apartment in Motoyama, where we used to live. H responded with sympathy for me, but it didn't feel like she understood what I was going through. How could she? I was the one whose children were now being driven around in some dude's Mercedes truck, not her. She had her own car. I had my bike, but I wasn't ashamed of that, until that day I saw that truck, with my children in it. Even though I was probably 5 inches taller than Roy Scheider, "K Papa", I felt small. *Really* small. I suddenly felt like my relationship with H was a sham, like my ex's relationship with K Papa *must have been better than mine.*

Another You By Tomorrow

Even though I was the one 'balling', the one with the magazine and music and events and whatever else, I suddenly felt like I was playing background to my ex-wife's flashy new life, without me. Worthless. Divorced middle-aged black dude in Japan who couldn't keep his dick in his pants, and whose kids are being daddied by some Japanese motherfucker with a dope car and money. *Loser extraordinaire.*

I began to feel like I had no chance, that I was completely outnumbered and outclassed. Then it dawned on me that my ex-wife had a team. Since both she and her dude were Japanese, and because her family was squarely on her side, they could all work together to make my life *really fucking miserable* in Japan. Then I started getting strange texts.

"You should be careful your behavior and your words, or you can't see your children anymore."

Or:

"You are not A's husband anymore. You should learn your position."

I was incensed. The texts didn't come from A's phone. *Some other number.* I knew it was her dude, who else? I also immediately realized the fact that dude had not only gotten into A's panties and lived in her (our) apartment, but that he'd also gotten into her head. A wasn't answering my texts and was *nowhere in sight* when I came to pick the children up, nor when I went back to drop them off. Neither was he. For months, I'd pick up the children at the grandparents', drop them off, and never hear a word from my ex-wife, nor see her or her guy.

Then one Saturday morning I get a text from A's mother that I shouldn't come to her house to pick up the children, I should go to the entrance to Higashiyama Zoo park across the street. *Sure,* I text back.

I arrive at the park, and I'm waiting on the curb in front of the supermarket, unsure, unsettled, as to what to expect. I'm looking forward to seeing Taiyo and Asia regardless.

The silver Benz suddenly pulls up directly in front of me. *I mean directly in front of me.* There's my ex-wife sitting comfortably in the passenger seat, wearing sunglasses, chillin' like it's nothing. She's looking directly ahead, through the windshield, as if I'm not there. Roy Scheider is also wearing sunglasses, like they bought them as a set. He exits the truck and comes around and opens the door for Taiyo and Asia. I'm standing in total shock, while my ex-wife sit five feet away with the window up.

Taiyo and Asia run up to me and jump into my arms.

"Daddeeeeeeeeee!"

They're both overflowing with the usual joy and exuberance they always have when we meet, but they seem oblivious to the weight of the moment. My ex-wife, *my wife*, is sitting nonplussed in the passenger seat of the silver Mercedes truck while her boyfriend is doing the dirty work of delivering my children to me, and she isn't acknowledging me whatsoever, *and she doesn't give a shit.* She's silently singing along to some stupid Japanese J pop music that's playing softly on the radio. Knives in my stomach.

It feels like her Beyoncé "I'm better without you" moment. I swear I felt like I was in the "Irreplaceable" video.

> *I can have another you by tomorrow*
> *Go ahead and get gone*
> *Replacing you was so easy*
> *You got me twisted*
> *To the left, to the left...*

A is sitting in her shining new Mercedes Benz, rocking sunglasses, delivering our children to me with her man, and we, me, Taiyo, and Asia, are going to go down into the dark subway and disappear while they speed off into the sun, shining, in their gleaming new Mercedes.

> *...Another you in a minute/Replacing you was so easy.*

From then on, that was how A delivered the children to me, each subsequent time on the last Saturday of the month. Either she was riding alongside Roy K Papa Scheider, or she'd sometimes not show up at all, but he would, and he'd open his fucking passenger door and my kids would come bounding out yelling *daddeeeee*, and then he'd speed off in his truck. Rage. I wanted to make the situation go away, but how?

Every time that last Saturday of the month came, I was filled with both anticipation and dread, anger built up and metastasized into feelings of hate and bitterness, not just for K Papa and A, but also for Japan and Japanese. I wanted to see my children, but somehow I didn't want that last Saturday to come, because I knew I'd have to deal with the fact that this motherfucker had completely replaced me, and that my ex-wife was throwing it in my face any chance she had, and that this same cat was texting me telling me to be careful and other bullshit.

The bitterness started to take over my life. I thought about it more, much more, than I thought about anything else. I'd wake up every day wondering how to fight the situation, and there was no "how"—there was essentially nothing I could do about anything, except try to be a decent father on that one Saturday a month.

Falling Apart

The rage inside me grew. This is when I started riding my bike to the Motoyama apartment in the wee hours of the morning three or four times a week. Most nights I couldn't sleep anyway, so I figured, *let's take a ride up to Motoyama and see what there is to see up there,* which was always absolutely nothing. Nothing to see, except the car that I'd bought A sitting in the parking lot in space number 6. Sometimes. One time the front fender looked askew, so I tried to straighten it. Another time there were flyers stuck inside the windshield wipers, I took them off. Then I'd always go through the same routine: walk the bike up the ramp, park it, look up at the dark apartment, walk over to A's car, inspect it inside and out—what I was looking for I had no idea—then I'd just lean up against my bike and look up at the window and wonder *what is going on in there,* that apartment where I used to live and call home with my family, and then I'd wonder if K Papa was up there with A and my children. The whole shit made me sick. I'd imagine meeting him somewhere and beating him to a pulp. I asked a friend named Khaine to come with me on a spying run to confront him wherever he worked, which never materialized. Khaine told me he was down for whatever, himself having been jilted by more than his fair share of Japanese women, but I was actually too scared to go through with it. Two foreigners, one black and one white, running up on some Japanese cat at his place of business on some *are you fucking my wife* jealous ex-husband shit. Yeah, right.

I visualized running into A somewhere and having a conversation with her about our children and their future and my place in it. None of these situations ever played out, but the idea of them became an absolute obsession for me. I wasn't thinking straight at all. I had hatred, defeat, bitterness, anger, and confusion coursing through my veins at all times. My teaching was affected, I started cancelling private lessons and became a sort of recluse. Sort of, but I still had to function. There was my magazine to attend to, my band TAOW was rehearsing our live show and I was writing ALL the material for the band. There were events to plan and organize, et cetera, but my vision was cloudy and my image of self was deteriorating, and all I could think about was what to do about the situation with my children.

I decided to seek counseling. I didn't think it was normal that I was apparently planning Japanese Roy Scheiders's demise. I didn't think it was okay that I was riding my bike at 4am, skulking around my ex-wife's apartment, lurking in the shadows smoking Japanese cigarettes back to back. I didn't feel good about the fact that I now thought of myself as a total fucking loser, despite all the really good shit going on around me. I felt ashamed of the idea that was starting to take root in my mind, I didn't want to hate anyone. I also wanted to kick my own ass for fucking up my relationship with my beautiful young Japanese wife, and for taking my children's father away from them. *I saw that I was my own enemy* in Japan. I started to think I was a huge laugh-ingstock. I was losing my self-esteem to my ex-wife and her Japanese family, who had put me back on the outside of their lives, and who had essentially taken my children with them. Losing my apartment. Los-ing my children. Losing my status. I figured everyone must be thinking I'm some kind of rogue outsider, coasting along the bottom edges and fringes of society. I guess I was, but I didn't want anyone to know that. *I didn't want to go nuts in Japan.*

I asked around about who I might be able to avail myself to, profes-sionally. I wasn't surprised that there was a lack of English-speaking mental health counselors available in Nagoya, as well as a lack of Japa-nese ones too, which wouldn't have been any help to me anyway. Japanese do not go out and pay strangers to listen to their personal psychological issues as a rule. In Japan, if you've got mental issues you're simply labeled as "sick" and you essentially have to work it out yourself. Many Japanese become *hikikomori,* shut-ins, for certain dif-ficult periods of their lives, others jump in front of trains. I hadn't planned to do either, but someone told me about a French cat who had committed suicide in Tokyo recently, as a result of not being able to contact his children after divorce. *I didn't come to Japan to die.* I couldn't end up like that dude.

Someone told me that the Kokusai Center had counselors available for things like extreme culture shock and simple legal issues. So I set up an appointment, and started having twice weekly visits with a tall, thin British dude who had moved to Japan only a few years earlier. *How the fuck is this cat who's only been here a few years gonna help me?* Turned out I was more help to him than he was to me, except that he told me to "focus on your projects, pour your energy into whatever you are creating" and "don't let the hate cause you to do anything that could ruin your life." I'd told him about the potentially violent ideas I was having related to A's dude. Told him also about how my hatred for A had turned into me thinking she was just plain stupid for not allow-ing me into Taiyo and Asia's life. He said instead of focusing on hurting the dude and thinking A was stupid, that I should be thankful to be able to see my children at all, and to focus on making the moments I did have with them as great as possible for us all. It all worked, for a while.

>Chapter 26

15 Minutes Of Fame

TAOW blows up

The Art Of War, my band, had recorded our first and only full album, *The Way*, almost entirely at Nakamura's studio out in Biwajima. After *The Way* was finished, our lead singer, Tzuru, decided to get married, move out of Nagoya, and thus leave the band. A friend of mine named Charles 2, "Soul Kitchen DJ," tells me about another singer who might be a good addition to the band. Her name will be E.B. I meet with E.B. at the Starbucks in Sakae around the corner from Sunshine Sakae and invite her to join the band to replace Tzuru. She's mixed race, half black and white, dressed like a combination suicide girl/punk junior high school student, she's madd cute, madd sassy, and madd jaded. She's perfect.

She accepts my invitation to join our band and it was on. Almost immediately she and Taro start smashing and everything was cool until it wasn't. E.B. is calling me crying in the middle of the night, wondering why Taro won't take her calls. Meanwhile, I'm going to my weekly head sessions with the lanky Brit at the Kokusai Center because I want to kill my ex-wife's boyfriend, who happens to look like...yeah, you know.

Taro, to his credit, is acting like nothing is going on, which is very good for the band and our music because he is all business, pretty much all the time. Taro's got a partner named Dan, whom he calls his "wife". Dan is also on point with the plan and buys a sick electronic drum kit. We start rehearsing at 123 Studios, which is conveniently located underneath Higashiyama Zoo, which of course, is directly across the street from my wife's family's house. Yup, right next to the subway entrance where my ex-wife's boyfriend was pulling up in his Mercedes to drop off my children. Every time we had a rehearsal, I was viscerally reminded of the bullshit I was going through with my ex and her new boyfriend, or whatever he was, and my children.

All summer long TAOW is holed up underground rehearsing once, twice, three times a week leading up to our show on September 11, 2011, at RADIX. The show sells out due to fantastic marketing by everyone involved, and also because our individual personalities had attracted a really eclectic mix of attendees to our show. Lots of people came out of the electronic/dance scene to see Taro and Dan, since they had built a following under the name SOLSKYE, and many people had already heard Taro play Shakuhachi. Chikayo, Dan's girlfriend, is truly mystically beautiful, she's like a Japanese Stevie Nicks, she brings together both male fans who are most likely sweating her, and female fans who want to see her do her thing on her electric piano. Thing is, she can really *play*. E.B. has a strong, surprisingly soulful voice, and a killer stage presence. Her just being herself earned her a group of 'fans' who follow her around, and her fans became our fans. Then there's me. Because I'd been DJ-ing, because I had RAN, and because I had a slew female fans who wanted to see me do anything at all, we were able to create a strong "buzz" in Nagoya. We had our first sold-out show to prove it.

We performed about a dozen shows over the course of the next year, and recorded another album's worth of material. None of which ever saw the light of day, even though they're great songs, better than "The Way", in their own right. We developed a harder edge musically, with Taro exploring boundaries in his production, along with my writing and E.B.'s lyrical contributions. But something was eating away at the band from the inside. Everyone was suffering from their own issues of identification and society. Everyone in the band was living on the fringes of society in one way or another. It was too much, way too soon.

Nothing ever matched the excitement, anticipation, and sheer energy of our first show. The "art" aspect of the band was in high gear, but so was the "war" part. Inner turmoil mounted and relationships frayed. Taro and E.B. ended their mini relationship soon after it started and that ending was dirty and affected the entire band. Dan and Chikayo were having issues as well, and it didn't help that I was growing insanely bitter with my situation with A and the courts. I started forgetting my own lyrics at shows and showed up *high as hell* to our dates and rehearsals. E.B. arrived drunk off her ass at our practice sessions and the tension between her and Taro was evident. The experience turned from stellar to sour quickly. Still, almost every time we met, Dan would ask, "When are we going to be famous?" as if that was a given, and I'd silently think, *When you learn to play drums, motherfucker,* but nothing was his fault by a long shot. In fact, it's safe to say Dan was the most solid, chilliest member of The Art Of War. He, himself didn't seem to have any war going on inside him, unlike the rest of us. *Must be why Chikayo always seems totally at peace.* But that was by far not our biggest issue.

Taro had invested cash into TAOW from the jump. He rented space, bought equipment and paid for studio time to record at Nakamura's place. I owed Taro money for my half of the dough he'd fronted, and he never let me forget it. Nothing is free. Our relationship became strained and H didn't want me to be too close to the band anyway. I was spending time away from her in studios and rehearsal rooms. If I wasn't at those places, I was somewhere by myself writing songs. Despite my beef with Taro, I had developed a tight relationship with the band.

However, soon the crowds at the shows became smaller and the energy we'd created dissipated. Everyone lost their passion for the great concept we'd created just the year before. Plus, we had no focus. E.B. was definitely on some suicide/depression/pain/angst/anguish shit, I was in my hip hop/reggae pseudo spiritual bag, Dan couldn't keep time on his drums, and Taro was thinking about *money*. In addition to all of this, we were having identity issues. We weren't sure if we were an electronic dance band, a gritty punk band, or a multiethnic hip hop band like the Black Eyed Peas, whom we constantly compared ourselves to. Sun Tzu's quote, "The supreme art of war is to subdue thy enemy without fighting," was entirely lost on us. We were fighting within ourselves and thus lost the war even before the battle had begun.

Eventually things just fell apart. Taro opened a café in Okazaki, Dan and Chikayo split up and went their separate ways, and E.B. got married and had a son. Fleetwood Mac didn't have *a thing* on us, but oh how fascinating it all was while it lasted, and TAOW became a microcosm of my entire life in Japan, in retrospect. Excitement. Energy. Elation. Then work. Then routine. Then displeasure. Then . . . explosion, or implosion, one or the other. Have you ever seen a good explosion, or implosion for that matter? *Are explosions ever good?* Ask yourself.

After the explosion, all the band members slowly walked away from each other like lovers saying goodbye on the shores of a beach somewhere.

We Are Family

That summer, 2011, Asia Jade had another birthday and we celebrated with a cake, gifts and a few friends at Tenpaku Park. I put an ad in RAN telling anyone with bi-racial children to come to the park. I was thinking of starting some sort of social group for the parents and children of bi-racial children in Japan. That's where I met the Twins, "D and D"—two cool cats from the states I had become friends with through the *gaijin* network in Nagoya. West Indian, from Brooklyn, and down by law, the twins and I became really fast friends. The older D had children of his own, a boy and a girl almost exactly the same age as my kids. D's ex-wife wasn't Japanese, she's from South America. They had split up just after my wife and I did. He had seen the ad in my magazine and brought his children to meet mine. Another cool cat, Mario Long, also brought along his "hafu" kids. Risa came with her children and it was a great party.

Later, I featured the younger D in the first issue of *RAN*; he and his girl were artists and had been designing T-shirts and painting dope frescoes on sneakers. They held monthly meetings at their apartment in Freebell and everyone was there. Rocco, Brian, Gavin, Nigel, Fred, Roger, Ryan, a couple white chicks, Willow and another one I can't remember. In addition to the crew of chummy foreigners, there were always a slew of cute Japanese girls present, of course. We'd all chill, smoke, drink beer and talk while D would write everything that was being said up on this huge double-sized white board. These meetings were like a classroom. Dozens of great ideas went up on those white boards.

Even though D was divorced, he told me that his ex-wife allowed him to see their kids basically whenever he wanted. He said they got along and there was no beef. I wasn't jealous, but I wondered why my shit couldn't be more like his.

I burned my wife, that's why. That's what I had to eventually just come to grips with. Not only had I cheated, but I'd gone absolutely crazy with the sheer amount of cheating I'd done. *So fucking brazen.* It was ridiculous, I didn't have just a mistress, I had dozens of them.

During our marriage, there hadn't been one single moment that I was being completely faithful to A. I had started the marriage thinking my penchant for dalliances, and scores of them, would simply fade away. I thought I'd "grow out of it" or something like that. I hadn't, and it destroyed my marriage. Inevitably, my indiscretions accounted for the hate that my ex-wife now held for me, it also accounted for her decision to limit how often I could see my own children, whom she knew I loved.

A knew I loved Taiyo and Asia. She knew they meant everything to me. We had discussed having those two children numerous times before they were ever conceived. I wanted them and I wanted them with her and when we had them I was a proud papa. But she didn't want me to have anything to do with them now. She'd found a new dude and he was more than enough papa for Taiyo and Asia and I was just an annoyance. This revelation bruised me. It choked my confidence and paralyzed my pride.

I tried to capture different emotions through listening to all kinds of music. MGMT's "Melancholy Man," H brought home this CD by a band called The Album Leaf, truly isolated music for soul isolation. Gil Scott Heron's heroin-soaked *Spirits,* heavy doses of Bob Marley and Miles Davis. Tribal Indian music, *shakuhachi,* and Tibetan singing bowls. And Stevie Wonder's *Innervisions.*

Someone I'm Not, Or Want To Be

I started meeting lots of cats with similar situations to mine. Lots of divorced dads who were having heinous issues with their Japanese ex-wives. I met an American dude named William who wrote a piece for me in *RAN* about his ex-wife trying to run him over with their car in his driveway. The only reason he got *partial* custody of his children was the fact that his ex-wife had tried to murder him. There was the infamous French dude who had offed himself because he couldn't see his children, and he lived right up the street from them, just like me. I met more and more bitter, "angry-at-the-Japanese-world" dudes.

Eventually, I found and joined a fabulous organization called *Children's Rights Network,* established to assure that all children maintain a meaningful and continuous relationship with both parents in cases of divorce, regardless of gender or citizenship.

At the CRN, we shared our stories about parental alienation, international parental abduction and straight out parental kidnapping. These organizations are amazingly helpful and have deep insight into the emotional psychosis of parental alienation, and the peculiarities of divorce in Japan. They helped me tremendously to stabilize my emotional imbalance.

Things were great at first, but this group and I became uneasy bedfellows. Suddenly, I was in a community of jaded, angry, self-righteous Japan haters, who also had a personal vendetta against Japanese women. These guys admittedly, buckled underneath the pressure of Japanese marriage in Japan, exactly like I had. These dudes became my running partners.

These guys were absolute assholes and a total bore to be with. They droned on and on about whatever mishaps or hardships they either had or kept having while in Japan. They were pissed to high holy hell about their lives in Japan, while staying very much *right the fuck there* in Japan. They were bitter, no fun to be around and I hated these dudes.

I know my shit wasn't a trip to Coney Island in Japan but at least I was being productive in it, and still doing my best to offer whatever father-ship, guidance and protection to my children that I could. I hadn't graduated yet to being a total complete asshole. I didn't want my heart to rot like those other dudes' had allowed theirs to do. Living lonely lives, making occasional appearances on the scene at one or two events a year, mostly subsisting on mediocre relationships and memories of whatever "golden era" of Japan they subscribed to. They seemed pathetic to me...*and I was becoming one of them.*

The Great Pretender

A, Taiyo and Asia, lived fifteen minutes from me. A bike ride through the back streets of Kakuozan, where Larry lived, up onto the main drag Higashiyama Dori and then up into the hills of Motoyama. Their apartment was my old apartment. I could never escape this, or let it escape me. Some other dude was living in *my* apartment, sleeping with *my* wife, lording over *my* children.   It was my worst nightmare come true, right there in Nagoya, and I was living it.

Meanwhile, there was still life to attend to. I was eight years in with no end in sight yet. There was shit popping off left, right, and center. I had a huge beach party with *RAN* and the staff right after Asia's birthday party. We rented a huge eighty-passenger coach bus and filled it with partygoers like, Yoko Kumagai and her family. Then by sea, we threw another event called "Beach Bang Boogie" with seventy-five bikini-clad internationals on a Saturday cruise. Of course, it rained.

We set up under a blue tarp and barbecued burgers, hot dogs, and chicken anyway. A friend of mine named Shannon had come to visit me from Orlando. She sat in the front seat of the bus and made everyone laugh, and helped cook on the beach. Through pictures folks had taken at the party, I noticed that my body looked slouchy. I was *madd* out of shape and feeling like shit. In the middle of my rained-out beach party with eighty people huddling next to each other underneath the flimsy blue tarp, I felt like I looked like shit whilst still DJ'ing and jumping around, pretending like my life was *the best thing ever.*

C And The Electric Piano

Taiyo has his fifth birthday in September. C, the classically trained pianist, buys Taiyo a brand new electric piano, with pedals and a wooden finish. Taiyo loves it from the start and C starts giving him monthly, half hour lessons on it. I wasn't a huge fan of sharing my children with the women in my life, but I didn't work too hard to avoid it either. Inevitably, any woman I was dealing with wanted to meet my kids. I talked about my kids to anyone who I came in contact with. I made it very clear that they were there, so on a few occasions I allowed the ladies in my life to hang out with me and my children.

C had always been generous, but when she bought the electric piano, and started giving Taiyo lessons on it, I was taken aback. I was ecstatic to have the piano in my house for Taiyo to be able to play. C came over a couple times a month and we'd watch a movie, talk a little, fuck, take a shower, maybe fuck again, then she'd climb up on the stool of her electric piano, and play classical music and jazz for hours until 3 or 4 A.M. sometimes. It was bliss and sent my mind reeling every time.

I told H the piano came from one of Taiyo's aunts and I supposed she bought it. The flat-screen and the microwave, I told her I'd bought those myself, even though C bought those too. I was still working sometimes, but I didn't have a full time job anymore. H was paying all my bills including my rent, while C was buying me furniture and electronics, including that electric piano.

>Chapter 27

A One Night Stand With Kermit The Frog

No strings attached

"Autumn came, with wind and gold." Nicky Edges asked me to DJ his Absolute Halloween party up in Toshincho, behind the Chunichi Building. *Absolute Halloween* is a Nagoya tradition and *absolutely* one of the best adult Halloween events I've ever been to. Somehow, Nicky and Babur manage to corral about a dozen clubs and bars into the event every year. All of the bars are strung together into a madd Halloween club crawl with Japanese Batman and Princesses and Demons and bloody vixens taking over the streets for a wild night of excess, costumes, and debauchery. My Halloween was no different.

I meet a young lady while I'm behind the CD turntables, Dj-ing. This cute, young Japanese girl looks like a sexy, iced-out Kermit the Frog.

We're in Red Rock, the Aussie-themed bar. Absolute Halloween is going *off.* Red Rock is small-ish, maybe 50 people can fit in there comfortably. However, there has to be 100 bodies smashed up in here tonight. Everyone's wearing Halloween costumes, painted faces, fishnets and short skirts. Everyone is partying their asses off.

I'm DJing. My face is painted white with a black star outlined around my eye, in homage to Ace Frehley of the legendary band KISS.

I'm rocking my tight purple hoodie with "Madd Lovely" embroidered on the back. Courtesy of H. The crowd is pumping, bodies are smashing and everyone's drinking. The music is banging and the energy is high. The place is absolutely rammed. Big John Ahern is dancing over near the bathroom and Ashley James, Steve Pottinger and Michael Kruse are at the bar drinking and laughing. *Joe Sichi is in the house.*

From behind my DJ decks, I see a young Japanese girl reading my magazine—most Japanese, young or old, can read English, but almost none can actually understand what it means. However, this particular young Japanese girl is completely and totally reading my magazine, because I can see her eyes scanning the words from left to right, then back again. I approach her and ask if she's reading. She looks at me and defensively says,

"...yes, why?"

I tell her it was my magazine. She freaks out,

"Really? Yours? You mean you are the editor?"

"No, I'm the publisher, it's my magazine," I say,

"I made it." I point to my name on the inside cover.

Trevor David Houchen, Publisher

"That's me," I say, pointing to my name.

"Wow, really? I go to a university to study English. I want to know more about your magazine!"

I toss her my card, with my information on it. Then I look across the restaurant and catch a glimpse of myself in a mirror. I'm instantly reminded that I'm wearing a purple hoodie on my head with my face painted to look like Ace Frehley. She's either into me or into Ace Frehley, either way, I go with it. We make small talk and I return to the booth.

I'm doing my DJ thing. Scratching, back spinning, talking on the mic, beat matching. All of it. *DJ Maddlove for real.* I look up a few times and notice that sexy Kermit is watching me, smiling, big giant smiles, whatever. I'm the DJ, so *everyone is smiling at me.*

Party ends. I'm packing up my DJ equipment scanning Red Rock for Kermit but she's gone. Oh well. Next day, I wake up and there's a message in my Facebook inbox:

"Hi. i'm Erika. i met you last night. i want to know more about your magazine, please contact me"

I mailed back "Let's meet," whatever, yadda yadda. She replies "When?" I say how about tomorrow night. She says okay.

Monday night, I meet her at the train station in front of Geos. It's 8 P.M. She slowly comes walking up the stairs and she's much cuter than she had been just a couple days before. She's a small-framed, high-maintenance looking Japanese girl, long fake eyelashes, (which for some reason I love), she's small, thin and wiry with short asymmetrical hair, blinged out but very feminine jewelry, a big grey turtleneck, tight grey jeans, pink pumps, and frosted pink lipstick. She no longer looked so much like Kermit the Frog.

We head into Geos and look for a movie to rent. We settled on Crouching Tiger Hidden Dragon because I love the fight scenes and the film is kind of romantic to me. We return to my place, I turn on some music and she quickly settles in. She stares at Taiyo and Asia's desks for a few seconds, as if she's creating a scenario of my life in her head.

The music is playing while I'm in the kitchen cooking pineapple chicken and vegetables. She's curiously looking at all my shit, even reading old copies of RAN I've got laying around. She's checking out my poster of the Hindu God Ganesh, my picture of the Mexican painter Frida Kahlo, and my black and white photo of Krishnamurti. She's running her fingers along the inside of my books of CDs, slowly eyeballing every CD.

We eat. She likes my food. Conversation is decent. She's got her legs crossed and her shoes off and her pretty toes are also painted pink. She speaks fast, in spurts, with decent English. Time passes and suddenly it's 12 midnight. *She's missed the train.*

She says, "David, can I stay the night?" *Of course you can Kermit, you already know.* We talk a little more. I show her some videos and pictures and sing a couple of my songs from TAOW. She's impressed. Maybe. I don't know. She starts getting tired. Maybe. I don't know. I ask her if she wants to go to sleep. She says yes. I ask her if she wants to take a shower. She took a shower.

She exits my bathroom looking like a sexy, wet, thin female Japanese *Kermit the fucking frog,* even though she didn't really anymore. I had the image of Kermit in my mind so to me, she was Kermit. She's wearing my white T-shirt and my camouflage long john pants. She's got really nice feet. *For me, that is a massive Plus.* We get in bed. She's talking a lot about something. Laughing too. But No touching. Yet.

We're on either side of my bed, futon I mean, propping ourselves up on our elbows facing each other. I pull her close to me. She likes it. But, something is weird. I don't know what exactly. I say to her,

"...something feels weird, but I like it anyway... I don't know if YOU like it, but I like it..." She laughs.

What felt weird was the fact that I'd met her two days before and now she was laying in my bed wearing my t shirt and long johns after having just taken a shower. Plus, we were talking to each other in English, staring at each other and laughing and it felt somehow like we'd known each other and had somehow played out this very same scene many times before, even though we hadn't.

Then I reached down and I put my hand in her long john pants. *My* long john pants. She's got a nice patch of pussy hair, like the majority of Japanese girls do, which is one of my favorite things. She clamps up her legs momentarily, but not too tightly. My hand is jammed in between her thighs.

She says,

"...no David, I don't know you so much . . ."

I let my hand lie still for a moment. Then I say to her,

"How do you say 'open your legs' in Japanese?"

I'm surprised I don't know how to say this by now. I must be an idiot. Wait, I've never had to say it since I've been here.

She tells me how to say it, I forget immediately. Then I remember, because she's laying there and looking at me and she's wanting me to say it. So I said it. But I say it in English first, and she just looks at me. Smirking. So I say it in Japanese,

"ashi hiraite"

She opens her legs immediately, and we both laugh out loud. *This is going well.* I place my hand gently down her pants and her pussy is already very wet. This is something I love about Japanese girls. She's got big pussy lips and a fat, engorged clit. I start brushing the palm of my hand up and down against her clit. Her legs spread open more, she's staring down at my hand and then looking back at me as if she has no control of what's happening.

She starts rocking her pelvis back and forth, grinding on my hand. Now she's bucking, making guttural sounds, arching her back and contorting. "UGH . . . UH. MMMM. UH . . ." She sounds like it's hard for her to catch her breath. *And all that shit.* She still has on her bra under my T-shirt.

"Do you sleep in your bra?" I ask.

She says no.

"Take it off." I say.

She says no again. I'd already had my hand on and in her pussy, but she won't take off her bra. *Whatever.*

Lots of Japanese girls seem to be okay with you having your hands down their pants, but seem to have issues with you touching their tits. So I go back to the pussy. Pushing, rubbing, toying, lightly rubbing, flicking, in and out, in and out, and in. She's bucking. Her pussy's good but *but I wanna see her tits.* I ask her again to take off her bra. She says no again. *Man come on. No?!* Whatever. Back to the pussy. Long johns come off. Panties come off. Naked below, T-shirt and bra above. Whatever. Back to the pussy.

She throws her legs up in the air. I'm now jackhammering her pussy with my fingers. She's breathing like she's running marathon. Kinda weird. I take off my shorts and she grabs my swollen junk. I come out of my shirt and ask her again,

"...take off your shirt Erika..." That was her name, Erika.

Finally she pulls the shirt over her head and unsnaps her bra in the back exposing a pair of small Japanese twenty-two-year-old tits. *I love those.* Sometimes. Tired of them other times. Tonight they're perfect.

I bend my head down, cup one in my hands and start licking her nips and swirling my tongue around her areola. She's looking down at me and her breathing picks up again.

"David, do you have a condom?" She asks.

"Sure" I say.

I get up and quickly retrieve a condom from a shoebox located on top part of my closet. I return to bed. She looks impatient. I place the condom at the tip of my...junk...and start rolling it down the shaft. She slides her body underneath mine. With her legs open, I gingerly place my cock at the outer edge of her pussy. She throws her head back and moans.

Slowly, I start thrusting in and out and she's arching her pelvis to meet mine as I came forward. Kermit knew what to do. She's doing this thing all Japanese girls do, they turn their heads either left or right, put their hands up to their mouths, close their eyes and act like you're doing some kind of surgery on them but without anesthesia, and they're watching you do it. They act shy and pouty, except when they don't, and it's very sexy, unless you've seen a thousand of them do it, which it seems I have, but it's sexy anyway.

Finally she asks me slowly and tenderly,

"David, isn't it enough for you?"

"...sorry...gomen..." I say.

I climb off. Her breathing slows down. We rest awhile, just laying there silently for what, ten minutes? Twenty? -during which time I pry off the condom.

"Erika, climb on top of my face." I request.

She's looks at me like she doesn't understand. I position myself underneath her, and she gets what I'm going for, and straddles my face. I held her hips, and she just seemed to kind of watch me do what I was doing. I had to lean my head up, which strained the back of my neck, so eventually I just stopped, she climbed off, and we fell asleep to some Indian tribal flute music. We never got around to Crouching Tiger.

Couple hours later, maybe 5 A.M., maybe 6 A.M., her alarm on her phone goes off, she gets up, gets dressed, and boogies out my door without saying much. Actually, just as she was about to open my front door to leave, she turns to me, bows, and very formally says

"...arigatou gozaimasu. Tanoshikatta desu." And then she's gone.

I fall back to sleep and then wake up alone a few hours later. I send her a text, "Did you get to home/work/school okay?" No answer. Few hours later, I send another mail: "How are you? R U ok? How's your day?" No answer. That evening, I send another mail: "Hey Erika . . . are u ok? Working? Busy? Send me a mail so I know you're okay." No answer.

Even though earlier, I went through a list of different types of Japanese girls, the truth is, there are basically only two types; there are the ones you can never get rid of, and there are the ones who disappear forever. She was the latter.

Lots of foreign guys in Japan think that they're players when it comes to Japanese women, very few ever consider the fact that *they're the ones getting played.*

Erika, my Kermit The Frog, never returned my text or called or anything. She did leave her big hoop earrings at my place, however.

>Chapter 28

GIVE ME THE NIGHT

The freaks come out

Fall 2011 I start working at this club in the club district of Nagoya. I'd had many gigs at clubs over the years in Japan—promoter, DJ, organizer—but this gig started off with me standing outside Plus Park from 10 P.M. until 5 A.M. in the bitter-ass cold doing "security" work. My gig was essentially threefold: ID anyone who looked underage, don't let in Brazilians, and stall the cops if they came. Ghost Will got me the gig, all love to Ghost all ways.

You see strange shit on the street at 3 A.M. in Japan. You see drunk-off-their-asses Japanese girls too fucked up to walk, throwing up all over themselves, and walking pigeon-toed in their high heels, which they can't walk in even when they're sober. You see those same girls curled up on the curb or in the fetal position on the sidewalk with their thongs showing gurgling vomit out of the corners of their mouths, with random dudes crouched down beside them smoking cigarettes and smiling, not a care in the world.

You see fat Abbot and Costello–looking Yakuza cats in gold Adidas sweat suits, wearing sunglasses and slippers, walking down the middle of the street carrying suitcases bursting with cash money, flanked by burly Japanese dudes dressed like Dan Ackroyd and Jim Belushi from Blues Brothers.

You see gigantic Japanese transvestites, 6 foot 5, with huge hair, sitting on baskets with their legs open, wearing pancake makeup, fanning themselves while half dozen airport-haired young Japanese dudes in small suits stand around smoking. Doing nothing.

You see skinny little knuckleheaded doped-up and drunk wild-eyed Japanese dudes brandishing broken bottles, going up against fat dopey-looking Japanese wannabe hip hop thugs wearing sagging jeans and rope chains.

You see overeager Japanese cops riding their bicycles at top speed in hot pursuit of . . . nobody and nothing at all, heads bent over the handlebars, necks craned, suits ironed, ties flailing, bolting down the block going nowhere fast. Idiots.

You see packs of young Japanese cats dressed in tight jeans and tighter jackets, wearing pointy, plastic, roach-killer shoes, with their hair gelled up to look like the opera house in Sydney, chasing down similarly dressed young zombied-out Japanese girls.

You see old Japanese cab drivers with their car windows rolled all the way up, engines running, parked, while they snore open-mouthed with the seats let all the way down, cigarette burning in the ashtray. This, during an "energy crisis". Meh.

You see middle-aged Chinese, Thai, Korean, and Filipino "massage" ladies, physically harassing drunk Japanese salarymen and forcing them to pay for quick hand jobs behind closed doors. You don't see the hand jobs, which is probably a good thing.

You see those same salarymen crashing into garbage cans, cars, poles, and people. They're piss-drunk, dazed and confused, and wearing the same suit they wore to work some fourteen, sixteen hours earlier. These same guys glare at you on the train and make oddball comments about you not being Japanese, as if the whole world should be Japanese. Assholes. You also see these same salarymen getting into loud arguments with each other that wind up as *weirdo staring matches*, because in Japan, Japanese dudes rarely ever throw a punch. It's all about who can speak in the most threatening manner, and who can throw their chest out the farthest, and inevitably it becomes . . . nothing. I never once saw two Japanese men actually physically fight

with each other. They've progressed, honed and refined their emotional apparatus so much that they don't have to fight. Or they're
pussies, one.

You see dolled-up middle-aged Japanese hostesses bowing at near
45-degree angles, doing their best to look entertained by these same
drunk, stupid salarymen. And through it all, 95 percent of these folks
don't notice you're there, watching it all. It's an entirely different scene
from the straight-laced, orderly, law-abiding, sanitized streets you see
during the day in Japan. And I dug it all.

Plus Park

My Japanese language skills had improved ridiculously. But it was
still hard for me to understand lots of what people were saying. *Ni-
hongo Wakaranaie.*

Even after eight years in Japan, I could still barely speak a full sentence of Japanese. I could however understand, maybe 30 percent of
whatever anyone who spoke Japanese to me was saying. This was
weird. I had thought I'd just somehow "pick up" the ability to speak the
language through osmosis, but it never quite happened to the degree
I wanted it to. As for reading or writing, I couldn't read a single *kanji*
anywhere, including on those Japanese IDs. As security at Plus Park, I
had no idea what I was looking for. The *tencho* (manager) didn't give
me any real training, all he'd said was that I was supposed to make sure
everyone had some kind of ID to get in. Cops in Sakae had recently
gotten *kibishi* (strict), and lots of eyes were on the club district because
a few weeks before I got hired, two Chinese had gotten into a fight and
the fight ended with one of them stabbed dead. That was enough to
put five or six Japanese cops on every corner for a few weeks.

With my shitty Japanese, I could barely understand anything the
customers said. I'd say to them, "*Mebunsho misette kudasai*"—Show
me your ID please—but if they tried to engage me in conversation,

which they often did, I was almost immediately lost. Some of the hottest Japanese women you have ever seen would come up and start talking to me, and I'd pretend I understood, but didn't have the slightest clue what they were saying. Maybe a good thing, the temptation was unreal.

I knew my being black was why I was put there; it gave the place an exotic flavor, and it said to potential troublemakers that they'd better think twice about starting some dumb shit, or else the two black security guards might just . . . might just what I never knew, but the threat was there. I figured I could make a few yen, we were making 9 thousand yen a night when I started. I could improve on my shitty Japanese, and maybe build myself up from where I felt I was at the time I took the gig. I was broke, almost desperate, madd confused about why the hell I was still in Japan despite knowing it was mostly about my children, along with the fear of the unknown back home. What I did know, was that I wasn't going back into those Japanese junior high schools as a teacher anytime soon.

I took the gig not only because I needed the dough, which wasn't great by any standards, but because I figured it fit more with my real personality than the elementary school/junior high school English teacher role I'd been playing in Japan until that time. Teaching folks how to say "how are you" and "this is an apple", had effectively begun to drive me crazy. I had mutated from what I was when I'd first arrived, into something completely different. I had blossomed into an artist, even a cultural ambassador. I could no longer fathom waking up early, taking crack-of-dawn trains out to the Japanese countryside, trying to teach Japanese kids how to speak English while they didn't give a shit about English. The reality of my job as an ALT was that more or less, I was just a tall black clown, and the Japanese junior high school students laughed in my face more often than not.

I knew there was more I should have been doing with my life at the time, I just wasn't sure exactly what it was, but, I did know I was attracted to Nagoya's street life. "Attracted to" is a mild way of putting it—it was more of an addiction. One of the reasons my marriage ended was because I couldn't keep my ass at home, *I had to be out on the streets.* Growing up in New York City does that to you, everything happens on the streets there, it just becomes a part of you.

At the time, Plus Park wasn't one of the more famous clubs in Nagoya, it wasn't "international" by any means, and didn't pretend to be. Its clientele was almost 100 percent Japanese, which was fine by me. Most of the other "international" clubs in Nagoya consisted of a few white boys, a few Africans, and a large Brazilian clientele.

Brazilians in Japan are loud, obnoxious, and they like to fight. They all think they're Royce Gracie. Every one of them swears they're some kind of MMA kickboxing fucking champion and they're eager to prove it on your face. They roll in packs. My man Ghost Willy had had a bottle smashed over his head by some Brazilian cat once while he was spinning at Rocket. The incident shook Ghost though, and he never went back.

Club Night in Nagoya / The Brazilian Invasion

On any given Saturday night in downtown Nagoya, when the clubs empty, you see hundreds, if not thousands, of all nationalities scattered and sprawled out along the streets. Africans, Brazilians, Japanese. Tall white dudes and short Indian cats. Turkish and Russian dudes. Australian cats and the rare American dude, of which I was one.

The Brazilians are the most notorious. All of them wear knockoff, hip hop gear and muscle T-shirts; with or without the muscle. You'll see them spinning the wheels of their tricked-out rice burners, while clutching their Brazilian girlfriend's fat ass. The Brazilian girls love the attention as they parade themselves in their always-too-tight clothing and too-small shoes. Or, you catch them inside the clubs, making a brazen display of themselves, making out, tongue-lashing each other, baggy jeans and baseball caps or tight skirts and high heels.

Hip hop has become the default international culture and it appears that everyone wants to be black. Until they either get bored of being what they're not, or, until they realize just acting black isn't really the same as *being* black. At which point they just drop the "black act."

Basically, Brazilians stay with Brazilians in Japan. It's all good. This one other Brazilian chick tried to holla a few times, but I was a bit scared of her. She was a Facebook stalker type, always wanting to chat, sending too many damn messages, calling me "baby" and "honey" and whatever else. I made out with her once randomly on some street. I was riding my bike home late, saw her, she called me over and mashed her face up against mine and pulverized my mouth with hers. Scary. I rode home in a state of semi-shock: *What the hell just happened?* She was nice I suppose, told me she was a Christian, had a gigantic megatron atomic-powered ass, but I'm not really feeling chicks who profess to be Christian in one sentence, and in the next moment are trying to vacuum my damn tonsils out in the middle of the street. Too much drama.

I never had any beef with any Brazilian cats; a few came to Plus Park, and I always let them in, even though when I got hired, Hiro told me not to let Brazilians in. *Fuck that racist philosophy,* I thought, even though they were trouble. *What if the policy was "no brothers allowed," could I support some shit like that?* Imagine me, black as night, standing there saying to the next brother, "Sorry dude, can't let you in, no brothers allowed." Funny thing is, there are LOTS of places that have exactly this policy in Japan, with African brothers working the door for establishments where they themselves and their friends are not allowed in. Could I be that cat, not letting in people because of their race or nationality? *Hell no.* One thing I don't like being is a hypocrite. Fuck that. Keep it real or keep it moving.

One night, these two brothers come in to the club. One of them looked like the R&B singer Omarion. The girlfriend of one of the Japanese DJs falls all over this dude and ends up going home with him that night. The next week, honey shows up with some African cat and is seen swapping spit with him at the bar while her Japanese boyfriend is spinning. No respect. This same DJ tried to institute a "No blacks allowed rule" after that incident. I could understand his pain, but this was the same cat who was walking around with loud-ass Jay Z sweatshirts and saying to me "wassup son," Here he is, getting paid and making his living off the back of the music brothers in the US were making, but getting angry because his girl fucked some dude whom *he* taught her to idolize. *Come on, son.* That "rule" he tried to enforce didn't fly, then he tried to institute a "No picking up girls" rule. *Nigga please.* Why would anyone come to a club if they can't pick up girls? That shit lasted exactly one night.

Hiro, the manager of Plus Park, had a huge head but was madd low key. He almost whispered whenever he spoke, and always had his hands stuffed into his pockets. He also had horrible posture, almost as if he was hiding from the world, but he was the head nigga in charge at Plus Park.

Hiro told Ghost and I not to allow Brazilians in because of their proclivity to go to blows. However, he also wanted Ghost and I to think we were part of his insider group, to get our loyalty in case anything went down. Sure, we were *gaijin* and always would be *gaijin,* but we were "special" *gaijin,* like "house niggers", and the Brazilians we were told to not let in were like the "field niggers". Was wild. This is how Japanese maintain a certain caste system over there. Yeah, we were foreigners, but we Americans are somehow better than the Brazilians and Africans and Indians, but forever still underneath the Japanese themselves. I saw this immediately.

When Hiro requested that we do this, I played along in Hiro's face, but I felt fucked up about it. You can call me whatever you want, but you cannot call me a hypocrite. I let them Brazil cats in just like they were anyone else. Romanians and Turks are another story though. Those cats reeked of trouble and were prejudiced against everyone.

More Sex For Sale

Plus Park is located on the third floor of a five story building in Sumiyoshi. On the fourth floor, there's another variation on the theme of sex for sale. It is a *deaikei*, a sort of "Let's Make A Deal" dating room, called Nana Café, Nagoya's most notorious. The word deai kei is actually two words put together to create one. Deai means "to meet" and "kei" means system, so these places were literally "meeting systems" where Japanese men could easily "pick up" young Japanese women.

These places make money on both ends, from the women and men. The dudes go there looking to meet a girl they can "date." They pay for increments of time, go into a room where there's a huge two-way mirror. In the room where the men hang out, the mirror is actually a window, but the girl's side is a huge mirror. The girls are all in another room separated by this mirror, where they just hang out and do what 20-something year old Japanese girls do. They're in there applying makeup, talking on their phones, looking at magazines, whatever, and the men on the other side are checking them out via the two way mirror. *Stalk much?* How weird. Legal peeping. Japan, after all. When the men see someone they're interested in, they let the girl know through some form of electronic communication and chat the girl up. If the girl is interested enough, or if the man throws enough cash at her, they both make an agreement to go on a "date," which usually lasts about an hour, with a quick blowjob in a car, a fast fuck in one of the twenty-four-hour karaoke joints scattered around the area, or they'd go to one of the many close-by love hotels and do their thing. Or, sometimes the Japanese men aren't actually looking for sex, they're simply looking for companionship, and any doe-eyed Japanese girl with no opinion on anything will do.

All night long while I'm standing outside the front door of Plus Park, 2, 3, 4am, there's be a parade of young Japanese girls looking no older than 18 or 19 wearing huge dark shades coming out of the elevator with different Japanese men. Young dudes, old men, guys who look like they've got a family at home, well dressed businessmen, student-looking dudes, and even homeless-looking dudes. If they had the cash they could have some fun with these skinny, non-descript, young Japanese girls.

Most of these young girls look lost and zoned out as they exit and enter the building with equally non-descript Japanese men. I'm not a prude, I got no issue with women selling whatever it is they have, to make their money, but lots of these girls looked like they were still in high school, some looked even younger. Their eyes were glazed, their bodies looked frail, their fashion was off, but night after night, they'd leave the spot with some dude, then return an hour or so later only to leave again.

I could never quite tell what was on the fourth floor. The building itself was covered with posters advertising NANA CAFÉ in huge colorful letters, and the mascot of the place is a duck, for whatever reason.

The fifth floor housed a bonafide Japanese soapland called Fran Fran. The advertisement for this place featured a half dozen nearly naked Japanese girls wearing bikinis, all in various positions, giving the obvious impression that THIS IS A PLACE WHERE JAPANESE PUSSY IS FOR SALE.

There are pictures of the various women who work there encased in a dingy glass display case next to the elevator, with all the relevant information: height, bra size, weight, age, obligatory blood type—I guess in case someone needed a quick transfusion—and a little message scrawled to the potential customers;, "I like having fun and meeting new people, let's enjoy together!" Shit like that. Fran Fran didn't have as many customers as Nana Café, but the product was the same, Japanese girls and affection for sale. Ghost Willy told me he went up there one night, got a massage, was offered some ass for a hundred bucks but turned it down. I believed him.

Somehow, I both felt sorry for and admired the girls who I saw coming out of Nana Café every night. I felt like they had taken their destinies into their own hands. These girls were living on two edges of

Japanese society. On the one hand, they're probably like all the other Japanese women in Japan, they probably adore Disneyland like their lives depend on it, and they're probably freaks in bed. Japanese girls go through three stages, shy stage, freak in bed stage, and crazy. I've never been one to put anyone down for what they do for their cash, money makes the world go 'round, right? Get it how you can, without hurting yourself or anyone else.

But yet and still, I wondered why they weren't home in their beds, or in their pink bedrooms, with their stuffed animals and pet dogs and *Hello Kitty* paraphernalia. Why weren't they curled up on the couch with their boyfriends watching a movie? Why did they have to be out in the cold selling themselves to strangers in the dead of the night?

I felt these girls had no love for the dudes they've been blowing, or whatever else, but I also felt they were like me. We were working the same street, same time and same objective; to get paid. It isn't easy to do what they were doing, physically, mentally, emotionally, or otherwise. We were both working undercover at night, with the moon and the stars as witnesses to our deeds.

>Chapter 29

THE GHOST

Fireworks

Ghost Willy and I worked the late-night shift together. Ghost was the dude who got me the job. A tall, strong African cat from Kenya who had put himself under my wing a few years back when I was DJing at C.R.E.A.M. I knew Willy as just another African cat trying to make it, trying to get over in the culture, and bag as many Japanese girls as possible along the way.

Many African cats in Japan are caking. The African dudes I met were hustlers to the core, every one of them. They arrive in Japan hungry for a better life. Their countries—Uganda, Ghana, Nigeria, Kenya, Tanzania, and others —offer them little hope or opportunity, so they arrive in Japan wild-eyed and starving for a chance. They adopt the swagger of American thugs, and lots of them go around telling the Japanese girls they meet that they're from New York or Los Angeles, hoping the American cache will get them laid. The Japanese girls are gullible and don't know the difference. They usually buy the lies and the African cats in some cases con the girls, siphoning cash from their bank accounts and doing dirty shit like that. I'm not saying ALL the African cats are like this, but many of them are.

Some African dudes work their asses off to become successful. Many of them have great lives in Japan, operating clothing stores and selling all the latest American hip-hop gear to young, Japanese wannabe ballers. Other African cats are involved in import-export, exporting anything from heavy machinery to cars to bicycles to food to clothing back home in gigantic barrels. Lots of dudes send money back to their countries in order to build houses and support families where no opportunity is the rule. Ghost was one of these cats, caught somewhere in between trying to do good and be good, but caught up in the undertow of being at almost the bottom rung of the ladder in terms of gaijin in Japan.

But Ghost was my dude. He wasn't to be fucked with but at the same time he was sensitive and fun-loving. Ghost is a cat who always has two or three chicks at his beck and call. But like most of the Africans in Japan, he's got a dark and sinister side as well. One night at work he showed me a video of himself smashing some dude's chick, while he was on the phone with the dude. Savage.

Only a few weeks after meeting Ghost, I ran into him after Djing at CREAM one night. I see him ambling around Sumiyoshi looking hollowed out, like he'd seen something he wasn't supposed to see, or had gotten some real bad news. I call out his name from across the street, "Ghost! Wh-sup witchya man?", and he walks straight up to me and tells me both his parents have just died in Kenya, and that his sister's husband had been beating his sister, and that he'd gone back to Kenya to square up the situation with his family, their home, and their belongings, and had just returned, and didn't know what to do with himself. He tells me he's feeling really sad and literally doesn't know how to go forward.

I don't know what to do man, my mother and father both just died, and I just came back from Africa. I'm the oldest, so I have to handle all their business and take care of my brothers and sisters, and one of my sisters is getting beaten by her boyfriend, I'm only twenty-four years old myself man, I don't know what to do, can you help me Maddlove? Please.

I don't know what to say, but Ghost is staring me in my eyes looking for answers. He respects me because he knows I'm a DJ, and also because he knows I keep my nose pretty much clean. Even though I was doing my dirt, my biz was nowhere on the streets at the time, I kept my movements as on the low as I could. Plus, I being from New York made Ghost see me as kin, since he called himself *Mr. New York.*

From that moment Ghost and I became brothers. I told Ghost he should stay out of the streets for a while, take care of his biz back home as best he could, and think of whatever he wanted to do and pursue it. A short while after Ghost approached me, I was managing Club Maverick, and remembered that Ghost had told me he wanted to get into the music business, so I gave him his first gig as a DJ at Mav.

Ghost showed up high or drunk a few times, but eventually refocused and grew into one of the most respected hip-hop DJs in Nagoya. More on Ghost in the next chapter...

>Chapter 30

STREET FIGHT AT PLUS PARK

Please don't poke me

P lus Park itself was a club, but only the actual patrons of the club knew that. It advertised itself as just a bar with music being played by a DJ. At the time, all of Japan's major cities were undergoing a sort of nightclub prohibition period. A couple Chinese cats had gotten murdered at a club somewhere in Osaka, and for the Japanese Koban, these incidents constituted a crime wave. Subsequently, clubs were under "investigation" all over Japan, and Nagoya was no different. Clubs had to close down at 1 instead of 2, and cops were all over the streets.

Plus Park didn't have a cabaret license, which meant that legally, no dancing was allowed in the club, so it had to advertise as being just a lounge or a bar where folks could come cop a drink and chill. Inside, the truth was different. The front part of the club was the bar, while the back bestowed a huge wall that contained a large dancefloor behind it. Our job as security was to stall cops in case they ever came through to perform their "investigations". We just had to stall them long enough so that the retractable wall could be put in place, and the customers could be ushered out the back door before the cops could see either what was really going on, or how many people were in the club.

Ghost was an expert at stalling the cops, and therefore, he was Hiro's boy, and therefore was able to get me the gig on his recommendation. Mostly, we stood outside in the freezing cold, me wearing my Navy Pea Coat that H had bought me, gloves, boots, jeans, scarves, long johns, checking Id's and bullshitting with the customers.

By American standards, there wasn't really much "action" happening outside of the club, aside from what was happening in the streets around us. But cops were always lurking, riding by bent over the handle bars on their bicycles. I was happy about the fact that there wasn't really much real trouble because for the most part, I'm not a fighting type of dude.

It isn't that I'm afraid of fighting, but my take on fighting has always been *even if you win, you might get hurt, fucked up, whatever, and what have you won really? No one's paying you and there's no applause or prizes, so what the fuck is it for really?*

A Japanese Girl Named Double M

At the time, I was seeing a Japanese girl who I named Double M. Double M was a perky young college girl, barely into her twenties, looking for something interesting to do and some interesting folks to hang out with. She was thicker than your average early 20's Japanese girl. Nice thick thighs and wide hips.

Double M, like most Japanese girls her age, lived with her parents. She would come to my place at Fukiage after her classes, and we'd spend the afternoon on my futon until she'd fall asleep. While she was asleep, I made calls for RAN, or practiced DJing, or did whatever. Our relationship wasn't that serious and I didn't even know her last name. She spoke a few words of English and whenever she came over, we barely said more than three or four sentences to each other. She'd show up, slip off her shoes, ask me if I was genki, then we'd head into my bedroom and get to business. She didn't offer me any drama and knew her place in my rotation. Truth is, she reminded me a little of M3, the photographer I had gotten pregnant. We enjoyed our little moments together, and then she'd bounce, and that was it. For a while.

A Side Note

A few months into the gig with Ghost, I tell him that I don't think the 9 thousand yen we're getting paid is enough. We were standing outside in the cold for 8 or 9 hours, which amounted to a thousand yen an hour. Bullshit money. Ghost asks me how much I think we should be getting paid and I tell him I'm not sure, but that I'm going to ask Hiro to raise our pay to 15 thousand yen a night. Ghost tells me to go ahead and do it. We both figured if Hiro didn't give us the 15 thousand, he'd compromise and meet us somewhere in the middle.

Hiro knew I was from New York, and he knew that New Yorkers enjoyed a sort of semi-celebrity status in Japan. Hiro also knew that I was a DJ and musician, so some nights, Hiro would ask me to get on the mic to hype the crowd. I figured I wasn't just a security dude anymore, *I'm apart of the entertainment*, so I'm thinking I deserve more dough.

One night, after being on the mic and ripping the crowd into a frenzy, I was feeling myself so I approached Hiro on a whim and asked him if we could get the 15 thousand. The crowd was large and in a great mood that night as a result of my mic skills, and Hiro agreed. I told Ghost and suddenly we're both making 6 thousand yen more a night than we were before. Real cool.

My Phone Takes a Ride to Tokyo

I get home one night from one of my gigs to discover that I'd left my cell phone on the Shinkansen. My phone had taken a trip on the dolo to Tokyo, where it stayed for about two days. When I realized it was missing, I had one of my students come with me to the Shinkansen station in Toyohashi to translate to the stationmaster that I'd left it on the train. Due to Japan's unparalleled respect and honesty when dealing with other people's property, they said they'd found it, and they'd mail it to me, but it would take about two days to arrive. Imagine that, they not only find your phone, but they mail it directly to your house. Japan.

For the next two days, I didn't have my phone. Those days were Wednesday and Thursday. Friday morning, my phone arrives early in the morning by delivery. When I open the package and turn my phone on, there were a dozen calls and text messages from Double M. All of her messages had a frenetic tone:

"Are you all right? Did my crazy ex-boyfriend do anything to you or your coworkers? Are you all right? Please tell me you are all right . . ."

She also mentions in one of her texts that she's been "running away from him for a long time, but now he's back again. He's a little danger-ous and a little big." *A little big? What the fuck?*

Danger Lurks Ahead

I didn't want to spend the day worrying about some *"little big" dude, who may or may not want to kick my ass,* so I immediately called Double M. She picks up the phone frantic, asking me if I'm okay and what had happened at work the night before at Plus Park. I hadn't worked at Plus Park the night before, since it was a weekday. I tell her nothing happened and asked her what did she hear happened. She tells me her ex-boyfriend returned to Japan from wherever he had been, and called her upon finding out that her "new boyfriend", *me*, was working at Plus Park.

I didn't know honey had an ex-boyfriend. I guess all women have ex-boyfriends. The thought hadn't occurred to me. It never does. She tells me that he "found out" that she had been seeing some new dude and that this new dude—me—worked at Plus Park and that he'd gone there to confront the dude—me—except while he was "confronting" me, I was stone-cold asleep in my bed.

She says while he was confronting me, he'd called her and cursed at me while he was on the phone with her. Double M said she tried to reason with him but he hung up on her. After several, unsuccessful attempts to call him back, she was scared something might have happened to me, except it wasn't me. I was in bed the whole time. Lucky, I guess.

I ask her who he is, she says he's American, in his mid-twenties. I ask her his name, she says "David or Joe..." she's not sure. Hm. I ask her what his last name is and she has no idea. *You've been seeing this dude for 6 months and you don't know his last name.* Nice. Then it comes crashing into my head that *I don't know her last name either.* Remember, it's very common for foreign dudes in Japan to invent aliases and fake histories in order to get gullible Japanese girls into their beds, or onto their futons. However, this guy, her ex-boyfriend, never fully understood the game. The game was created for all to play, including his girlfriend, ex-girlfriend. He's got a rotation that he's fitting her into, and *so does she.* You attract what you are.

I ask her where he lives, she doesn't know this either. Chances are they had been carrying out their entire "relationship" in love hotels. I ask her again what he looks like, she says he's black, "a little big", and that's all she can offer. At this point, I didn't know he was African, because Africans in Japan go by aliases all the time. Plus, she'd already told me he was American, and I had no reason to doubt her.

I ask her how long they've been dating, she says about six months. I ask her his occupation,

"Where does he work?"

She doesn't know. She tells me she broke up with him a few months prior because he was "crazy", and she heard he'd went back to America, but now he's suddenly returned, possibly to reclaim her [period] However, these plans had been altered by someone who works the door at Plus Park. She says he'd called her a week before claiming he wanted to repay her some of the money he owed her. Yeah. *Right.* A dude who has been told to kick rocks shows up and wants to repay you what he owes you? Out of the kindness of his heart? Sure.

The words "a little big" are swirling through my head. What does it mean exactly? Is he a little tall? Is he a little fat? Is he a little muscular? Is he a little all three? This is exactly what I don't need. Some mysterious dude who knows where I work, whose girlfriend, or ex-girlfriend I'm now sleeping with, is looking for me and probably wants to hurt me. All this, on the account that I'm banging who he *thinks* is still his girl. The whole shit pissed me off.

The Mystery Man About Town

"You mean to tell me, you dated this dude for six months and you don't know shit about him? You don't know his last name or where he works or if the first name he told you is real or not?" She says no.

I ask her, what type of dates have they been on?

"Where have yall gone?"

She says they've been to a few clubs, shopping and some restaurants. I tell her *if* dude is after me, not knowing shit about him puts me at a distinct disadvantage. Information, as they say, is crucial. I was trying to assess who dude was, the level of threat he posed, and who I might know that knew him, but she had nothing for me.

The whole shit pissed me off more. Why didn't I know about this estranged ex-boyfriend? Why didn't I know she was running from anyone? Should I have known? This is one of the issues with dating Japanese women, and vice versa. Everyone is taking everyone else at face value in Japan. No one is asking smart questions. Everyone is trying to get what they can as fast as they can and the results of this situation aren't good. You don't think to ask these questions at the beginning of a relationship in Japan, but maybe you should.

She asks me if I'm angry and I tell her *hell fucking yes* I'm angry, even though ostensibly, she hadn't done anything wrong. Fact is, I just didn't need the drama. I wasn't feigning for pussy nor was I especially "getting" anything out of my relationship with Double M that I couldn't stand to lose. I tell her that I don't want to see her anymore because I just don't need the drama. I tell her to work it out one way or another with the little big dude and then, when things between she and him are figured out, to give me a call. I tell her not to call me or mail me in the meantime, and to forget about us. I figured it wasn't worth it.

Some dudes don't realize that they are "ex" boyfriends. The girl "moves on" but the dude doesn't and all kinds of trouble can come from a situation like that. Who needs it? Either way, I tell her to step off. However, she doesn't listen, she attempts to contact me a few times that day but I don't respond. She's leaving messages and texts saying she's "worried" about me and "scared" of "what might happen."

Mystery Man Reveals Himself... *"You F**ked Me."*

After we get off the phone, I call Ghost Willy to ask him if he had worked the night before and what had happened. Sure enough, Ghost tells me some African cat named Joe had stepped to him on some "are you fucking my girl" shit. Ghost tells me that the shit had gotten ugly because, "little big" African Joe had made all kinds of threats to Ghost and since Ghost don't back down it had almost turned into a fistfight. Fortunately, Ghost was able to convince the dude that he really didn't know what he was talking about, and dude eventually stormed off saying he'd be back. Problem was, Ghost really *didn't* have any idea what dude was talking about. This very fact, is what saved Ghost that night. From what exactly, I'm not sure. Ignorance was indeed bliss, because the dude didn't know my name and never mentioned it to Ghost.

I told Ghost that the dude had been looking for me, and not him, and that it was me who was sexing "his girl." And then the whole thing made sense. Ghost tells me,

"Yo, T, the dude is the dude who came here a few times wanting to sell herb. You know the dude. He drives a silver Mercedes."

"He knows you." Ghost says.

And so I had a face and person to go with the "crazy ex-boyfriend." Little big African Joe was this forty-something-year-old African dude who I barely knew, but knew of. Dude drove around in a silver Mercedes and tried to come off as some kind of "boss." He wore nice clothes, spoke with some sort of affected American accent, and always looked clean. Dude always spoke about "who he knew" and "where he'd been" and "what he could do". I never had beef with son. In fact, he had interesting stories about his time in Japan and we'd had a couple drinks together a few times in The Hub, an English-style pub in the heart of downtown Nagoya. Dude was always on some "I'm making more money than you and doing things around here that no one knows about" type shit, but I didn't give a fuck about any of that, never meant anything to me. But son had stressed me one time for thirty dollars for a bag of weed. And he was exactly what Double M said he was, "a little big." He was about my height, maybe an inch shorter, but probably about forty pounds heavier. Dude had a square head, a barrel chest and dark perfect-looking skin.

One night at Plus Park, a few months before our "situation", this Japanese cat had come to the door, shouting some ol' Japanese, gangsta shit to me. Out of nowhere, the "little big" dude emerged from the crowd and got into a shouting match with the Japanese gangsta cat. This was apparently in a show of support for me, but all I thought while it was going on was *this whole shit isn't necessary, and why is dude yelling at this Japanese cat for no reason?* At the end of that episode, "little big" dude made like he was calling someone on his cell phone in a threatening manner. He walked slowly up the street, disappeared into his car, and I didn't see him again for months. I guess that was the time he had gone back to "America", or wherever.

The night after my phone call with Ghost, there were three of us working the door at Plus Park. Myself, Ghost, and this new, older African cat named "Harry". Around midnight, African Joe pulls up in his silver Mercedes, gets out and calls me over to the curb near his car. I tell Ghost to keep an eye on what's going on, meaning the door and more importantly me. I walk over to the dude, thinking he's going to start some shit right then and there. Instead, dude starts nonchalantly talking to me about some "good shit" he wants to give me, if I'll help him to get rid of it. Weed.

Then African Joe eyes Ghost Willy and tells me that Ghost is an asshole, a son of a bitch, and a snitch. This heats me up immediately. He's talking about my boy Ghost right in front of me, apparently not knowing I knew what had happened the night before. How could he not know? Maybe he still believes that Ghost is the perpetrator. I play along and listen.

In my mind, I'm wilding. I'm not saying anything, just nodding and listening, thinking *doesn't this dude know I'm the guy who is fucking his girl?* Eventually, his shit makes me sick so I tell him I have to get back to my job. He says he'll be back with some stuff for me later that night, I'm like *yeah, whatever nigga.* Then, Ghost says to him, "Yo, can I talk to you for a minute?" and he and the dude disappear into the parking lot next to Plus Park for about fifteen minutes. I hadn't had a chance to tell Ghost what he said before Ghost called him over. So I waited.

When they were done, I asked Ghost what went down. He says dude didn't give him a chance to talk. Ghost says dude made the same promise to him that he had made to me. He told Ghost that he "had some good shit that he wanted to share with his brothers," words to that effect. He'd made no mention about the night before, nothing, no apology, no explanation, nothing, it was as if it didn't happen. This was truly baffling. I figured the African Joe had to know Ghost wasn't the one, or maybe he just decided to let it go. African Joe was told that the guy that had been fucking his girl worked at the front door of Park Plus, so why didn't he at least approach the new guy Harry? Why didn't African Joe exercise the process of elimination? I mean the only other person it could be at this point was me. But there I was, right under his nose, and son is telling me he was going to bring me some weed?

Something was wrong. The night played itself out with me and Ghost on our p's and q's at the front door, and dude kept coming and going, coming and going, driving around the block and pulling up in front of the club all night, like he was watching us, planning some shit.

Plus Park closes at 5am. At about 4am, Hiro always asked me to go inside and help shut down the club when the lights came on. I'm now inside the club, standing along a wall near the dance floor, watching and waiting for the lights to come on. Suddenly, I get a call on my phone from Ghost, who tells me to come outside, African Joe is there and wants to talk to me. I'm thinking *okay, it's on*. Joe had apparently cased the club the whole night and now wanted to get down to business.

I hang up with Ghost and before I could get a chance to go outside, I feel someone grab my arm from behind. Before I turn around to see who it is, I feel the hot breath of a distinct deep voice with a thick African accent whispering slowly into my ear,

"You fucked me. Come outside."

I turn around and it's African Joe. I look him in his eyes and tell him he'll have to wait fifteen minutes until the club finishes, then I'll come out. Dude was obviously heated, sweating, a little jumpy, controlled fury. Strange thing was, I wasn't in the least bit nervous or scared, I was more tired than anything else. I remember yawning the moment dude walked away. I'd been standing all night outside and had been in that loud-ass club for the last hour and my head was throbbing, ears bleeding, legs like mush. Just tired, and now, this.

The Poking Thing Pisses Me Off

After the club clears, I walk outside and there's Joe, standing with two other African cats. One is Malcolm, a muscle-bound dude who everyone knew, and the other dude is this guy who's been to the club before and who's caused a lot of stupid static because he'd lost one of his "five thousand dollar gold rings" in the club while he was dancing on a pole like an idiot. This other dude's name is Martin, but I didn't know that at the time. What I did know was that this dude had major pull with the African community as a whole, and with the Nigerian community in particular. Dude pushed a fat, black brand-new Hummer, the only brother in all of Nagoya making the kind of loot to be able to do this. I'd seen dude around a few times; one time in particular I remember seeing dude slap the shit out of some other African in the street like the other dude was a little kid. Dude was supposedly a "boss", and the leader of the entire Nigerian community in Nagoya. Dude was not only a player, but he was *The* Player, and apparently Joe was his boy.

I walk up between the three of them and say directly to Joe, "Yo, son, you want to talk to me?" He says yeah, I say cool, let's go talk. We walk about ten feet away. Malcolm, Martin, and Ghost are watching us. The new guy Harry, is still upstairs ushering the last few people out of the club. The parking lot is filling up with everyone who had been in the club.

I knew Malcolm because everyone did. Big bodybuilder dude who was a fixture on the streets. As far as the Martin dude, I didn't know him at all except for what I knew of him. Ghost knew of the Martin cat from his notorious reputation as the leader of the Nigerians, but since Martin was with this silly African Joe character, Ghost had no love for him on that night either. It was 5 A.M., the club was emptying out, the sun had just risen into the sky, and there was madd static on the street.

Dude and I are standing a few feet from his little crew. He's not saying anything, just looking at me.

"Yo, you want to talk, let's talk." I say.

Dude says some wild, dumb, incomprehensible shit. Something stupid. I think he asked me again if I wanted to talk to him, *you want to talk to me*???-like it was incomprehensible to him that I wanted to talk to him, even though he'd just come up and grabbed me inside the club and said he wanted to talk to me.

"Yeah, man, that's why I'm here, you want to talk to me right?" I say.

He gets a look of disgust on his face, throws his arms up in the air, turns around and walks away, back to his boys. I'm standing there wondering what the fuck is going on. His boys then say loud enough for me to hear,

"Don't walk away from the man, he's here trying to talk to you. Go and talk to him."

He turns back around and I'm staring at him.

"You want to talk to me?" He asks again.

"Yes my dude, let's talk." I reply while squinting my eyes.

I was planning to ask dude how long he's been with the chick, or if he knew the chick, and to make sure it was the same chick. I was planning to tell him that I'll step aside and he can do whatever he wants with the chick, since I had already told her we were through. I would have just stepped aside, told him I didn't know the girl was "his" girl, and let it be that. But that's not how it went down.

"Let's go over here and talk." He says.

He gestures to the parking lot where all the people had gathered to smoke, talk, laugh, drink and vomit. We walk into the same alley, away from his boys and away from Ghost.

"So wassup." I turn and ask.

He takes a step towards me.

"You're a snake" he says and pokes me in my chest.

I didn't quite hear him clearly, the "snake" word came out sounding weird.

"I'm a what?" I say.

"YOU'RE A SNAKE..." He shouts and pokes me in my shoulder again. *Something is about to pop off out here*, I'm thinking.

"First of all, don't touch me, second, fuck are you talking about man?" I say.

I'm willing to be at least partially deferential—after all, I was boning this chick whom he did have some "relationship". I could understand how he'd be heated to find out that the dude boning "his" girl was the same dude who he had offered herbs to just hours before.

He says it again, even louder this time, like he was trying to draw attention to us,

"YOU'RE A SNAKE AND YOU'RE FUCKING MY GIRL, AND YOU TOLD HER I'M A DRUG DEALER...", and he pokes me *again*. *Three pokes.*

He's standing a foot in front of me, right in my face, poking me, loud talking me, calling me names, and I'm tired, pissed, and confused, but *son keeps poking me.*

Finally, I say,

"Dude, first, you don't have to keep touching me. Second, I don't know who 'your girl' is, and third, I didn't tell anyone anything about drugs or anything like that, fuck are you talking about man?"

Then he steps even closer to me, pokes me again and practically screams,

"YOU'RE A SNITCH!"

He keeps his finger on my shoulder where he'd been poking me. I take a step back, look dead at him and say,

"YO, I TOLD YOU NOT TO FUCKING TOUCH ME, MAN."

Then he lunges at me, I side step and crack him in his head, then all of his boys come running over. They try to come between us, but the dude keeps lunging at me and every time he does this, I take a step to the side and crack him in his head. He's swinging at me wildly and I'm just popping him in his face until finally he falls to one knee. By this time, I'm completely furious.

"COME ON NIGGA! COME GET SOME MOTHERFUCKER! I'LL KILL YOUR WHOLE FUCKING FAMILY BITCH NIGGA!"—shit like that, and Ghost is holding me back, telling me to "calm down, calm down T, just calm down."

I notice that my bandana has fallen off near where dude was kneeling. His two boys are attending to him, so he does not see the bandana, until he does. Dude picks up my bandana, stands up and walks toward me with it in his hand. He extends his arm as if he's going to hand me the bandana but lunges at me instead. I side step his goofy ass, and crack him in his head repeatedly until he falls to his knees in a daze. His boy Martin helps him up and then Martin proceeds to slap dude in his face. Finally, Martin grabs dude by his throat, yelling at dude,

"I TOLD YOU NOT TO FIGHT! I TOLD YOU NOT TO FIGHT!"

African Joe is down on his knees in the crowded parking lot taking Martin's slaps to his face like he deserves it. Everyone is now watching. I didn't know what was going on. African Joe is down on his knees and Martin is standing over him beating him like he was his child. His mouth is bleeding, his eye is swollen and he's getting slapped, punched, pushed and screamed on by his dude in front of the crowd that had just emptied out of Plus Park. Ghost is pushing me saying,

"Go home Trevor. Just go home." I wasn't sure what to do.

Suddenly, Martin stops slapping African Joe and walks towards me while mumbling something that I assumed was bad. Ghost is standing between us but Martin still manage to start with that same POKING shit. Instinctively, I push his hands away and scream,

"NIGGA YOU DON'T KNOW ME, DON'T FUCKING TOUCH ME!" Martin's eyes widen. He looks at me as if I was a student that just pushed the Principal. He then leans in, looks me directly in my eyes and with the utmost sincerity says to me,

"You want to fight me?"

Then from nowhere, the new guy, Harry shows up and says gently to me,

"Trevor, he's defending you, you shouldn't want to fight with him, he's on your side."

I'm confused, heated and tired. Joe is still kneeling on the ground with his head down and Martin is glaring at me and I'm just not sure what's going on.

Meanwhile, Ghost and Harry are both pleading with me,

"Just get your stuff and go home, Trevor."

So, I pick up my blue bandana from the pavement, walk to my bike and pedaled my ass all the way up Wakamiya Dori towards home.

I continued to work at Plus Park for a few days after that but, naturally, Hiro had heard about the fight, and since the block was now very hot, he told me he had to let me go, which was actually fine with me.

>CHAPTER 31

THE RELUCTANT DRUG DEALER

Trappin' In Japan

I'm not a great salesman. Not even a really good one. But still, I know that everything in life comes back around to sales of some sort. You've gotta sell yourself to your job, your boss, your partner, your friends, and even yourself. You sell your ideas, your dreams, your goals and the image of yourself, to yourself. You sell your time, your expertise, your knowledge, your strength, your unique traits and abilities, *motherfucker, you got something for sale?* Yes, in fact I *do*.

You can make a lot of money selling the right shit to the right people. However, I've always been turned off to sales jobs, seems like a crass way to get cash. Especially if you're working on pure commission, you have to rely on the needs and desires of your customers and whether they want to part with their dough. The art of persuasion is a con and I'm a dude who's on a quest for truth and the two don't mix, cons and truth. Can't serve two Gods no matter how hard you try. With sales, there are just too many variables for me. I think the main reason why I don't consider myself a good salesman is because I've never been much of a consumer. I don't get sold easily, never have, and therefore I feel like it's a hard shot to try to sell someone some shit they might not want or need. But.

A gram of weed in Japan goes for a hundred bucks. That's *ichi man* yen. Easy money. Most, if not all of the weed you can get in Japan is the absolute worst shit you have ever seen or smoked in your entire life. It's all stress weed. I never saw one single bud, *not one,* in Japan, until I was the one selling them to my friends in Nagoya.

A gram of weed for a hundred bucks. If someone could get some good Cali weed into Japan, that dude would make ridiculous money. The profit would be sick. That same gram sells for like ten bucks in LA, top-shelf herb goes for maybe twenty a gram. You're talking about potential 1000 percent profit, if you can get the product into the country. Fuck, someone put me on. *This is a no-brainer.* Or so I thought. This was the allure.

I knew a few heads selling herbs because I was a buyer. I knew how much they were charging me, the aforementioned ridiculous prices, so I knew what I'd be charging others. Herbs are like green gold in Japan, because it's not easy to find anyone selling, it's so hush hush, and mostly, if and when you get caught with herb, selling herb, et cetera, you're going to jail for a potentially very long time, and the Japanese cops may just beat your ass in addition. My man R who is now in Saudi Arabia, got busted, and subsequently deported for selling weed in Japan, and now he can't return to Japan. Drugs are not tolerated in Japan the way they are in the US, and definitely not the way marijuana is sold openly and over the counter in California. You're a social pariah if you smoke weed in Japan, never mind that alcohol is the nation's nightly news. Smoking, selling, discussing, using, experimenting with, or fraternizing with anything illegal whatsoever is sorely frowned upon in Japan. You shouldn't do it, period.

The way I was getting my stash, if I didn't get it from D, was I'd have to call a number, tell the voice on the other end where I'd be at a certain time, then go there and wait for the delivery.

After waiting for about a half hour, an Iranian or Turkish salesman would pull up in his car, tell you to get in the backseat, drive off, and you'd make the transaction in the car while driving. Usually, you're in the backseat because for whatever reason your salesman doesn't want you in the front seat next to him, because you being foreign might somehow implicate him in some illegal doings, even though he's every much as foreign as you, which makes the whole shit all that much more conspicuous.

Picture this frazzed-out, Iranian cat wearing a sparkling white muscle shirt, looking like a cross between John Travolta, Freddie Mercury, and Ali Shaheed Muhammad. Driving around in a long, light green, lowered Lincoln Town Car, with me, the dread head, in the back seat, broad daylight, bumping Tupac loud as fuck, cruising down the streets of Nagoya making a weed sale. I don't know why we never got pulled over for these outrageous shenanigans, but we didn't. We may as well have been two purple Plutonians, floating down the street on a long green hoverboard.

Although the Iranians and Turks lacked present-day fashion sense and didn't know the meaning of water, nor soap, they were still totally cool, plus they got me stoned.

My Plug Is Named P

Then this cat I knew named 'P' randomly emails me from California one day:

Trevor,
It's P from LA. It's been a long time. You still in Nagoya? I'm going to be in Nagoya from December 8 for three months. I'm bringing some California love.
You won't be disappointed. Hopefully we both can fly for free for a few months.
If you get one ring from my number it's because it's prepaid and I am out of time, so if you can please give me a shout after you get the one ring. It means my plans are set!
Thanks bro.
P

I meet P at some bar, or some party, or someone's apartment, or somewhere. He's a shortish cat with an obvious Napoleon complex. He has a big nose, a huge head and really tall dark hair, which gives him maybe 3 extra inches on his height. P can never stand still. He's always gesturing with his hands but on occasion, he'll catch himself and immediately shove his hands into his pockets as if he's apologizing for gesturing too much. He looks like a big-headed, half Japanese Ben Stiller, with brown hair who thinks he's really fucking cool.

P's dope-selling proposition dropped out of the sky at exactly the right moment. I talked him into a total 50/50 split, plus he fronted me the herb. So whatever I sold, I got half, and paid nothing for it. Total profit. Free herbs. Can't lose. *Cool deal,* I thought.

The days of riding in the backseats of long green Lincoln Town Cars was dead.

If You Build It

Cats appeared out of the woodwork asking for my cabbage. P slowly morphed into a loquacious idiot bragging about how much pussy he was getting, constantly misquoting Snoop Dogg and dancing the shaky leg like the nerdy half-Japanese, half-American white boy from Orange County that he was. I'd met him in Japan at a club through another friend, and P and I found ourselves taking a smoke break outside the club the night we met. We got to talking, and he whipped out a joint and asked me if I wanted a hit. We became smoking friends, but P was kind of an overbearing weirdo. He was overly critical, overly confident, and articulated his words too precisely. He reminded me of a young English or Social Studies teacher trying to be cool in Japan. While smoking weed.

Whenever we met at the train station, he'd give me maybe half a dozen Ziploc baggies of the stuff fully wrapped up and in perfect little buds. Mostly, in Japan, if you're buying herbs you're not getting buds, you're getting what we'd refer to as "stress weed" over here. The quality was inevitably low but you take what you can get. There was a rumor that lots of these Iranian and Turkish cats swallowed small packets of herb and then shit them out once in Japan, which made the whole process mildly nauseating, but again, you take what you can get.

I asked P how much he had brought over from Cali, and his response was "pounds."

"Dude, how are you getting pounds of herb through customs with all this shit?" I ask.

"Cologne, lots of cologne." He respond.

He said the dogs couldn't smell the stuff because it was vacuum-wrapped and the plastic was doused with heavy doses of Perry Ellis cologne, *Perry*, see? -and since he was a big-headed half-Japanese white boy who spoke fluent Japanese no one ever suspected him of shit. I was kinda jealous about that, for about a minute.

One time, I was returning from a short trip to California, where I'd spent lots of time burning trees on Venice Beach. Knowing the strict Japanese laws on marijuana possession, I made sure, as sure as I could, that I had no traces of herbs either in my carry-on bag, or on my person, or in my stowed baggage. Except, I had burned in my man Fred's car on the way to LAX the day before. The smell had nestled itself into my clothes, and the drug dog at the Nagoya airport promptly identified me as a carrier. I was immediately taken back into a small room with two or three Japanese airport officials. They rifled through my belongings, and only came up with some pure essence frankincense body oil. Upon asking me what that was, I told them I was a practitioner of meditation and needed the oil to help me go into a trance. Eventually, they found literally two tiny crumbs of herb in my bag and told me that if I got into any trouble, of any sort in Japan, at any time, for any reason during the duration of my stay, that I'd be immediately deported. They had their eyes on me from then on.

There were many times that I should've been deported. Like the time when my Vietnamese girlfriend in the Valley sent me some black pornography. The porn was discovered by the folks who check the mail, and they called me down to the post office and asked me what the obviously pornographic DVD was, and I told them it was family videos, and they believed me. Whew.

So P tossed me the Ziploc baggies of pre-weighed cabbage and I went to selling it. However, I was petrified of carrying it around and the fact that I was high off my own supply every time I had to make a delivery made the paranoia unbearable. The paranoia wasn't that low-grade, can't-quite-pinpoint it, uncomfortable paranoia you get when you smoke weed. It was an industrial-powered, very, very real and visceral, sweat buckets pouring down my forehead, running from every cop car I saw, heart beating wildly and chest heaving, hiding behind garbage cans kind of trembling with fear paranoia. The fact of me not only being high, but also carrying pernicious amounts of trees, had me literally booking down the street and ducking into pachinko parlors in order to hide from anyone who I thought might have suspected that I was walking around with these four or five little Ziploc baggies of perfectly formed marijuana buds that smelled like Perry Ellis cologne.

I could only handle it for a few weeks, and even those few weeks caused my beard to grey prematurely. Every time I'd return to my apartment in Fukiage, I'd creep up first to see if there were any cop cars outside my apartment. Then I'd check around to see if anyone was watching me go upstairs. Once upstairs, I'd check to see if my door was still locked, half expecting it to be open, then I'd slink inside and check my stash to make sure it was still there. Once I'd concluded that everything was normal, I'd sigh a humongous "whew," pack a bowl, blaze, and make some calls.

Somehow, I never got busted, and they say that miracles never cease ... but that's something I'd never do again in Japan again. *Unless I had to.*

Your Wish Is Your Command

The twins were turning me on to customers and I was throwing them fat buds for it. They put me onto this one cat, a dude from Philadelphia. The twins told me he was interested in buying quantity, so I said sure, put me on to dude. I was slowly becoming Nagoya's plug.

The Philly cat and I met one day in Sakae. He pulls up in a small family car, jumps out of the whip looking very serious. He's wearing a two-tone cardigan sweater, stuffed deep into his pants, which were belted up tight around his waist. He's a brother, maybe around my age, and he's got on a pair of those cheap goofy-looking old-school Oakley sunglasses with the strap. Them joints have never been cool. I'm waiting for him on the sidewalk leaned up against my bike smiling. The twins said dude was going to be buying quantity, I wanted to make a good impression.

He approaches me and gruffly looks me up and down, like I'm somebody not really worth his time.

"So, hey, you're ah, Trevor, right?" he says.

He's not looking at me, in fact, he's looking in the other direction, again, like *fuck this guy and whoever he's with*. He's got his body facing mine, but his head is looking down the street towards Shirakawa Koen, and his top lip is curled up in that *who the fuck do you think you are* kind of way we do in NYC. I guess Philly and NYC have some things in common. This dude was trying to let me know that he was cooler than me, and that he didn't really need to be there, even though there he was buying herbs off me.

"So whatchya got?" he asks me a bit too fucking loudly, finally turning towards me. I'm thinking *dude, you know exactly what I got, man. D told you the price, so let's just make this sale so we both can get the fuck outta here.*

"I got . . . it, man. You know. I got it, man. You want it?" I answer affirmatively.

He looks at me, then looks back towards the park.

"I wanna see it," he says.

He's still got his lip curled up and he's arching his eyebrows. I'm thinking *if I was in the states this exact nigga right here would be five-o.* But I'm not in the states, and there ain't no black cops from Philly in Japan.

"Okay nigga. You can see the shit," I say.

Fucking dickhead. I open my backpack and show Philly dude the Ziploc'ed baggies of fat fresh Cali kush still in buds. This motherfucker looks into my bag and squeals like a five year old girl. Dude literally let out a high pitched squeal and his eyes lit up like he was seeing the ice cream man for the first time.

"How much are they again?" he asks.

He looks dead in my face now but without the lip curl and without the sneer. Now, he just looks madd eager.

"Dude, they're *ichi man* yen for a gram. It just got here a few days ago, it's going to go fast, so if you want it . . ." I say.

Dude shoves his hand into his back pocket and pulls out three *ichi man* yen bills. He hands me the money, I open the backpack, he sticks his hand inside and grabs three bags. I close the bag and turn to take off.

"What's your number?" He asks.

I tell him my digits and just before I put my foot on my pedal...

"Hey, you got time to listen to a CD?" He says.

A CD? "What kind of CD?" I ask.

He goes over to his car door, opens it, and pulls out a blue CD in a plain white CD jacket. Gold letters in script emblazoned on the blue CD label read: "*Your Wish Is Your Command.*"

"Give this a listen when you have time." He says.

He hands me the CD.

"Sure, man." I say.

I stuff the CD into my backpack, and hop on my bike.

"Whenever you need, holla at me directly yo, you don't have to go through the twins anymore," I tell him.

"I will," he says.

He then quickly gets in his whip and drive's off.

I get home later and listen to the CD. It's a motivational self-help CD along the lines of Tony Robbins, but something was different about it. Or maybe I *wanted* something to be different about it. I was selling herbs in Japan, divorced from my wife, who was living with some dude named K Papa in my old apartment. I was going to counseling and staying up late nights essentially stalking my family. I was "soothing" myself with ongoing trips to the massage ladies in Sakae and Imaike.

Even though my magazine was blowing up and I was writing music, I didn't feel really great about myself. I was stung by how absolute my ex-wife's disdain for me was. H and I were on again I suppose, but I was wondering how long we could last, or I could last. I was starting to think maybe it might be time for me to start thinking about actually leaving Japan.

I listened to the CD. The gist of it was, you can have absolutely anything you want, if you just think about it hard enough, and did things you like doing, to keep your emotional apparatus working in a receptive mode. And as long as you are continually grateful and expectant, and can spend some time every day concentrating on whatever it was you want, you'll get it. This shit sounded like the gospel to me.

I asked myself what I wanted, what I really, really wanted, and it dawned on me that maybe I wanted to get the fuck out of Japan.

So I started concentrating on getting out of Japan. Those 14 CDs in that beat up blue CD case became my religion. I listened to them raptly, every day, took notes, concentrated, vibrated, and visualized my ass off. I felt like I had a secret and my secret was that I was going to return to Los Angeles.

Yes, Los Angeles. Why LA? Why not New York? *No, man.* Nix that right away. Too cold. And Brooklyn isn't Brooklyn anymore. Where would I go? The Bronx? GTFOH. Manhattan? There's no place in Manhattan I can afford. Not going back to Queens, and that leaves what,

Staten Isle? Huh? Be serious—nah, no NYC for me. So I fixated my plans on LA.

California Dreamin

I imagined myself on Venice Beach, smoking herbs with my man Ra the artist. I imagined trading crazy flat-earth conspiracy theories with my other dude J Frassini. I imagined weed shops and Fat Burger and Hollywood Boulevard and massage parlors with Dominican and El Salvadorian chicks working there. I thought about endless sunshine and Jamba Juice and California Pizza Kitchen and movie stars. I imagined my own previous life in LA, but without the strife that accompanied it. I thought about acting and craft services and The Doors. I convinced myself that I had decided *to move back to LA.*

>Chapter 32

THE SHOW GOES ON

I'll write a song for you

I had written songs while I was in TAOW about my past, present, and future relationships. I wrote about how I'd fallen in and out of love with my wife. I wrote about the crushing isolation of Japan for foreigners. I wrote about innocence, addiction, dreams, race, obsession, and desperation. I wrote about searching for meaning and understanding and spirituality, about forgiveness, desire, and paranoid psychedelia. *And it all had become my life.*

Back in Japan
i'm looking forward trying to escape my past
she's waiting for me in a Tokyo café
sitting by the window as she's sipping a latte
i told her i would make it there in an hour
told her we could get away we could run away
we could find a way we could be together
somehow, someway, someday...

Words are prophetic even when you don't mean them to be. Written words, in a notebook, journal, or diary, have power. You imbue them with your energy and they take on a life of their own and through some kind of weird osmosis energy metaphysical power, the words you write come true in ways you can't fathom.

maybe she could save me . . .

i told her i would take her back to LA
where the sun shines on the boulevard
everybody has a dream and the people look clean
and the living is easy but sleazy. I can see it now we're on the runway
waiting for the big time, waiting for our big break
waiting for the sunshine, stage show, bright lights
long nights . . . back in japan
Taow
"the way"

Toyohashi, Hitzone, and H

In the fall of 2011, Ali, who had produced the beats for my song "*Anata No Namae Wa Na'an Desu Ka*" approached me with a gig. He was performing with a live band out in Toyohashi and asked me to fill in for a few weeks. He offered me *ichi man goh sen* yen per gig, about 150 US dollars, plus meals and perks. Seemed like a no-brainer. He also offered me a couple songs to record to, and since TAOW had since burned itself out, I needed the outlet to continue my music.

La Haina is a dark, cavernous club with ornate chandeliers hanging from the ceiling. To the right of the stage, there's a huge karaoke screen mounted on the wall, and sometimes, when the crowd sang English songs, you'd see English lyrics on the screen, but only rarely. The Filipina women are always singing loud, emotional, songs in Tagalog, and whenever they sing their songs they adopt an emotionally defiant attitude as if to say *you better not fuck with me anymore*. There's a hardness to the Filipina women, something must have happened to them. The Brazilian chicks' primary goal is always to have as good a time as they can, laugh at everything, flirt with everyone, and be as loud as they possibly can.

The band and I spent most of our time offstage walking around the club, taking pictures with the crowd and eating fried tilapia fish. Then, whenever Zon, the bandleader, felt that the crowd was ready for us to take the stage, he'd get behind his drum kit, press a button, and

"HitZone," took the stage and killed the crowd with R&B, salsa, funk, hip hop, reggaeton, and soul classics.

Ali is the lead singer on most of the tunes, Abe handled leads on a few tracks, and my job was to handle the raps while Zon kept the beat on his drums. It was surreal, me on stage performing Damian Marley's "*Welcome To Jamrock*" and rapping Fat Joe's "*Lean Back*" and *ragamuffin stylee* on Shaggy's "*Angel.*" One of the crowd favorites was Daddy Yankee's "*Gasolina*"—we'd set it off with that jam and the level of the club amped up from there. We played the hottest R&B/hip hop hits of the day: Outkast's "*I Like The Way You Move*," plus funk classics like The Commodores' "*Brick House.*" Everything from Earth, Wind & Fire to Flo Rida, Usher to Snoop and Dre. Performing again was sexy as hell and made me feel like a rock star, just like when TAOW was at its peak. At any given moment there'd be two or three sexy Brazilian or Filipina ladies on stage with us, shaking their asses. During breaks, Ali would disappear with one of the girls who had been dancing on stage with us. He could usually be found with a chick either backstage, in his car, or getting head in a bathroom stall. Ali was a dichotomy. He was a bible banging Christian who liked getting blowjobs in bathroom stalls from Filipina club hostesses, but a good guy at heart and a talented producer and great performer. Ali and I were often at odds about one thing or another: music, women, politics. Flamboyant and materialistic but talented, Ali and I were like feuding cousins, maybe because he's got Trinidadian roots and I've got Jamaican blood, maybe. Maybe not.

Zon, would beat it back to the band house and chill in his room, or sometimes he'd have some "Bob Marley" and we'd go sit in his whip and get blazed, talking about politics, music, films, and the future. Zon was a lot more intelligent than anyone gave him credit for, sensitive, low key, and had a sharp sense of humor. He kept me grounded. He'd pepper me with obscure questions about Nia Long—"Where was her character in 'Love Jones' from?"—or Eddie Murphy—"Do you think that motherfucker was really getting blown by a dude?"—or spit out on-point Bernie Mac impressions—"I ain't scared of you motherfuckers, I'm blessed!" We became really good friends and I appreciated his advice, gentle nature, and friendship.

Abe, was a family man who was a lot more serious than the rest of us. After our sets, Abe would disappear and I had no idea where he went. Then, just before we were supposed to take the stage, he'd reappear with his saxophone. Cool cat.

Me, sometimes I'd hang out in the club, other times I'd return to H's car, or we'd go back to the band house together and spend the breaks in my room. She never hung out in the club when we performed, I suppose because she didn't like seeing the women in the club throwing themselves at us. These moments with H were maybe my favorite times we had together. We were outside Nagoya, I was performing, and she was my ride or die. Things in Nagoya seemed far away whenever we were in Toyohashi, the music and the crowds and La Haina and the band made me feel like my issues with my ex-wife and my children didn't exist for a couple of days.

HitZone often ended the night, at 5 A.M. most times, with my original, "*Anata No Namae Wa Na'an Desu Ka*". The crowd would go absolutely nuts on the hook, which I had written in five minutes: "*Anata no namae wa na'an desu ka/tsuki atteru hito wa imasen ka/isshoni odo te kure masu ka/anata no namae wa na'an desu ka.*"

Then, with the sun rising, H and I took off in her car back to Nagoya blaring Coldplay on her car stereo, me singing the lyrics at the top of my lungs.

> *So I look in your direction*
> *But you pay me no attention do you*
> *I know you don't listen to me*
> *Cause you say you see straight through me, don't you...*

The drive back to Nagoya took over an hour, so we listened to the entire Parachutes album and I'd sing every word. More often than not, I'd look over at H while my car seat was let all the way down, and she'd be crying, tears streaming down her pretty face, silent sniffles, her mascara streaming down the sides of her cheeks, with the morning sunlight streaming in through the windshield.

Things with H were . . . strange. I needed her, and I guess she needed me somehow. We'd become addicted to each other, codependent, but not in a great way. She'd embedded herself into my life such that I couldn't really do anything without her. I suppose lots of dudes in Japan cream themselves for the situation I had with H. She's paying my rent, buying me shit, taking me places, buying and cooking my food, acting as my Japanese mouthpiece, totally "taking care" of me. But why? I'm a grown ass man. I'm not incapacitated in any way whatsoever. I can do for myself. But I wasn't.

I needed her for *RAN*, I needed her to take care of my business and speak on my behalf to clients. I "needed" her to help me pay for my life because once her money started flowing I had long since given up on the idea of working a full time job for myself. I needed her to help me take care of my domestic issues. I needed her to shop for me, read my mail, make my calls, help me with my banking, handle my utilities, and more. I had voluntarily given up my independence and sabotaged my own ability to *do me* in Japan. As I said, lots of foreign guys in Japan strive for this situation. They become semi-delusional hookers, prostituting themselves to lonely Japanese women, effectively selling their souls, and their dicks, for cash. They think that they are players but before they know it, they've been castrated by that cute, innocent, submissive Japanese girl they met at the club. I had become one of them.

H willingly did all this and more, but I wasn't in love with her and she knew it. I was using her but at the same time she was using me. She had made too many investments and had been with me for too long to give up, even though she clearly wasn't getting what she wanted out of our relationship, whatever that may have been. Honestly, I didn't know what she wanted. She never talked about marriage, children, or even about us moving in together. Her considering leaving her parents' home in Gifu was never even put on the table. Seemed like she just wanted us to keep doing what we had been doing, which was seeing each other 3 or 4 times a week, with no real plan for anything different in the future.

Even though H and I weren't necessarily "enjoying" our relationship, neither of us could imagine how things would be if we separated. We'd been "together" at this point for longer than I'd been married to my wife. Six years, the longest relationship I'd ever been in, but it was stiff and frayed at the edges, like an old worn out cloth that you keep using even though you should have thrown it out long ago. There wasn't much more we could do together, save get married and/or have a child, but neither option was anywhere in either of our plans.

I couldn't get my heart over the fact that it was my relationship with H that had mostly done in my marriage. Even though there were scores of women besides just H. Even though the woman my ex-wife had caught me with wasn't H, still, I felt like my relationship with H was to blame for the downfall of my marriage. I felt since H was still around, *right there next to me*, it was easy to blame her.

No matter how much she helped me, no matter how giving, generous, caring, and useful H was to me, I couldn't shake the idea that she was a marriage wrecker. I remembered asking H a few months into our relationship, at the very beginning, to leave me alone. She'd said no. I remembered telling her I didn't want a sexual relationship with her anymore after one of those episodes in her car behind Higashiyama Koen, so she'd decided she'd become my "assistant." She wouldn't let go, wouldn't let *me* go. She persevered relentlessly and got what she wanted, which, I guess, was me. But I wasn't there with her. We were both floating around in our separate worlds together. The life I'd built with my family was gone and in its place stood H. I both hated her and needed her, and the combination made me bitter and conflicted.

But not H. She didn't seem even slightly perturbed about what we were doing, nor what I'd lost. She tried to make up for my obvious lackluster attitude towards her and "us" by lavishing me with clothes and jewelry and all the money she was spending. She was paying for my affection and she knew it and I knew it and this made me even angrier. My respect for her slowly eroded more and more, and I began to see her as having low self-esteem and as being too needy. She told me stories about how her alcoholic father had abused her mother, physi-cally and emotionally, in her childhood. She reminded me that she'd grown up in the Gifu countryside with her younger brother and hadn't even seen Coke in a glass before she was eleven years old. She said her childhood had been strict and that she'd worn a mouth brace to sleep every night for her entire teenage life. She painted a picture of herself as an innocent country girl whose abusive father had tormented her and her mother when she was growing up and it all translated to me as someone who would do anything to be able to feel needed, wanted, loved by someone. I was H's someone, marriage and children be damned. But at the same time, I was impressed by her loyalty and devotion to me. No one in my life had ever shown me half as much attention as H showed me. No one, not even my wife gave as much of herself to please me, to make me feel special, or to cater to me, as H.

She chaperoned me all over the place at the drop of a dime and took me to shows, movies, shops. She made sure I ate well and whenever I had any medical issues she took me to a doctor. She even had me go in for a complete medical evaluation, for which she paid for. Three times. She painted her own original designs on my clothing and also painted huge colorful pictures of eagles, unicorns, flowers. She painted a giant mural of New York City, and all these hung on my wall above my DJ equipment at my apartment in Fukiage. She'd make sumptuous dinners and did my laundry and cleaned my apartment and she was the absolute best assistant anyone could ever have. It was as if she found her existence more significant based on my apparent need for her.

H did everything she could to win my affection, but to me, she just wasn't the one.

>Chapter 33

I'm On A Bullet Train

Headed to nowhere fast...

The Toyohashi gig rolled over into 2012. TAOW was done but I was still writing and performing music with HitZone and Ali was giving me beats to work with. Three of the beats he gave me metamorphosized into my next full CD project, *Full Time Hustler,* which I recorded at G Conkarah's studio near Rokubancho station.

I felt with all I was doing at the time allowed me to call myself a full time hustler because no one in Nagoya was doing it the way I was. I was everywhere, Nagoya's P Diddy.

The completion of my album helped me to get more live gigs after the ashes of TAOW had burnt out. I did shows in Tokyo, Osaka and all around Nagoya.

America...Fame...My Heart Still Beats for You

Meanwhile, at my apartment, I'm listening to the *Your Wish Is Your Command* CDs every chance I got. I put up a vision board on my wall with pictures of LA and printed out color 8 X 10 photos of Denzel Washington, Morgan Freeman, and Samuel Jackson. I decided I was going to return to Hollywood and become a movie star. I put all my shit into boxes, clothes, pictures, books, and CDs, pretty much everything I had accumulated in my almost 9 years in Japan. I didn't know exactly when I was leaving, how I was leaving, why exactly I was leaving, or where I was going, I just had an inner feeling that my time in Japan was just about up. I was seeing a decade start to loom on the horizon and wondering just how much longer I could stay. Barack Obama was still president in the US and I figured it might be the only time in my lifetime there would be a black president in the US. This was one of the reasons I used to justify leaving Japan. I re-read the Declaration of Independence and the Constitution's Bill of Rights. I convinced myself that America was indeed a great country and made myself proud of being an American, all over again, or, for the first time.

But the international group of friends I had in Nagoya seemed to have something against America and Americans specifically. I recorded "American Man" on my *Full Time Hustler* album as a *shut-the-fuck-up* to them and their gripes with American people. The irony wasn't lost on me. I had arrived in Japan almost 8 years earlier with my own major issues with America, in fact when I arrived to Japan I was almost embarrassed to be an American, and here I was in my next to last year in Japan *defending* America and walking around with a newfound chip on my shoulder about being an American. Wild.

Communication as a Weapon

By now, my ex-wife wasn't communicating with me at all, or, if she was, it was all in Japanese. I couldn't read it and she knew it. She was "speaking" to me in Japanese, but she was not using it to communicate *with* me, she was using it *against* me. She was being silent as far as I was concerned, and her short sporadic messages came months in between. She was freezing me out of her life even moreso, all while I was depositing money into her bank account every month so I could keep seeing Taiyo and Asia.

Meanwhile, her boyfriend "K Papa" was dropping Taiyo and Asia off at Higashiyama Koen once a month and it was eating me up inside but there was nothing I could do. I didn't want to become a bitter old foreigner but it seemed the entire situation was getting the best of me. I wanted to smash dude's face in every time I saw him, but I knew that'd land me in jail or worse. He and A were playing their card and shoving it down my throat and I had to remain calm through the whole arrangement. I felt like the whole town was laughing at me, and my heart felt like it was shrinking.

At the same time, it seemed like suddenly I could both speak and understand a lot more Japanese. It was like it happened overnight, except for me my "overnight" actually had taken 9 years to happen. I could clearly remember those first few years when I could barely put together a full sentence, but now I noticed how much of the language I'd learned. It was coming out of my mouth without me even thinking about it. Suddenly there wasn't any lag time spent in my brain with me having to translate what people were saying word for word, entire phrases and paragraphs now registered in my mind with no effort at translation. *I was speaking Japanese.* Everywhere I went—restaurants, post office, bank, cell phone store, gym, clubs, bars, offices, schools, elevators, shops—I was able to speak and communicate almost freely with anyone at any time. *How the fuck did this happen?*

It happened. Almost through osmosis, the language was inside my head, and the culture had embedded itself inside me too. But I hadn't invited it in, like a parasite it had burrowed itself underneath my skin and into the language center of my brain. I hadn't practiced, hadn't gone to school, hadn't taken formal classes, but somehow, the language had spilled its way into the canals of my brain.

I found myself actually thinking in Japanese whether or not I wanted to wherever I was. *Sono kuruma ii desu yo*, that's a nice car. *Nani shiyou ka na*, what am I doing later? *Samuii*, it's cold outside. *Ima nanji*, what time is it? *Onaka ga suita*, I'm hungry. *Kanojo dare*, who is she? *Coco doko?* Where am I? *Dekimasuyo*, I can do it. Et cetera.

I was thinking basic thoughts in Japanese and when I stopped to consider it, which I often did, it was really, really weird. I got all the little hiccups, tics, sound effects, pauses, the *wa, ta, ga, ha, sa, wo, no, do, ko, sho*, nuances in Japanese. These sounds and others, plus the parade of formalities and gestures, resided in my brain and my body expressed them without me thinking about it. I was becoming Japanese, like that dude in *District 9*. Even the way I did nothing besides fume about my situation with my ex and K Papa and my children was a Japanese reaction, which is to say, no reaction at all, on the outside at least. I had fully incorporated the Japanese tatemae/honne value system into my own behavior.

The grunts, growls, sneers, cackles, coughs, moans, groans of Japanese men became instantly understandable to me. Not only did I understand them, I was making those same noises. I was bent over and bitter and apologetic for my existence all at once. I wasn't sure what I really felt anymore anyway because I had submerged how I felt under the social constructs of everyday Japanese polite behavior for so long that my own real feelings seemed to escape me. I was becoming numb and going dead inside. I was caught up in the Japanese matrix, wanting to be Neo, but without any of Neo's special powers. Superman in a land where the national product is kryptonite. Unlike when I had first arrived in Japan, when it had felt like anything was possible, now, it felt like nothing was possible, and while all the foreigners I knew were falling over themselves trying to be as Japanese as they could, I wasn't. I was desperately trying to hold onto myself, but it seemed to me as if my body and mind were being taken over by an unwelcome foreign entity. I was living a real life version of Invasion of The Japanese Body Snatchers.

I couldn't ask questions, because you're not *supposed* to ask too many questions about anything in Japan, even if you really need to know, it's just not polite. Never ask a Japanese person *why* unless you want to see his head explode. It's a deer caught in headlights reaction. There is no "why" in Japan, there is only *do like everyone else, and never wonder why*. There's a "form" and formula for every situation in Japan, and if the formula doesn't exist, then the situation isn't supposed to exist either. I found myself carrying out the same social rituals Japanese perform with each other, confusion, mock surprise, blurry *unawareness, wishy washiness, being vague, all the while knowing this isn't how I behave, this isn't me*. I learned the social games Japanese play with each other and I played along, but I couldn't *let on* that I knew how silly it all was. I had to play dumb over and over in all kinds of situations where just being direct and honest would have worked so much better. I did everything I could just to not seem too aggressive, but the straitjacket of Japanese formality and politeness was chafing my fucking skin off, literally and figuratively.

I was faking it all the way through, all day, every day, and so was everyone else. I thought I had figured out how to disguise my blackness, and my foreign-ness, underneath a phony affected Japanese exterior, with perfect Japanese, but I was still a black foreigner every day, all day, everywhere I went. A gaijin, even though I had the language *and* the nuances down pat.

Sometimes it felt like there was a tiny Japanese dude living inside me, who was trying to break free of all the black skin he was surrounded by. Every time I interacted with anyone, Japanese or foreign, this tiny Japanese dude living inside me took me over, controlling my voice, words, expressions, and gestures. I both needed and hated this dude, similar to how I was feeling about H.

I found myself struggling with what I was supposed to say or how I was supposed to act. More often than not, the Japanese cultural language, gestures, and behaviors came out of my body involuntarily. It felt like I was a living, breathing, black marionette, a puppet controlled by the strings of Japanese society. It sounds like I'm over-dramatizing what was going on but I'm not, it was crazy. Sometimes I found myself bowing to my foreigner friends. I caught myself saying *"sumimasen"* to my Mom on the phone while we were talking numerous times. I started apologizing profusely, saying *"gomen nasai"* to everyone and anyone, for any reason, or no reason whatsoever. I apologized to the host at restaurants for showing up and asking if any tables were available. I apologized to the waitress for ordering food. I apologized to anyone who caught my eye on the streets. I apologized for anything I either said or did or wanted to say or do. I started being unnecessarily and overly apologetic just like the Japanese, and then I started feeling really, really bad about just being alive. I started walking with my head down and my shoulders slumped. I started ignoring my own emotions and wasn't sure what I felt about anything anymore. I was afraid of my own opinion on things. The only things I was sure about was that I was angry at my ex-wife, I was angry at her new boyfriend, and I was angry at H, even though *I needed her.*

Japan has one of the highest suicide rates in the modern world. Seppuku may not be as prevalent now as it was in Japanese history, but it still very much exists. They literally *kill themselves* over shame and for feeling sorry, and I was starting to feel *very* Japanese, very shameful, and *very* sorry. I was losing myself, caught between the *me* I thought I knew and some new me that seemed to be fighting it's way to the surface. A hybrid Japanese version of myself.

The language, the culture, the battle with my wife, the ongoing relationship with H, *the women*, the food, the rules, the air—the whole Japanese experience had sculpted and refashioned me into someone that I didn't quite recognize. It felt like I was literally splitting into two people, or *three.* It began to feel like I was doing daily battle with this new person who was fighting his way through my skin. He spoke his own language, had his own gestures, and he thought in an entirely different way than I did. He carried himself differently than me, and he showed up whether I asked him to or not. I wasn't 100 percent sure who he was, but I often heard him speaking perfect Japanese in my voice and I wondered just *who the fuck was talking.*

I went to sleep at night hearing Japanese in my head and I was dreaming in Japanese and the first thoughts I had when I woke up were in Japanese. My life had turned into a Japanese Groundhog Day.

Even with my children, I began to wonder if they truly understood what I was saying to them, whether I said it in English or Japanese. I wondered if they too thought their dad was a gaijin. Then I wondered since they are technically half gaijin, *do they hate half of themselves?* Obviously at their young age, I could never think to ask them a question like that, but that made it worse for me. Who *could* I ask? I was caught up in my head and had questions about my own sanity and comprehension and it all made me feel like I was more alone in Japan than I'd ever been. Sometimes I'd catch my son staring at me and his eyes seemed to be asking *what is daddy?* Not who is daddy, but *what.* I didn't quite know myself. I freaked myself out.

In my mind, I figured the Japanese were laughing at us behind our backs, and sometimes, in front of our faces. The idea of me trying to be them and having them laugh at me infuriated me. I wasn't going out like that. Soon my idea of returning to the US became an obsession.

I'm listening to *Your Wish Is Your Command,* over and over. I decided I was headed back to Los Angeles and I started listening to the Mamas and the Papas' "California Dreamin'" again and again and again and again. *All the leaves are brown/and the sky is grey/I'd be safe and warm/If I was in LA/I'm California Dreamin'...*

>Chapter 34

SPRING SUMMER FALL

2012: Sex Circus

I'm leaving, but I'm totally enslaved to my sex tick.

Morally bankrupt. Delinquent. Slutty. Vice ridden. Bastard. Womanizer.

Fall of 2012, my shit was jumping. Over the course of one month, I had four events lined up. I had started an improvisational movie and film themed English class called "Hollywood English Club". I had full scripts of actual Hollywood movies such as "Pretty Lady", "Sleepless in Seattle", "Bodyguard", "Top Gun", and "When Harry Met Sally" delivered to me from a bookstore I knew of on Hollywood Boulevard. I was slated to DJ a party for a newly formed international motorcycle club. It wasn't really a motorcycle club though, just a bunch of foreigners who had all gotten t-shirts and jackets emblazoned with the name of their club, but without actually having any motorcycles. Goofballs. I rocked the mic in an event my dude Vinnie Vintage had organized, called "Autumn Jam", and I participated in that years Aichi Film Festival. I definitely had it going on, and I was swimming in deep waters of Japanese flesh.

Trippy Love Bizarre

Desensitized and tired of "just having sex", I started coming up with weird things for these women to do whenever they came to my place in Fukiage.

I'd have one squat nude for as long as she could, just to watch her do it. Another one I'd have stick out her tongue and say "ahh" and let me examine her tonsils. Another one I'd make her do as many push-ups as she could, then make her try to do handstands against the wall. If she could, I'd see how long she could stay there upside down, while the blood rushed to her head. Nude. Another one I'd have play hours of jazz piano into the twilight hours. Nude. This one is showing me yoga poses. You guessed it, nude. That one is singing R&B songs with me saying "oki koe", *louder voice*, over and over, until she's screaming the lyrics at the top of her lungs in my apartment. Nude. Another one is watching lesbian porn with me.

I had a rule that any woman who stepped foot into my apartment had to immediately take a shower. I told them it was a medical condition that anyone in my apartment had to sanitize themselves, or else I'd get sick. They all asked for towels and t-shirts.

It was wearing me out. I was exhausted most of the time, almost dreading meeting these women. But I *had to have it,* even if I didn't really want it, or couldn't do it. Nothing was getting me high anymore. I was insatiable.

Alphabet Soup

There were a number of different *A*s, several *N*s, half a dozen *M*s, about 9 *Y*s, maybe another half dozen *S*s, a couple Ks, a few Rs, a few *T*s, and only one *H*. H was a standalone. However, over the past 6 years, she changed. H had evolved.

She was no longer the shy, submissive, skinny and awkward girl whom I'd met at the record store. She'd become confident after having conducted all those business meetings with both Japanese and for-eigners on my behalf. She had gained weight and the extra pounds on her thighs and ass made her absolutely fine. She'd also changed her fashion, exchanging her frilly dresses for tight dark blue jeans that hugged her new curves ridiculously. She had become thick in all the right places, and was now wearing contact lenses instead of the glasses she'd had on when I first met her. She'd also changed her make up. Before, she looked positively plain, but now, she was rocking frosted lipsticks and dark eyeshadows. Her posture also seemed to have changed, she now walked with her head upright and looked straight ahead, as if she were on a mission. Whenever we went anywhere she sashayed her new figure with style and grace and heads turned as if she were a celebrity. It turned me on to see how she'd re-made herself. It was as if I'd gone to bed one night with Thelma from Scooby Doo and woke up with a Japanese Janet Jackson in her prime. And everyone noticed. One time this drummer cat named MB tried to step to H when I wasn't around and I had to check him, telling him *yo my dude, whether or not you see me with H, she's still my girl, keep your dis-tance.* It seemed to me like I was seeing her for the first time even though we'd been together for 6 years. She had transformed herself, but still, I had my little menagerie of women, my alphabet soup, all vy-ing to be number one.

M34 *Spins* The Night...This One Time

M34, my Beyoncé R&B lounge singer came over at 3:30 A.M. wanting to fuck or whatever. I was pissed because I told her I didn't like her coming over so late and leaving immediately afterwards. Annoyed, even though it was MUCH better that she left right afterwards because if she DIDN'T, there was always the chance that my main girl, H34 would show up. I knew if H34 arrived early to find M34's big-haired naked ass sleeping in my bed it would have been dangerous for all of us. Either way, telling M34 that I wanted her to stay the night, even though I knew she *couldn't* because she had to be home by 7 A.M. to send her daughter off to school, made her think I had more feelings for her than I did. This misunderstanding inevitably caused more problems than it was worth.

For the last few months that I've been seeing M34, our meeting would end with her crying and telling me that I'm not treating her like a lady. Because, according to her, lots of guys wanted her to be their girlfriend. I know it was true because she's all over my Facebook and my friends are always asking me, "Yo Trev, who is that honey on your FACEBOOK page wearing your magazine's t shirt man? She is fine!"- or whatever. But it wasn't nearly as good as they thought it was, and she wasn't nearly as "fine" as they thought she was. But you can't quite say that to your friends about some pussy you're getting, that *they* think is hot, but you know isn't really, unless you want to downgrade your own status.

Anyway, at this point, I didn't give a righteous shit who wanted what from her. To be honest, it was becoming difficult for me to get my dick hard enough to even sleep with her anymore. This contributed to the fact that she was coming over so late. Then H34 would come over and want the same thing a couple hours later, and I'd be exhausted. Or, I'd have to keep myself awake UNTIL 3:30 A.M. . . . . it was all exhausting. Plus M34's recent crying and bitching was making it not worth it anymore.

For the last five or six months of 2012, from July into December, nine women had been making their rotation into my house and my bed. Ironic. 9 is the exact number of girlfriends the Dash cat who I met at Mos Burger had told me he had, and at the time, not only did it sound preposterous, but it also sounded sleazy and just plain fucked up. But now, either it wasn't sleazy and fucked up anymore, or, more likely, I had become sleazy and fucked up.

Just a few years ago Dash told me he had nine girlfriends and I not only thought he was lying, but I also wondered if he did have nine girlfriends, just exactly wtf he needed all nine of them for? I constantly asked myself quietly, *nigga how can you fuck nine chicks and keep them all satisfied?* It was killing me. It was *all* killing me.

Seasonal Man

It was the holiday season in Japan, and Japanese women are "supposed" to be with a man during the holidays. That's just how it is. And for all of the women I had, I was their holiday man.

M34, N32, A26, H34, S36, Ms. S-40's, C33, Y 22 and Y44. Initials and ages. H34 was the mainstay. N32 had been around for a while. A26 was sometime-y. Y44 had just come on board. M34 had been going on for a few months. S36 and I had been at it a few months as well, maybe six months. Ms. S was sort of unbelievably sexy in a mean dominatrix sort of way. And she paid me. Y 22 never let me put it all the way in but always wanted it anyway. Annoying. H34 was the long-term relationship. We'd been together almost 7 years at this point. I was tired. I don't know why I dragged myself through this "fucking" cycle. It was wearing me out. It's usefulness was getting shorter each go around. The whole thing—meeting some woman, playing the same ditzy game of "what kind of food/music/sports/movies do you like", dealing with their bizarre personalities, trying to get them in bed, succeeding, then wishing they'd leave me alone—all of it became positively annoying. It felt like it was making me old, hell, maybe I was getting too old for it, not sure. Was a time I could stretch out a group of women for months, years, hold onto all of them through all kinds of weather, *her and her*, this one, that one, and the next one too, but not anymore.

M34 was the singer. She was gorgeous. Tall, tan, glamorous, high maintenance. Big white teeth and long legs, she looked like a Japanese Beyoncé, without the hips, tits, and ass. Sang like her too. She had a daughter ten years old. M34 had big, soft bubble lips, beautiful, straight bright white teeth—she shined, but she was flawed. It wasn't the kid, M34 had a deep streak of sadness in her. Japanese have this word that sort of encapsulates their life-view, *shouganaie,* which means basically "Oh well, nothing we can do about it, just accept your fate quietly." It's a defeatist way of looking at life if you ask me, but it's very Japanese.

M34's sad streak showed itself whenever we talked about dreams and music and travel and such. Tears welled up in her big brown eyes anytime I mentioned dreams and goals. She knew she was stuck singing R&B cover songs at 3 A.M. in dive bars and tiny "live houses", surrounded by fat, drunk, middle-aged Japanese dudes. She saw my picture on Facebook and holla'd at me while I was in LA for the summer. After a few months back and forth on Facebook, we met one night when she was on break at her singing gig. She was wearing a long traditional Japanese gown with her hair done up. We sat on some steps in front of an office building down near Fushimi station and talked a little. Instant attraction. The damaged middle-aged black dude from Brooklyn, and the beautiful but flawed single Japanese mother. Both of us nursing dreams that had long since come of age, and left.

Drop-dead gorgeous, but she's always telling me "Japanese men *watashi suki ja naie*," Japanese men don't like me. She was too tall for them, too dark, she said. She laughed loud and easy and had perfect caramel skin, but Japanese men don't like women who laugh out loud and they prefer white skin, the whiter the better. First time we ever fooled around was in the front seat of her tiny car on a rainy day in a video store parking lot. She was driving me home from school, we had stopped to get some Mos Burger, she was eating some fries, looked really cute, and I leaned over to kiss her. Next thing I knew I was lapping at her flat, but somehow perky tits while the rain pelted the windshield.

Our rendezvous were glorious, yet infamous. But now, she was complaining that I hadn't broken up with my girlfriend yet. She had no idea how many girlfriends there were.

"I never said I'd break up with my girlfriend for you," I'm telling her.

Why do women always want you to break up with your girlfriend for them? So they can become the girlfriend you are cheating on with other girls like them? Come on, *stay in your lane.*

She was crying that stuffed-up halting cry that kids offer when they can't get a full sentence out, speaking in an unintelligible staccato Japanese. It was actually kind of hilarious to watch her, but I couldn't laugh in her face. That'd be rude. But she looked and sounded ridiculous.

Truth was, right now I was trying to eighty-six M34. Perhaps it was the lateness of the hour or the over-expectation of sleeping with her. I liked her, but she was starting to get on my nerves with her demands that I break up with my girl. One day she showed up at my apartment in the middle of the afternoon with a long overcoat on and shiny lingerie underneath. It was underwhelming. She'd brought some groceries, which all the women do every time they come over, thinking they're doing something good, but it wasn't good, because every time they brought groceries, whatever we didn't eat right then I had to throw away. Couldn't let H34 come over and see groceries that she hadn't bought, big mistake. Imagine that. You've got several women all bringing you bags of groceries that you can't keep because you can't let the other ones know that someone else is bringing you groceries. Insane. Japanese say "mottaie naie", don't waste anything, but I was wasting *so much*, and it wasn't just food.

Unforgettable N32

N32 was the erotic nude model. Also had a daughter, eight years old. Guess we connect, me and the Japanese single moms running around looking for . . . something. N32 was extremely sexy, but even more flawed than M34. N32 had a potpourri of mental issues. Some of her issues may have been real, but others, like her temporary, spontaneous, intermittently recurring "memory loss" may have been a loose fabrication, to say the least. Add the fact that "sometimes" she couldn't hear out of one of her ears, and the fact that "sometimes" she seemed to lose consciousness spontaneously, well, man, I just couldn't buy that shit. It's like a dude being able to say, "Well, you know, sometimes I just forget shit, sometimes I don't, it comes and goes, and sometimes I suddenly black out and can't hear what you're saying, you just gotta deal with it." Fuck outta here. *You remember this dick right?* N32 played the role of the damaged woman to the hilt. Then there were the "voices" she heard in her head. Good thing the voices were inside her head, because she couldn't hear shit with her right ear, so had the "voices" been coming from outside her head, she may not have been able to hear them. Whenever I saw her I had to position myself so that I was on her left side. Pain in the ass.

Every few months N32 traveled to Europe to take naked pictures with a host of photographers—French, Swiss, German, Italian, Dutch, all of whom I had to assume were banging her. Thing was, her travels had made her culturally and artistically aware, which I really dug. I guess we identified because we both were into film, photography, art, and we were both misfits. She was on the fringe of Japanese society because she appeared nude and tied up in erotic photography, and didn't give a fuck who knew. She was smart and self-educated. Making a name for herself in the circles of people who dug that kind of stuff. When she was in Japan, she did kimono modeling, served tea, and held "classes" of some sort. . . I don't really know how she made her dough. She was mercurial and trippy. Had a big toothy smile though, and fucked like a banshee. Came three, four, five times every time, and announced it too. Gushed. Screamed. Sucked on my neck like a friggin' vampire, shook and shuddered. The whole nine. N32 was sexy and dangerous, but she used her various bag of mental afflictions as both a defense and an offense. Brilliant. What better way to give yourself the advantage in any relationship, than to invent a host of psychological problems that immediately places you in the role of the victim, one of which is that sometimes you can't remember what you did, said, where you went, promises you made, vows you exchanged? Fuck outta here.

Before I had the pleasure to encounter N32, a couple friends of mine were fighting, literally, for her attention. J and G, two brothers, one from New York, the other from Africa. Apparently G was hitting it but not doing it right, I suppose, and brought her to a bar one night where J was holding court. J was a brash and aggressive native New Yorker and martial artist who claimed to have been a cop in the city. Who knows the truth? That night in the bar, J steps right up to N32 while she was with G, grabs her arm, and puts her into some sort of arm lock. N32 was impressed, and away she went with J, leaving G standing there wondering wtf had happened. Next thing J is banging N32 silly, and he introduces her to erotic photography, being tied up with the ropes shit, and takes her to "happening bars." Happening bars are sex clubs where people fuck each other out in the open. N32 seemed to dig that shit, or not. Who knows?

The day I met her I wasn't impressed that much. The nutcase friend of mine JP dragged me over to where she was to introduce me to her, apparently he was also smitten with her. She had her daughter with her and we shook hands. I barely looked at her—at the time I didn't need another woman in my life. Shortly, after meeting N32, I decided she would make a good story in RAN. I can see it; a single Japanese mother moonlighting as an international erotic nude model. You don't meet those every day. I knew the images would work in the magazine. Glossy pictorial about her and her exoticness.

We met at my house for an interview, and I swear at the time I had absolutely no inclination whatsoever to sleep with her or anything of the sort. But, when you're sitting at your kitchen table at 11 P.M. eating soup and drinking green tea, and across from you there's a super-hot woman talking about how sexually liberated she is and how she likes to be dominated, well, things and plans go awry. We talked for a few hours and I found myself completely beguiled by her. She was coy, and demure, and polite, and smart. No signs whatsoever of her hearing affliction, or forgetfulness, or any of the battiness she eventually revealed to me.

After the interview I got up and walked over to her and asked her to open her mouth and she did and that was that. Normally I'm turned off by women who have slept with anyone I know, but N32 had this undeniable sexuality about her and I couldn't help myself. Plus, I had become a sort of sex addict by that time, preying on just about any Japanese woman who came anywhere near me. That first night and truly all of our nights together were amazing. She was insatiable, giving, tender, vulnerable and extremely affectionate—these are adjectives most Japanese women are not, mostly. Mostly they're just there, letting you do whatever you want, but N32 was a very active participant. Too bad she was stark raving mad most of the time.

How can you trust someone who claims to lose their memory at any given time? You can't. You just can't. I kept N32 at as much distance from me as she kept the rest of the world from her. Shit, if she weren't so goddamn hot it'd have been so much easier. It always is, if they're not hot. But N32 was hot. Felt for her though, sorta envied her ability to expose herself, literally and figuratively, then hide behind her various "mental issues." Can't fault crazy people for what they do right? It was like N32 was pleading insanity for her whole life. That way, nothing stuck. She had covered herself with emotional Teflon. Smart girl. A Japanese Teflon nude erotic model. Nice. And she just left my house, *again*, to go back home to be with her daughter.

She was lucky to have parents who would take care of her daughter whenever she took off for Europe to take pictures. It was her freedom. Her shot at freedom anyway, that's how she saw it. She was getting older though, those tits would start sagging soon—and then what? The memory loss wouldn't be quite so cute when gravity started tugging at those tits. Whatever, though, that might never happen, right?

Afternoon Delight with Ms. S

Ms. S was another Mom. Short, brassy, cocky, if a woman can be described as such, and also sexy. She pushed a pearl-white, four-door Mercedes and lived in an exclusive part of town. Her countenance was like that of a gymnast who knows she's stacked, and she was shaped similar to one too, as much as a middle-aged Japanese woman could be. Short cropped haircut, dainty but tough, Ms. S looked like a hot, Japanese version of a young Marlo Thomas, but with shorter hair. Alluring but snappy, her attitude wasn't what you'd consider "pleasant," one might even call her cocky, but like all Japanese, she was polite. She carried herself with a slight chip on her shoulder, which could be seen as her being bitchy. Never dull, she coincidentally always wore something with glitter on it, every time we met. She never told me how old she was and never told me her first name, she just told me to call her "Ms. S", so I did. That was fine with me. She said she had inherited a business after divorcing her husband. Her business was to provide all the snacks and refreshments for the dozens and dozens of pachinko parlors in Nagoya. Pachinko is an obsession of many Japanese. The game itself is similar to pinball, except unlike American game rooms, where there might be one single pinball machine, pachinko parlors have literally hundreds, if not thousands, of pachinko machines lined up in neat rows in spaces as big as a supermarket. On any given night you'll find young, old, cool, *otaku* (nerd), male, female, all spectrums of people, seated at one of the rows upon rows of pachinko games. Pachinko's allure is lost on me, but not on the millions of Japanese who stake their pachinko claim every night of the week.

I first met Ms. S after posting my picture on a Japanese website for English teachers. *Don't it always seem to go...*This happened to me on several occasions in Japan. The English teacher/English student amorous relationship isn't as frowned upon in Japan as it is in Western countries. In fact, in many cases it would have taken much more effort to *avoid* some kind of sexual relationship with some of my students than it would have taken to attract it. I like to think this.

Ms. S was one such case. I had an ad placed with an online teachers' dispatch service that matched students with teachers. My picture, some teaching credentials, a little personal contact information and that was it. You can make as much money teaching privates in Japan as you can at a full-time day job. Most of my day gigs got me around twenty bucks an hour, whereas if you could find the right "private", you could earn up to ten thousand yen an hour teaching a group of elderly, a group of women, businessmen, et cetera. A hundred bucks an hour, a couple times a week to teach the ABCs in a swanky, modern Japanese house out in the Japanese countryside is a really good idea.

My Privates

Privates, man, this is the way you want to go in Japan if you're teaching English as an occupation, and even if you're not. Students varied. Nine-year-old half-Chinese, half-Japanese little girl prodigy, whose father was an avid motorcyclist with a lisp. Forty-five-year-old, fat, Japanese father with thick glasses who barely uttered a word, but wanted to give you his forty bucks for spending an hour with him. Finally, the cute twenty-seven-year-old, Jazz singer, whose mouth, during one of our lessons—looked so alluring that I lost my senses temporarily and casually slipped my fingers into it while she was repeating the vowels to me. When she got to the letter "O", her mouth seemed to hang open a moment too long, and her lips were glistening. I could see her tonsils, and somehow, some way my index finger found it's way into her mouth and onto her tongue. What's stranger than me doing this, was her reaction, which is to say, there was no reaction, which is to say, Japanese women just don't quite know how to say NO. In fact, Japanese think the whole "no" thing is an American cultural phenomenon. Imagine this scene anywhere in the Western world. A teacher reaches into his student's mouth mid-sentence and squirms his fingers around in said student's mouth and casually retracts his fingers and the lesson continues as if it didn't actually happen. It would be what movies are made of, or the nightly news, story at eleven.

I admit to being guilty of gross inappropriateness and total unprofessionalism. I relate this incident strictly from a looking back perspective. I would not repeat this, nor do I recommend it, all that I'm saying is this is what happened on that day in that place.

My lessons with the Jazz singer continued after that, which one might think is evidence of tacit approval of what I did, but again, Japanese do not like to offend and do not like to confront. Maybe she liked it, who knows. Either way we met for about a month after that, at the end of which time she went to China to sing. Chances are if you're reading this, you've got some interest in Japan either culturally, academically, carnally, historically, or financially. The Jazz singer student was shaped like a human saxophone, or, maybe her voice reminded me of a saxophone. Saxophones are supposed to be the sexiest musical instrument ever designed. I don't know why I'm comparing her to a saxophone actually, but there was something definitely saxophone-esque about her.

Privates is the smart foreigner's way to make extra ends. Get some. Get a couple.

Ms. S Was One Such Private

One day I'm checking my status on the teacher website and I see a notice reading "a student is interested in you!" which can mean any number of things. She might be interested in you as a teacher, she might be interested in you as a husband, she might need a boyfriend to hang out with, or she might want to have sex with you as payback for something, someone else has done to her. What else? Guess.

I reply to the notice and within a few hours Ms. S and I had set up a day, time, and place to have our first lesson. First lessons, "Trial Lessons" as they're called, are usually at no cost to the student. It's a chance to meet each other, a chance for the prospective student to feel you out, and for you to do the same. Some students have preferences of age, nationality, race, temperament, accent, or teaching style. I'm not saying by any standard that most potential private students are looking for anything other than a good English lesson, but some definitely are. There are a good number of total absolute asshole foreigners running around Japan taking advantage of students, and ruining the nobility of the profession for everyone. I hope I wasn't one of these guys, but I guess I was. Even though I did end up sleeping with a few of my students, still, I saw private lessons as a chance to get some extra dough. Mostly anyway. But from jump, Ms. S had other plans for us, and I got the dough anyway.

We met at the Aeon mall, near Chikusa, which was a short bike ride from my place in Fukiage. I had no special thoughts on the way to meeting Ms. S. I figured she was another middle-aged woman who needed a hobby, or a boyfriend, or both. Again, me, I needed the dough. I wasn't on the hunt for any extracurricular activities, but I also wasn't averse to any either. I was getting my share and wasn't in any special need at the time, but lord knows, it's hard to turn down pussy. I hate the power of the pussy.

I arrived and took the escalator to the upper level where she was sitting with her back to me in the food court. There were several women there at the time, but I knew when she saw me she'd know it was me, not too many six-foot-tall black dudes with dreadlocks walking around the Aeon mall in Chikusa. When I noticed her, she noticed me, and gestured for me to join her. She was seated at a table wearing a velvet-looking pleated black skirt and black turtleneck laced with diamonds, fat white pearls in her ears too. Black high heels with sparkling anklets, and the requisite Louis Vuitton bag, nails done and hair cut just right, she looked rich, rich as in wealthy.

I sit down across from her and for about thirty minutes, the allotted trial lesson time, we did the usual small talk: She asked me where I was from?-New York City, asked me how long I'd been in Japan?-A few years, asked me what kind of music/movies I like?-All-romance, asked me how tall I was?-six one—"*hyaku hachi ni ju senchi,*" 182 centimeters—and asked me what my favorite Japanese food was?-*niku jaga,* beef and potatoes. I'm a simple man. I asked her the same, and proceeded to tell her how I carried my lessons.

"*I usually start with small talk, then if there are any questions about anything you'd like to ask you can ask me, like something you might have heard or read during the week, or seen on TV or in a movie. Then we go into a specific lesson of grammar, like modals or future perfect tense, which we'll do for maybe twenty minutes, so I ask my students to please prepare a notebook or something to write with. We'll work on that until you understand, then maybe we'll discuss current events. I might bring a newspaper and ask you to read it and we'll talk about it, or we can use a textbook also if you like, I have several really great textbooks. Or we can just sit and talk for an hour about anything you'd like.*"

This last type of lesson is called "free conversation," and naturally since it was theoretically the easiest, it was my favorite. But sometimes it was a bitch too, because Japanese don't like talking and don't really have what any Westerner might consider to be "good" or even "normal" conversation skills; however, it requires the least amount of preparation, so it's easy. I also asked students to keep a weekly journal, since this allowed them to use reading and writing skills also, I said. I wasn't sure if she was paying attention to me or what I was saying. She was just sitting there, still as a statue, chirping out one or two words at a time in choppy English. Her pronunciation of what she could say was very good though, almost too good, like she'd learned exactly those statements and how to pronounce them perfectly. Mostly though, for the entire trial lesson time, she just sat staring at me until our time was up, at which point I looked at my watch,

"So, what do you think? Would you like to continue to take my lesson? We can meet here again in a week at this same time if it's convenient for you. You can think about it if you'd like and contact me by text or email." I say.

As I'm about to get up and leave, she smiles and blurts out,

"What kind of porno do you like?"

"Uh, sumimasen? Gomen. Can you repeat please?" I say.

Did this ho just ask me what kind of porno I like? She says it again, but with more conviction this time, and in perfect English,

"What kind of porno do you like?"

What kind of porno do I like? I'm thinking.

"Yes. What kind of porno do you like?" she repeats.

Okay. She's said it three times now, so she's definitely saying what I think she's saying. I was startled, but didn't show it. I wasn't sure how I should react, should I feign shock? Wait, what's this "feign" shit? I *was* shocked. Or, should I be casual and just answer the freaking question? I figured if I let her know I was shocked, she might think I was green and might not want my lessons. Then I thought, if I answer like it's an everyday question, she might think I'm *ecchi* (horny, desperate), and it might be a test, so since I want this woman's cash, forty bucks an hour for talking, I couldn't do that either. I casually sidestepped the question by replying,

"Um, I don't watch much porn . . ." (which, at the time, was true) "...and um, I, ah, don't really have a preference . . ." I say.

I actually prefer mature amateur BBW porn, but that's neither here nor there. I also like foot porn, but who doesn't nowadays.

Now, that I had somewhat answered, Ms. S was wide awake and engaged. She straightened up her back and sat upright in her seat smiling coyly and leaned in closer. My answer didn't satisfy her.

"You don't have to be shy, it's just a question, what kind of porn do you like? I know you watch porn." She insists.

"Actually, I don't watch much porn, because I don't have time since I'm working so much." I insist.

I figured this was the best answer since it was true, depending on your definition of the word "working." The truth was, I wasn't watching porn because I was getting so much real sex that I was overdosed on real sex, and I didn't need to be watching it on my computer too.

"I don't like American porn, it's too hard, no imagination, not soft, Japanese porn is soft . . ." she says.

So are Japanese women, I think to myself.

"Really? So...you don't like American porn. Um...okay." I reply.

I don't know what to say. I'm at a loss. I didn't know how to proceed, and honestly, I still wasn't thinking about doing anything sexual with Ms. S. I didn't quite know where she was going with all this and I was just confused and bemused at the same time. Here's this petite Japanese businesswoman decked out in diamonds and pearls asking me what kind of pornography I like forty minutes after we've met. She wasn't smiling much, just curious. We sat there and talked about porn for about half an hour more, her asking me

"What do you do when you watch porn?"—*Uh . . . I . . . watch?*—her alluding to wanting to know about my masturbation habits,

"Do you watch alone or with someone?"—*Um, alone, I guess?*—her alluding to wanting us to watch porno together, I guess?!

"Why do you watch alone? You don't think it's sexy to watch with someone?"—*uh . . . I never tried?*"

"Really? You should try! It's fun. Please tell me what are your favorite types of porn?"—*Uh, I told you, I don't have a favorite type really, I don't know about it so much . . . uh . . .*

Finally, after she discovers I'm not going to give up any information on my own porno habits, she gives up, tells me she'll text me when we'll meet again, gets up abruptly, turns and leaves.

We met about three more times in that same mall, on that same floor, at that same time. We had our one-hour lesson, and then each time immediately after, she'd ask me questions about my sexual habits, if I had a girlfriend, what we did together, how many girlfriends I had, et cetera. She always showed up dressed to the nines with something glittery on her body. She told me she had had a black boyfriend whom she had met in Hawaii when she was on vacation. She said she had also been married to a Japanese businessman, but got divorced— "It just didn't work" is what she said. In the divorce, her husband had given her part of his ownership of the business that serviced the pachinko parlors. I asked her what she did with her days, since her daughter was in elementary school.

"I drive around to the pachinko parlors and let the owners see me," she said matter-of-factly.

Everything she said was matter-of-fact, as though there were no other way it could be. She was confident and curt, even with her questions about my sexual history and preferences. We'd have the one-hour lesson, she'd take notes, the lesson would end, she'd then ask me questions about my dating life and try to get me to talk about porn or sex, then she'd produce a little envelope with my four thousand yen in it, slide it to me on the table, get up, and disappear.

For that first month we met, it became obvious to me that she wanted something more than just an hour-long English lesson. In fact, that first trial lesson told me exactly what she wanted. She was asking questions about my sexual likes and dislikes, she told me her previous boyfriend was black, and she always showed up looking really, really good, as if what we were doing was dating rather than learning English. Naturally, it had occurred to me to try to make a move, but at this point, I didn't want to screw up the forty bucks an hour I was getting from her. But one day after the lesson, I asked her

"Would you rather have these lessons at my house?"

"Sure," she said.

And immediately, we walked outside to her shimmering white Mercedes, drove to my place. Once inside, she looked around, saw my beat-up old computer,

"Is this what you watch porn on?" she ask.

"Sometimes. But I told you, I don't watch much porn." I answered.

She looked at me yearningly. I walked over to her, bent down to her height, and started kissing her. She reacted like she hadn't been kissed in a long time. She lunged at my tongue and started undoing my pants like a madwoman, dropped to her knees and went to town. I wasn't totally "ready," pulled away a little, and on her knees she shuffled forward to keep me in her mouth, gasping, gobbling, neck forward like a turkey searching for food. Middle of the afternoon, broad daylight, and this wealthy Japanese woman is sucking me off like a drowning man—woman—gasping for air.

We met at my place instead of the mall for our weekly lesson in the middle of the afternoon every week for the next two or three months. She'd arrive dressed up like she was either going to or had just come from a dinner date every time. Her and I would sit at my table and have our hour-long lesson, she'd slide me the envelope, then we'd head into my *tatami* mat bedroom and bone for an hour or so. Afterwards, I'd go into the bathroom to wash up, and return to find her fully dressed. We'd say our goodbyes, and she'd disappear until the next week. No phone calls, no messages, and no contact whatsoever until our next lesson. Every time, the same routine. Until one day,

"Are you going to break up with your girlfriend?" she ask.

Uh oh. I said no, to which she replied,

"Okay, no more sex. We are just teacher and student from now on, okay? No more touching, kissing, nothing. Teacher and student. That's all."

I was cool with it. The honest truth was the forty bucks was more important to me, at this point, than the sex. I say "at this point" because this was happening several years into my time in Japan. Had this happened early on, I would have immediately jumped at the opportunity, but now, I knew there'd be eventual problems. I knew she'd one day want more than just the no-strings-attached sexual relationship we were having, and that day had come. She came over a few more times, but I didn't make any moves towards her and could tell she wasn't happy with our new plain old teacher-student relationship. Finally, after a few non-sex visits,

"Don't you miss what we were doing? You know, if you touch me, I won't refuse you . . ." she says. So I did.

I ran my hand along her back and she heaved a loud, breathy sigh as if to say *this is what I've been waiting for,* and again, dropped to her knees, undid my pants, and took me in her mouth.

Once our deed was completed, I went to the bathroom to wash up or whatever, and upon my return, there she was again, fully dressed as if nothing had happened. I walked her to the door, she put on her shoes and left.

After a few more sessions like this, one day she texted me saying she couldn't do it anymore. That she was angry that I had taken advantage of our relationship and that she wouldn't be taking my lesson again after that. This, even though it was her who had prompted our discussions about porn from our very first lesson. I texted back, "Okay, I understand. I'm sorry about everything. Please forgive me and good luck with your English studying." And that was it. Didn't hear from her again until one day I was shopping in the Osu Kannon mall, just about a week before I left Japan. She was surprised to see me and I was sure she had found another "teacher". We walked around a little, did some shopping, I told her I was leaving Japan, we said our goodbyes, and that was that. Truthfully, I was a little upset that our thing had to end so soon. Whipping around in her Mercedes was fun, and the weekly sex sessions, plus the forty-dollar fee, it all fit neatly into the lifestyle I had at the time.

No Laughing Matter

A26. Young Japanese debutante. Working at the airport. Sparkly, well dressed, every time we made out she laughed all the way through. She told me she laughed whenever she was nervous. She came around about once or twice a season. Sent me a random phone mail asking me what I was doing Thursday night at 11 P.M. That's code for, "I want to come over, drink some tea and then maybe have an orgasm." S'cool. Spoke decent English and said she had spent a year abroad in New Zealand. New Zealand is popular with Japanese women. She was very pretty with lots of makeup on, as many Japanese women are, but she had blotchy skin. Thing with A26, was that she had big tits and there aren't that many Japanese with big tits. Her pussy got as wet as a sponge, and her randomness was somehow attractive. She was no problem because she came, and then she went. Didn't ask many questions, but when she spoke, it was a bizarre combination of that fucked-up New Zealand accent, mashed up with *Engrish*, which is the Japanese version of English. Sounded exotic but also sounded like she had marbles in her mouth or something. I liked A26. Wished she'd do something about her skin, but she was cool. Once she showed me pictures of her parents and I'll be damned if her Mom wasn't just as fine as she was.

A26 and I both knew what time it was and she wasn't asking for anything that I couldn't give.

One time she came over, stayed a few hours, we did our thing, and then she left. A few minutes later, she returned because someone had broken into her car and stolen her car radio. Strange. Very random. Car break ins and burglaries in general aren't at all common in Japan, in fact, my entire time there this was the only time I'd ever heard of it. To this day I swear it was H34 who did it. But I couldn't go asking H34 if she had broken into A26's car, because then H34 would know I had someone at my place, and plus how do you ask your girlfriend if she's broken into another one of your girlfriend's car? I let it go. A26 didn't come around much after that. She drifted out of my rotation and I didn't mind. Sometimes I miss her laughter.

Drummer Chick Who Worries Too Much

Y44 was another single mother. Her daughter was nineteen or twenty. Y44 worked as an office lady, but was learning to be a drummer. She wanted to be in a rock and roll band. Gotta give props to anyone learning to do anything, but a forty-four-year-old Japanese single mother learning to be a drummer? Pretty cool. I met Y44 at a show I was doing when I had just returned from a short visit to NYC. Y44 was in the audience seated at a table with a friend and had her eyes glued to me the entire time I was performing. She gave me that glassy-eyed, *I-want-you-right-here-and-now-but-I'm-kinda-too-old-to-even-be-in-this-club-aren't-I* look. Another Facebook fan. Did the mailing thing for a few months until we finally met in person. She immediately told me that she loved me and that I was "the hottest guy in Nagoya."

Very first time we met she came to the crib with a bottle of red wine. We chatted for a little while, and then she said the magic words: "Can I take a shower?" Beautiful words, those. She took a shower and then we smashed. It was average and her skin was kind of loose on her body. She rambled on and spilled the wine. Literally. It was as if she was a nervous pussy cat, in a room full of rocking chairs.

She started creeping me out very early on by telling me she loved over and over, like an obsessed fan. If that wasn't enough, she also told me she was "worried" about me, which made me think she knew something about my life that maybe I didn't know, which was also creepy. I told her I didn't need her worrying about me, since according to the Your Wish Is Your Command CDs, worry most likely attracts whatever you're worried about right into your life. And since those CDs had become my bible, I couldn't go astray from the message for fear that it might mess with my plans to leave Japan. The last thing anyone needs is someone else worried about them when there ain't a damn thing to be worried about. Keep your worries to yourself. No, in fact, better yet, *stop worrying about shit when there ain't shit to worry about.*

The "worry" shit, plus the "I love you" confessions spooked me right off the bat, so I told Y44 we ought to just be friends, which she accepted. She said she'd return to fantasizing about me, which was fine with me.

Y44 was a fine lady but she seemed emotionally unstable, like she was always on the verge of tears, or always on the verge of an orgasm, or both. She was just . . . odd. I couldn't put my finger on it, and didn't want to.

Hell Raises In Starbucks

One early evening, Y44 text me to meet her at Starbucks. We meet. It was going well, she didn't seem angry, which I was happy about. *Cool, we can end this little thing like it never even started, perfect.* Like I said, I was getting tired of all this clandestine running around trying to fuck every woman I met. The curtain seemed to be coming down on that stage of my life, and she was one of the last acts. So we're at Starbucks talking. She's wearing some faux lacy cardigan that middle-aged Japanese women wear just before they move into becoming old ladies. And a big ugly tan coat that looked like it was made of wool. She looks ten years older than forty-four. *I'm glad we're finishing this,* I'm thinking. But she has nice gentle eyes. She's accepted the fact that we have to discontinue our relationship and I'm thinking *whew Trev, dodged a bullet.* Suddenly she looks around and leans in closer to me and says,

"I want to go to your house and make love right now," in a really sickeningly sweet cutesy way that I was sure was a figment of my imagination.

So I pretend to not have heard,

"What did you say?" I ask.

"Your house, take me to your house," she asks.

"No," I blurt out.

Just no. That's it. Nothing special, nothing less or more, just plain old no.

"Why not?" she asks.

She sits startled without lifting her head up from that faux sexy angle.

"What did you say?" I respond.

I search for my answer before her question comes out again.

"Why can't we go to your house?" she pleads.

Now I'm pissed because I've just explained that we should just be friends and she has just accepted this. I thought we had an understanding of where we were (weren't) going from here and so I said really fast, loud, and matter of fact,

"BECAUSE I HAVE A GIRLFRIEND AND MY GIRLFRIEND LIVES AT MY HOUSE AND I CAN'T TAKE YOU THERE. SO NOW YOU KNOW I HAVE A GIRLFRIEND-AND PLUS, BECAUSE I TOLD YOU WE ARE FINISHING OUR RELATIONSHIP."

She gets this horrified look on her face like she had just shit herself or I just shit myself or someone shit ON her, and she says,

"WHAT? EXCUSE ME? WHAT DID YOU TELL ME NOW?" as loudly as I had.

I repeated myself again in a lower tone, since everyone was now staring at us,

"I said I have a girlfriend, and that's why we aren't going to my house," I repeat.

Fuck it. I was feeling self-righteous in a good way, like I was right for a change. I felt like,

Listen honey, we fucked once or twice, four or five weeks ago, it wasn't all that, and no I am not taking you to my house. And where have you been the last half hour while I was telling you that our little relationship or whatever it is or was is over?! What don't you understand?

She stands up over me, in a huff. She's wagging her finger at me like I'm in grade school telling me I'm treating her like a prostitute. I'm looking up at her and everyone in Starbucks is looking at us. I then calmly ask her how it is that I'm treating her like a prostitute. She tells me that I'm treating her like I can have sex with her at my discretion.

I then move in where I'm sure she can hear me, then softly, but firmly say to her,

"...listen, I didn't invite you to Starbucks, you invited me and I didn't ask you if we could go to your house, you asked me if we can go to mine. And since it is my house and I am the boss of my house and myself, I have decided no we cannot go to my house today or ever again. Okay? Now, please stop talking so loud and sit down."

She instantly flies into a rage, jumps up and storms out of Starbucks. A few days later, a friend of mine tells me his wife's friend overheard a conversation of a woman who had broken up with her black American boyfriend in Starbucks. I never knew the lady and I were "boyfriend and girlfriend". That's why you have to be careful, because you never know what label or term other people around you are giving you at any time. I'm glad I didn't continue that "relationship" because in retrospect she acted like a serial killer. Although I've no idea what serial killers act like, if I had to paint a picture of a middle-aged Japanese female serial killer, I'd paint a picture of *her* wearing that long, heavy, tan wool coat and that frilly blouse. And I'd give the serial killer fake blue eyes, exactly like she had.

My Sad Beyoncé Singer

M34 came by a few weeks later. We were planning to do a song together during a show I was planning at Plastic Factory. The plan was, she'd come over after her singing gig one morning, and I'd give her my disc for her to learn the songs.

She arrived at 3:15, took off her clothes and slid into my bed. Almost immediately, she informed me that she was on her period, which was fine with me and I told her so. I got up, gave her the CD and got back in bed. She seemed pissed about something. She put on her clothes and left.

Forward a week later, she's at my house again, but this time at 10pm. She's telling me we can't do anything sexual anymore, which was also fine with me. An hour later she tells me she's sleepy and next thing I know she's peeling off her clothes and slipping underneath my covers. I slid underneath the covers with her.

As soon as I laid down, she threw her leg across my waist. I laid still for five seconds and then reached my hand slowly between her legs. I allowed my hand to hover over her panties for five more seconds and then as soon as I was about to touch her, she grabbed my hand with a lighting fast kung-fu grip. She says *"seri ga iru,"* she has her period, again. She had her period last time she was over a week ago, and now, a full seven days later, she still has it. I ask her how long does her period usually lasts. "Every woman is different". Sure. We spent the next 2 or 3 hours discussing the ins and outs of her erratic menstruation cycle.

We finally fall asleep but not before I asked her to drive with me to Yatomi Station in the morning to pick up something from my plug P. P and I had pre-arranged a small transaction that was supposed to net me about 350 bucks, which I needed for Christmas.

The next day, we wake up around 10 and she tells me she has to go into Sakae for something. We drive into Sakae and she parks in front of La Chic, goes inside and spends an hour doing I don't know what. Then we drive down to her live house and she parks on the curb and goes inside and spends another hour in there. Finally, she comes out and we set out for the hour and a half ride to Yatomi.

When we arrive, I call P and he comes down to Yatomi station and I make the pickup, and then I get back into her car for the ride back to Nagoya and M tells me she's hungry so we go to Mos Burger and eat. After that, she tells me she's got to go take care of some business with her daughter and her mother and asks me if I mind waiting at Mos Burger "a little while" and I say sure. I'm there 3 hours before she finally returns. She doesn't apologize for the wait and asks me if I'm ready to head back to Nagoya. *Of course.* We climb into her little car and start the drive back.

Since we'd spent the previous night talking into the wee hours about her period, I was tired, and she wasn't saying much anyway. So,

I decided to shut my eyes in the car while M drove us back into Nagoya. Big mistake.

When she sees that I'm trying to cop a few z's, M starts berating me for falling asleep, for making false plans, for not eating at the breakfast table with her, for not caring enough about her period (!)—for not being sensitive to her situation with her daughter, for treating her like she's just a "sex friend", and whatever else she could come up with. She's scolding me in Japanese and she's got the pedal to the metal in her tiny car, flooring the acceleration. We're tearing down these small Japanese roads with her tiny car careening to the edges of the road. All the while she's yelling at me in Japanese, crying, and she can't catch her breath. I look down at my phone and notice that H has text me several times throughout the day. I look back at M and big fat tears are bursting out of her eyes like little water balloons exploding from her tear ducts. I'm sitting beside her quietly with my hands in my lap like a child who is being yelled at by his mother. The sun is setting and it's getting dark and her little car is shaking and rattling in the wind. I'm in Japan with skinny, Japanese Beyoncé and she's whipping her car along dark narrow Japanese roads. She's blubbering through cascading tears, and *I don't know what the hell she is talking about.*

Finally, we arrive at my place and before I can exit the car, she looks at me, still crying. She'd been crying for the entire ride home, and asks me if she can be my girlfriend. I shake my head,

"I'll think about it" I say under duress.

Next day, she mails me bright and early that we "need to talk". We meet at a family restaurant to talk about what to do about our "relationship" and I don't want to do anything anymore. She tells me she can't perform with me at Plastic Factory and I say fine and we end our thing right then and there and I'm relieved.

Runaway Girl

N32, the erotic nude model, had told me she was a dancer so I asked her to be part of my show instead. Smart move.

I didn't know it at the time but this was to be my last performance in Japan. I wanted to present a three-dimensional, interactive theatrical performance featuring the dynamic between the sexes, which would also involve the audience in some way. During my final song, "Runaway," I wanted N32 to come out and appear as a sort of damsel in distress, which was what she was anyway.

I wanted her to be in the crowd during the entire performance, without me knowing where she was. I would then find her and sing "Runaway" directly to her. We'd feign some "connection" between us, then I'd take her hand and she'd join me on stage. While singing to her, she'd undress slowly, then she would perform some sort of nude "lonely" dance. As the song is ending, she'd run off stage, out of the club, literally *run away*, and I'd stand on stage and pretend to have lost the love of my life. Some Michael Jackson shit.

I figured with her ability to appear fearless in exposing herself for photographers combined with her lack of fear of being nude, plus the fact that we'd been fucking for a few months, it'd be erotic and the audience would be able to read our real connection. I thought she'd be perfect for a song about a lost soul. That, plus I'd been thinking about her since our last encounter. We hadn't done it for a while, and I kind of wanted to end the night in between her shaking legs, multiple orgasms and suction grip oral skills. It didn't quite work out that way.

I Didn't Say Goodbye

H34 wanted to come see me perform. She didn't know it would be my last performance in Japan, but then, neither did I. She always wanted to see me perform, but there was always a very high chance that either someone in the audience had been in my bed before, and in many cases, the *night* before, or someone in the audience *wanted* to be in my bed and may indeed have ended the night there. H34 hadn't been too happy when the piece on N32 came out in my magazine, semi-nude pictures accompanied by an article wherein I probed N's sexual history. H hadn't wanted the magazine to have anything sexual whatsoever in it, we'd fought about it numerous times. She said if I allowed nudity and sexual content in the magazine, it'd be harder to sell ad space. Of course, she was right, but I wanted to make a statement. What kind of statement I wasn't sure, but I didn't want to limit what I put on the pages of my own magazine.

That night, I couldn't let H34 see me talking openly to N32, since N32 had no inhibitions and had gotten drunk before the performance. During the performance of "Runaway", while N32 was dancing in the audience and I was staring squarely at her, I could see H34 staring at me with disapproval. When N32 finally made it to the stage and started to disrobe, I signaled to her not to take off her clothes, and instead embraced her. At the end of the song, N32 ran off the stage and instead of running out of the club, she runs into the bathroom. Immediately after the show was over I left the club without finding N32 to say goodbye, which was a massive mistake. On the drive home, N32 called me crying hysterically asking me why I didn't say goodbye. She was right.

I didn't say goodbye because I couldn't let H34 see me saying goodbye because I knew H34 was watching me like an owl and I thought if she saw me that close to N32 she'd figure out right away that we had much more going on than just a song. But I also couldn't quite tell N32 I didn't say goodbye because of H34, so I told N32 I was "looking for her" to say goodbye, but couldn't find her.

There I am in H's car with her sitting right next to me in the driver's seat, with N32 on the phone sobbing loudly and uncontrollably for five straight minutes. I tried as best as I could, in a clandestine manner to calm her down, but she wouldn't stop crying. Crazily, I asked H34 to take me back to the club so I could "say something to someone". I didn't know what else to come up with. I knew H34 knew something was going on, but H mostly played along with my stupidity, which is one reason we had lasted so long. She was always compliant in turning a blind eye to my obvious shenanigans. She obliged, turned around and drove back to the club. I asked her to wait in the car while I went inside to speak to N32. She did.

I enter the club, look around, don't see her, and head for the unisex bathroom. Inside, I hear muffled sounds of crying coming from one of the bathroom stalls. I open the door, and there to my surprise is N32, leaned up against the wall sobbing. She's sniffing while holding a wad of wet toilet tissue, blackened from her mascara.

I tried to console her by putting my hand on her shoulder and pulling her in close to me, but nothing was working. Finally, I ask "...what are you doing in the bathroom and why are you crying?" She wouldn't stop. It seemed like she couldn't hear me, and then I remembered maybe she couldn't hear me because maybe this was one of those moments when she had gone deaf in one of her ears. Or maybe, it was because we were in the bathroom at a loud club. There were people banging on the stall door, wanting to get inside to use the toilet. The door finally jars open and inside are the very two people who were just onstage a few minutes ago pretending to be crossed lovers. But in reality, they really *were* crossed lovers, and now we were in the toilet having a huge cryfest. The sight must have been mind-blowing for an already high clubber. All this while H waits outside with the car running.

N32 is hunched over the open toilet bowl while black tears stream down her porcelain-white face. She's sobbing and telling me not to touch her. I really just wanted to go home, eat H's chicken soup and go to bed. But there I was, asking her to calm down while my girlfriend waits outside with the car running, and now,

"What the fuck are you doing in here?" some girl asks (in Japanese) while standing over us.

Great. My presence is not making the situation any better. N32 is crying harder and the moment seems to last eternally.

Eventually, I somehow managed to calm her down. I tell her I that I have to go and that I'd call her the next day. She nods her head and I leave and go outside to find H34 still waiting in the car. We went home, I ate H's delicious chicken soup and went to bed.

The next day N32 texts me at the crack of dawn and tells me I should get a better job and pay more for my children. She asks me why I lied to her and questions me about my bad character. She compares me to some dude who stole her credit card from her. Finally, she tells me she's "leaving" me and that "we should have no further contact". Again I was relieved. *Runaway girl.*

Remind Me What I Missed

S36 was maybe the most "normal" of all of them, excluding H34. I met her at a barbecue party in the park one Sunday, nothing special, then a few months after that I met her again on the subway at 7 A.M., after working all night at Plus Park. I boarded the train at Sakae and there she was,

"Hey, I think I know you." I said.

"Hey, I think I know you too..." She replied in almost perfect English.

She was cool, smart and funny. She reminded me that I was funny too, which was huge for me. During my entire time in Japan, I had pretty much forgotten how to be funny. The fact that S36 laughed at my stupid jokes about talking octopuses and whenever I'd ask if my belly was getting fat made me remember a little better whom I had been before arriving in Japan.

S36 was really laid back and intellectually curious. She wanted to move to Canada because she said her mother hated her. I never asked her why she thought that. She rode a motorcycle, a woman riding a motorcycle in Japan isn't very common, and it turned me on.

We struck up a quick intimate relationship. However, S36 told me that the love of her life had moved back to Canada, and that she wasn't able to get over him. I guess I was a substitute for him so I never made much of an attempt to hide the fact that I was seeing other women, but it pissed her off that I'd leave H34's shampoo and conditioner and feminine products right out in the open whenever she came over. I figured by now, all these women had to know about each other. All except H34, who I at least tried to protect, but who probably knew more because she spent the most time at my house. She would find either short brown hairs in the shower (S36's), or long brown hairs on my *tatami* mats (M34's), or food that I didn't buy in the fridge (C33). Since A26 didn't come over that often, and since Y44 didn't last too long, I don't think she ever knew about them, but then again, she might have broken into A26's car and stolen her radio. N32, other than the naked pics in my magazine and our steamy performance at Plastic Factory, kept herself pretty much hidden. I think. Weird thing was, N32 and H34 had the most in common with each other, in terms of their looks.

I continued seeing S36 for a while until she couldn't deal with my brazen attitude about the fact that I was seeing other women. Eventually, her texts stopped coming and so did she. I miss her.

Where Are They Now

A26, I saw her at a Christmas party, during which she held my hand tightly under the table where no one could see. Felt nice.

N32, her face and image pop up on my Facebook every now and again. When we last spoke, she was still doing the erotic model slash damsel in distress European tour. Unfortunately, and very sadly, I also heard that she might have committed suicide.

Y44, I've no idea.

S36 moved to Canada.

Y24 lived out in the Ichinomiya countryside and also worked at the airport. I met her at Shooters while shooting a web series called "English Teachers" in which I was cast as "Victor", the evil owner of a rival English school. Y24 was Japanese innocence personified, and for whatever reason under the sun, she liked me. I liked her too, she was unjaded and worked very hard to speak the little English she could, and we enjoyed a mostly platonic friendship until one day she came over to my place and begged me to let her be my girlfriend, which I couldn't do, and then she broke down crying on my futon asking me over and over "why can't I be your girlfriend/why can't I be your girlfriend/why can't I be your girlfriend". Y24 and I never really had what anyone would consider true sexual intercourse. Mostly, we'd meet somewhere in Sakae or down behind Nagoya Station and we'd go behind some building and just make out.

The thing is, I wasn't even trying very hard to accumulate this near harem of women into my life, it just seemed to happen against my better judgement, and without my consent. All these flies buzzing around me made me feel like a piece of shit, and yet there I was right in the middle of it.

But H was the keeper. It wasn't until towards the very end of my time in Japan that I was able to actually see H for who she was. However, by that time it was too late, we'd already settled into a sort of need-and-greed relationship. I was hooked on H like an addict gets hooked on drugs, and she was hooked on an idea of our relationship that had never actually existed.

My Addiction to H Grows

Even through my goings and comings with all these different women, H was still there. She had a key to my apartment, which I'd reluctantly given her, but she wasn't allowed to just drop by. She gave me my space, and still, gave me so much more. I scheduled my liaisons' with the other women so that I still had enough time to devote to being with H a few days a week. None of the other women came anywhere close to being able to replace H, and I suppose that's partially what kept her loyal to me. Besides, by this time, we'd been "together" for over seven years. She'd gone through my divorce with me, she'd cared for my children, cooked for them, fed them, watched them, translated things back and forth between them and I. She'd driven me all over Nagoya a thousand times, paid bills for me, paid my rent, bought clothes and jewelry for me, cared for me when I was sick, and taken me to both the doctor and the dentist. She'd helped me with my taxes, my insurance and my magazine. She'd arranged business deals and traveled with me to and fro. Her loyalty and tenacity through all my bullshit was astounding, no, *ludicrous.*

Near the end of my Japan sojourn, I finally felt like I was actually falling in love with her. The ashes of my burnt out marriage still smoldered, but I had grown to set aside my resentment for H, even though it had taken nearly 4 years to do. Yet even while I felt I loved her, I felt I had to break free from her. Our relationship was crippling my sense of independence, she was enabling me by telling me I didn't have to learn any Japanese and paying for my existence and I felt I wasn't growing anymore. I even felt that my outlandish coterie of women was partially her fault. I told myself the reason I had so many women was because my heart had been splintered apart because of my divorce, which deep inside I still partially blamed her for. I needed her, but still hated that very fact.

I didn't know what to do. Stay in Nagoya, with H, and continue holding her hostage for having contributed to the demise of my marriage? Break up with her and stay in Nagoya? She wouldn't let me do that, and I myself could barely imagine staying in Nagoya and her not being there, which pushed me on in my decision to leave altogether. But *how . . .*

>Chapter 35

FLASH MOB WEDDING

May have set a World Record

Winter 2012

One of my best dudes in Nagoya at the time, was an American cat named William. William, who'd also had issues with alcohol and who'd nearly been run over by his ex-wife and who'd given me sage advice about my divorce, asked me to be his best man at his wedding. Thing was, his wedding was going to be a flash mob wedding. At the time, I had no idea what a flash mob was.

The wedding took place on Christmas Eve, in the middle of Nagoya station, with Big John Ahern as the Justice of Peace. Other attendees included, Dave Olaf, Adam Demby, Tim Lennane, William's lovely bride-to-be, about three thousand ecstatic Japanese onlookers and yours truly. But I almost forgot about it.

H woke me up for our morning session before she took off for work. After she left, I laid back down to go back to sleep. With no alarm set, I instinctively woke up at exactly the time William had asked me to be at the station. I jumped up, showered, and booked it to the train station.

When William and his wife came sailing down the escalator in the middle of the stations, thousands of onlookers had gathered to watch the flash mob style wedding taking place right in front of the golden clock. Sumiye, William's wife, went back up the escalator after they'd exchanged their vows and she tossed her bouquet of flowers over the balcony, and suddenly there were hundreds of Japanese women pushing each other to grab the falling bouquet of flowers. The flowers floated and twirled before finally succumbing to a sea of female hands outstretched towards the ceiling. The flowers were torn and sprayed everywhere inside the station. A beautiful disaster.

William was standing proud with his new wife, surrounded by friends and all the spontaneous pageantry. The moment couldn't have been more perfect if it had been orchestrated for a movie scene.

The whole mise-en-scène literally made me tear up. Here was a guy whose wife had literally tried to run him over with his own car, and who had at least temporarily kicked his alcohol dependency, and which was most amazing to me, was one of the few foreigners who was able to beat the system to win partial custody of his kids. William had somehow gotten a second chance at life in Japan and I was happy for him. Kudos man.

And there I was, capturing it all on my stupid smartphone. I used an image of their wedding as the cover of the last issue of *RAN,* which I put out in January 2013. I thought it was one of the most spectacular moments I had ever seen. I think it's in the *Guiness Book of World Records.* If it isn't, it should be.

William and his wife subsequently moved out of Nagoya and into Tokyo where by all accounts he and his wife are doing well.

Two Videos, One Swan Song

At the beginning of 2013, I was finished recording my *Full Time Hustler* CD. Conkarah, my Japanese-Jamaican producer, suggested we shoot videos for it, so we chose the tracks "Runaway" and "Fireworks." I'd already had the debacle inside Plastic Factory to go with "Runaway," I figured why not shoot a video, the song already had drama associated with it.

I asked the tatted up Japanese Suicide Girl who had been selling me spice to be my lead female in the video. I hired Steve Pottinger, to whom I think I still owe thirty thousand yen to, to shoot it for me. My treatment was simple, we'd wake up at the crack of dawn, before the sun rose, head down to Nishi Ki in Sakae, and shoot out the empty garbage strewn streets, the ones with the SEX FOR SALE posters advertising nude mature Japanese flesh, the same streets where at night the Korean and Chinese massage ladies sell hand jobs to drunk salarymen. We'd shoot all day into the evening and capture the noisy crowds and the mixture of personalities on the urban Japanese streets of Nagoya and the subway stations. We'd then end the shoot back on the streets of Nishi Ki with the lights, taxi drivers, hostesses, and all the seedy characters of the area.

We did that and more. I woke up and contacted Akane before the sun rose. I go down into Sakae and head to the spice shop and find her crashed out on the couch. Honestly, I wasn't sure whether or not she was sleeping or unconscious. She'd probably spent the night smoking spice and doing whatever else with the wild variety of customers who came into the shop all throughout the night. I wake her up and she immediately hands me a fat spice joint. I smoke it, and instantly get the same nauseating fire-hot brain burn I had gotten before. Akane smiles and takes the joint from me, hits it, and we both proceed to totally fry our brains at zero dark thirty in the morning before my music video shoot.

"Runaway" Video Shoot

We get to Sakae first, and start shooting just down the street from Plus Park. The first scenes of the video are silent images of the moon in the azure Nagoya sky. Garbage bags are bunched up on the street waiting to be picked up. Big black crows feast on trash while Akane lay sprawled out on the sidewalk, looking exactly as burned out as she really was. We shot the taxis and caught real hostesses scrambling to make it to the first train home in the morning.

Juvenile motorcycle gangs who do nothing really "bad" besides engage Japanese cops in a loud, slow motion "chase" down dark roads. Japanese taxi cabs double park on narrow streets with their cars running and their doors open waiting for someone to pay a fare.

The skewed social dating landscape provides ample opportunity for a mind-boggling array of pay-for-play, phony romance arrangements. Japan is a country where the absolute most doofus looking white boy you ever saw can be seen walking down the street with the most strikingly gorgeous Japanese woman in the world.

And it's all there in the *Runaway* video. Type in "Runaway Final 2012" and you'll see the results of what a day of being burnt out on spice in Japan looks and sounds like.

"Fireworks" Video Shoot

The "Fireworks" video was different. Conkarah rented an aluminum can–crushing warehouse to shoot the video in. It was the middle of February, which is the coldest month of the year in Japan, by far.

We're in this huge, empty, aluminum-crushing plant, with giant forklifts and mountains of aluminum cans stacked to the ceiling all around us. I'm shirtless with a bandana covering my face, holding an aerosol blow torch and standing in front of a barrel with five-foot flames shooting up into my face. It's freezing cold, but absolutely exhilarating.

In the video, I'm standing over a blazing fire erupting out of an old oil can, spitting my lyrics, shivering while trying not to look cold, "*Firecracker/Fireworks/Flamethrower/Don't get your feelings hurt....*" My teeth and bones were shattering but at the same time my skin was almost catching fire from me standing so close to the flames shooting out of the barrel. Meanwhile, Conkarah and Percy, a Jamaican cat that

Conkarah knew who worked at the plant, and who had hooked up the location for us to shoot in, are standing off to the side laughing at my freezing/burning ass while passing a joint between them, shivering themselves.

I figured this was as good a swan song as any. I was done with it all, the girls, the clubs, the spice, the emotional and mental anguish of fighting with my ex-wife over the children, the language difficulties, the stressful "go nowhere" teaching jobs, the two faced "friends" I had accumulated, the bowing and apologizing and "sumimasens" and constant wondering about whether I was saying the right thing, to the right people, at the right time, the gaijin label, it was all too much.

One day, I found myself with 600 bucks cash in my pocket and I wandered into a travel agency in Sakae and bought myself a one way ticket to Los Angeles and that was it. I contacted a friend I had barely known in LA and asked him if I could crash on his couch for a spell once I returned to Los Angeles and the deal had been set. I had set myself up to return to the big bad United States of America in early April, and I was terrified.

>Chapter 36

THE WIZARD OF OZ

A quick, stressful trip to Australia

You never know who you'll meet, who you'll need to be there at any given moment in your life. People show up in the strangest places, at the strangest hours, as if they were put there to save your life.

Samantha, my very first roommate in Japan, had long moved back to Melbourne, Australia. She'd been inviting me to Australia for years, and when I told her I had decided to move back to the US, she told me she'd pay for me to come visit her. She offered to pay for my hotel and transportation, and said the only thing I had to pay for when I arrived in Melbourne was my food. Let's *go*... jump from space ...

Ouch!!

It's 5 A.M. here in Nagoya. It's dark outside, the sun hasn't come up yet. I'm wide awake, like I have been at this time every day for the past week. It's actually been an incredibly trying month for me. Starting with my nasal surgery, which led to (so it seemed) a massive toothache. The pain got to be so unbearable, that H had to take me to see her Dentist. *I am saved*, so I thought, until her Dentist told me that any procedure to rid myself of the pain would be GREATER than the toothache itself. Imagine a Dentist telling you that, THIS IS REALLY GOING TO HURT A LOT.

Come to discover that Japanese Dentists, are not too fond, for whatever reason, of local anesthesia. And putting someone completely under is almost anathema, especially for something as simple and presumably endurable as a simple tooth pulling. Hearing the Dentist tell me in Japanese how much it would hurt sounded much worse than hearing it in English would have sounded: "*sugoi ittaie,*" he said, which terrified me, especially after having just recently gone through the torture of the nostril excavation surgery. So I decided not to have the procedure, hoping somehow to stave off the pain until I returned from my impending short trip to Australia, which was, overall, a painful trip in itself.

Welcome To the Land Down Under, "Where Women Glow and Men Plunder"

When I arrived in Australia, I was greeted at the airport by my old roommate Sam. What I didn't know was that she had been angry, bitter, and resentful for most, if not all of her time in Australia since having returned from Japan. I quickly discovered that Sam was planning, I guess, to take out her displeasure with Japan on me during my stay with her in Oz. Had I known that, I might not have gone to Australia, but a free trip abroad is a free trip abroad, no matter how you slice it. After convincing H that nothing would happen between Sam and I, which I meant, I flew to Oz on Sam's dime.

Sam and I spent the first three days in a hotel room in Melbourne with me complaining incessantly about my painful-ass tooth. Eventually after three days of relentless pounding pain inside my mouth, on that third day Sam took me to an Australian dentist who yanked my tooth out with pliers while her assistant held me down. This entire scenario seemed to piss Sam off even more. I guess I can understand it in retrospect—you pay for someone to come visit you and they end up arriving with a madd toothache, complain about said toothache from arrival, and make noise after 11 P.M. in the room where you're both staying to boot. Add to it, you've paid for someone to come visit you under the pretense that "I'm going to get some," and you don't get anything.

I just wasn't feeling her *like that*. I guess that was my mistake. *Big* mistake. Sam and I had been nothing more than friends, and I really had no idea she expected something *more* than just friendship, even though she'd paid for the trip and the hotel. I can be a dumbass like that sometimes.

Still, I made no moves on Sam and was somewhat oblivious to the moves she had been making on me. She suggested we put our beds together and "sleep next to each other," which we did, but I didn't do anything. She showed me her tits, walked around half naked, and continuously made suggestive remarks about . . . everything, but I wasn't biting, which frustrated her. Add to this the fact that Sam wanted to be IN BED and almost SLEEPING before midnight. I didn't want to go to sleep so early, and now you've got a recipe for disaster. I wanted to stay up and listen to music or go out or . . . something. Sam wanted us both in bed, either together or not, by eleven or twelve. It kind of sucked. *But I'm in Australia!* New country, new city, new everything. I wanted to see nightlife, but Sam wanted to sleep? Or have sex? Or . . . what? I really wasn't sure.

The night of the Great Tooth Pull, I decided I wanted to go out for myself, see some shit, see something. *Hell*, I figured, *I might get lost*, but I was already lost, so come whatever, I was going to go see something for myself. Another mistake.

I went out walking one night near our hotel and bought some stuff—shit is incredibly expensive in Melbourne, we're talking eight bucks for a small bottle of apple juice and some chips. I bought the expensive-ass snacks and returned to the room to discover that Sam was pissed that I'd come back so "late." It was a little after midnight.

She chewed me out, told me to go to bed and to BE QUIET. She told me expressly that she didn't even want to hear me so much as go take a piss. The next day we flew out of Melbourne to go to Sydney.

She'd scheduled us to spend four days in Sydney, sightseeing and whatever else there was to do there. We flew the short flight to Sydney from Melbourne seated next to each other in total silence. It was the most uncomfortable two hours I'd spent maybe ever.

When we arrived, still not speaking, we quietly checked into the hotel she'd booked for us. We got up to our room, unpacked, and Sam told me she was going to go check out the harbor, which is beautiful, and promptly walked out and left me in the room by myself. I took a shower and decided to go out and walk around gorgeous Sydney Harbor, check out the breathtaking Sydney Opera House, and spend some time exploring downtown Sydney by myself for a few hours.

I returned to the room later that evening and, upon sticking my key in the door and entering the room, found Sam sitting straight up on her bed, arms folded over her sleeping gear, face scowling, and she promptly told me to get out. She was heated. She told me she was "sick of seeing my face" and said she didn't care where I went or what I did.

"GET. AOUT. NAOW," she says. Loud and clear, but not yelling.

Get out? Of here? Right now? And go ... where?

We're in Sydney, right? Sydney, Australia, right?

Sam didn't care. Every question I asked her made her more upset, until finally she was screaming

"JUST GET AOUT TREV-AH. NOW. JUST GET AOUT!"

So. I left. I go downstairs to the lobby with my little bag and use the computer to try to contact H, via email. I have no idea what I'm going to tell her or how—

"Hey, Sam kicked me out of the hotel room here in Sydney because I was ... making too much noise?" or *"Sam kicked me out because I don't want to fuck her"?*

Both excuses seemed equally ridiculous, so before I contacted H, I checked my Facebook and looked up Darren Kemp. Darren was the Australian cat with whom I had written *Cherry Blossom Trail* with while living in at Freebell. I hadn't seen or spoken to Darren in years.

Maybe five, maybe more. He'd disappeared and we hadn't kept in touch too tough, but now, I needed him. Bad.

I sent him a message:

Hey Dar, it's Trev. I'm in Sydney at a hotel on the harbor.
Brother, if you're anywhere you can get this message, please respond.
I'm in trouble.
I need your help.
Trev

I'm pacing the lobby wondering just what Sam could have been thinking upstairs in her room. Chances were she was fast asleep and didn't give a shit about what I was doing or not doing, or where I was or wasn't.

I walk over to the bar in the lobby and order a ten-dollar ginger ale and sit, and wait for what seems like forever. I'm checking my inbox three, four, five, six, ten times, every five minutes, but no response from Darren.

Of course he's not answering, I'm thinking, *what do you expect, dickhead? You haven't spoken to Darren in years, you don't even know if he's in Australia, or even if he's in the hemisphere or on the planet. WTF are you going to do now?*

I had no idea where he was. He could have been in Vietnam, could have been in Thailand, could have been in Japan, he could have been anywhere. I'm twirling the mixing stick in my ginger ale while staring at my bag on the floor near the bar. *What the fuck do I do?* I'm wondering to myself. I wasn't sure how to get out of this without contacting H. My hands are tied. Looks like I have no choice.

How could I tell my girlfriend that the girl she hadn't wanted me to go see to begin with, had kicked me out of our hotel room in Sydney?

I decide to check one more time before sending her a message hoping she'd bail me out, *again,* but . . . Darren had answered me. *Sonofabitch.* I'll be damned if Dar didn't leave his phone number in my inbox telling me to call *right now.*

I run to the front desk and ask the clerk if I can use the phone and Dar answers immediately,

"Hey mate, whe' ahh ya?" he asks.

I tell him the name of the hotel and he says he lives an hour drive away. He gives me his address and tells me to take a taxi to his place.

With ninety Australian dollars in my pocket, I take a forty-five-dollar cab ride to his house near the beach. I had forty-five bucks left to my name in Australia, with a week left to go—the plan was to spend four days in Sydney with Sam and the final three in Melbourne at Sam's family's house (which I wasn't sure I'd ever see)—before I returned to Japan. But Dar had rescued me, and I figured it was going to be all good. *Unreal.*

The Fucking Wizard of Oz

People appear suddenly in your life when you least expect it. Be kind to everyone.

When the taxi pulls up to his house, Dar is standing there smoking and smiling, looking like a million bucks to my eyes. He was as easygoing and mellow as he'd been years earlier when we'd smoked joints rolled with weed and tobacco. Dar's big smile and sincere eyes immediately brought me back to the stairs of Freebell where we'd talk about movies and he'd share his wild stories about Thailand and Vietnam.

Darren tells me he left Japan years earlier, and had moved back to Sydney to live with his family after discovering he had terminal cancer. The doctors had told him he had three years to live, "but that was three years ago, and I've never felt better!" he says, smiling.

He looks tanned and happy, like a retired golf pro or George Hamilton. Either way, I felt like I was seeing Santa Claus when he offered up a rolled pinner joint, with tobacco and weed. We got high right there and then, while sitting on the steps of his apartment under Sydney's hot sun. I'm in a state of thankful bliss.

Those days I spent going around Sydney with Darren were great. His entire family, his Italian Mom and his half-Aboriginal Dad, treated me fantastically. His sister and her husband took me out to dinner and his nephew Ryan told me how great an Uncle Darren was. Dar, for a person who was literally living on borrowed time, was the best host anyone could hope for. Always full of interesting stories, always a keen listener, always mellow and cheerful. Dar made me completely forget my situation with Sam, and made me forget the fact that I had decided to leave Japan when I return from Australia. He was a wonderful friend who saved my life.

My last day with Darren, he told me he had planned to do some more traveling. He said that he'd been writing more film ideas, and was planning to hook up with his friend who was in an England jail. He said his friend was slated to be released soon and they would both get their share of whatever cash they'd stashed away on one of their capers.

Dar was beaming and looked great, but I had noticed that whenever we went out walking for long periods of time he had to stop often, sit down, and catch his breath. He *looked* like he was fine, but he wasn't...but you'd never know it from his constant laid-back, casual attitude and the ever-present smile on his face. Dar carried himself like he was the holder of some really cool, really great secret that only he knew.

After our few days together, Dar rode back to the hotel with me in a cab. Jay Z and Justin Timberlake's song "Holy Grail" was booming out of the cabbie's car speakers when we pulled up to the lobby. When we arrived, I retrieved my wallet to pay the cabbie and Dar said he'd already taken care of it. I realized the last time I'd opened my wallet was to pay the cabbie who dropped me off in front of Dar's place four days earlier. *I hadn't even opened my wallet* since the day I had contacted Dar four days before. His family and he had taken care of everything.

I get out, Dar gets out the other side, and he's wearing a pair of cool Aviator shades. We gave each other a hug, he says "Cheers, mate! Stay in touch," gives me a thumbs up and a big wide-toothed smile. He climbs back into the taxi smiling before disappearing over the horizon and driving off into the distance. I watched the taxi slowly vanish in a state of humble shock about what I'd just experienced. Life man.

"Man, that guy is the fucking Wizard of Oz," I hear myself saying out of nowhere.

Sam and I Reunite, and I Say Goodbye to A Dear Friend

Samantha and I flew back to Melbourne, and I still had four or five days left before I was to return to Japan. Being that I had no place else to go, I spent those last four days in Sam's parents' home, but all I could think about was Darren. Sam's parents were hospitable and kind, generous and friendly, unaware, I suppose, that Sam had been the exact opposite of all that since pretty much the moment I had arrived in Australia the week before. Sam's Mother had recently beaten breast cancer and was recovering. Her Father was a jovial dude, the type who wakes up at 5 A.M. every day and goes out into his garage to fix something, or make breakfast for the family—he was a great cook as well.

Luckily, I had my own room, Sam's brother had moved out, and I was staying in his room. I tried my best to keep quiet, to stay out of Sam's way, but still, Sam told me I was taking showers too late, told me I shouldn't "roam the house" at night. My "roaming" consisted of me going to get a drink of water in the kitchen, which her Father told me I had all access to.

For those next few days I tried without success to steer clear of Sam, who was grumpy and irritable. I had nice conversations with her parents and we watched the tsunami movie *The Impossible* about a family who gets ripped apart from each other in the 2004 Indian Ocean tsunami, but is reunited by film's end, against impossible odds. Great film. While Sam's parents were great, she was not, and I counted down the days to my return to Japan.

That last night in Melbourne, Sam treated me to a live concert given by *The Jacksons*, in the Melbourne Convention Center, and it was spectacular.

The next day, we woke up early, she took me to the airport, we ate breakfast together at one of the airport shops, and I was off, back to Japan. Burnt bridges and rainbows in Sydney.

When I returned to Japan I felt like DiCaprio on Shutter Island. *Was everyone else around me crazy, or was I?* I went to Oz hoping to have a relaxing, mellow sightseeing tour with maybe a kangaroo or two; instead I got kicked out of a hotel, went homeless for two or three hours one afternoon, and then got rescued by my friend who was dying of cancer. The whole thing was just too bizarre. And now, I was Back in Japan, again.

Six months after I returned to LA, Ryan sent me a message one day saying,

"Dazza died last night. Trevor, we wanted to let you know because Darren always talked about you."

It wasn't shocking, or even all that sad for whatever reason. Dar seemed to live the life he wanted to live, went to the places he wanted to go, indulged in all he wanted to, and had kept his integrity and had great relationships until he passed.

When I heard the news, I was in LA, already stressed, trying to readjust to a life of uncertainty. I looked at the message and selfishly thought to myself, *Man, if Dar were here now, he'd rescue me from all this shit.* R.I.P. pal. You saved my life in Australia once, and I'll never forget it.

You're the fucking Wizard of Oz, man.

>Chapter 37

GOODBYE TO MY CHILDREN

"I'll see you again, soon"

W hen I returned to Japan, I had a little more than a week left before I was scheduled to leave for good.

All my belongings were packed up, ready to go on the airplane. All the jeans, T-shirts, jackets, wristbands, posters, jewelry, hats and belts that H had made or bought for me, packed tight in a couple of huge black duffel bags. The week went by briskly.

I threw myself a Sayonara party at Lea Lea Hale. All the superstar *gaijin* were there. C2 was on the mix. Keiko, Lea Lea's owner, was all smiles, but couldn't believe I was really leaving—no one could, myself included. *How am I going to do this?*

The idea of actually getting on the airplane was giving me chills, it was orders of magnitude, and more nerve wracking than it had been that month before I left Cali for Japan. I'd created a life here in Nagoya. I had lifelong friends that I'd met here. I had an ex-wife and two children, I was running a business, *I had a dozen girlfriends,* and everyone knew who I was. I'd made it! So, why was I leaving? Folks couldn't believe I was leaving. Neither could I, and then...suddenly, I had one week left.

I hadn't seen Taiyo and Asia Jade since the year began because my ex-wife had informed me by text that I couldn't see them anymore until I caught up with my child support payments. I had stopped paying as a result of learning that A's new boyfriend had seemingly taken my place. *But I just wanted to say goodbye...that's it.*

The next day would be the only opportunity I would have to see my children before taking off for Los Angeles the next week.

So, I decide I'm going to her house, literally to her front door, where I had not been for at least the last three years. To see them, or to see her, or to see *something*. I was leaving Japan and I had to say something to my children about it. I was not just going to vanish silently, I was just *not going out quite like that.*

I arrive to the apartment with H. It's dark and I have no idea when or if I'll get to see my children. I decide to wait on the other side of the tall bushes across from the steps that lead up to the apartment. I wait an interminable amount of time crouched behind the bush, squatted up against the chain-link fence, holding my knees close to my chin. I'm officially stalking now and thinking anyone who might see me might call the police, but still, *I have to see my children.*

Time passes slowly. It's deathly quiet and I've lost track of how long I've been waiting. It might have been 20 minutes, it might have been two hours and while I'm crouched behind the bushes my entire trip flashes in front of me. The day I arrived, Aki and Eiko, SKI and the students, the onsen trip and the naked old Japanese ladies, my apartment in Higashi Ku, Freebell, RAN, the rafting debacle, me performing with TAOW, the girls, my fight with the African, Sam, Darren, Australia, everything. My knees are hurting from being bent down so long and I chuckle to myself thinking *but Japanese people can stay bent down like this forever...*

Then...

I hear soft voices coming up the hill on the other side of the apartment building. My heart rushes, I fade further behind the bushes, then I realize *I'm not supposed to be hiding.* I'm here to see my babies and to let them see me, so I stand up tall and come out from behind the bushes. I'm now in plain view. I wait until I see them come up over the hill through the little playground with the little yellow toy slide and the tiny wooden jungle gym. This is the playground I'd taken them both to many times before.

Taiyo sees me first. He looks up towards the small sand filled playground and even though it's dark he spots me immediately. In midsentence, Taiyo halts his engaging conversation with his sister Asia,

"Eh? Daddy?!" he blurts out.

Asia looks up and says the same thing, but sweeter, in her airy baby girl Japanese voice,

"Daddy da!"

They look at each other and run to me. I scoop them up into a big hug. It's twilight and A's boyfriend approaches and as soon as he spots the three of us hugging, he's on me. He's pointing at me, his voice louder than it needs to be. He's irate, I'm an unwelcome surprise, Japanese hates surprises.

"*Nande coco ni irun desu ka? Nani shi ni kitta'an dsuka? Coco ni kuru beki dewa arimasen. Shi'tteru? Keisatsu ni denwa shimasu.*" He says.

He takes out his phone and starts dialing. *Do whatever you have to do.* I'm confident, but I don't know why. Could be that my children were happily wrapped in my arms. I could smell Asia's hair and face, but Taiyo looked slightly perplexed. He knew something wasn't right.

Suddenly H is there. I had told her to stay in her car but she showed up at exactly the right time, like she always had. While K Papa is waiting for someone to answer, H approaches him with small talk. Whatever she's saying dude apparently was not trying to hear. And now he's talking to the cops. H throws me a look of serious concern.

"Trevor, hurry up before the police come."

I smile at H, trying to pretend it was just another evening, not one where my kids would be seeing their dad possibly for the last time into an unknown future.

I'm doing my best to stay calm because Taiyo and Asia are wrapped in my arms while "K Papa" is talking to the police. He's describing the "*gaijin*" who has trespassed on "his" property and doesn't belong there.

He's actually telling them an "intruder" is on the premises. He's giving them the address while looking at me, Taiyo and Asia.

Finally, after not saying much to my children, I ask Taiyo if he's *genki* and he says "un," and I ask Asia the same thing and she repeats what her brother said exactly, "un."

Taiyo's fidgeting with his jacket, he knows this isn't "normal," but Asia is playing with my hair and for her, it was pretty normal. It's just me, her daddy, and that's all she really knows.

I ask them what they did today, where had they gone, what they ate, if they were cold. I tell Asia her hair looks pretty, she says "Daddy *mo*'—daddy too, twirling my locks in her hands.

I don't know what else to say to them. I'm speechless. I'm smiling but *I have no more cute words for them.* How do you tell your children that you're leaving the country? Leaving them, and that you don't know when, or if, you'll ever see them again?

I know leaving is my own choice, no one is forcing me out, no one is asking me to leave, it's all my choice. But I'm not being the father I want my children to see. If I stay in Japan under the present circumstances, with the way my heart is feeling, who knows how I might end up, what I might do. I've made the choice to leave, and now it's time to tell my children.

I'm kneeling down, cradling them both on either side of me. Taiyo is fidgeting and Asia is whispering something in my ear. K Papa gets off his phone and says the police are on their way. I'm doing what I can to ignore him. H stands between my family and this man, K Papa. And suddenly, flashing red lights appear down below the small hill. The police have arrived.

They Are Holding Large Flashlights

Two Japanese cops in caps and boots quickly approach where we are. They immediately shine beams of light directly into my face while I'm still kneeled down in front of the fence, by the bushes, holding

Taiyo and Asia. Since I'm the gaijin, they know immediately who to approach. I'm the foreigner.

The two cops ask me what I'm doing there. Taiyo and Asia shield their eyes from the bright light. They're confused and scared. I can see Asia wants to cry. She's not playing with my hair anymore. I can see Taiyo's face silently saying *this is my daddy, he didn't do anything wrong.*

"Nande coco ni iru'n desu ka?" *Why are you here?* One cop asks.

Even though the Officer is standing right in front of me, above me, his voice sounds like a whisper.

*I came to see my kids. That guy is not their father. I want to talk to my wife. I love my children. Why are **you** here?*

These thoughts are racing through my mind. My knees hurt. I drop my head. I look directly at both of my children,

"Watashi wa ashita America ni kairi masu. Tsugi itsu kaite kuru no ka wakarimasen." "Kodomo tachi ni sayonara wo i i'ni ki mashita."

I'm going to America tomorrow. I don't know when I'll come back. I came to say goodbye to my children. I say.

The Officer silently looks at my children and I kneeled on the ground. He then slowly lowers his flashlight, the beam is now facing the ground. The Officer takes a breath, and walks away towards his partner, who is conversing with K Papa.

K Papa is standing watch a few feet away, looking on sternly and triumphantly with his arms folded. He looks like an angry, short Japanese Roy Scheider. He's waiting for the Japanese cops to put a stop to what I'm doing, but they didn't.

The cop who had his flashlight shining in our faces five seconds ago walks over to him and gently, but firmly asks, "

Kodomo tachi wa kare no kodomo desu ka?" Are those his children?

K Papa slowly unfolds his arms and hesitatingly answers,

"Sou desu," *That's right*, K Papa says.

But K Papa is now offended, he points me in protest,

"...da-ke-do! Kare wa . . ." *But he is....*

The Officer puts up his hand in K Papa's face as if to say *It's okay,* and K Papa immediately backs down, glowering at me.

I have a moment or two to say something to my children, am I supposed to say goodbye? H knows this is it too, she looks at me, Taiyo and Asia and tears start rolling down her face. She can't take it. She turns and walks away. Taiyo and Asia notice H's tears.

My knees are burning. I look up at Taiyo and my eyes feel like they're about to be really wet. I tell him I'm leaving, that I'm going back to America, and that I don't know when I'll return to Japan.

I tell him he's a big boy and that he'll start first grade in a few weeks. I tell him to be careful and to always be nice to his sister.

"Okay, daddy" Taiyo says in perfect English.

As my son continues to speak, I look through the lights towards the playground. I never imagined that I would feel the threat of the Japanese police 10 feet from the swing where my babies and I had played a hundred times before.

I turn to Asia, *she's so cute,* and at the same time she's confused. The cops wait a few yards away near the stairs with K Papa. I tell Asia I love her and that I'll see her again soon,

"Okay, daddy," she says. Very sweet.

My eyes immediately well up with tears. I stand, take a deep breath and look directly at the cops with K Papa. I'm neutralized. Crushed. I look over at H, her hand is covering her mouth and she's crying openly. I signal to her with a nod, *it's time.* She walk towards her car, passing in front my children and I, she's choked up and tries hard not to look at us. Walking backwards, I follow, waving goodbye to Taiyo and Asia Jade. They stand next to each other, all alone together, waving back at me. Taiyo is fidgeting on the fence and Asia is mimicking Taiyo. They stand alone, bathed in the light of the Japanese police officer's bright flashlight. Just them two.

And.

I don't know if I'll ever see them again.

I haven't seen them since that evening. Haven't seen their faces, forced only to keep their mental images alive in my own head.

I haven't heard their voices since those last moments of darkness, with two Japanese cops shining their flashlights on us, while H stood between us and the chain-link fence, with tears streaming down her face.

I haven't touched their skin, I don't know how they're doing in school, and I don't know what their hobbies are. I don't know what they're either doing or not doing.

How can some mothers, not allow some fathers to have any relationship with their children?

Fade

I'm sitting in front of my computer in my apartment, with my belongings strewn about the place. I'm supposed to be leaving Japan for good in just about a week.

With exactly no money, just a place to go, and a "dream". I envision my new life in LA. I had 8 by 10's on my wall of Denzel Washington, Morgan Freeman, Samuel Jackson, and Johnny Depp because I was trying to convince myself that I was leaving Japan for something better, a new opportunity, *I'm going to become like one of those guys.*

Now it's time to go. I feel broken up. Wrecked. If I weren't me, I might be suicidal. Truly.

I wrote this to avoid the mental haunted house my mind puts me through in the wee hours of the morning after a week of very little sleep. I'm emotional because my ex-wife now has a reason to get a restraining order against me, which could be the very real and potent reason why I may never see Taiyo and Asia Jade again.

It feels like I'm dying.

Not only physically, but in some other way too. Emotionally, it feels like the spirit version of me is dissipating, or something like that.

Leaving here, dissolving my life, parceling off my stuff, leaving my girlfriend, leaving my children, it feels like I'm purposely vanishing myself, killing off my life in Japan, and I'm not all too sure why.

But I am sure that even if someone called me tomorrow morning (today), and offered me some fantastic position here in Nagoya, some new life, I'd probably turn it down, because I am not happy here, and haven't been, for quite some time.

>Chapter 38

MISSION

Accomplished?

They wanted me to change. They told me so. They paid me good for my language but still wanted me to speak theirs. They shunned me and applauded me at the same time. They gawked at me and scolded me and praised me and ridiculed me. They fetishized me even while I fetishized them. They gave me a chance and weren't openly hostile to me but they lowered the ceiling of opportunity and wanted me to lobotomize myself. They wanted me to be more and less American, more and less black, more and less Japanese, all at the same time.

They wanted me to be like them, not *kind of* like them, but exactly like them, and they loved and hated the fact that I wasn't, even when I tried to be. Nothing, quite, was ever good enough, and it never would be. I'd have to be good enough for myself somehow, even with the daily microaggressions "sticking out like a nail" and all that, due to my *gaijin* identity.

H didn't seem to want me to change, except when she did, which wasn't so much. She never really helped me with the language, and accommodated my English more than anything—maybe she was just learning the language after all. Maybe she was just taking my private lesson for a really, really long time. I don't want to think that. I want to think she enjoyed speaking English with me, I want to think we spoke English because it was our default language, not because I was her eight-year private teacher. I want to think even though I couldn't bring my heart to love her like she wanted me to, that she's been by my side all this time because she likes me, not because I'm American, or black, or because I speak English, but just because she digs me. H spoke English to me almost all the time. She kept the Japanese language, and as much of the culture, with lots of its harsh realities at a distance from me. She was my bodyguard, and my soul guard, and my health guard.

Still, I learned lots of the language, more than I ever thought I could or would. I got myself to where it sounded like I was *pera pera*—fluent—because I spoke the tiny bit of Japanese, I knew exactly like they knew. I sounded like them. It was damn near perfect. But I didn't look like them, and I wasn't like them. Even though I bowed and said "*sumisen, gomen nasai*" before I spoke Japanese, like they do, and even though I apologized for my existence, like they do, and even though I apologized for having opinions and for thinking and feeling, like they do, I still wasn't like them, wasn't *one of* them.

I didn't react, even after eight or nine years of living there. Every single day someone reminded me that I wasn't Japanese, by moving away from me in restaurants or not sitting next to me on the subway or not recognizing me in the *conbini* that I'd been to a thousand times. *Microaggressions*, is what the media and the learned elite call it. Fucked-up-ass racism and lots of annoying stupid bullshit is what I call it. There are folks who couldn't stand being stared at for five minutes, I was stared at for ten years. How do celebrities do it? Everywhere you go, everywhere you look, someone is staring. I don't think celebrities are being laughed at though. Are they? It bent me, but didn't break me. Or did it?

There are Japan apologists, foreigners who live in Japan who are angry that other foreigners don't like being treated like foreigners, especially after ten years. Those foreigners, who aren't, weren't, and will never be Japanese themselves, ostracized me exactly the same way the

Japanese did. They work so hard at being Japanese that they feel entitled to hate non-Japanese, even more than Japanese do. Japanese are masters at the art of secrecy and deception and at hiding their true feelings, if they have any. But foreigners aren't. We're supposed to say what we feel when we feel it. We're supposed to let you know if we disapprove of your behavior, and many of my own closest friends started doing exactly that right to my face. They used their right to speak their minds to tell me that they didn't like that I wasn't trying hard enough to be Japanese. They didn't like that I was outspoken. They didn't like that my magazine was successful, and that I was recording music and doing well. They started acting really funky, giving me funny looks which made me feel like I had contracted leprosy, but I was one of "them." Many of them were angry that I was there with them, like I'd invaded their own private little foreign country and I was poisoning the atmosphere with my presence, exactly like they were.

At the same time, the Japanese society ostracized me for just being me and then for being a divorced foreign black man. Whatever had happened in my marriage was assumed to be my fault, and whether or not it was, wasn't the point. "You're the foreigner, what are you doing here in the first place? You must have fucked up." That was the attitude, it's written all over their faces.

No, I'm not Japanese. But I tried. So hard. I kowtowed and drooped my shoulders so as not to be so tall and scary. I shaved off a few octaves of my voice to sound less threatening. I smiled when I didn't want to smile, just to be polite. I tried my best to be invisible, to compact myself into a smaller, paler, less amped and less woke version of myself. For society, for my wife, for her family. But I couldn't change completely. In the beginning, my wife loved me because I was adventurous, spontaneous, courageous, outgoing, a bit flashy maybe, funny, wild, and entertaining. Then suddenly she hated me for all those exact reasons, and I couldn't understand it. It was an emotional and social sleight of hand that I couldn't figure out. A deft magic trick.

I Know Who I Am

I left for work in the morning as Trevor and returned home as Trevor, but my wife wanted Takashi or Masato or some other motherfucker to return home. I didn't even want to be "Trevor-san," like many Japanese women had decided to call me.

My wife wanted me to be Japanese, and fuck if I didn't want me to be Japanese too. She wanted me to be like the white boy Scott from Nebraska, or Mike from Ohio, or Oliver from New Zealand, who thought they were successfully becoming Japanese, but who weren't, aren't, and never will be.

But still, *I wanted to be Japanese*. Because I knew that was the way to my wife's heart. That was the way to her family's heart too.

That was the way for me to be accepted and being accepted is everything in Japanese culture.

I couldn't do it, *be like them*. I thought I had some deficiency, maybe I couldn't learn as well as them other cats who learned to read, write, and speak the language, and who spent half their days bowing and *sumimasen*-ing their asses off. I thought they were smarter than me, more international, more something, whatever. I beat myself in my head trying to catch up to the white dudes over there who were speaking fluent Japanese. I thought the Japanese were more accepting of them than me, but they weren't. Those dudes were fooling themselves. They seemed all too willing to give up the personality they had arrived with, good or bad, in favor of trying to melt into Japanese society. But the joke was on them, because no matter how deep they bowed, no matter how much *hiragana* and *katakana* they could read and write, no matter how well they wore their *jinbei* or wooden sandals or ate whatever Japanese food they loved, they'd never be Japanese. The same Japanese who were staring at my black ass in the street were staring at them too, no matter how Japanese they thought they'd become.

Japan tried to steal my identity, even though there were many times I tried to lose it purposely. I tried to give myself away, tried to shake off my skin and my nationality and myself, but it wouldn't go away.

They wanted me to whitewash myself, and even though I tried, I couldn't, the paint wouldn't stick. But I did try. I cried in the mirror looking at my black self, wondering why I couldn't change. Why couldn't I learn the language better? Faster? Why didn't I want to just stay here and get better at being Japanese? Was I standing too tall? I was the nail that sticks up and gets hammered down. But I wouldn't let myself be hammered down, even though I tried.

Lots of times I wanted to peel off my black skin and find a little Japanese man living underneath, but he didn't exist.

They wanted me to trade my individual soul for their collective soul and I just couldn't, but lord knows I tried.

When I realized I would never be Japanese enough, when I realized I couldn't shake my personality and my culture, when I finally paid homage to that NYC Jamaican-American blood coursing through my veins, when I realized that dark, aggressive, powerful nature wasn't going anywhere, I realized I couldn't stay.

At that moment, I began forgiving myself for what had happened with my wife. I had been looking for her to forgive me, but I began to forgive myself, because I realized I was just being me, why apologize and feel bad about it.

I slowly unfurled my own honest feelings about who I was, a black Jamaican American. And who they were and who they weren't, and who my wife had thought I was or would become, but I just couldn't do it despite trying—it dawned on me that she'd never forgive me. Because Japanese don't forgive. That's why. Simple. It isn't a high virtue in their society, forgiveness. Being unforgiving is quintessentially Japanese, and my wife was out to show me exactly how Japanese she was, and so I had to find forgiveness for myself.

I knew if I learned more, I could allow myself to separate from H, who in turn knew that my learning less was a better situation for her, because in me not knowing shit, she wielded the *Power of Knowledge* over me, and knowledge plus the intelligent application of it is *everything*.

Warts and All

I knew if I learned, I could be a better papa to Taiyo and Asia. I knew it would be easier to communicate with them, and I thought maybe they'd think I was "normal," since being Japanese was the norm. I felt bad about being who I was, since I knew Taiyo and Asia's mom and her family appeared to be normal to them, so I didn't want them to think their dad was abnormal, or some kind of weirdo. If they thought I was a weirdo then that might lead to them thinking that they were weirdos too. Can't have that. I wanted to be around for them, so that when Japan made them feel that they weren't normal, they could run into my arms and understand that they were part of me. That even if I wasn't normal for them, I still loved them. I wanted them to know that they could be whatever they wanted to be, even if it wasn't "normal", whenever they were with me. I wanted us all to be abnormal together.

I wanted to learn how to be more Japanese so I could teach them that not being "100 percent" Japanese is normal. But learning how to be more Japanese doesn't at all equate with actually being Japanese. I decided *fuck it,* I'm not Japanese, I'll never be Japanese, so maybe I'll be better off leaving, going back to big bad America, where I can say what I feel and be who I am, warts and all. Even though I wasn't sure when I'd see my children again, I needed to take care of me, and then, maybe when I felt better about myself, I might be able to return and see them somehow, someday.

... ahh ... my beautiful Japanese wife. Where is she? When I met her she was innocent. That jet-black short hair and that goofy jagged-toothed smile. Those tight jeans and tight sweaters. Her wild laughter and incredulous naïveté. Where had she gone? And our

children, our two beautiful half-Japanese, half-black, half-American, half-Jamaican kids, all four quarters of them, not "hafu". Just two beautiful little human beings caught in the middle of a war, not only between mother and father, but also a war of cultures and ideas.

In the crosshairs of racial intolerance and useless old forms, sure, I was a total asshole, but . . .

> Chapter 39

Back To Los Angeles

Electric Lady Land

The night of my flight back, H is laid-back and low-key. She's either holding her emotions in or has none whatsoever. Either way, I can't put my finger on her behavior.

My apartment is empty. I've given so many of my books, clothes, furniture, toys, posters, kitchen stuff, equipment, decorations, and music to friends that it must have been a bonanza for them. *So many things I bought, collected, was given, needed, looked at, played with, worn, sat on, slept in, cooked with, used in some way or another, so many things that had become a part of me—all gone now.*

Unreal. It all disappeared and left me with a big *whooooooosh,* like it was sucked out the window in the middle of the night by some giant spaceship.

I've got a few black duffle bags of clothes, and a big box that H promised to take care of for me until we'd meet again. We had promised each other to always be together. I told her I'd always keep her and she'd always be in my life.

We'll meet forever.

We're in the hotel at Chubu airport. We eat some dinner and try to act like it isn't a suicide mission disguised as me just "going back home." We slightly succeed. H has on tight jeans, a turtleneck that I had bought her and a denim jacket, owing to the fact that it's early April and still cold in Japan. *Kafunshou* season is on the way, but *fuck you* kafunshou, I'm thinking to myself, *you won't catch me this year, I'll be gone!*

We're in the hotel room and the absolute last thing on my mind is sex but H wants it, more as a ceremonial send-off than anything else, and for this very reason I can't do it. *I don't want to be sent off.* Plus, I'm just not feeling sexual at all. I just don't want to do it. *More sex?* I don't need it, it just doesn't seem necessary.

But we do it and afterwards, I'm worried that H could possibly meet Y24 at the airport—Y24 is the young slightly nerdy girl I've been seeing on and off, who H knows, and has known about, in an ancillary fashion, for some time.

Or wait, no, maybe we'll run into A26! A26 also works at the airport. She's the big-titted cutie whose Prius was broken into when she was over at my crib in Fukiage. Seeing either or both of them at the airport on my last day in Japan with H is extremely possible and makes me shudder, and feel good about my decision to leave for a moment. Still though, I think, *What might happen if H sees them? Or they see us? What will I do? What will they do? What will we do?* Then I fall asleep.

Next day, my flight is scheduled for around midday, and I wake up at 8 A.M. feeling like I'm in a horror movie. I'm sweating. Naked. Breathing heavily. I just had another dream about my ex-wife and the babies. I still have those dreams till this day. *I love having them.* However. There, in that hotel room, the dream was less a dream and more a nightmare. My wife no longer exists, my children are gone and I've destroyed my family. I shoot up out of bed, naked.

I can't do it! I can't do it! I can't leave yet!

I'm sitting up in bed heaving, trying to catch my breath, and I'm frantic.

Only In My Dreams

I've had dozens of dreams where my ex-wife and I are communicating freely without hatred or anything negative whatsoever. *We like each other and talk to each other*, in my dreams.

In my dreams, I can see my *okaasan*, my former mother-in-law, her face is as clear as day. She's glaring at me. Her lips are curled in derision. Why? I do not know, but that's how I remember her. I can also see her husband, my *otohsan,* as well. His face looks vacuous, like he's neither here nor there. We're all sitting at their kitchen table, my wife's dad is drinking an Asahi beer, and there's lots of Japanese food at the table. My wife is standing near the sink looking so absolutely hot that I have no idea how I got her, where she came from or why she likes me. Our insanely cute children are playing with their *obaachan* near the TV...

But none of this is real. It's just a dream. I'm not in my wife's family's dining room. I'm in a small hotel room at Chubu Airport *and I'm about to leave Japan.*

Pre-Flight Meltdown

My chest is pumping, I'm sweating. I fling the sheets from my naked body, yank open the door and run into the hotel hallway, screaming,

"H, I can't do it! I don't think I can do it! I don't know why I'm leaving! This is crazy! This is crazy!" I shout.

This *is* crazy.

H chases after me with the sheet wrapped around her naked body,

"Trev-ah! Trev-ah! Come inside! Are you okay? Come inside!" She's whispering and shouting at the same time.

I'm crumbled against the wall, down on my knees, naked and shivering, looking up at H.

"I don't think I can do it, I can't leave! I don't think I should leave now!" I say.

I'm pleading, looking up at her for some answers. She's coming towards me, clutching the dark burgundy hotel bedsheets around her body, while her other hand is stretched out towards me.

I can't catch my breath, my eyes are bulging, I feel exhausted and broken, but the day has come, *I have to leave Japan today.*

I have to get on the airplane, say goodbye—possibly *forever?*—to Japan, to H, to my children, to my magazine, my events, my stuff, to all the ideas and time and effort that went into *RAN* and my music. To women, friends, streets, places, moments, to my apartment in Fukiage that I loved, to the accumulated wealth and everything I had acquired over my almost ten years in Japan?

Say goodbye to it all? *How could I do it?*

H comes over and helps me to my feet and gently guides me back inside the room. We both sit down quietly on the edge of the bed. H is silently rubbing my back and lays her head softly on my shoulder. We sit like that in silence for a while.

I get myself together. Take a shower. Put on my clothes. Silently pack my stuff into my backpack. Wallet. Phone. CD Player. Nose spray. Lip balm. Sunglasses. Toothbrush. Toothpaste. Keys—*to where?* To my apartment in Fukiage. To my old bike. Keys I'll never need again. I drop the keys into my bag anyway.

Tears Flood the Airport

We make our way into the airport towards my terminal. As I'm walking into the foyer, who do I see but Y24. She's smiling a big cheesy smile and here I am walking up with H and my bags to leave Japan forever. As I walk past Y,

"You're really leaving, Trevor? Really?" she asks.

Her smile is breaking, it looks like she wants to cry underneath her smile, it chokes me up.

"Yes Y, I think I really am. But I'll be back!" I say.

Y starts to cry, H is right behind me ignoring Y's very obvious tears. I give Y a hug. She pushes me off her and tells me to *hayaku,* or I'll miss my flight.

I walk further into the terminal. I attempt to check my bags in. I have too much stuff. I have to pay more or leave something. Cool. *I'll leave this big cardboard box of stuff, because I'm not actually sure what's going to happen to me. I might have to come back,* I think to myself, *and I'll need that stuff,* I tell myself.

I don't want to leave.

It's good that H has to take control of my extra stuff—it's virtually guaranteed to be taken care of and it assures me that I'll see H again, one day.

I wait at the front of the line until the Service Agent signals to me that it's my turn to head to the service counter. It's time. A Japanese clerk asks me for my boarding pass and identification. H can go no further. I look directly at her, *I'm really leaving now.* Right *now.*

Huge watery tears well up in my eyes, and run down my face. I crumple into H's waiting arms and cry. Hard. My face is buried in her chest and I'm sobbing.

"I'm sorry I'm leaving. I'm sorry. I'm so sorry. I love you and I'm so sorry I'm leaving . . . you're my wife forever . . ."

H is crying too, but at the same time she's comforting me. I raise my head with my sobbing eyes and slobber kiss H, turn, and walk into the boarding tunnel.

As I'm walking deeper into the tunnel, I straighten up, wipe my face, and greet the smiling Japanese flight attendant solemnly.

On board the airplane, there's a bunch of Japanese people putting their personal items in the cabins above. They talk softly to each other. They seem happy. The air is cool, still and eerily artificial.

I take my seat next to the window, lean back, press play, and peep Jimi singing "Electric Ladyland."

The nose of the airplane lifts off the ground, and in a flash, Japan is thousands of feet below me.

ABOUT THE AUTHOR

Trevor David Houchen is a Brooklyn, New York City born actor, musician, writer, teacher, and former publisher of RAN MAGAZINE, a pop culture arts related international magazine based in Nagoya, Japan.

After leaving NYC with his family at 17, Trevor spent the next decade living in Gainesville, Florida, where he earned his Bachelor of Science Degree in Broadcast Journalism from the University of Florida.

He then returned to his native New York to pursue his dream of becoming a professional writer, contributing to several magazines.

From New York City, he then traveled to Los Angeles in order to begin an acting career, which was temporarily suspended when he decided to travel east to Japan.

He now lives in Atlanta, Georgia, where he owns and operates a private ESL school with his wife, and continues to write, act, and create music.